CRISIS INTERVENTION
THEORY AND PRACTICE
A Clinical Handbook

CRISIS INTERVENTION THEORY AND PRACTICE
A CLINICAL HANDBOOK

Ann Wolbert Burgess, R.N., C.S., D.N.Sc., F.A.A.N.
Professor and Director of Nursing Research
Boston University School of Nursing

Bruce A. Baldwin, Ph.D.
Clinical Associate Professor in Psychiatry
University of North Carolina School of Medicine
and
Director, PsychSystems Consultation Services
Wilmington, North Carolina

PRENTICE-HALL, INC., Englewood Cliffs, New Jersey 07632

Library of Congress Cataloging in Publication Data

Burgess, Ann Wolbert.
    Crisis intervention theory and practice.

    Bibliography: p.
    Includes index.
    1. Crisis intervention (Psychiatry)   I. Baldwin,
Bruce A., joint author.   II. Title.
RC480.6.B87   616.89'025   80-26311
ISBN 0-13-193466-X
ISBN 0-13-193458-9 (pbk.)

Editorial/production supervision
  and interior design: Eleanor Henshaw Hiatt
Cover design: Frederick Charles, Ltd.
Manufacturing buyer: John Hall

©1981 by Prentice-Hall, Inc., Englewood Cliffs, N.J. 07632

Printed in the United States of America

10   9   8   7   6   5   4   3   2   1

PRENTICE-HALL INTERNATIONAL, INC., *London*
PRENTICE-HALL OF AUSTRALIA PTY. LIMITED, *Sydney*
PRENTICE-HALL OF CANADA, LTD., *Toronto*
PRENTICE-HALL OF INDIA PRIVATE LIMITED, *New Delhi*
PRENTICE-HALL OF JAPAN, INC., *Tokyo*
PRENTICE-HALL OF SOUTHEAST ASIA PTE. LTD., *Singapore*
WHITEHALL BOOKS LIMITED, *Wellington, New Zealand*

To my uncle,
Frank Wolbert, M.D.,
who taught and practiced humanistic medicine
A.W.B.

To my father,
Walter C. Baldwin, Jr., D.D.S.,
who inspired intellectual interests
and the curiosity to pursue them
B.A.B.

CONTRIBUTING AUTHORS

Frederick L. Ahearn, Jr., Ph.D., Boston College School of Social Work, Chestnut Hill, Massachusetts 02167

Gordon D. Armstrong, Ph.D., University of Minnesota, Minneapolis, Minnesota 55455

Simeon Rizo Castellon, Ministerio de Salud Publica, Managua, Nicaragua

Judith N. Eastman, ACSW, Division for Disorders of Development and Learning, University of North Carolina, Chapel Hill, North Carolina 27514

Charles R. Figley, Ph.D., Family Research Institute, Purdue University, West Lafayette, Indiana 47906

Elaine L. Goolsby, ACSW, Division for Disorders of Development and Learning, University of North Carolina, Chapel Hill, North Carolina 27514

A. Nicholas Groth, Ph.D., Sex Offender Program, Connecticut Correctional Institution, Somers, Connecticut 06071

Carol R. Hartman, R.N., D.N.Sc., School of Nursing, Boston College, Chestnut Hill, Massachusetts 02167

Lynda Lytle Holmstrom, Ph.D., Department of Sociology, Boston College, Chestnut Hill, Massachusetts 02167

Ida M. Martinson, R.N., Ph.D., School of Nursing, University of Minnesota, Minneapolis, Minnesota 55455

Sharon K. Meginnis, Ph.D., Student Health Service, University of North Carolina, Chapel Hill, North Carolina 27514

Barbara Eck Menning, R.N., M.S., Director, Project RESOLVE, Belmont, Massachusetts 02178

Gary B. Mesibov, Ph.D., Departments of Psychiatry and Psychology, University of North Carolina, Chapel Hill, North Carolina 27514

Carolyn S. Schroeder, Ph.D., Division for Disorders of Development and Learning, University of North Carolina, Chapel Hill, North Carolina 27514

Jessica Segre, Ed.D., Somerville Mental Health Center, Somerville, Massachusetts 02143

Ellouise Bruce Sneed, R.N., M.S.N., Family Nurse Clinician, Mandeville, Louisiana 70448

Joseph L. Steinberg, L.L.B., Attorney-at-Law, Hartford, Connecticut 06103

Janet Urman, ACSW, Student Health Service, University of North Carolina, Chapel Hill, North Carolina 27514

Hollis Wheeler, M.A., Incest Consultation Network of Western Massachusetts, Amherst, Massachusetts 01002

CONTENTS

FOREWORD

The concepts of *crisis* and *crisis intervention* have had enormous impact on all fields of mental health since they were introduced—or re-introduced—by Erich Lindemann in his work with the survivors of Boston's Coconut Grove Fire over 30 years ago. The reason for this impact has primarily been that these concepts have proven to have great practical value in application to a wide range of phenomena, ranging from college graduation to acute psychosis. Gerald Caplan's work has further extended the value of these concepts by establishing crisis intervention as a major organizing principle for developing community mental health services.

The usefulness of the crisis concept is that—in contrast to most other psychological theories—it provides the clinician (or social scientist, or whoever) with a *focus* with which almost any behavioral event can be economically analyzed. As the director of a community mental health clinic, I have had a great deal of experience with the use of crisis concepts in clinical settings. Almost every client who presents to the clinic can be regarded as being in some form of crisis, and by analyzing this crisis, clinicians can rapidly develop a focus that allows them to formulate a plan for effective and time-limited intervention. Given the complex and long-standing problems that many clients have, the possibility of finding a focus—in the "here and now"—which can serve as a starting point for clinical work is most welcome. Moreover, given the limitations of available clinical resources in the community we serve, it is vital that we have a capacity to formulate short-term therapies that are efficacious and readily applicable. Thus, crisis intervention is doubly valuable in the mental health setting.

In addition, crisis intervention theory, as this volume clearly demonstrates, is valuable in many other settings as well. Health clinics, emergency rooms, military installations, and schools can all be settings in which the application of crisis theory can prove to be helpful for both clients and staff.

Despite the enormous potential of the crisis intervention concept, the literature on crisis intervention to date has been limited in two important ways. First, there has never been developed a truly comprehensive crisis theory, with a meaningful typology of crises, and strategies of instrumentation for each type. Second, there are many significant areas of potential application of crisis theory that as yet have not been adequately investigated and described. *Crisis Intervention Theory and Practice* addresses itself to both of these limitations admirably.

The first part of the book consists of Bruce Baldwin's extraordinarily lucid presentation of an integrated crisis theory, with descriptions of six types of crises, and formats for intervention in each type. I have been teaching crisis intervention for many years and have reviewed the literature thoroughly, and I have never found any work that even approaches the comprehensiveness and practicality of Dr. Baldwin's. He has drawn from a wide range of sources, brought them together, and filled in the gaps to make an integrated whole. Having used a draft of this work to teach crisis intervention to staff and students in the past year, and having found it to be extremely successful, I would recommend it highly for teaching purposes, and feel it can be used readily by students at any level of sophistication.

The second part of the book expands upon Dr. Baldwin's concepts through exposition of particular examples of each crisis type. The authors have taken great pains to seek out examples of crises that have not been discussed in depth elsewhere; but that are of great current interest nevertheless. Of particular note are Dr. Burgess's powerful sections on the crises of rape victims and potential rapists. In addition, there are, among others, well-written discussions of crises of infertility, sexual abuse, incest, divorce, mothers returning to work, multiproblem families, and Vietnam war combat stress. These stimulating and timely discussions flesh out the theoretical framework and make the practice of crisis intervention come alive.

For these reasons, I feel that *Crisis Intervention Theory and Practice* is truly a seminal work on the subject of crisis intervention, through its presentation of innovative theoretical concepts and practical clinical applications and its lucid, well-written, well-organized format. I therefore do not hesitate to recommend it to you, and trust that you will enjoy it as much as I have.

Kenneth Minkoff, M.D.
Director, Somerville Mental Health Clinic
Somerville, Massachusetts

PREFACE

The study of human response to critically stressful experiences is an increasing area of focus for all mental health care clinicians. Multidisciplinary conferences as well as clinical research are dealing with crisis intervention practice. Results of such study have yielded important data for clinicians in their work with patients and families in crisis.

Crisis situations are critical points of attention in health care delivery. Various health education groups who practice primary prevention have as their objective the teaching of strategies and alternatives for avoiding potentially stressful situations. Clinicians who intervene in a crisis may also practice secondary prevention by detecting early cases of emotional illness and by making effective referral to appropriate treatment agencies.

All clinicians should be knowledgeable in the concepts and principles specific to crisis practice. Community mental health staff are in daily contact with people who are in crisis. The patient who is hospitalized is in a transitional crisis in that his or her normal life style is disrupted. A family member dealing with the news of the death of a loved one is in a crisis state. The stresses of environmental conditions create for many people crisis situations of an economic nature.

In Part I, "Conceptual Framework," we describe how crisis intervention as a therapeutic model has only recently been accepted by mental health professionals as a treatment of choice for many clients seeking help in a range of counseling services. Effective crisis intervention requires adapting the practitioner's theoretical framework and personal style to the structural limitations of the crisis model. This model is conceptually easy to understand, but it is quite difficult to translate the concepts of crisis theory into effective practice. The intent of this section is to provide the practitioner using the crisis approach with a foundation for the theory and practice of this model. There is focus on the development of coping behaviors, and the functional value of coping mechanisms as a means to stabilize psychological functioning (i.e., to preserve emotional homeostasis). Consideration is given to the various reasons that cause coping behaviors to become ineffective, or inoperable, and that result in coping failure (i.e., emotional crises). The state of crisis is examined in terms of psychological characteristics and the opportunity for growth produced by an emotional crisis.

The assessment process is carefully described. A model for assessment and understanding maladaptive responses to stress is developed that has direct implications for the crisis intervention process and eventual crisis resolution. Emphasized is the process of working through the determinants of maladaptive coping and replacing those ways of coping with others that are more adaptive. The role of the precipitant of emotional crises as a primary support for maladaptive responses is explored.

The importance of establishing structure in crisis intervention is emphasized, specifically the necessity for establishing time/goal contracts as part of therapy. The rationale for contracts is a general theme, as is the development of appropriate contracts that will facilitate crisis resolution. The relationship between client motivation and acceptance of responsibility for crisis resolution and time/goal contracts (i.e., using Parkinson's Law in psychotherapy) is explored. Structural aspects of contracts as well as problems encountered in contracting are discussed.

In Part II, "Typology of Crises," we have used the conceptual framework for crisis intervention to understand client populations in crisis who have been previously neglected both in clinical practice and in the professional literature. We believe it is essential to reexamine those life issues that produce stress and vulnerability and thus discuss parenthood as well as infertility, divorce, returning to work, child abuse, victim issues in rape and incest, offender behavior, earthquakes, war combat stress, home care for the dying child, and the multiproblem family. Within the chapters that deal with the specific classes of crises, we attempt to apply the assessment process and describe general intervention strategies.

We sought experts to present their clinical knowledge in this section of the book and have included representatives from a wide variety of disciplines. We have written this book for the interdisciplinary groups of mental health care providers: nurses, psychologists, social workers, psychiatrists, educators, clergy, lawyers. Mental health professionals are constantly faced with the task of helping clients deal with a wide variety of trauma, losses, and crises. Applying the convergent model of crisis theory to the six classes of crises is a step toward more effective treatment intervention.

We extend our appreciation to the many people with whom we have worked in the various phases of our research and practice.

This text would not have been complete without the guidance and advice provided by the Prentice-Hall staff, especially our editor Fred Henry. We are indebted to Eleanor Henshaw Hiatt, who directed the editorial production of the book, for her constructive and thorough work on the project, and to Margaret McNeily, who copyedited the manuscript.

Our warmest thanks go to our children, Elizabeth, Benton, Clayton, and Sarah Burgess and Travis and Elissa Baldwin for their patience throughout the project. And above all we owe a special debt to John N. Wolbert, Allen G. Burgess, and Joyce Baldwin for their discussions, suggestions, encouragement, and support throughout all phases of the manuscript development.

A.W.B.
B.A.B.

I

CONCEPTUAL FRAMEWORK

A convergent model of crisis intervention theory and practice is described and presented throughout this book. This model optimizes the strengths of the two divergent models of screening/assessment and problem solving, yet minimizes the weaknesses of each. This convergent model, based on the work of Gerald Caplan (see Caplan 1964 reference at the end of Chapter 1), has a past-present-future orientation.

In addition, this part of the book includes chapters on the conceptual framework for crisis intervention practice, an assessment format for emotional crises, a structural design for practicing crisis therapy, and intervention techniques—individual, group, self-help—for crisis intervention practice.

1

INTRODUCTION TO CRISIS INTERVENTION: TOWARD A CONVERGENT MODEL

During the last decade, the growth of the community mental health movement has closely followed the development of innovative approaches for meeting mental health needs in the community.[1] An important part of this trend has been an increasing interest in crisis intervention, a therapeutic approach developed from the pioneering work of Lindemann (1944), Caplan (1961, 1964), and many others. Crisis intervention theory has now been extended and elaborated into a soundly conceptualized and effective model for the practice of brief therapy. Further, clinician consistency during the course of crisis therapy has been demonstrated (Beers and Foreman 1976), a consistency that closely corresponds to the tenets of this theoretical model.

However, there remains a significant disjunction between the increased use of crisis intervention in clinical settings and the specific teaching of this model in training programs for mental health professionals of all disciplines. It is unfortunate that, with few significant exceptions, crisis intervention and the principles on which it is based as a structure for brief intervention have not been taught directly and systematically to students in professional mental

[1]A substantial part of this chapter, through page 22, is reprinted with permission from B. A. Baldwin, "Styles of Crisis Intervention: Toward a Convergent Model," *Journal of Professional Psychology*, 11 (1980), 113–120. Copyright 1980 by the American Psychological Association.

health training programs. Students too frequently graduate from their training programs with only general conceptions of crisis therapy and with minimally developed skills in the practice of such therapy.

As a result, crisis intervention has become at once a widely used and often abused approach to brief therapy. For many mental health professionals, *crisis intervention* has become a generic term encompassing a broad range of therapeutic practices, and specific aspects of this model remain vague and nebulous (McGee 1968). Although this approach is now a treatment of choice for many clients, there has not been comprehensive examination of models for training effective crisis therapists nor enough active consideration of the place of crisis intervention in graduate training programs. In the field, the clinical practice of crisis intervention remains inconsistent and at times ineffective as practitioners not adequately trained in this approach are required to use it.

MYTHS AND MISCONCEPTIONS ABOUT CRISIS INTERVENTION[2]

A major source of confusion that compromises the effective use of this model arises from the myths and misconceptions currently associated with this model. Misinformation has contributed to the lack of a clear conceptualization of this approach by mental health professionals and has promoted a good deal of confusion in the practice of crisis therapy by the clinician. Dispelling the myths about crisis intervention is a prerequisite for examining the implications of this model in training and clinical practice. Among the more common myths and misconceptions about crisis intervention are the following.

Myth: Crisis intervention is only for responding to psychiatric emergencies

In this common myth, crisis intervention is confused with emergency services in which medical or psychiatric resources must be mobilized immediately to treat clients in situations where serious medical and/or psychiatric consequences can result if treatment is delayed. Although the effective crisis therapist is trained to deal with acute psychiatric emergencies, this type of crisis is usually only a small part of the crisis situations presented by clients. Response to psychiatric emergencies is at one extreme of a range of crises that vary in intensity and that are all part of the practice of the well-trained crisis therapist.

[2]This section, ending on page 7, is reprinted with permission from B.A. Baldwin, "Crisis Intervention in Professional Practice: Implications for Clinical Training," *American Journal of Orthopsychiatry*, 47(1977), 659-670. Copyright 1977 by the American Orthopsychiatric Association, Inc.

Myth: Crisis intervention is a "one-shot" form of therapy

In this case, crisis intervention is viewed as a single-session type of therapy to defuse a stressful situation without necessarily requiring follow-up or therapeutic continuity. In actuality, most effective crisis intervention involves a series of therapeutic contacts, usually ranging from one to eight in number (with only a small proportion of the total requiring just a single contact). Caplan (1964) stated that most crises are time-limited events that average four to six weeks in duration, and it is during this time span that a series of therapeutic contacts takes place to adaptively resolve the crisis.

Myth: Crisis intervention is a form of therapy practiced only by paraprofessionals

During the sixties, there was a great proliferation of youth-oriented drug crisis services staffed primarily by paraprofessionals. During this period, crisis intervention became closely associated with drug crisis services and was seen as a specific response to drug-related problems among youth. Training programs in these alternate services were usually limited (McCord and Packwood 1973), and *crisis intervention* was a term used to describe a range of helping interventions within the "crisis center." However, this type of crisis intervention contrasts markedly with the model now used by professionals. Crisis intervention as practiced in the alternate services (Baldwin 1975; Glasscote et al. 1975) emphasized present problem solving while often neglecting consideration of the psychodynamic determinants of crises. Although there are areas of overlap, the problem-solving style of crisis intervention differs in a major way from the emerging convergent model where the clinician addresses the psychodynamic issues involved in client crises.

Myth: Crisis intervention represents only a "holding action" until longer-term therapy can begin

This frequently encountered misconception stems from a perception that crisis intervention provides only a limited supportive relationship to help stabilize the crisis client until "real" therapy (i.e., long-term therapy) can be arranged. It is seen as a primarily supportive intervention and not as a therapeutic model in its own right. In actuality, crisis intervention is a soundly conceptualized therapeutic model that provides an effective framework for the practice of this form of brief therapy. As a result of this recognition, crisis intervention has increasingly been used as a treatment of choice for many clients, and in many cases is the only therapy required.

Myth: Crisis intervention is effective only for primary prevention programs

Crisis intervention had its origins in the early work of professionals interested in the primary prevention of mental disorders (i.e., reducing the incidence of new cases of mental impairment in the community) as espoused in the philosophy of those who originally defined many of the constructs underlying this approach (Caplan 1961; Caplan and Grunebaum 1967; Lindemann 1944). There is now more awareness that levels of prevention of mental disorders overlap considerably and that specific programs may have impact in the community at several levels. With this in mind, it is not surprising that crisis intervention has been used effectively in secondary prevention of mental impairment (i.e., reducing the duration of cases of mental impairment that occur in the community) and at the tertiary level as well (i.e., helping those who have recovered from mental disorders to return to full participation in community life). This multilevel use of crisis intervention at present contrasts with its early affiliation with primary prevention programs. In fact, today some researchers believe that crisis intervention is practiced primarily at the secondary prevention level (Silverman 1977).

Myth: Crisis intervention does not produce lasting change

Crisis intervention is at times perceived to be only a present-oriented expedient, one that is useful in defusing situational crises (usually through environmental manipulation) but ineffective in producing lasting change. There is little recognition that substantial change often occurs during the resolution of emotional crises, when even brief therapeutic interventions may disproportionately influence adaptive change and personal growth. A client's reaction to an emotional crisis is not irrevocably determined by previous experience, and a new psychological or emotional equilibrium established through crisis resolution may not only be at a more adaptive level but may also prevent future crises from occurring (Paul 1966). There is increasing emphasis in crisis intervention on identifying underlying conflicts represented in crisis situations and using the crisis as a vehicle for adaptively resolving these determinate conflicts or issues.

Myth: Crisis intervention requires no special skills for the well-trained therapist

Among professionals who hold to this pervasive myth, crisis intervention is perceived to be an "easy" form of therapy requiring no skills beyond those of the clinician well trained in longer-term therapy. Although the practice of effective crisis intervention requires many of the skills of the longer-term therapist, there are additional skills necessary for the practice of crisis therapy that are inherent to this theoretical framework. The skills associated with the crisis model must be integrated with the more traditional skills of the clinician for effectiveness in crisis therapy. By extension, those who believe that few or no special skills are necessary for crisis intervention may stand in the way of introducing specific training in this approach in professional training programs.

These often interrelated myths and misconceptions about crisis intervention have produced confusion, doubt, and ineffective use of this model among many mental health professionals who have been well trained and who are quite competent otherwise. As this therapeutic model becomes more accurately perceived among professionals, its potential for helping and its application in various clinical contexts can only be enhanced.

DIVERGENT MODELS OF CRISIS INTERVENTION

When the clinical practices of both professional and paraprofessional crisis therapists are examined, it is apparent that there are several distinct "styles" of crisis intervention now in use. These divergent styles reflect the training of their respective practitioners and the particular philosophy of change on which these approaches are based. These contrasting styles have contributed to the development of crisis theory by defining the intervention process from differing theoretical and philosophical frameworks. In addition, these styles have also highlighted some of the strengths and weaknesses inherent to each model.

With various styles of crisis intervention now in use, two models that represent polar extremes are discussed to provide perspective on the convergence phenomenon now being observed. The screening/assessment model and the problem-solving model reflect contrasting approaches to client crises at both theoretical and practice levels. An overview of the characteristics of each of these disparate approaches to crisis intervention as they have contributed to the convergent model is presented in Table 1-1.

Table 1-1
Overview of the Major Dimensions of Two
Divergent Styles of Crisis Intervention as Related to an
Emerging Convergent Model.

	Screening/ Assessment Model	Convergent Model	Problem-Solving Model
1. Time orientation	Past-Present	Past-Present-Future	Present-Future
2. Assessment	Traditional diagnostic	Crisis assessment	Little formal assessment
3. Response to client psychodynamics	Broad spectrum	Focal emphasis on precipitant	Minimal response
4. Therapeutic emphasis	Evaluation, support, emergency services	Crisis resolution	Present problem solving
5. Time frame	1-2 sessions	1-8 sessions	Open-ended
6. Therapeutic structure	Structured, therapist defined	Structured, negotiated with client	Relatively unstructured
7. Outcome criteria	Referral facilitated, services coordinated	Restoration of or increase in precrisis functioning	Problem resolved
8. Common problems	Little treatment beyond client support	Defining time frame/ relevant goals, maintaining focal emphasis	Dependency/regression issues, Therapist overinvolvement
9. Level of training	Professional	Usually professional	Usually paraprofessional
10. Typical clinical context	Emergency rooms, walk-in clinics	Outpatient clinics, community mental health centers	Switchboards, suicide prevention services

Note: Variations in the above three models for crisis intervention are recognized but are conceptualized here so as to clarify the dimensions on which they differ from one another.

The Screening/Assessment Model

The screening/assessment style of crisis intervention derives from the medical model as it is interpreted within a psychotherapeutic context. The medical model emphasizes treatment of an underlying disease process within the client. As a result of this treatment philosophy, the screening/assessment model stresses thorough evaluation of the client through a rather comprehensive diagnostic process. The client, although experiencing an emotional crisis that reflects a present problem situation that has produced stress, is seen to have underlying problems that have only become manifest in that situation. As Blaney (1975), discussing the medical model in terms of psychotherapy, states:

> The visible evidences of the disorder are but manifestations of an underlying condition (not necessarily organic). This claim employs a direct analogy from physical illnesses, and dynamic psychiatry has accepted it with a vengeance. [P. 911]

In this model for crisis intervention, structure is created primarily by the therapist to accomplish an in-depth evaluation of the client with attention to the client's past experiences and psychodynamics, family and social history, and medical background. Following this evaluation, the client is then referred as appropriate to other services or community resources for treatment. In those instances when the client presents with a medical and/or psychiatric emergency, available resources for treatment are mobilized immediately. At times, during and after an emergency intervention process, the therapist may also function as a coordinator of services required by the client (Baldwin 1978). However, the primary task of the therapist when this style of crisis intervention is used is to evaluate the client's past and present functioning and to help the client obtain appropriate treatment.

Because of the emphasis on screening (or triage) and assessment, little therapy is provided when this model is used. Support is given during the evaluation process, and any insight developed may be helpful to the client. However, the emphasis is on diagnostic evaluation, and treatment is secondary to this process. The time-limited nature of the evaluation process (usually 1–2 therapy hours) also places severe limitations on treatment possibilities. At times, clients feel that their presenting problems are not addressed because the focus in the therapeutic contact tends to remain on exploration of the past. Because of this, many clients do not follow through with referrals initiated by therapists who use a screening/assessment style of crisis intervention.

The screening/assessment model of crisis intervention is a viable form of therapeutic contact that is necessary for certain clients, particularly those with deep-seated or chronic psychopathology. It is also an often mandated style of crisis intervention due to clinic policies that limit service primarily to evaluation and referral. This is frequently the case in walk-in services or hospital emergency rooms. However, although necessary in certain cases, the screening/assessment model is an incomplete form of crisis intervention and must not be confused with crisis intervention as practiced by the skilled crisis therapist. In several important respects, the screening/assessment model of crisis intervention is more related to walk-in intake interviewing as practiced in professionally staffed clinics than to crisis intervention even though such services are often called "crisis clinics."

The Problem-Solving Model

The problem-solving model of crisis intervention was standard in the alternate services, staffed by paraprofessionals, that developed during the last decade. This model stands in contrast to the screening/assessment approach to emotional crises. The problem-solving model had its origins during the sixties when the rise of the counterculture signaled changing life styles and a challenge to traditional values. Influential in the development of alternate services were questions about the ability (or willingness!) of mental health professionals to help youth involved with this subculture. There were also serious questions about the responsiveness of established service delivery systems to the special problems of youth at this time.

Clark and Jaffe (1972) discuss the rise of the counterinstitution as the result of professionals attempting to "help" young people by seeking to modify their behavior to correspond to the normative values of society. The result was the development of distrust between youth and mental health professionals. Yet, there were casualties of the counterculture that required intervention to deal with alienation, drug crises, and the adjustment problems associated with new life styles and values. A direct result was the development of alternate services (Baldwin 1975) that functioned outside the established mental health service delivery systems in the community.

These alternate services experimented with new styles of crisis intervention and with innovative service delivery systems. One significant innovation in these services was use of peer counseling as a primary service modality. Young people were trained in basic helping skills to help other youths experiencing crises. Training usually emphasized a humanistically oriented, client-centered approach that stressed active listening, establishment of an empathic relationship with the client, and dissemination of information. A problem-solving approach was used in which a peer counselor helped clients to define and evaluate different courses of action as a response to a problem, to decide to act on one of them, and then to follow through with the decision. Because of the client-centered emphasis in training, little attention was given to the need for the counselor to structure the counseling contact. Any structure created in the counseling interaction (e.g., time of meetings, goals, time contract, etc.) was usually at the client's initiative.

The service delivery system in the alternate services also tended to deemphasize structure. When responding to clients' problems via telephone "hot lines" or walk-in contacts, no appointments were needed, and the counseling contacts were typically left open-ended. The client could call or return for additional counseling as often as needed for as long as needed. This type of service delivery provided immediate accessibility to consumers and complemented youth culture values.

The basis for crisis intervention in the alternate services was present problem solving to help clients to adjust to the current realities of their lives. The relevance of past experience and of the psychodynamics that affected present functioning was frequently denied. As a consequence, any evaluation of the psychodynamic aspects of clients' problems was ignored in order to respond only to the immediate problem of concern as defined by the client.

Deemed important was the "here and now" rather than the past, and "categorizing" clients into psychiatric diagnoses was considered to be "dehumanizing" and to be avoided. This present problem-solving emphasis (and the denial of the relevance of past experience and psychodynamics) was a direct reaction to the underlying disease-process assumption of the medical model that was associated at the time (sometimes unfairly!) with mental health professionals. Also rejected in the alternate services was the assumption that long-term treatment was required for most clients to better adjust to their present realities.

This problem-solving style of crisis intervention was not without its problems. By responding only to a client's present problem, many times the underlying determinants of the client's difficulties were not perceived, and an opportunity to resolve the crisis at a deeper level was missed. Indeed, some aspects of the highly client-centered approach used in the alternate services was counterproductive. The unwillingness (supported by absence of necessary training) of peer counselors to structure and focus the counseling contact frequently permitted the helping process to become quite diffuse. Client dependency was often encouraged (directly or indirectly) by overnurturant peer counselors. Excessive client support, without concurrent encouragement of client responsibility for growth, tended to subtly reinforce client regression instead of encouraging adaptive coping in response to a problem situation.

Another factor that compounded these problems was that the humanistic philosophy in these services was often distorted into an assumption that complete client acceptance by the counselor was somehow inherently therapeutic. Imposition of any structure in the helping relationship by a counselor was equated with lack of acceptance and excessive counselor control. As one consequence, young and often idealistic peer counselors became overinvolved in the helping process and were at times manipulated and used inappropriately by their clients (Torop and Torop 1972). This led in turn to disillusionment and high dropout rates (or staff burnout) in the alternate services (Freudenberger 1974, 1975).

TOWARD CONVERGENCE

In recent years, there has been a trend toward convergence of the different styles of crisis intervention. Of particular interest is the convergence of the approach to crisis intervention represented by the professional practitioner and that of the paraprofessionally staffed alternate services. This convergence has resulted in a more unified and accepted conceptual framework for crisis therapy, a framework that is eminently usable by the practicing clinician and by those in training. At least part of this convergence has resulted from the rising prominence of community psychology and from the increased sophistication of community mental health programs.

The convergent model optimizes the strengths of both the screening/ assessment and problem-solving approaches to crisis intervention and minimizes the weaknesses of each. This model, based on the work of Gerald Caplan (1964), has a past-present-future orientation. There is selective attention given to any reactivated conflict from the client's past experience that may have precipitated the present crisis (Hoffman and Remmel 1975). Data, either past or present, that are not directly related to the client's present crisis have no place in the crisis intervention process (Morley, Messick, and Aguilera 1967). Such data are not allowed to diffuse the focus of crisis intervention.

There is also a future preventive emphasis in the use of this model based on the assumption that a present problem situation can be used to work through a reactivated conflict from the past (i.e., the precipitant) that has in part determined the client's failure to cope with a resulting emotional crisis. By defining and working through the precipitant with selective attention to psychodynamics *and* learning more adaptive ways to respond to a present stressful situation (i.e., problem solving), the probability of a future similar crisis is reduced.

The time orientation also has implications for the crisis assessment process. Although the traditional diagnostic evaluation is not usually part of crisis intervention, there is assessment of all dimensions of the client's present crisis situation. The crisis intervention process by definition focuses on the client's stress, whereas in other forms of brief (and long-term) therapy, the emphasis is on the person (Stuart and Mackey 1977). Butcher and Maudel (1976), among others, seriously question the efficacy and relevance of traditional assessment procedures in crisis intervention as these may distract the therapist's attention away from the crisis and ways to resolve it.

Further, the self-limiting nature of most emotional crises permits a time frame of only one-to-eight therapy hours for the crisis resolution process. These hours are structured and focused through the collaborative effort of *both* client and clinician. During the crisis assessment process, there is mutual definition of the problem and of the specific goals to be reached for crisis resolution, and an agreement on a period of time to work toward these goals. This is the contracting process so necessary for the effective use of this approach. Diffusion of the crisis therapy results when an effective time-goal contract is not defined with the client early in the therapeutic contact.

The goals of the convergent model of crisis intervention are also different from those of other brief therapy models and long-term psychotherapy. The general goal of crisis intervention is to help restore the client as quickly as possible to the level of functioning that existed prior to the crisis rather than to effect a "cure." If an underlying conflict (precipitant) can be worked through during the crisis resolution process, this is an additional benefit to the client and will help reduce the probability of additional crises of this type.

At times, therapists find it difficult to terminate clients in crisis therapy and to help them to return to daily life with unresolved problems not related to the present problem situation. Yet, helping the client to regain the level of precrisis function remains the standard criterion against which success in crisis intervention is evaluated. In any service using crisis intervention as a therapeutic modality, it is understood that some clients will require referral for additional therapy or for other services following the time-limited and goal-structured intervention process.

THE EFFECTIVE
CRISIS THERAPIST

Therapists who are learning crisis intervention may experience varying levels of difficulty adjusting to the convergent model. Without systematic training in this approach, therapists tend to fall into the weaknesses of both the screening/assessment and the problem-solving approaches to crisis intervention. Therapists with strong traditional training may spend too much time doing an extensive and complete evaluation of the client before any "therapy" is offered. This defeats the purpose of crisis intervention because most emotional crises are time-limited states, and help must be quickly available if adaptive resolution is to occur. Other therapists who are novices or who are insecure in their therapeutic role often fail to provide any structure and adopt a passive role in relation to the client. As a result, the crisis therapy spreads into other irrelevant problems, or turns exclusively to exploration of the past. The ability to create and maintain an effective time-goal contract in crisis intervention is a major determinant of outcome.

The well-trained crisis therapist, on the other hand, should be able to use certain aspects of both the screening/assessment and the problem-solving models with selected clients. For example, a choice might be made to use a screening/assessment approach when the therapist cannot continue to see a particular client through to crisis resolution (because of vacations, not enough training to deal with a particular type of crisis, the problem is not appropriate for clinical services, etc.). Providing support and evaluating the client might also become the response of choice when the presenting problem is a psychiatric and/or medical emergency and other treatment resources must be immediately mobilized.

At the other extreme are client crises that are primarily situationally determined. In such instances, the crisis therapist may elect to use the problem-solving style of crisis intervention to facilitate adaptive crisis resolution. This is a particularly helpful model for intervention when there is no clear precipitant, when the locus of stress is primarily external to the client, and when the client has had a reasonably good precrisis level of functioning.

For the practicing clinician, crisis intervention can be placed into realistic perspective only if it is considered a *limited framework* for therapeutic intervention in contrast to a major theoretical orientation to psychotherapy, one that is relatively broad based. This is particularly true of the convergent model for crisis therapy. Crisis intervention as a model is neither a theory of personality nor a comprehensive theory of psychotherapy. It is, rather, a limited but important framework for responding to a normative life event: the emotional crisis. As a result, crisis intervention as a therapeutic model cannot be discussed in the same terms as more inclusive therapeutic approaches such as psychoanalytic psychotherapy, behavior modification, relationship therapy, or the Gestalt orientation.

Crisis intervention as a structural framework for a limited form of therapy to resolve emotional crises is based on a sound body of principles, corollaries, and techniques inherent in the convergent model. However, this corpus of knowledge and techniques primarily defines limits within which the crisis therapist uses a more comprehensive psychotherapeutic orientation modified for application within the crisis framework. In sum, crisis theory and technique provide the context for the specialized use of the therapist's preferred orientation to psychotherapy.

In the course of professional training, the skills of the clinician are essentially developed at three levels: (1) the *conceptual skills* provide the framework for understanding client problems and for developing strategies for change; (2) the *clinical skills* are the techniques for implementing an effective therapeutic strategy and are an extension of the conceptual framework; and (3) the *communication skills* are necessary to enhance information exchange in the therapeutic relationship and to create a non-threatening, open relationship. Effective crisis therapy at each of these three levels requires: (a) the general skills of the well-trained clinician, and (b) the special skills of the well-trained crisis therapist.

Understanding the relationship of crisis theory to the more comprehensive theoretical orientations to psychotherapy, it follows that there can be behaviorally oriented crisis therapists, Gestalt-oriented crisis therapists, or psychoanalytically oriented crisis therapists, all of whom may effectively practice this form of therapy. In each case, the therapist has adapted a general therapeutic orientation and the skills associated with that orientation to the framework of crisis theory and the skills inherent in this model. Thus, the convergent model of crisis intervention can be practiced effectively from many theoretical bases provided that the clinician makes the necessary modifications to accommodate the structural limitations of this approach.

BURNOUT AND
THE CRISIS THERAPIST

It would be remiss in this introduction to crisis intervention to neglect a discussion of the pressure experienced by the crisis therapist. The stresses of crisis intervention lead to a particular vulnerability of the crisis therapist that must be addressed—that is, burnout. As more clinics adopt crisis intervention as a primary treatment modality, and as more professionals use this approach in clinical practice, the danger of burnout increases since more time each day is spent in this type of work.

The effects of continued intense involvement with clients in acute distress are cumulative on the clinician and become a significant liability if measures are not taken by the clinician *and* by the organization to prevent burnout. As Larson, Gilbertson, and Powell (1978) so aptly state in this regard,

> The mental health environment . . . , as currently structured, facilitates burnout. In fact, the present attitude seems to be one of not respecting, in terms of themselves, those same principles of mental health that therapists espouse for patients: The need to set limits on the demands of others, the need to balance work and social needs, the need to foster self-respect, and the need to reject the notion of being all things to all people. [P. 564]

The burnout syndrome as a psychological phenomenon among mental health professionals has only recently been recognized. Freudenberger (1974, 1975) first conceptualized burnout when he recognized it among the staff of alternate services and free clinics in the late sixties. In those services, he noticed that volunteers tended to leave after about one year because they had "burned out" as the result of intense involvement with clients and the need to give constantly to clients experiencing acute distress.

More recently Maslach (1978a) and others have recognized that burnout also occurs in a wide range of professions, not the least of which are the mental health disciplines. In fact, burnout seems particularly endemic among those in the social service and health professions because of the often emotionally charged nature of helping in this type of work (Pines and Maslach 1978). In these professions, clinicians are required to respond to clients experiencing acute crises, as a major aspect of their professional responsibility. Because of this, burnout among mental health professionals, particularly the crisis therapist, becomes a very real and powerful vulnerability if not anticipated and if preventive measures are not taken.

Pines and Maslach (1978) define burnout as "a syndrome of physical and emotional exhaustion, involving the development of negative self-concept, negative job attitudes, and loss of concern and feeling for clients" (p. 233). This description is very similar to Freudenberger's earlier observations of the reactions of volunteer staff members in alternate services. However, there is a significant difference. The burned out professional (in contrast to the volunteer) does not as easily have the option to terminate because of the personal, economic, and educational investment in a particular profession. The professional, to survive emotionally, must recognize the possibility, even the probability, of burnout and must initiate necessary steps to slow down or arrest the progression of this syndrome.

Shubin (1978) cautions that the first signs of burnout may be so subtle that they are easily dismissed. As the symptoms intensify with time, they may then be blamed on other (usually external) factors rather than on personal burnout. In the first stage of burnout (Maslach, 1976), there is experienced characteristic physical tiredness and emotional exhaustion. This is often accompanied by somatic symptoms of stress such as headaches, gastronintestinal distress, or other aches and pains. There may be increased susceptibility to physical illness, and absenteeism may increase. Often experienced as well is insomnia and the inability to truly relax and "get away" emotionally from work.

Slowly this phase evolves into a second stage in which therapists "lose all concern, all emotional feeling, for the persons they work with and come to treat them in detached or even dehumanized ways" (Maslach 1976, p.16). In turn, this devalues the clinician as a competent professional, and self-esteem diminishes because of these negative feelings about clients. There is often a concurrent physical and emotional withdrawal from clients. Many different mechanisms develop to emotionally keep clients and their problems at a distance. A minimum of effort and energy is put into work with clients, and the individual burning out becomes oriented to "just getting through" another day.

Up to this point, burnout can be controlled, and can be reversed, if the proper steps are taken. However, in at least some individuals, burnout progresses to a third and probably irreversible phase. This is the stage of terminal burnout (Maslach 1978b). It is characterized by deep cynicism about people in general and clients in particular, accompanied by a feeling of total disgust with the work that has created burnout. At this stage, some professionals move to other types of employment, particularly to positions that do not involve working directly with people in distress. Others stay on as burned-out professionals to continue working in the same or similar positions to the detriment of their clients, their profession, and themselves.

There are a number of signals that indicate a particular professional is in the process of burning out. Some of the most common signs are the following:

1. Limiting or reducing the time spent with clients and making more or earlier referrals.

2. Adopting rigid "by the book" approaches to client problems rather than developing individualized treatment protocols.

3. Referring to clients in dehumanized, technical ways rather than as people, or using "sick" humor in reference to clients and their problems.

4. Use of intellectualization or compartmentalization as defenses to reduce the emotional impact of client presentations.

5. Increased emotional lability of the therapist, often accompanied by emotional outbursts (sometimes directed toward clients), which signal loss of emotional control.

6. Turning excessively to other staff members for help in coping with emotional or physical problems or with professional responsibilities.

7. Developing uncharacteristically rigid ways of thinking and/or loss of ability to adapt to change.

8. Cynical attitudes about oneself and about really doing anything helpful with clients who are perceived to be incapable of change.

9. Minimizing time spent at work or spending more than usual time at work but getting less and less accomplished.

10. Feeling bored as clients seem to fuse and are perceived to be more and more alike rather than individuals.

11. Increasing use of drugs or alcohol to cope with job pressures and as a way to "unwind" after work.

12. Increasing interference with one's family or social life as the stresses of work spill over into these areas.

Although no single sign of burnout is indicative, when many of them are present together, it should be recognized that burnout is in progress. When burnout occurs, a number of steps can be initiated to alleviate this problem.

Interventions can be made at both the individual and institutional levels as responses to burnout among clinical staff. At the individual level, the following interventions have been suggested (Freudenberger 1974, 1975; Maslach 1976, 1978a, 1978b; Pines and Maslach 1978; Shubin 1978).

1. Develop an on-the-job support system with coworkers to discuss difficult cases, and to provide support and encouragement and an opportunity to vent frustrations.

2. To the fullest extent possible, vary professional activities during the day to prevent seeing client after client in emotionally charged therapy sessions.

3. Keep yourself professionally involved and growing by engaging in new projects, developing new skills and techniques, attending training programs, or becoming involved in the activities of your professional organization whether at a local, regional, or national level.

4. Adopt a "decompression routine" (not alcohol or drugs) to ease the transition from work to leisure time. Meditation, relaxation techniques, jogging, or even a walk is most helpful in this regard.

5. Learn to enjoy yourself outside work and develop other interests or skills that have nothing to do with your professional life. These activities help to rejuvenate yourself physically and emotionally and help you to withstand work pressures more easily.

6. Consistent with the crisis intervention approach, clearly structure your therapy by creating a time-goal contract and to set appropriate expectations for the intervention for both you and your clients.

7. During the day, take short breaks to give yourself some relief, and make it a point to get out of the office for lunch. Spend time during the day (perhaps lunch) with friends (not necessarily coworkers) and avoid any "shop talk" during conversations.

8. Cultivate the capacity for "detached concern" that is so necessary for self-maintenance in crisis therapy and will enable you to provide more objectively the care your clients require for adaptive crisis resolution.

When crisis therapy becomes a primary treatment modality as is occurring more and more often at present, the institution must also be sensitive to the possibility of burnout among its professional staff. To prevent or reduce the effects of burnout among clinicians, there are a number of specific steps that can be initiated at the organizational level (Freudenberger 1974, 1975; Kahn 1978; Maslach 1976, 1978a, 1978b; Pines and Maslach 1978). Among these steps are the following:

1. Educate the staff about the possibility of burnout, the signs and signals of burnout, and the individual preventive measures that can be taken to alleviate the effects of burnout.

2. Keep the staff-to-client ratio within reasonable limits. Also structure clinical responsibilities so that the client load is shared and see that chronic and acute care do not become the sole responsibility of just a few staff members.

3. Create institutional support for crisis services with rewards and encouragement for staff engaged in this type of work. (*Note:* In many service settings, crisis intervention and emergency services are an unwanted "extra" responsibility in addition to regular responsibilities and operate without adequate support by the organization. This increases the possibility of burnout.)

4. Build in opportunities for lateral job transfers for those clinicians who are burning out and also provide enough flexibility so that clinicians can periodically restructure their clinical responsibilities to some extent.

5. Sponsor retreats or other organizational activities for staff training and development. Fostering clinican input into organizational policy and development is also helpful in providing a sense of personal value and legitimacy to clinical work. Periodic social activities for all staff are also helpful.

At the present level of knowledge about burnout, it is not known whether this syndrome can be completely prevented. However, with foreknowledge and preventive measures instituted, its progression can be significantly slowed. Sensitivity of the organization to burnout and to its prevention among crisis therapists is helpful not only to extend the effectiveness of the clinicians engaged in this important work but also to provide quality care to clients seeking help from the service.

Because of the emotional intensity of crisis therapy, clinicians who do this type of work as a major part of their professional responsibilities are prone to burnout, and protective measures must be adopted. Ultimately, education about burnout will be necessary in the graduate training programs for mental health professionals. Until that time, it is up to the individual clinician and the employing organization to initiate measures that prevent (or slow) burnout among staff members engaged in crisis intervention.

CONCLUDING REMARKS

In summary, the convergent model of crisis intervention is the basis for most crisis therapy practiced by mental health professionals. However, either the evaluative approach of the screening/assessment model or the problem-solving approach of the alternate services may be relevant for certain clients in the practice of crisis intervention. The well-trained crisis therapist is able to use all three models effectively in clinical practice as appropriate to the needs of particular clients. Neither the screening/assessment model nor the problem-solving model for crisis intervention by itself is a complete approach to crisis therapy.

The evolution of a variety of distinct models for crisis intervention toward one convergent model has accelerated during the past decade. One result of this convergence has been modification of service delivery systems to optimize the effectiveness of this approach. For example, in clinical settings now structured to accommodate the screening/assessment model, opportunities for clinicians to work with clients long enough for crisis resolution (in lieu of referral) are being provided. In other clinics, waiting lists are being eliminated or reduced to help clients gain the necessary accessibility for help in resolving their crises that are time-limited.

The convergent model of crisis intervention is also being adopted by the alternate services that continue to provide valuable community-based crisis counseling. In the alternate services that have begun to adopt the convergent model, creation of structure and counselor attention to selected psychodynamics involved in the client's crisis (i.e., the precipitant) have now become accepted practices. Such structure permits increased counselor ability to guide and focus the helping process in the direction of adaptive crisis resolution. Using the tenets of the convergent model for crisis intervention has also secondarily eased staff burnout in the alternate services.

In the future, the convergence phenomenon in crisis intervention can be expected to continue. As a therapeutic model, it does not carry with it the social stigma often associated with "psychotherapy"; it has become an important part of community mental health, although it has not yet reached its full stature in clinical training programs. However, the increased prominence of crisis intervention has permitted the benefits of training in this model (Baldwin 1977; Wales 1972) to become more recognized and established as a valuable part of the clinical training of mental health professionals from all the disciplines. Further, this convergence has been an impetus for continuing research into the theory and practice of crisis therapy and is a trend that is expected to continue.

In short, crisis intervention may represent an important change in therapeutic emphasis since it is a model based on mental health and adjustment rather than being oriented to psychopathology and the past. To an increasing extent, emotional crises are viewed as normative psychological events that occur even among the well adjusted rather than as a sign of psychopathology per se. It is likely, in a technologically oriented and impersonal society, that crises may become even more frequent as a response to rapid social change and changing life styles (Shields 1975). The adjustment-oriented mental health professional represents a new role in contrast to the traditional one that emphasized treatment of the deviant, the mentally ill, and the seriously disturbed (Freudenberger 1973).

REFERENCES

BALDWIN, B. A., "Alternative Services, Professional Practice, and Community Mental Health," *American Journal of Orthopsychiatry,* 45 (1975), 734–43.

———, "Crisis Intervention in Professional Practice: Implications for Clinical Training," *American Journal of Orthopsychiatry,* 47 (1977), 659–70.

———, "A Paradigm for the Classification of Emotional Crises: Implications for Crisis Intervention," *American Journal of Orthopsychiatry,* 48 (1978), 538–51.

BEERS, T., and M. FOREMAN, "Intervention Patterns in Crisis Interviews," *Journal of Counseling Psychology,* 23 (1976), 87–91.

BLANEY, P. H., "Implications of the Medical Model and Its Alternatives," *American Journal of Psychiatry,* 132 (1975), 911–14.

BUTCHER, J. N., and G. R. MAUDEL, "Crisis Intervention," in I. Weiner, ed., *Clinical Methods in Psychology.* New York: John Wiley & Sons, Inc., 1976.

CAPLAN, G., *An Approach to Community Mental Health.* New York: Grune & Stratton, Inc., 1961.

——— *Principles of Preventive Psychiatry.* New York: Basic Books, Inc., Publishers, 1964.

CAPLAN, G., and H. GRUNEBAUM, "Perspectives on Primary Prevention: A Review," *Archives of General Psychiatry,* 17 (1967), 331–46.

CLARK, T., and D. T. JAFFE, "Change within Youth Crisis Centers," *American Journal of Orthopsychiatry,* 42 (1972) 675–87.

FREUDENBERGER, H. J., "The Therapist Faces the New Life Styles of His Patients," *Journal of Clinical Issues in Psychology,* 5 (1973), 2–5.

———, "Staff Burn-out," *Journal of Social Issues,* 30 (1974), 159–65.

———, "The Staff Burn-Out Syndrome in Alternative Institutions," *Psychotherapy: Theory, Research and Practice,* 12 (1975) 73–82.

GLASSCOTE, R., et al., *The Alternate Services: Their Role in Mental Health.* Washington, D.C.: Joint Information Service of the American Psychiatric Association and the National Association for Mental Health, 1975.

HOFFMAN, K. L. and M. L. REMMEL, "Uncovering the Precipitant in Crisis Intervention," *Social Casework,* 56 (1975), 259–67.

KAHN, R., "Job Burnout: Prevention and Remedies," *Public Welfare,* 36, no. 2 (1978), 61–63.

LARSON, C. G., D. L. GILBERTSON, and J. A. POWELL, "Therapist Burnout: Perspectives on a Critical Issue," *Social Casework,* 59 (1978), 563–65.

LINDEMANN, E., "Symptomatology and Management of Acute Grief," *American Journal of Psychiatry,* 101 (1944), 141–48.

MASLACH, C., "Burned-Out," *Human Behavior,* 5, no. 9 (1976), 16–22.

————, "The Client Role in Staff Burn-Out," *Journal of Social Issues,* 34 (1978a), 111-24.

————, "Job Burnout: How People Cope," *Public Welfare,* 36, no. 2 (1978b), 56-58.

MCCORD, J., and W. PACKWOOD, "Crisis Centers and Hotlines: A Survey," *Personnel and Guidance Journal,* 51 (1973), 723-28.

MCGEE, T., "Some Basic Considerations in Crisis Intervention," *Community Mental Health Journal,* 4 (1968), 319-25.

MORLEY, W. E., J. M. MESSICK, and D. C. AGUILERA, "Crisis: Paradigms of Intervention," *Journal of Psychiatric Nursing,* 5 (1967), 531-44.

PAUL, L., "Crisis Intervention," 50 (1966), 141-45.

PINES, A, and C. MASLACH, "Characteristics of Staff Burnout in Mental Health Settings," *Hospital and Community Psychiatry,* 29 (1978), 233-37.

SHIELDS, L., "Crisis Intervention: Implications for the Nurse," *Journal of Psychiatric Nursing and Mental Health Services,* 13 (1975), 37-42.

SHUBIN, S., "Burnout: The Professional Hazard You Face in Nursing," *Nursing '78,* 8, no. 7 (1978), 22-27.

SILVERMAN, W. H., "Planning for Crisis Intervention with Community Mental Health Concepts," *Psychotherapy: Theory, Research and Practice,* 14 (1977), 293-97.

STUART, M. R., and K. J. MACKEY, "Defining the Differences between Crisis Intervention and Short-Term Therapy," *Hospital and Community Psychiatry,* 28 (1977), 527-29.

TOROP, P., and K. TOROP, "Hotlines and Youth Culture Values," *American Journal of Psychiatry,* 129 (1972), 730-33.

WALES, E., "Crisis Intervention in Clinical Training," *Professional Psychology,* Vol. 3-4 (1972), 357-61.

2

CRISIS INTERVENTION: AN OVERVIEW OF THEORY AND PRACTICE

Crisis intervention, after almost four decades of development, has only recently gained widespread acceptance among mental health professionals.[1] As a flexible, albeit limited, approach for response to a normative event, the emotional crisis, it has been successfully adapted to a wide range of counselling settings. While recognizing that crisis theory and practice is still evolving, the impact of this approach on mental health practitioners and on service delivery systems in mental health cannot be underestimated. At least one researcher (Ewing 1978) believes that crisis intervention is part of a "third revolution" in mental health (after the advent of psychoanalysis and the development of psychotropic drugs). While it is impossible to assess the full impact of this model on concepts of mental health and on the practice of psychotherapy at the present time, it is a growing influence that has already created some change in approaches to helping.

[1]This chapter, through page 50, is reprinted with permission from B.A. Baldwin, "Crisis Intervention: An Overview of Theory and Practice," *The Counseling Psychologist,* 8 (1979), 43–52. Copyright 1979 by *The Counseling Psychologist.*
This overeiew of crisis theory and practice is limited in two respects: (1) it emphasizes the crisis model as used by mental health professionals and does not address the models used by paraprofessionals, and (2) it focuses on the general principles that define the crisis model rather than on use of this approach with particular types of client problems or use in various types of counseling settings.

Crisis intervention had its conceptual origins in the work of Eric Lindemann (1944; Cobb and Lindemann 1943) who designed a program to prevent unresolved or pathological grieving among survivors and relatives of those who perished in the Cocoanut Grove fire of 1943. However, it was Gerald Caplan (1964) and his colleagues who carried forward the pioneering work of Lindemann through the forties and fifties when there was little professional interest in and support for crisis intervention theory and practice. Many of the concepts underlying crisis theory have been used for long periods of time, but they have only recently been formalized into a model for helping. There is evidence that even Freud used a form of crisis intervention with some of his patients (de la Torre 1978; Trilling and Marcus 1961) while developing the concepts of psychoanalytic theory.

It has only been in the last fifteen years that crisis intervention, perhaps given impetus by the community mental health movement, has captured the attention of mental health professionals from the several disciplines. Kardener (1975) points out that crisis theory and technique did not develop during the last decade, but the pressures of increased consumer demand and limited professional resources forced examination and adoption of approaches that had been previously developed. Crisis intervention, perhaps more than any other model for helping, is strongly interdisciplinary in both theoretical development and in practice. In the future, it may become a unifying influence among mental health professionals of all disciplines.

However, at least one writer (Smith 1978) who has recently reviewed crisis intervention at its present level of development believes that this approach has not yet reached the status of a unified theoretical model. It is a helping framework still under development at both theoretical and applied levels. In contrast to other reviews of crisis theory, the intent of this chapter is to overview the already established principles of crisis intervention in theory and practice for the mental health practitioner who has not been exposed to this approach in the past. It is an attempt to bring together from diverse resources the concepts that define this model.

CRISIS THEORY
AND COPING PROCESSES

An understanding of crisis theory must begin with the concept of homeostatic balance and the relationship of coping processes to stable psychological functioning. The principle of homeostasis is borrowed from physiology and is defined by the need to preserve stable chemical or electrolyte balances within the body necessary to sustain life. When these balances are upset, self-regulatory mechanisms are triggered that help to return these balances to healthy levels for the individual. Crisis theory is based on this principle applied to psychological functioning.

For each individual, there exists a reasonably consistent balance between affective and cognitive experience. This homeostatic balance between affective and cognitive functioning may vary considerably from person to person, however. The primary characteristic of this balance is its stability for that individual, a stability which is "normal" for that person and which becomes a frame of reference against which to evaluate changes in psychological functioning. A healthy homeostatic balance requires stable psychological functioning with a minimum of dysphoric affect and the maintenance of reasonable cognitive perspective on experience and the retention of problem-solving skills.

However, each and every day, experiences are encountered in which homeostatic equilibrium is disrupted, and negative and uncomfortable affect results. Often this increase in affective discomfort is accompanied by diminished cognitive capabilities. Caplan (1964) defines these experiences as "emotionally hazardous situations." An emotionally hazardous situation occurs when a shift or change in the individual's psychosocial environment alters relationships with others, or expectations of the self, in ways perceived to be negative. The rise in stress that results from emotionally hazardous situations motivates the individual to bring into play coping mechanisms or problem-solving behaviors that help to reestablish the usual and stable homeostatic balance for that individual, and the dysphoric affect is consequently diminished or eliminated.

Coping processes are those psychological self-regulatory mechanisms that when used by the individual facilitate return to homeostatic balance following the impact of an emotionally hazardous situation. As such, they are critical to the emotional well-being of the individual and essential in maintaining stable functioning. Coping begins at the moment of birth and continues until the interruption of death. Most individuals through development and experience learn a repertoire of coping behaviors that are used as responses to various types of emotionally hazardous situations when they are encountered. Coping mechanisms, which encompass a wide range of behaviors, are defined as:

> those maneuvers used by individuals to reduce, to control, or to avoid unpleasant emotions in order to re-establish a state of homeostatic balance and facilitate return to normal functioning for that person. [Baldwin 1978b]

Coping behaviors occur at various levels of awareness of the individual using them, and coping behaviors at different levels may be used simultaneously as responses to stressful situations. Perlman (1975) describes three basic levels at which copying behaviors are used: (1) the unconscious level of coping that includes the mechanisms of ego defense, (2) the preconscious coping mechanisms which are those almost automatic responses to stress that can be quickly brought to conscious awareness, and (3) the conscious coping behaviors that are in full awareness and that are used selectively as the result of an active decision process. In crisis intervention, because of its focal and time-limited nature, interventions are planned primarily at the levels of conscious and preconscious coping.

By the time adulthood is reached, most individuals have developed a range of coping behaviors, some of which are adaptive and some that are less than adaptive. Maladaptive or immature coping responses are typically used in those situations in which the individual feels vulnerable. At best, coping is the process of mastery of a particular problematic situation. At worst, coping behaviors serve primarily to protect a vulnerable sense of self without mastery of the situation. Coping behaviors cannot be dichotomized into categories of adaptive and maladaptive, but should rather be viewed as a continuum with behaviors manifesting various levels of adaptiveness depending on the person and the situation. When the individual encounters a situation in which there is significant psychological threat and great personal vulnerability, coping behaviors are more likely to be self-protective than oriented toward mastery.

When the individual experiences an emotionally hazardous situation and is unable to effectively utilize previously learned coping behaviors, or to reduce stress using novel problem-solving behaviors, then an emotional crisis may ensue. Caplan (1964) believes that an emotional crisis is evoked when the "usual homeostatic, direct problem-solving mechanisms do not work, and the problem is such that other methods which might be used to sidestep it also cannot be used" (p. 39). Silverman (1977) believes a crisis is the result of "an interaction of a stress event and a perceived lack of resources either to overcome it or to accommodate to it" (p. 293). In short, an emotional crisis is a disruption of homeostatic balance "manifested by cognitive uncertainty, psychophysiological symptoms, and emotional distress" (Hirschowitz 1973, p. 37). In summary, an emotionally hazardous situation becomes an emotional crisis when there is failure to cope effectively.

There are several distinct phases in the life cycle of an emotional crisis (Baldwin 1977b), and these are summarized as follows:

Phase 1: Emotionally Hazardous Situation

a. There is a rise of uncomfortable affect that signals disruption of homeostatic balance.
b. This unpleasant affect produces motivation to reduce it and to return to a normal state of psychological homeostasis.
c. Previously learned and used coping behaviors are brought to bear on the situation in attempts to reduce unpleasant affect.
d. In most instances, learned coping behaviors are successful in returning the individual to homeostatic balance in a short period of time.

Phase 2: The Emotional Crisis

a. Previously learned coping behaviors are tried but are found inadequate or ineffective as responses to the crisis situation.
b. Unpleasant and uncomfortable affect intensifies, and cognitive disorganization increases over time.
c. The individual is motivated to attempt new and/or novel coping behaviors or problem-solving techniques.
d. The individual seeks out others for support and for help in resolving the crisis.

Phase 3: Crisis Resolution

Adaptive Resolution

a. With help, the individual defines issues, deals with feelings, makes decisions, or learns new problem-solving or coping behaviors.
b. Underlying conflicts represented in or reactivated by the crisis situation are identified and at least partially resolved.
c. Internal and external sources of support are mobilized, and the individual's resources for resolving the crisis are defined.
d. Unpleasant or uncomfortable affect is reduced, and the individual returns to at least a precrisis level of functioning.

Maladaptive Resolution

a. The individual does not seek or find adequate help to define issues, deal with feelings, make constructive decisions, or learn new problem-solving or coping behaviors.
b. Underlying conflicts represented in or reactivated by the crisis situation remain unidentified and unresolved.
c. Internal and external sources of support for the individual are not mobilized, and needed resources remain unavailable.
d. Unpleasant and uncomfortable affect is reduced somewhat, thereby defusing the immediate crisis situation, and the individual returns to a less adaptive level of functioning than in the precrisis period.

Phase 4: Postcrisis Adaptation

Adaptive Resolution

a. The individual becomes less vulnerable in a particular problematic situation because underlying conflicts have been resolved and will not be reactivated in such situations.

b. The individual has learned new and more adaptive coping behaviors or problem-solving skills that can be used as responses to future stressful situations.
c. The individual's general level of functioning may have improved, and personal growth and maturation have occurred.
d. The likelihood of future emotionally hazardous situations of a particular type developing into an emotional crisis is reduced.

Maladaptive Resolution

a. The individual remains vulnerable or becomes more vulnerable in particular problematic situations because underlying conflicts have not been resolved and will be reactivated in future, similar situations.
b. The individual has learned maladaptive, self-defeating, or neurotic mechanisms to cope with stressful situations.
c. The individual's general level of functioning may be reduced to a less adaptive level than in the precrisis period.
d. The likelihood of future emotionally hazardous situations of a particular type developing into an emotional crisis is enhanced.

Eastham, Coates, and Allodi (1970) in their review of the literature on the concept of crisis defined many of the problems associated with use of this term and included an overview of ego-integrative, developmental, life-space, communications, and interpersonal/sociocultural models that use this term in somewhat different ways. Bloom's (1963) study further highlighted the tendency of therapists to define crises primarily along the dimensions of a known percipitating event and an acute onset. It is apparent that emotional crises differ from one another in terms of whether the locus of the stress that results in a failure to cope is an external event or primarily internal and results from the particular vulnerabilities or preexisting psychopathology of the individual (Baldwin 1978a). However, in spite of these definitional problems, there does seem to be some agreement that a crisis state does consist of a particular constellation of behaviors and symptoms manifested regardless of the internal or external locus of the stress that produced the crisis.

Halpern (1973) in his study attempted to confirm this viewpoint. He selected four clinical groups presenting with crises (i.e., those involved in the process of divorce, students in personal crisis, those recently admitted to a mental health institution, and individuals who experienced a recent loss of a family member). To each individual he administered a test consisting of ten groups of statements based on clinical descriptions of crisis behavior. These groups of statements were based on the following dimensions: (1) feelings of tiredness and exhaustion, (2) feelings of helplessness, (3) feelings of inadequacy, (4) feelings of confusion, (5) physical symptoms, (6) feelings of anxiety, (7) disorganization of functioning in work relationships, (8) disorganization of functioning in family relationships, (9) disorganization of functioning in social relationships, and (10) disorganization in social activities. Each of these statements was rated a more or less valid description of present behavior and feelings as compared to the precrisis period.

The result of an analysis of variance revealed that each of the crisis groups demonstrated behaviors characteristic of a crisis state that was markedly different from precrisis functioning. Halpern (1973) concludes:

> Were this hypothesis not validated, the concept "crisis" would be meaningless when applied to individuals because their behavior could not be differentiated from that of any individual selected from a noncrisis population. The lack of significant differences between the various crisis groups is also of importance to crisis theory. It suggests that there is a significant amount of communality in the behavior of individuals in a wide variety of situations which have all been labeled "crisis situations." This result lends credence to the generality of the crisis model. [P. 347]

COROLLARIES OF CRISIS THEORY

Beyond this overview of crisis theory, there are a number of corollaries to crisis theory that are helpful in understanding emotional crises in more depth and that provide a foundation for crisis intervention. Ten basic corollaries of crisis theory are the following:

1. *Because each individual's tolerance for stress is idiosyncratic and finite, emotional crises have no relationship per se to psychopathology and occur even among the well adjusted.*
Emotional crises are more or less normative events that are experienced by almost everyone at some point during the life span. Each individual has a specific tolerance for stress depending on general level of adjustment, the internal and external resources available to that person, the flexibility of learned coping mechanisms, and the degree and type of stress being experienced. Emotional crises may be experienced by the well adjusted when stressful situations are encountered in particular areas of personal vulnerability (i.e., in those areas where coping behaviors are weak or absent) at critical points in time. It is true that the less well-adjusted individual is likely to experience more emotional crises than those with better levels of adjustment. However, an individual experiencing an emotional crisis cannot be assumed to be significantly maladjusted or to manifest psychopathology based solely on the existence of an emotional crisis.

2. *Emotional crises are self-limiting events in which crisis resolution, either adaptive or maladaptive, takes place within an average period of four to six weeks.*

When an emotional crisis occurs, the individual becomes highly vulnerable due to the intense state of unpleasant affective arousal and the cognitive disorganization that characterize the crisis state. The critical question in responding to emotional crises is not whether the crisis will be resolved; it will. The only question is whether the crisis will be resolved in an adaptive manner that will contribute to greater emotional maturity and stability of functioning in the future, or in a maladaptive fashion that will render the individual more vulnerable and prone to more crises of a similar nature in the future. Caplan (1964) has stated that the vast majority of crises are resolved within a period of four to six weeks because in most instances the individual cannot tolerate a crisis state for longer than that period of time. Even regressive, maladaptive, or neurotic coping behaviors share the quality of partially reducing stress (without resolving the situation) and therefore may be learned in lieu of more adaptive coping behaviors if the resources necessary for adaptive crisis resolution are unavailable or unused.

3. *During a crisis state, psychological defenses are weakened or absent, and the individual has cognitive and/or affective awareness of material previously well defended and less accessible.*

By definition, an individual experiencing an emotional crisis is not coping effectively with a present stressful situation. Coping occurs at several levels (Perlman, 1975), and during a crisis, failure to cope may be present at any or all levels. One result of coping failure is enhanced awareness of feelings and memories from the past that are helpful in understanding the crisis at a psychodynamic level. Often these data are not accessible to the individual, and by extension to the therapist, when that individual is not in a crisis state. The individual, because of this heightened affective and cognitive awareness has an opportunity to deal with these past experiences as part of the crisis resolution process. However, in many instances, motivation during the crisis state is directed to return to a precrisis state in which this material is again suppressed or repressed rather than to using the accessibility of this material afforded by the crisis to work toward a deeper and lasting resolution.

4. *During a crisis state, the individual has enhanced capacity for both cognitive and affective learning because of the vulnerability of this state and the motivation produced by emotional disequilibrium.*

During a crisis state, the individual needs support and help, often manifested as increased dependency, and these needs must be understood and met as part of the crisis intervention and resolution process (Hirschowitz, 1973; Wolkon, 1972). Because of the distress experienced by the individual in crisis, there is an enhanced capacity to learn new coping behaviors or problem-solving skills and to modify previously learned but maladaptive coping responses in the direction of increased adaptiveness. The net result of increased dependency and the motivation produced by painful emotional disequilibrium is an enhanced receptivity to help from others (Schwartz 1971) and the capacity to learn at both cognitive and affective levels more quickly than during noncrisis states. Learning that occurs during a crisis state tends to last, and those coping behaviors adopted during the crisis tend to be repeated during stressful situations in the future. It is this enhanced capacity for learning that represents both the danger and the opportunity that are frequently associated with emotional crises.

5. *Adaptive crisis resolution is frequently a vehicle for resolving underlying conflicts that have in part determined the emotional crisis and/or that interfere with the crisis resolution process.*

Because of the affective and cognitive awareness that often accompanies crisis states, unresolved conflicts and traumas from the past that have been reactivated by a present experience can be identified and at least partially resolved as part of the crisis intervention process. Often these reactivated experiences create the disproportionately intense affective states that determine the failure to cope with a present situation. Hoffman and Remmel (1975) have defined these reactivated, but unresolved, experiences that are part of many emotional crises as the *precipitant* (in contrast to the precipitating event). The precipitant surfaces when there is presently experienced a situation that is somehow analogous to a past trauma or conflict, or when there is anticipation of such an experience. As part of helping the individual to respond more effectively to a present situation, the individual is helped to face and resolve the underlying conflicts or traumas that are present. Frequently, fear of facing a present stressful situation directly is determined by fear of facing past traumas or conflicts. It is this fear that is often found to motivate and support use of maladaptive coping responses. Without understanding of and response to the precipitant of the crisis, adaptive resolution may be significantly impeded, and an opportunity for personal growth and maturation of the individual may be lost.

6. *A small external influence during a crisis state can produce disproportionate change in a short period of time when compared to therapeutic change that occurs during noncrisis states.*

Because of the vulnerability and receptivity to help produced by a crisis state, the individual in crisis has an opportunity to move therapeutically at a faster pace than would be possible than when a crisis state is not present. The result is that gains made during crisis therapy may be disproportionately great when compared to therapeutic movement occurring during noncrisis states. Rapoport (1962) summarizes this aspect of crisis therapy succinctly when she states: "A little help, rationally directed and purposefully focused at a strategic time, is more effective than more extensive help given at a period of less emotional accessibility" (p. 30). However, for such gains to be made, the individual in crisis must accept the opportunity for change that is brought by the crisis state. If this opportunity is not used effectively for growth, a disproportionate change in the direction of maladaptive learning may occur that will require great therapeutic effort to modify once the crisis state has passed. It is this capacity for rapid and disproportionate adaptive change (and the prevention of similar maladaptive change) that is part of the economy of crisis therapy from the perspective of both therapist and client.

7. *Resolution of emotional crisis is not necessarily determined by previous experience or character structure but rather is shaped by current and perhaps unique sociopsychological influences operating in the present (Paul 1966).*

In crisis intervention, the resolution is not necessarily determined by the past. When an individual is in crisis, previously used responses to stress are either inadequate or ineffective as coping behaviors. Often these responses are characterological in nature and part of the character armor of that individual. These may be long-standing and deeply ingrained patterns of behavior that may ordinarily be quite strong and very rigid. However, because these responses are not effective in the present crisis situation, preexisting characterological patterns do not determine the outcome of crisis resolution or the behaviors that bring such resolution. It is the individual's social and psychological resources and the adequacy of help received during this period of personal vulnerability and psychological defenselessness that are primary determinants of crisis resolution rather than past learning or character structure per se. Further, in those individuals with strong characterological defenses, it is during a crisis state that change must be facilitated quickly before that awareness is again sealed over and accessibility to psychodynamic material is lost and with it the stress that is a primary motivation for change. In such individuals, it is sometimes more therapeutically economical to attempt change only during crises when there is emotional openness and motivation for change.

8. *Inherent in every emotional crisis is an actual or anticipated loss to the individual that must be reconciled as part of the crisis resolution process.*

In assessing emotional crises, it is assumed that there is an actual or potential loss to the individual that must be conceptualized and responded to as part of the therapeutic strategy for crisis intervention and resolution (Hitchcock 1973). Strickler and LaSor (1970) are more specific in stating that in every crisis there is a loss involving: (1) self-esteem, (2) nurturance, or (3) sex-role mastery. They believe that one of these losses is usually dominant in any given crisis, although elements of all three may be present to some extent. At another level, there is additional loss to the individual as part of adaptive crisis resolution. As part of the new learning that occurs during crisis intervention, there is loss of old and familiar, albeit maladaptive, responses to stress or to meeting personal needs that are given up as growth occurs. Identifying and reconciling these losses as part of the crisis resolution process reduces resistance to change. The process of adaptive change involves risk to the individual, and to the extent that losses to the individual can be responded to as part of the process of change, the risks of growth can be more readily accepted.

9. *Every emotional crisis is an interpersonal event involving at least one significant other person who is represented in the crisis situation directly, indirectly, or symbolically.*

An emotional crisis is never a completely intrapsychic phenomenon even though the locus of stress that precipitated the crisis may be primarily internal. Emotional crises always have an interpersonal dimension that must be assessed and understood prior to the intervention and resolution process. The significant others involved in the crisis may be from the present or the past or both. Those individuals may be directly or indirectly involved in the present situation. Sometimes significant others are part of the precipitant of the crisis (Hoffman and Remmel 1975) and help to understand the relationship of past traumas or unresolved conflicts to a present stressor. At other times, significant others are represented psychodynamically as introjects, or in the form of values or behaviors that have been adopted by the individual in crisis from a significant other. In these instances, others exist primarily within the individual in crisis at a symbolic level but remain powerful determinants of the crisis that must be understood before an effective intervention can be made. Identification and clarification of the interpersonal dimension of an emotional crisis are essential to effective crisis assessment and necessary to the plan for adaptive crisis resolution.

10. *Effective crisis resolution prevents future crises of a similar nature by removing vulnerabilities from the past and by increasing the individual's repertoire of available coping skills that can be used in such situations.*

In many instances, crisis intervention and adaptive resolution have past, present, and future components. The primary emphasis in crisis intervention is resolving a present problematic situation that the individual is unable to cope with effectively. However, in order to resolve such a situation, the precipitant of the crisis must be identified when present and worked through as part of helping the individual in crisis to cope with the problem situation that has reactivated these past conflicts or traumas. There is selective attention to the past in crisis intervention in response to the precipitant. Yet, response to and work with the precipitant that links present to past also has future connotations. As the precipitant is resolved, the decreased vulnerability of that precipitant allows the individual to experience future similar situations more easily. Further, the new coping skills that are a key aspect of resolving the present situation also become a buffer against future crises of a similar nature. Optimally, the individual who has successfully and adaptively resolved a crisis will experience future similar situations only as emotionally hazardous situations for which there are available and effective coping behaviors that can be used to reestablish homeostatic balance quickly.

TYPES OF EMOTIONAL CRISES

The classification of emotional crises has been a significant gap in the development of crisis theory. If a present-oriented crisis resolution is needed, then a classification system for different types of crises must be developed in order to deeply understand crises in the present and provide direction for planning effective intervention strategies. In the past, crisis therapists, particularly those traditionally trained, have relied on diagnostic evaluations more characteristic of longer-term psychotherapy. Butcher and Maudel (1976) believe that traditional assessment processes tend to focus both client's and therapist's attention on the past and on psychopathology in lieu of attention to the present problematic situation that the client has been unable to cope with effectively. Kardener (1975) believes that

> the question to be answered remains, "Is this event, or sequence of events, what caused the patient to seek help now?" Chronic difficulties which reflect no recent change, while contributory, are less likely to be the salient factors sought. [P.7]

Kardener further believes that the therapist must be aware that often the past is used as a means to avoid dealing effectively with the present. Morley, Messick, and Aguilera (1967) take essentially the same stance in their belief that while accurate crisis assessment is necessary, relatively little attention need be paid to gathering case history information not directly related to the present crisis situation.

The general consensus among crisis theorists is that full psychodiagnostic evaluation in crisis therapy is not only an uneconomical use of time, but may also be counterproductive to the process of crisis intervention and adaptive crisis resolution. There is some precedent for classifying crises, but the classification schemes developed are quite general and reflect dichotomies or trichotomies rather than a continuum as suggested by McGee (1968). For example, Jacobson, Strickler, and Morley (1968) divide crises into generic types that follow a particular pattern in the resolution process and individual crises that are determined by the unique psychodynamics of an individual in a particular situation and that follow no predictable patterns. Aguilera and Messick (1974) divide crises into "maturational" and "situational," and Morrice (1976) follows this trend by dichotomizing crises into those that are primarily developmental and reflect transitions and those that are accidental and caused by the unexpected hazards of life.

There are several tripartite divisions of emotional crises. For example, Schneidman (1973) divides crises into intratemporal types that are typical of a particular "time of life," intertemporal crises that occur during transitions from one developmental stage to the next, and extratemporal crises that occur independently of developmental issues. Silverman (1977) has also developed a trichotomy of crises by dividing them into those that are primarily physical-environmental in origin (e.g., accidents, fires, natural disasters), those that have social-environmental roots (e.g., busing, discrimination, and migration), and personal crises (e.g., birth, marriage, divorce).

These classification systems are more or less arbitrary, and dichotomizing or trichotomizing emotional crises is too general to be helpful in "diagnosing" crises in ways that will have direct implications for treatment strategies.

Baldwin (1978a) has developed a classification paradigm for understanding emotional crises in terms of six basic types or classes that fall along a continuum. With movement from Class 1 to Class 6, crises become more serious, and the locus of stress that produces the crisis shifts from external stressors to internal conflicts of the individual that reflect psychopathology. Each of these six classes of crises is presented with a definition and a general treatment strategy basic to that type of crisis. The therapist responds with a treatment plan at the most serious level of crisis detected during the crisis assessment process.

Class 1: Dispositional Crises

Definition

These crises (Butcher and Maudel 1976) are defined by distress resulting from a problematic situation in which the therapist is asked to respond in ways peripheral to a strictly therapeutic role, and the intervention is not primarily directed to an emotional resolution. Intervention may involve referral, information dissemination, administrative action, or psychological/medical education.

Intervention Strategy

The general strategy for responding to dispositional crises involves clarifying the client's problematic situation and providing the services needed or requested by the client while giving or mobilizing as much support as is appropriate. During this process, it is essential that the crisis therapist rule out the possibilities that (1) the client is making an indirect request for help at an emotional level that cannot be acknowledged directly, or (2) the client has failed to anticipate serious implications of the situation that may have a detrimental impact on later emotional functioning. If either of these factors is present, the crisis situation is responded to at the appropriate level of intervention.

Class 2: Crises of Anticipated Life Transitions

Definition

These are crises that reflect anticipated, but usually normative, life transitions over which the client may or may not have substantial control (e.g., leaving home, becoming a parent, mid-life career changes, retirement). The client may present for help prior to, during, or after the life transition has taken place. However, in all cases there has been substantial forewarning and time for psychological acknowledgement that the transition is forthcoming and, optimally, time to prepare for the changes that result.

Intervention Strategy

The primary task of the crisis therapist is to develop with the client an in-depth understanding of the changes that have or will take place, and to explore the psychological implications of these changes. Support is provided as needed, and anticipatory guidance is used to help the individual plan adaptive coping responses to problems that have resulted from a life transition or anticipated problems that the client will encounter as the result of a transition. Recently, there has been a trend toward use of group approaches to help those experiencing various types of life transitions (e.g., preretirement groups, LaMaze groups, group approaches to college orientation).

Class 3: Crises Resulting from Sudden Traumatic Stress

Definition

These crises are precipitated by strong, externally imposed stresses or traumatic situations that are unexpected and uncontrolled and that are emotionally overwhelming to the client (e.g., rape, sudden death of spouse or family member, accidents with physical dismemberment). Usual coping behaviors are rendered ineffective due to the sudden, unanticipated nature of the stress. There may be a refractory period during which the client experiences emotional paralysis and coping behaviors cannot be mobilized.

Intervention Strategy

In this type of crisis, the client has usually functioned in a reasonably stable fashion prior to the sudden impact of the traumatic stress. The general intervention strategy is to provide or mobilize support for the client during the refractory period (i.e., the time between the impact of the precipitating stress and the ability to mobilize coping behaviors), which may be more prolonged in this type of crisis than in any other. Following the refractory period, the client is helped to emotionally acknowledge a situation that has usually not been encountered previously and for which no specific coping behaviors have been learned. Particular attention is given to helping the client to acknowledge and express negative emotions that result from the stressful situation. Anticipatory guidance is used to aid the client in planning for and coping with changes that result from the traumatic situation experienced.

Class 4: Maturational/ Developmental Crises

Definition

These are emotional crises resulting from attempts to deal with interpersonal situations that reflect a struggle with a deeper, but usually circumscribed, developmental issue that has not been resolved adaptively in the past and that represents an attempt to attain emotional maturity. These crises usually involve developmental issues such as dependency, value conflicts, sexual identity, emotional intimacy, power issues, or attaining self-discipline. Often there is a repeated pattern of specific relationship difficulties that occurs over time in those presenting with this type of crisis.

Note: Every type of emotional crisis involves an interaction of an external stressor and a vulnerability of the individual. However, it is in Class 4 crises that there is a shift from a primarily external locus of stress that produces the crisis to an internal locus determined by the unique psychodynamics of the individual and/or preexisting psychopathology that becomes manifest in particular problematic situations.

Intervention Strategy

Developmental/maturational crises may be encountered at any time during the life cycle and are not specific to any particular time of life. Basic intervention strategy is to help the client to identify and conceptualize the underlying and unresolved developmental issue that has been instrumental in producing the crisis situation (i.e., the precipitant of the crisis) as part of the crisis assessment process. Emphasis is then placed on helping the client to respond to the present problematic situation more adaptively while simultaneously aiding in the resolution of the determinant developmental conflict. It is in this type of crisis that the therapist has an excellent opportunity to blend present interpersonal difficulties with a focal psychodynamic issue (with its etiology in the past) into a productive growth experience for the client during the intervention process. If response in developmental crises is only to the manifest problem of the client, while the developmental precipitant is ignored, the opportunity to prevent future similar crises may be lost. Rosenberg (1975), writing on the treatment of developmental crises, has defined a very effective treatment model for this type of crisis that incorporates many of the concepts of crisis theory and practice.

Class 5: Crises Resulting from Psychopathology

Definition

These are emotional crises in which preexisting psychopathology has been instrumental in precipitating the crisis or in which client psychopathology significantly impairs or complicates adaptive crisis resolution. The emotional crisis is primarily determined by reactivated and unresolved client problems rather than by external stressors per se. This type of crisis is often seen in those with borderline personality disorders, severe neuroses, characterological problems, and psychoses that are nonorganic or not drug-induced. In most instances, those presenting with Class 5 crises have multiple problems or difficulties that significantly impair more than one area of functioning in contrast to those with maturational/developmental (Class 4) crises.

Intervention Strategy

Crises that result from preexisting client psychopathology are almost always of the "individual" (as contrasted to the "generic") type described by Jacobson, Strickler, and Morley (1968) and follow no predictable pattern. The client's problems become manifest, usually within a relationship context and trigger strong (and previously learned) maladaptive coping responses. These are usually ineffective in reducing the severe stress that results, and there is disproportionate incapacitation of the client's ability to function.

The crisis therapist responds primarily in terms of the present problem of the client with emphasis on problem-solving skills and environmental manipulation (Morley 1965). The therapist gives support but is careful not to produce or reinforce client dependency or regression by allowing the therapeutic process to become diffuse. The therapist acknowledges the deeper problems of the client, and assesses them to the degree possible within the crisis therapy context, but does not attempt to resolve problems representing deep emotional conflicts. Through the process of crisis intervention, the client is helped to stabilize functioning to the fullest extent possible and is prepared for referral for longer-term therapy or other services once the crisis intervention process has been completed. Referral (or coordination of services) is facilitated as actively as necessary by the therapist with follow-up (Flomenhaft and Langsley 1971; Sudak et al. 1977) to insure therapeutic continuity.

It is quite difficult for the crisis therapist to work with clients with multiple or deep-seated problems in a limited but helpful way without becoming so involved with the client that referral is difficult or impossible following crisis therapy. The skill of the therapist in structuring and limiting the crisis intervention process is critical in this type of crisis. In many crisis clinics, one-third or more clients seen will involve a Class 5 level of intervention with referral for additional services required for treatment of the client's problems.

Class 6: Psychiatric Emergencies

Definition

These crises result from situations in which general functioning has been severely impaired, and the client is rendered incompetent or incapable of assuming personal responsibility. Medical as well as psychological intervention may be required. These crises may involve intoxications (e.g., street drugs, alcohol), impulse control problems (e.g., suicidal, homocidal impulses), or acute psychoses.

Intervention Strategy

The psychiatric emergency is a most difficult type of crisis to handle as there may be less than complete information about the situation available, the client may be minimally helpful or disruptive, and there is great urgency in understanding the situation in depth and in beginning effective treatment. Fortunately, informants with some knowledge of the situation accompany or bring such clients for treatment in many instances and can be most helpful in planning appropriate psychological and medical services.

The basic intervention strategy for this type of crisis involves: (1) assessment of the client's psychological and/or medical condition as rapidly and as accurately as possible, (2) clarifying the situation that produced or led to the client's condition, (3) mobilizing all mental health and/or medical resources necessary to effectively treat the client, and (4) arranging for follow-up or coordination of services to insure continuity of treatment as appropriate. It is in the psychiatric emergency that the skills of the crisis therapist are tested to the limit as there must be capacity to work effectively and quickly in highly charged situations and to intervene where there may be life-threatening implications of the client's condition. In a psychiatric emergency, the crisis therapist accepts primary responsibility for initial decisions and/or treatment.

THE PROCESS
OF CRISIS INTERVENTION

Defining the process of crisis intervention is difficult due to the different kinds of emotional crises presented to crisis therapists and the varying degrees of applicability of the crisis model to different types of crises (Baldwin 1978a). Several crisis theorists have attempted to define the process of crisis intervention (Hoffman and Remmel 1975; Morley 1965; Smith 1978), usually in general terms. In their review of the literature on crisis intervention processes, Beers and Foreman (1976) found only two basic models (Aguilera and Messick 1974; Rusk 1971) for this critical aspect of crisis therapy. They concluded the Rusk model to be more comprehensive in terms of "explicitly mapping the sequence of counselor activities" (p. 87). In their comparative research on the process of crisis intervention, Beers and Foreman trained counselors in the Rusk model and in a brief focal therapy approach. Both groups were found to follow the Rusk intervention pattern when time segments of crisis interviews were compared.

Baldwin (1978c) has developed a model for conceptualizing the crisis intervention process that combines the sequence described by Rusk with others principles of crisis therapy. This model for crisis intervention has four basic stages and is defined in terms of specific affective and cognitive therapist tasks for each of the stages. Most crisis intervention takes place in one to eight therapy hours, and the time required for therapist and client to move through this sequence varies within these limits. Further, completion of each stage in movement toward crisis resolution may also vary from client to client. The four stages of this model for understanding the crisis intervention process are as follows.

Stage 1: Catharsis/Assessment[2]

Therapist Tasks: Affective

1. The client is encouraged to acknowledge and to express feelings generated by the crisis situation.
2. The client is helped to explore and to define the emotional meaning of the precipitating event that produced the crisis.

[2]A structure for guiding a crisis assessment interview is provided in an excellent article by Naomi Golan (1969).

3. The therapist directly provides or helps to mobilize appropriate support for the client.

Therapist Tasks: Cognitive

1. The therapist helps the client to restore a realistic perspective of the crisis situation and to define viable options or courses of action available.
2. The client is helped to conceptualize the precipitant or psychodynamic meaning of the crisis situation that links present to past (when this component of a crisis is present).
3. Limited but relevent background information is obtained from the client to help in understanding more fully the crisis situation.

Stage 2: Focusing/Contracting

Therapist Tasks: Affective

1. The client is helped to develop an awareness of those feelings that impair or prevent use of adaptive coping behaviors in response to the crisis situation.
2. The therapist strives to develop a therapeutic alliance with the client with emphasis on client responsibility for adaptive change and eventual crisis resolution.

Therapist Tasks: Cognitive

1. The therapist obtains from the client agreement on a concise statement of the core conflict or problem that has produced the crisis.
2. The therapist and client together define a time and goal contract for the crisis resolution process.
3. Therapist and client agree on a tentative therapeutic strategy or plan to attain the goals necessary for crisis resolution.

Stage 3: Intervention/Resolution[3]

Therapist Tasks: Affective

1. The therapist defines and directly supports client strengths and adaptive responses to the crisis situation.

---

[3]Delineation of specific therapeutic tactics useful in crisis intervention can be found in Butcher and Maudel (1976), Rusk (1971), and Schwartz (1971).

2. The client is helped to work through feelings that support maladaptive coping responses (i.e., resistance) which prevent adaptive crisis resolution.

3. The client is supported in and helped to respond directly and appropriately to the crisis situation in terms of both issues and feelings (i.e., direct communication with significant others involved is encouraged).

Therapist Tasks: Cognitive

1. The therapist directly teaches or helps the client to develop new or more adaptive coping responses or problem-solving skills.

2. The therapist helps to define client progress (or lack thereof!) in working toward defined goals and crisis resolution.

3. The therapist prevents diffusion of the therapeutic process away from the focal problem and the goals defined for crisis resolution.

Stage 4: Termination/Integration

Therapist Tasks: Affective

1. The therapist elicits and responds to client termination issues but does not prolong the therapeutic process because of them.

2. The therapist reinforces changes in client coping behaviors and affective functioning and relates these changes to adaptive resolution of the problematic situation.

Therapist Tasks: Cognitive

1. The therapist evaluates with the client goal attainment or nonattainment during the crisis intervention process.

2. The therapist uses anticipatory guidance to help integrate adaptive change and to help prepare the client to meet future similar situations more adequately.

3. The therapist provides the client with information about additional services or community resources needed, or makes a direct referral for continuing therapy as appropriate.

In addition to facilitating client movement through these stages toward crisis resolution, the therapist must also accept goals for crisis intervention that are different from those of longer-term psychotherapy. It is *not* the task of the crisis therapist to effect major changes in the client, to deal with *all* the client's problems, to restructure personality, or to resolve deep-seated conflicts or chronic problems. There is a single general goal for crisis intervention that becomes the sole criterion for success in this form of therapy. This goal is to facilitate return of the client in crisis to at least a precrisis level of functioning as quickly as possible even though this level of functioning may not be optimal for that individual (Jacobson 1970). Any gains made by the client beyond restoration of precrisis levels of functioning is a therapeutic bonus that will be helpful in preventing future crises.

In addition to the general goal of crisis intervention, there are several subgoals that are part of successful crisis resolution.

1. The individual in crisis is prevented from using or learning maladaptive coping responses and/or regressing, thereby avoiding maladaptive crisis resolution.

2. The individual in crisis is aided in learning new and more adaptive coping responses that will result in reintegration at a more mature and stable level of functioning in the postcrisis period.

3. The individual in crisis is helped to use the crisis experience to become aware of and to resolve underlying conflicts and/or ambivalence that are manifest in and that determine the crisis.

4. The individual in crisis is helped to integrate changes resulting from adaptive crisis resolution at both cognitive and affective levels to expand the repertoire of available coping skills.

CONCLUDING REMARKS

Crisis intervention in both theory and practice represents a significant interface between the practice of psychotherapy and the principles of community mental health. In a recently completed national survey of crisis services provided by community mental health centers, Miller and Mazade (1978) found a rapid expansion of such services which was expected to continue in the future. In addition, there has also been a recent proliferation of crisis services in the community directed to particular types of crises (e.g., rape crises, services for battered wives, problem pregnancy counseling, etc.). The recent increase in both general and specialized crisis services reflects public awareness of particular community problems that has been a continuing impetus to the development of such services since the early sixties.

Although crisis intervention was originally associated with primary prevention programs, to perceive crisis intervention today only in terms of primary prevention is a commonly held myth and an unduly narrow perspective (Baldwin 1977a). It is true that many crisis intervention programs are designed for primary prevention. Their emphasis is on defining subpopulations at risk in the community and providing services that will prevent the occurrence of problems. However, more recently these programs have shifted to group formats that are more therapeutically economical, although individual-oriented crisis services at the primary prevention level remain prevalent.

Most crisis services developed during the recent period of rapid proliferation have become more oriented toward secondary prevention of emotional disability. These secondary prevention programs provide services in the community to those already experiencing problems and have the goal of reducing both the severity and the duration of such problems. Silverman (1977) believes that at the present time the majority of crisis intervention services are directed to the secondary prevention level, particularly those in general outpatient services and those in community mental health centers.

Perhaps the most exciting new trend in crisis intervention is development of services at the level of tertiary prevention that are directed to institutionalized individuals in need of help with reentry and reintegration into community life. Several studies (Decker and Stubblebine 1972; Rubenstein 1972) have clearly demonstrated that crisis services established as part of aftercare programs are helpful in considerably reducing the incidence of rehospitalization of psychiatric patients. In addition, at least one crisis-oriented model has been developed for use within inpatient settings (Jones and Polak 1968) and reflects another emerging trend in tertiary prevention applications of the crisis model.

Although the crisis intervention approach is very flexible and can be adapted to a range of helping services and types of client problems, there are several general principles of crisis therapy that transcend setting, target population, and type of problem. An understanding of these principles is essential for both effective crisis intervention and for crisis service programming.

1. *Material not directly related to the client's present crisis has no place in crisis intervention* (Morley, Messick, and Aguilera 1967). Because of the time-limited nature of crisis intervention, there is not enough time for full psychodiagnostic evaluations even if they were considered helpful. In crisis therapy, it is necessary to select and use only information relevant to the present crisis (including past antecedents) for crisis assessment to initiate the intervention process. It is almost axiomatic in crisis intervention that the therapist must proceed on the basis of incomplete information. Required are rapid assessment skills that include the ability to sift relevant from irrelevant information obtained from the client. Rapid assessment skills are essential to effective crisis intervention, but also are perhaps the most difficult to master when learning to use this model.

2. *Crisis intervention is active and direct but not unnecessarily directive* (Baldwin 1977a; Morley, Messick, and Aguilera 1967). It is necessary for the crisis therapist to quickly and actively engage the client in an effective helping

process. The crisis therapist must be direct with the client, but not become unnecessarily directive or controlling during the process of crisis intervention and resolution. At the other extreme, the crisis therapist who adopts a passive and overnurturant posture may inadvertently encourage client dependency and / or regression in lieu of accepting responsibility for and actively working toward crisis resolution. In those instances, however, when there is little time available for crisis resolution, direct suggestions or advice may become part of the therapist's intervention (Butcher and Maudel 1976). Novice crisis therapists sometimes encounter difficulty in directly and actively engaging the client in lieu of adopting excessively passive or directive postures.

3. *The crisis therapist must be skilled in a range of therapeutic techniques and change modalities* (Aguilera and Messick 1974). To practice crisis intervention effectively with diverse client crises requires not only flexibility but an eclectic approach to client problems and the helping process. Therapists trained in different therapeutic orientations can use the crisis model by adapting to the structure and limits of this approach (Baldwin 1977a). However, the therapist familiar with many different types of therapeutic interventions, no matter from what theoretical system they are derived, will have more flexibility and capability to effectively help more clients within the time-limited framework of crisis intervention. Kardener (1975) has aptly summarized this important point:

> Short-term therapists must be reasonably conversant with a variety of treatment modalities or seek appropriate collaborative consultation. It is the responsibility of the therapist to fit the therapeutic message with the needs of a given patient, and his particular desired goal, and not the patient's responsibility to fit a unimodal therapist! [P. 8]

4. *Effective crisis intervention requires a minimum delay between initial client contact and the beginning of treatment.* It is clinically known and has been experimentally validated (Wolkon 1972) that successful outcome in crisis intervention is related to the accessibility of the client to early treatment. Delay of treatment increases the probability that new learning by the client will be maladaptive, and the opportunity for growth and adaptive learning that will prevent future crises may be missed. Clinics or mental health facilities with waiting lists or delay between intake and treatment are not able to effectively use the crisis model due to these counterproductive aspects of their service delivery systems. Further, those facilities that require extensive background data and a full diagnostic evaluation before treatment is initiated also find it difficult to use the crisis model. It is at this point that administrative mandates and therapeutic necessities clash. Many facilities are struggling to find ways to solve this problem at present.

5. *Defining goals for crisis resolution and the time available to attain those goals must be made explicit in crisis intervention.* A core skill for

effective use of the crisis model is defining with the client a time and goal contract for the crisis resolution process. Nelson and Mowry (1976) find time/goal contracting in crisis intervention helpful in defining role relationships, for clearly defining problems, and for creating structure that helps to control client symptomatology. Montgomery and Montgomery (1975) believe that contracting helps to surface client resistance to change, and the feelings that support or determine maladaptive coping responses can be identified and responded to as part of the goal attainment (i.e., resolution) process.

Further, Appelbaum (1975) has applied Parkinson's Law ("Work expands or contracts to meet the time available for its completion") to psychotherapy. He believes that client motivation for change is increased when time limits are defined early in the therapeutic process. This is critical because in crisis intervention, time is of the essence both in terms of the self-limiting nature of crises and in the therapist time available to help the client work toward resolution. The effect of creating time limits for the crisis intervention process may also be helpful to the therapist in maintaining focus for therapy and for monitoring progress toward goals. A statement of Parkinson's Law adapted to the crisis intervention model might be the following: "The work of adaptive crisis resolution expands or contracts to meet the time available for completion as defined by the limits created for the crisis intervention process" (Baldwin 1979b).

6. *Restoration of cognitive perspective and mastery is critical to effective crisis resolution.* During an emotional crisis, strong dysphoric affect disrupts homeostatic balance and progressively impairs cognitive functions that are critical in maintaining objective perspective of the situation and in effective problem solving. This leads to an increase in feelings of hopelessness, helplessness, and to the distortion of viable options or alternatives (and the capacity to exercise them!) as a means to resolve the crisis. Rapoport (1965) suggests that helping the client to restore cognitive mastery of the crisis situation is critical early in the intervention process. Increased objectivity allows the client to feel more in control, less confused, and more able to move toward resolution. Frequently, the structure created through crisis assessment and the contracting process (e.g., particularly defining the core problem, goals for resolution, and issues preventing resolution) are helpful to the client in restoration of cognitive mastery. Hansell, Woodarczyk, and Handlon-Lathrop (1970) have gone further and developed a decision counseling method that is a primarily cognitively based approach to crisis intervention and resolution.

Crisis intervention is a professionally challenging model that requires a firm grasp of therapeutic processes, comfort with a variety of therapeutic interventions, a knowledge of psychodynamics, and a secure sense of self-as-therapist. Training preprofessional students in crisis therapy is most productive when initiated at an advanced level of training. When begun too early in professional training, the need for quick, decisive action, the rapid pace, the necessarily active role of the therapist, and the inherent accountability of the therapist when using this model may produce anxiety and erode the confidence of the therapist-in-training (Baldwin 1979a). Wallace and Morley (1970) discovered two basic types of problems in training preprofessional crisis therapists:

> The initial problems involve anxiety and a need for specialized skills, whereas the advance problems involve consistent use of the crisis model, facilitating expression of feelings, and the promotion of growth versus dependency. [P. 1485]

Yet, training in crisis therapy at an appropriate level of expertise can produce rapid professional growth in the preprofessional student. Wales (1972) has noted significant growth in psychologists trained in this model as part of their professional development. Baldwin (1979) has suggested a number of unique aspects of crisis therapy training and believes that

> . . . the limitations of the crisis intervention model . . . bring to the fore a number of issues for trainees that when resolved are translated into valuable clinical skills and an enhanced professional maturity. [P. 164]

Crisis intervention as a model for brief therapy is still rapidly evolving with a convergence of several professional and paraprofessional lines of development (Baldwin 1980) that optimally will result in a more complete system of constructs that will increase the effectiveness of this approach. There is growing evidence that even very brief interventions are helpful to clients (Dorosin, Gibbs, and Kaplan 1976; Katzenstein 1971). Cummings (1977) produced evidence that has demonstrated a highly favorable cost-therapeutic effectiveness ratio for these very brief therapeutic interventions. It is not unfair to state that it is not only the therapeutic effectiveness of crisis intervention but also the cost-effectiveness of this type of approach that will become a major impetus to its future development and widespread use.

An understanding of the crisis model and the skills to practice crisis intervention effectively may become an increasing asset in the therapeutic armamentarium of the mental health professional in the future. It is hoped that this overview of the basic tenets of the crisis model may improve the effectiveness of those already using this approach as well as those who may be in the process of learning it. For others, it is hoped that some questions were answered but also that some questions were raised that will result in the stimulation of further research on this emergent model for brief psychotherapy.

REFERENCES

AGUILERA, D. C., and J. M. MESSICK, *Crisis Intervention: Theory and Methodology.* St. Louis: The C. V. Mosby Company, 1974.

APPELBAUM, S. A., "Parkinson's Law in Psychotherapy," *International Journal of Psychoanalytic Psychotherapy,* 4 (1975), 426–36.

BALDWIN, B. A., "Crisis Intervention in Professional Practice: Implications for Clinical Training," *American Journal of Orthopsychiatry,* 47 (1977a), 659–70.

———, "Phases of Emotional Crisis." Unpublished training materials, 1977b.

———, "A Paradigm for the Classification of Emotional Crises: Implications for Crisis Intervention," *American Journal of Orthopsychiatry,* 48 (1978a), 538–51.

———, "The Process of Coping." Unpublished training materials, 1978b.

———, Stages of Crisis Intervention." Unpublished training materials, 1978c.

———, "Training in Crisis Intervention for Students in the Mental Health Professions," *Professional Psychology,* Vol. 10 (1979a), 161–67.

———, "Crisis Intervention, Parkinson's Law, and Structure in Psychotherapy." Manuscript, 1979b.

———, "Styles of Crisis Intervention: Toward a Convergent Model," *Professional Psychology,* Vol. 11 (1980), 113–20.

BEERS, T. M., and M. E. FOREMAN, "Intervention Patterns in Crisis Interviews," *Journal of Counseling Psychology,* 23 (1976), 87–91.

BLOOM, B. A., "Definitional Aspects of the Crisis Concept," *Journal of Consulting Psychology,* 27 (1963), 498–502.

BUTCHER, J. N., and G. R. MAUDEL, "Crisis Intervention," in I. Weiner, ed., *Clinical Methods in Psychology.* New York: John Wiley & Sons, Inc., 1976.

CAPLAN, G., *Principles of Preventive Psychiatry.* New York: Basic Books, Inc., Publishers, 1964.

COBB, S., and E. LINDEMANN, Symposium on Management of Cocoanut Grove Burns at Massachusetts General Hospital: Neuropsychiatric Observations," *Annals of Surgery,* 117 (1943), 814–24.

CUMMINGS, N. A., "Prolonged (Ideal) versus Short-Term (Realistic) Psychotherapy," *Professional Psychology,* 8 (1977), 491–501.

DECKER, B. J., and J. M. STUBBLEBINE, "Crisis Intervention and the Prevention of Psychiatric Disability: A Follow-Up Study," *American Journal of Psychiatry,* 129 (1972) 725–29.

DE LA TORRE, J., "Brief Encounters: General and Technical Psychoanalytic Considerations," *Psychiatry,* 41 (1978), 184–93.

DOROSIN, D., J. GIBBS, and L. KAPLAN, "Very Brief Interventions—A Pilot Study," *Journal of the American College Health Association,* 24 (1976), 191–94.

EASTHAM, K., D. COATES, and F. ALLODI, "The Concept of Crisis," *Canadian Psychiatric Association Journal,* 15 (1970), 463–72.

EWING, C. P., *Crisis Intervention as Psychotherapy.* New York: Oxford University Press, 1978.

FLOMENHAFT, K. and D. G. LANGSLEY, "After the Crisis," *Mental Hygiene,* 55 (1971), 473–77.

GOLAN, N., "When Is a Client in Crisis?" *Social Casework,* 50 (1969), 389–94.

HALPERN, H. A., "Crisis Theory: A Definitional Study," *Community Mental Health Journal,* 9 (1973), 342–49.

HANSELL, N., M. WODARCZYK, and B. HANDLON-LATHROP, "Decision Counseling Method: Expanding Coping at Crisis-in-Transit," *Archives of General Psychiatry,* 22 (1970), 462–67.

HIRSCHOWITZ, R. G., "Crisis Theory: A Formulation," *Psychiatric Annals,* 3, no. 12 (1973), 36–47.

HITCHCOCK, J. M., "Crisis Intervention: The Pebble in the Pool," *American Journal of Nursing,* 73 (1973), 1388–90.

HOFFMAN, D. L., and M. L. REMMEL, "Uncovering the Precipitant in Crisis Intervention. *Social Casework,* 56 (1975), 259–67.

JACOBSON, G. F., "Crisis Intervention from the Viewpoint of the Mental Health Professional," *Pastoral Psychology,* 21 (1970), 21–28.

JACOBSON, G. F., M. STRICKLER, and W. E. MORLEY, "Generic and Individual Approaches to Crisis Intervention," *American Journal of Public Health,* 58 (1968), 338–43.

JONES, M., and P. POLAK, "Crisis and Confrontation," *British Journal of Psychiatry,* 114 (1968), 169–74.

KARDENER, S. H., "A Methodologic Approach to Crisis Therapy," *American Journal of Psychotherapy,* 29 (1975), 4–13.

KATZENSTEIN, C., "The Effectiveness of Crisis Therapy." Unpublished doctoral dissertation, University of Chicago, 1971.

LINDEMANN, E., "Symptomatology and Management of Acute Grief," *American Journal of Psychiatry,* 101 (1944), 141–48.

MCGEE, T. F., "Some Basic Considerations in Crisis Intervention," *Community Mental Health Journal,* 4 (1968), 319–25.

MILLER, F. T., and N. A. MAZADE, "Crisis Intervention Services in Comprehensive Community Mental Health Centers in the United States," *Proceedings of the IX International Congress of Suicide Prevention and Crisis Intervention,* 1978, pp. 273–84.

MONTGOMERY, A., and D. MONTGOMERY, "Contractual Psychotherapy: Guidelines and Strategies for Change," *Psychotherapy: Theory,*

Research and Practice, 12 (1975), 348–52.

MORLEY, W. E., "Treatment of the Patient in Crisis," *Western Medicine,* 3 (1965), 1–10.

MORLEY, W. E., J. M. MESSICK, and D. C. AQUILERA, "Crisis: Paradigms of Intervention," *Journal of Psychiatric Nursing,* 5 (1967), 531–44.

MORRICE, J. K. W., *Crisis Intervention: Studies in Community Care.* New York: Pergamon Press, Inc., 1976.

NELSON, Z. P., and D. D. MOWRY, "Contracting in Crisis Intervention," *Community Mental Health Journal,* 12 (1976), 37–44.

PAUL, L. "Crisis Intervention," *Mental Hygiene,* 50 (1966), 141–45.

PERLMAN, H. H., "In Quest of Coping," *Social Casework,* 56 (1975), 213–25.

RAPOPORT, L., "The State of Crisis: Some Theoretical Considerations," *The Social Service Review,* 36 (1962), 211–17.

ROSENBERG, B. N., "Planned Short-Term Treatment in Developmental Crisis," *Social Casework,* 56 (1975), 195–204.

RUBENSTEIN, D., "Rehospitalization versus Family Crisis Intervention," *American Journal of Psychiatry,* 129 (1972), 715–20.

RUSK, T. N., "Opportunity and Technique in Crisis Psychiatry," *Comprehensive Psychiatry,* 12 (1971), 249–63.

SCHWARTZ, S. L., "A Review of Crisis Intervention Programs," *Psychiatric Quarterly,* 45 (1971), 498–508.

SHNEIDMAN, E., "Crisis Intervention: Some Thoughts and Perspectives," in G. Specter and W. Claiborn, eds., *Crisis Intervention,* New York: Behavioral Publications, 1973.

SILVERMAN, W. H., "Planning for Crisis Intervention with Community Mental Health Concepts," *Psychotherapy: Theory, Research and Practice,* 14 (1977), 293–97.

SMITH, L. L., "A Review of Crisis Intervention Theory," *Social Casework,* 59 (1978), 396–405.

STRICKLER, M., and B. LASOR, "The Concept of Loss in Crisis Intervention," *Mental Hygiene,* 54 (1970), 301–5.

SUDAK, H. S., J. B. SAWYER, G. K. SPRING, and C. M. COAKWELL, "High Referral Success Rates in a Crisis Center," *Hospital and Community Psychiatry,* 28 (1977), 530–32.

TRILLING, L., and E. MARCUS, eds., *The Life and Work of Sigmund Freud.* New York: Basic Books, Inc., Publishers, 1961.

WALES, E., "Crisis Intervention in Clinical Training," *Professional Psychology,* 3–4 (1972), 357–61.

WALLACE, M. A., and W. E. MORLEY, "Teaching Crisis Intervention," *American Journal of Nursing,* 70 (1970) 1484–87.

WOLKON, G. H., "Crisis Theory, the Application for Treatment, and Dependency," *Comprehensive Psychiatry,* 13 (1972), 459–64.

3

CREATING STRUCTURE FOR THE CRISIS INTERVENTION AND RESOLUTION PROCESS

Training programs for crisis therapists are still not widespread, although specialized skills, in addition to the skills of the well-trained clinician, are required for the effective practice of crisis intervention.[1] A critical area for clinicians learning or using the crisis model is the creation and maintenance of the structure necessary for a focal therapeutic process that results in adaptive crisis resolution (Baldwin 1979a, 1979b). Without the specialized skills of the crisis therapist, the use of the crisis model is seriously compromised and at times is counterproductive to the client's welfare.

The use of structure developed through an active, collaborative process between client and therapist has been of relatively recent origin, particularly among psychodynamically oriented practitioners. It has only been since the advent (and acceptance) of brief therapy approaches that structuring the helping process has been legitimized and valued as a necessary clinical skill. The crisis model, requiring definition of the focal problem and time and goal boundaries for resolution, cannot be used without addressing the issue of structure.

[1]This chapter, through page 68, is expanded from B. A. Baldwin, "Crisis Intervention, Parkinson's Law and Structure in Psychotherapy." Presented at the XVII Interamerican Congress of Psychology, Lima, Peru, July 1979.

However, defining the boundaries for crisis intervention and resolution requires special skills that are not typically taught in graduate training programs. These are also skills that challenge many of the tenets on which longer-term therapy are based. Crisis intervention mandates an action orientation of the therapist instead of the more passive and open-ended approach characteristic of more extended psychotherapy. In the various brief therapy models now becoming more popular among professionals, structure is explicitly defined early in the therapeutic process as an agreement between client and therapist that defines both time and goals for the ensuing therapeutic process.

There is a somewhat surprising gap in the literature on crisis intervention relating to structure in the therapeutic process. Students learning to use this model experience great difficulty unless the skills required for structuring and focusing the intervention and resolution process are developed. It is often said that the concepts on which crisis theory and practice are based are easily understood but are deceptively difficult to place into practice effectively. Nowhere is this more true than in the development of the structure needed early in the intervention process as a requisite for the effective practice of crisis therapy.

TWO TYPES OF STRUCTURE
FOR CRISIS INTERVENTION

Many therapists experience difficulty using the crisis model because of misconceptions about this approach (Baldwin 1977). Two basic premises of crisis intervention must be clearly understood to use this model well. First, clients are not typically selected for crisis intervention. It is used in walk-in clinics or in other services where such procedures are not feasible. The crisis therapist must adapt this model to a wide range of clients presenting with different types of problems and different levels of "crisis." The well-trained crisis therapist must be prepared to respond to these different types of crises while recognizing that this approach does not "fit" equally well to all (Baldwin 1978).

A second premise is that the crisis model is defined more by the structure and focus created for a time-limited intervention process than by the presenting problem or affective characteristics of the client. It is necessary for the therapist and client working together to define the issues, the goals to be attained, and a time framework for working toward them. Related to this premise is the assumption that no matter what problem the client is facing, an intervention can be defined and accomplished that will be helpful (albeit in a limited way) to the client within a short period of time. This requires organizing and structuring the intervention process through a cooperative effort of client and therapist for maximum helpfulness.

The structural boundaries that define this model, and that are required to use it effectively, take two forms. The first form, created during crisis assessment, is *definitional structure.* The crisis therapist, in conjunction with the client, defines key issues, client resources, and coping responses being used by the client. This definitional structure is helpful to the client in organizing the crisis experience. Creating this structure often includes an educational component that is necessary in crisis assessment. It removes cognitive distortions by restoring a more objective perspective of the situation and helps to define it as a solvable problem. It counters the feelings of helplessness and hopelessness that are often characteristic of the client in crisis. In this respect, creating definitional structure is an initial therapeutic intervention.

The second type of structure follows the definitional structure of crisis assessment and is termed *contractual structure.* The client and therapist agree on goals that will resolve the crisis, a time frame to work toward defined goals, and a therapeutic strategy to attain those goals. This is the agreement created between therapist and client that (optimally) results in resolution of the crisis and development of more adaptive coping responses by the client. Within the framework of contractual structure, the techniques of many therapeutic orientations can be used effectively (Baldwin 1977).

Essential Qualities
of the Crisis Therapist

In order to create both definitional structure and contractual structure for the crisis intervention process, the therapist must create appropriate expectations early in the therapeutic process. No matter what the orientation of the crisis therapist, three qualities, as discussed below, are essential for use of this model and in communicating the style of crisis therapy.

The Crisis Therapist
Must Be Active

The therapist who engages a client in time-limited interventions must actively become involved with that client. The crisis therapist must confront issues and relate directly to a client without becoming unnecessarily controlling of the client or of the therapeutic process (i.e., telling the client what to do, giving advice, etc.). The therapist must quickly create an optimistic therapeutic ambiance while developing a therapeutic alliance in which the client accepts responsibility for change. Often in crisis intervention

" . . . therapists feel responsible for arriving at particular solutions for the patient, rather than helping alleviate stress through support and providing directions for effective problem solving" (Stuart and Mackey 1977, p. 529). Novice crisis therapists find it difficult and threatening to create the defining structure for crisis intervention with its necessary directness and active therapist involvement in the change process.

The Crisis Therapist Must Be Accurate

By definition, the crisis therapist must assess the crisis situation quickly and must intervene on the basis of less than complete initial information or knowledge of the client. Time is not available to obtain a complete history or to conduct a thorough psychodiagnostic evaluation. Extensive evaluations are often counterproductive in crisis therapy because of their emphasis on the past and on psychopathology (Butcher and Maudel 1976). The crisis therapist must quickly and accurately discover the relevant issues that have determined the crisis situation and conceptualize them clearly. Relevant information must be obtained and screened from the irrelevant. Client problems not related to the present crisis must be acknowledged but set aside. To do this requires the capacity to quickly and accurately focus the intervention process and not "be seduced into exploring interesting but tangential material" (Stuart and Mackey 1977, p. 529). The screening of information obtained from the client, and learning how to ask for key data or information, are the essence of the accuracy required by the effective crisis therapist. This screening process, which results in rapid focusing on relevant issues in the crisis, is one of the most frustrating aspects of learning and using the crisis model, especially for novice therapists.

The Crisis Therapist Must Be Accountable

For effective crisis intervention, the crisis therapist must place personal therapeutic expertise and skills "on the line." In crisis intervention, the therapist experiences a cogent sense of accountability. Wallace and Morley (1970) have described this as the "responsibility/accountability" issue that the crisis therapist must face when confronted by individuals in crisis and for whom they must intervene quickly and effectively. In this endeavor, and through the structure of the contract designed to resolve the crisis, the crisis therapist becomes visibly accountable for the therapeutic process when goals, time frame, and a therapeutic strategy are defined in advance. This accountability issue is much easier to disguise or mask during relatively unstructured or open-ended forms of therapy where the pace is more leisurely and it is left to the client to define therapeutic goals. The therapist who uses the crisis intervention model must accept the responsibility that is inherent in the use of this model. Interestingly, it is this accountability that is an influence that helps the therapist prevent diffusion of the therapeutic process in crisis intervention.

STRUCTURE IN CRISIS ASSESSMENT

It is in crisis assessment that the stage is set for the crisis therapy, and for the contracting that is necessary to focus and delimit the crisis resolution process. While obtaining the information necessary to understand the client's crisis, definitional structure is produced. From this defining structure, the client develops expectations for both the style and the focus of the therapeutic process that follows.

By definition, when an emotional crisis occurs, the individual's homeostatic balance is disrupted because previously learned or new coping behaviors prove ineffective. With continuing vulnerability, the client's coping behaviors turn more to protection of the self rather than to mastery of the situation (Silverman 1977). As dysphoric affect intensifies over time, there is increasing cognitive disorganization and progressive impairment of problem-solving ability (Caplan 1964). The individual in crisis is increasingly less able to mobilize personal resources, to maintain an objective perspective of the situation, or to use existing problem-solving skills effectively.

During crisis assessment, interventions to help reestablish homeostatic balance, from the emotional disequilibrium characteristic of the crisis state, can begin. By structuring and defining the parameters of the problem situation, these structural interventions help to restore to the client a perspective on the problem and the capability to mobilize internal and external resources and bring them to bear on the problem. In short, hope is generated as perspective is created through definitional structure (Korner 1973).

Organizing the client's perceptions of the problem situation is of therapeutic value in crisis assessment. Rapoport (1962) believes that the individual in crisis " does not know how to think of his problem, how to evaluate reality, and how to formulate and evaluate the outcome of the crisis and possibilities for problem solving"(p. 28). Creating definitional structure is a therapeutic intervention, and it becomes the foundation for creating a time and goal contract for crisis intervention and resolution. Golan (1969) has delineated specific questions for the crisis therapist to ask during the intake (assessment) interview in crisis intervention that help to create the structure necessary for the use of this model.

Four Major Areas
for Structural Intervention

During crisis assessment, there are four major areas in which the experience of the client is defined and organized before therapeutic contracting for crisis resolution can begin.

Defining the Core Issue
or Problem

For many individuals in crisis, there is loss of perspective of the problem that precipitated the crisis. There is progressive negative escalation of the magnitude of the problem and concomitant feelings of loss of control, of hopelessness, and of helplessness. Helping the individual in crisis to focus on and clearly define the problem is essential in crisis assessment, and is a critical factor in planning effective intervention and resolution. It is necessary for the client and therapist to define the core problem, and to agree upon a concise and accurate statement of that problem. This helps to reduce the problem to a reasonable perspective by removing any distortions produced by the crisis state.

Defining Coping Responses

In assessing the client's coping responses, it is critical to differentiate healthy and adaptive coping behavior from those behaviors that are self-defeating or maladaptive. Implicit in this process is differential reinforcement of adaptive and maladaptive coping responses, which will help the client gain a realistic perspective of the problem. Also, by examining maladaptive or ineffective coping behaviors, the therapist often gains insight into the fears (i.e., resistances) that are determining those responses and that must be worked through as part of the crisis resolution process (Montgomery and Montgomery 1975). In many instances, the client has some awareness of these fears but may not have conceptualized them clearly.

Defining/Mobilizing
Client Resources

The client's available internal and external resources must be defined and mobilized. The client's personal strengths, previous learning experiences, and skills that can be used or brought to bear on the present problem situation are defined and their use encouraged. When in crisis, there is often a tendency to focus only on negative affect and personal shortcomings rather than on effective use of problem-solving skills and other assets available to help resolve the crisis.

Similarly, there are often external resources that can be mobilized with encouragement and help from the therapist. Sources of support for the client such as friends, a pastor, or parents may be arranged. Appropriate community resources to aid in resolving the client's problem can also be mobilized and necessary information provided. The client is helped to emotionally acknowledge that resources are available that can be used to respond to a problem that initially seemed overwhelming.

Psychological Education

As part of the assessment process, mental health education cannot be neglected. It cannot be assumed that clients are aware of the dynamics of their personal emotional and psychological functioning, or that they know what constitutes emotionally mature responses in a given situation. Defining directly what emotionally mature behaviors are in stressful situations is very helpful to the client in understanding the crisis more fully (e.g., anger that is not expressed often produces depression). Helping the client to understand the implications and consequences of maladaptive coping responses is also part of the educational intervention that is often part of the crisis assessment procedure.

Many crises are made worse by a lack of basic information about emotional maturity on one hand, or by inadequate client information about psychological "cause and effect" relationships on the other. Clients who have not been exposed to role models demonstrating emotionally mature responses to stresses or to problem situations often find psychological education very helpful. Through this educational process, clients often gain a rationale to initiate responses useful in resolving the crisis (e.g., the need to say *no*, to take time off and enjoy oneself, to become more active during sexual encounters, etc.).

These four structural interventions during crisis assessment serve dual purposes. First, the therapist gains information necessary to understand the crisis at the level of the present problem as well as its psychodynamic determinants. And second, from the client's perspective, these interventions help to reduce an emotionally disruptive experience to a solvable problem with hope and optimism taking the place of helplessness and hopelessness. This organization of the client's experience in the crisis situation is accomplished through initial therapeutic interventions that create definitional structure and that form the basis for the contract necessary for crisis resolution.

CONTRACTING IN CRISIS INTERVENTION

Contracting delimits and focuses the therapeutic process and is necessary for crisis intervention. There are three basic stages in the contracting process, each of which is discussed below.

Stage 1: Creating the Contract

Several tasks must be accomplished when developing a therapeutic contract, and the ease of these tasks depends on the adequacy of the definitional structure created during crisis assessment. To contract effectively, the therapeutic process must be defined along two major dimensions according to Nelson and Mowry (1976): First, mutual obligations between the client and the counselor should be defined, and second, the therapy should be carefully delimited. To create this therapeutic "set," three components of the contract must be addressed; these include (1) the specific goals for crisis resolution, (2) the time limits for the therapy, and (3) the therapeutic strategy to attain those goals within specific time limits.

Developing Specific Goals

The client and therapist must develop from the core statement of the problem a set of goals that will result in crisis resolution when attained. These goals are often helpful to the client in thinking about the problem in very specific and concrete terms rather than globally (e.g., "I want to be happy again"). Goals should be few in number, no more than two or three, and should be behaviorally specific, that is, defined in terms of tasks or behavioral changes rather than defined in affective terms (e.g., "feeling better").

It is incumbent upon the therapist to limit goals to those that can be reasonably obtained during the time-limits of the contract. If goals are left unspecified, diffuse, too general, or too many in number, failure to attain these goals will be counterproductive to the crisis intervention. For those clients with multiple problems who are treated using the crisis model, the most relevant problem, or part of a problem, must be defined as the focus of the therapy, and the intervention should be limited to this aspect of the total problem.

Defining the Time of Termination

The next task of the therapist and client is to agree on the time frame within which they will both work toward attainment of defined goals. Sometimes these limits are defined by administrative policy as in those clinics that have a limit of six or eight or perhaps ten visits. In other services, it is the responsibility of the therapist and client to define a reasonable time frame for crisis resolution and to acknowledge the date or time when termination will occur.

Goals for crisis intervention and the time limits for attaining those goals are highly related. For example, the therapist must keep in mind the outer limits of time available when developing goals for crisis resolution with the client. It is also necessary for the therapist to define clearly and explicitly with the client the fact that the therapy *will* end at the specified time, and not leave an "open door" to continue therapy after the crisis is resolved.

If the goals are relevant to the issues in the crisis situation and are attainable within the time frame defined, less resistance will be presented by the client. If appropriate, it is desirable at this time to acknowledge that additional therapeutic intervention beyond the crisis therapy may be required to deal with other problems once the crisis is resolved and the client's functioning has stabilized. Sensitization of the client to this possibility is often helpful as therapist and client work toward the limited goals of crisis intervention.

Deciding on a Therapeutic Strategy

At the time the contract is negotiated, it is necessary for the therapist to discuss with the client a tentative therapeutic strategy to attain the defined goals. This process elicits the cooperation of the client and also prepares the client for the type of therapeutic intervention that will take place. The crisis therapist, to be maximally effective, must be skilled in a range of therapeutic techniques and change modalities to meet the needs of many different kinds of clients presenting with many and varied types of problems (Aguilera and Messick 1974). Kardener (1975) strongly takes this position:

> Short-term therapists must be reasonably conversant with a variety of treatment modalities or seek collaborative consultation. It is the responsibility of the therapist to fit the therapeutic message with the needs of a given patient, and his particular desired goal, and not the patient's responsibility to fit a unimodal therapist! [P. 8]

It is axiomatic in crisis intervention that the narrower the range of the therapist's intervention skills, the less that therapist's capacity to meet the needs of the range of clients presenting for crisis intervention. Consequently, there is need for more referrals for longer-term psychotherapy or for other services. The eclectic therapist, on the other hand, skilled in a variety of therapeutic interventions and able to apply these techniques selectively, is able to use the crisis model maximally as a treatment of choice, and this often reduces the number of referrals beyond the crisis contact. Fortunately, many different therapeutic orientations can be used with great effect in crisis intervention.

Stage 2: Maintaining the Contract

Once the contract has been negotiated, the "work" of the therapeutic intervention and crisis resolution lies ahead. Many problems become manifest in this phase of crisis therapy. In fulfilling the contract, there are three priority therapeutic tasks: (1) preventing diffusion of the therapy, (2) dealing with client resistance, and (3) enhancing client skill development or task mastery.

Preventing Diffusion of the Intervention/Resolution Process

It is easy to allow crisis intervention to become diffuse even when a time limit and goal contract have been created. This may occur actively or passively, consciously or unconsciously, by either the therapist or the client. Diffusion may represent resistance by either the therapist or the client, *or by both*. Frequently, therapists diffuse the therapeutic intervention by emphasizing the past and neglecting the present stressor that must remain the focus of the intervention process. At other times, the therapist inadvertently slips into the techniques and style of longer-term therapy by adopting a more passive therapeutic posture and loses the necessary active involvement in present problem solving with the client.

Sometimes clients escape to the past and blame or scapegoat others, or bring in other problems not related to the present crisis that diffuse the therapeutic process. Wallace and Morley (1970) found in their training program that one of the major supervision issues centered on helping their trainees (and by extension their clients!) to adhere to the structure of the crisis model throughout the entire intervention process. It is essential to exclude extraneous problems, unrelated client concerns, and nonrelevant information from the therapeutic process when using this model. The therapeutic energy of both client and therapist must concentrate on attaining the defined goals that represent more adaptive coping responses and that reflect determinant issues that produced the failure to cope (i.e., the crisis).

Responding to Client Resistance

Goals for crisis intervention are defined in terms of establishing adaptive coping responses to a present stressful situation. Such goals often arouse client resistance to adoption of these new behaviors. Clients in crisis therapy fall into one of two basic categories: (1) those who are encountering new situations for which no coping skills have been previously developed, and (2) those who are using maladaptive coping responses because healthier coping behaviors are threatening. In both cases, resistance to facing change or to giving up the security of past responses to stress, albeit ineffectual, becomes manifest.

Resistance often has psychodynamic implications as well. When there is reactivation of past traumas or conflicts, resistance may result from the fear that emotional pain would be experienced even more intensely if adaptive and mature responses were made (i.e., if the issues or the situation were confronted directly rather than avoided). Those unresolved conflicts or past traumas that support maladaptive responses, defined as the precipitant of the crisis (Hoffman and Remmel 1975), are primary determinants of resistance that must be addressed by the crisis therapist during the resolution process (Montgomery and Montgomery 1975). If the therapist responds only to the surface "problem," resistance may be magnified and may prevent adaptive resolution of the crisis through the development of more effective coping behaviors. It is this capacity to work with the manifest problem of the client, while also responding to the precipitant and to client resistance, that distinguishes the professional crisis therapist from the paraprofessional.

Enhancing Skill Development or Task Mastery

The therapist, while responding to and working through client resistance, also focuses on helping the client to attain those skills needed for mastery of the crisis situation. The therapist may directly teach problem solving or decision making, or may enhance skills through such techniques as role playing, assertiveness training, or relaxation training. It is also not uncommon for therapists to give homework to the client as part of crisis intervention. All of the above techniques help place responsibility for change on the client and help maintain active client involvement to attain the agreed upon goals of the crisis contract.

It is this action orientation and emphasis on skill development that will often identify the client's resistance to change that must be addressed as part of the therapy. This reflects the axiom that the more active the therapy, the more quickly resistance will become manifest. However, this resistance can be used to help define and conceptualize relevant issues inherent to the crisis situation or conflicts reactivated by a particular event that impair or prevent adaptive crisis resolution. Working with resistance is only a means to the end of helping the client to develop more adaptive coping behaviors, and second, removing a vulnerability that may prevent future crises. For some, however, the emphasis on skill development and task mastery is threatening, especially to clients whose "wish to be treated far outweighs the wish to be cured" (Levinson 1977, p. 483).

Stage 3: Terminating the Contract

Terminating the contract at the end of the time period specified for crisis resolution involves several therapeutic tasks that are an important part of the crisis model (Baldwin 1979b). These tasks are discussed below.

Responding to Client Termination Issues

In any form of psychotherapy, termination issues arise. Although crisis intervention is short term and therapeutically limited, termination issues are often present and must be dealt with at the end of the therapeutic contract. The vulnerability and the consequent dependency of the client in crisis (Wolkon 1972) bring termination issues to the fore. Termination of crisis therapy is therapeutically compromised if the time frame for the intervention process has not been made clear from the beginning or if crisis resolution is permitted to become diffuse. As in any therapy, termination issues may have therapeutic value if handled well, but they usually do not warrant extension of the therapeutic process beyond time limits defined in the initial contract.

Conversely, there are therapists who experience difficulty with separation issues. They prolong termination or undermine client termination by attempting to deal with new problems, by not responding to termination issues, or by extending the therapeutic contract. This is a therapist issue that is not only counterproductive to the use of the crisis model but is also a form of "patient-making" that ignores the real needs of that client.

Sometimes, this therapist problem stems from an inability to accept the very limited goals of crisis intervention, that is, to restore the client to the level of functioning that existed prior to the crisis. Further, those therapists who are overly nurturant and who inadvertently reinforce regression and dependency rather than mastery (Wallace and Morley 1970) very often find it quite difficult to separate from clients who have made very little "progress," or who still have "problems." Coming to terms with termination issues is critical to the use of the crisis model, but this task is one that novice crisis therapists often find quite difficult because of the special limitations of this approach.

Evaluation of the Client's Progress

In addition to response to termination issues, the last therapy hour is also used to evaluate the client's progress toward defined goals (or lack of goal attainment). Frequently, sources of resistance become clearer and can be discussed in detail during the termination interview. However, definition of client progress is difficult if there has not been strict adherence to the structure and limits of the crisis model. When there has been adherence to this model and to the goals for crisis resolution, exploring lack of client goal attainment can result in therapeutic growth and significant learning by the client. It is incumbent on the therapist to initiate this evaluation of what has occurred (or not occurred) during the intervention process defined by the initial contract and to use it productively as part of the therapeutic process.

Use of Anticipatory Guidance

During the final stage of therapy, there is need for anticipatory guidance (Caplan 1964; Caplan and Grunebaum 1967) to help integrate client gains by conceptualizing them clearly, and to help the client to anticipate applying new responses in future similar situations. It cannot be assumed that adaptive crisis resolution per se enables the client to use new responses when encountering a similar problem. However, use of anticipatory guidance is quite helpful as a technique for integrating more adaptive coping skills.

Anticipatory guidance as a crisis intervention technique does help to prevent future crisis by reinforcing client mastery. Yet, use of this intervention is often omitted. Clients respond to it well, and find it very useful to conceptualize in advance adaptive responses to problem situations. When this intervention is used, adaptive responses are more likely to occur in the future. Similar problems are then reduced to the status of an emotionally hazardous situation for which coping skills are available in lieu of progression to an emotional crisis (Caplan 1964).

In summary, Nelson and Mowry (1976) found contracting in crisis intervention useful in: (1) defining role-relationships of therapist and client, (2) defining problems, responsibilities, and alternatives and decisions facing client and therapist, (3) limiting the time available for therapy, and second, reducing the client dependency that often develops, (4) eliminating or controlling some of the client's symptoms that often impede problem solving, and (5) by dealing with "here and now" problems, avoiding some of the stigmatizing labels associated with the need for help. It is clear that therapeutic contracts in crisis intervention are an essential part of the structure required for the effective use of this helping model and a necessary skill area for the crisis therapist.

THERAPEUTIC STRUCTURE
AND PARKINSON'S LAW

Experienced clinicians are familiar with those clients who make rapid therapeutic gains when an externally defined end point for therapy draws close (e.g., the therapist is leaving, a training experience finishes, extended vacations or sabbaticals begin, etc.). The therapy moves from a "plateau" to more active involvement by the client, and consequent therapeutic gains are made as termination approaches. This is the operational effect of Parkinson's Law in psychotherapy (Appelbaum 1975). This law is derived from the sociological principle defined by Parkinson that states: "Work expands or contracts to fill the time available for its completion."

Although this law was not originally developed for application to change in psychotherapy, it is now recognized that Parkinson's Law is a motivational influence in psychotherapy that may work for or against client attainment of therapeutic goals. If Parkinson's Law in psychotherapy is to be used to enhance client change, then the time available for the "work" of therapy must be specified and acknowledged by the client. That is, an end point (termination date) must be defined in advance if the motivational influence of this principle is to be used in crisis therapy. Parkinson's Law in psychotherapy is part of the justification for time/goal contracting when using the crisis model.

Adapted to crisis intervention, Parkinson's Law in psychotherapy might be paraphrased as: "The work of adaptive change expands or contracts to meet the time available for its completion as defined through structure and limits created early in the therapeutic process." Appelbaum (1975) believes that both in psychotherapy and in other types of contracts completing the necessary work is unconsciously timed or phased to fit the time available. Within the framework of crisis intervention, the time available for the therapeutic process, whether mandated by clinic policy or by negotiated agreement between client and therapist, is a critical part of the contracting process if the motivation created by such limits is to facilitate adaptive client change.

Parkinson's Law is also a motivational influence on the clinician. By creating a clearly defined time framework for therapy, the clinician becomes more accountable for what occurs during the course of crisis resolution. Under such conditions, the therapist is less likely to diffuse the intervention process because of the accountability generated by stating time and goals in advance. The process of time/goal contracting forces recognition of an end point by both therapist and client that harnesses the motivational influence of Parkinson's Law for both.

Conversely, Parkinson's Law can effectively work against therapeutic change. If psychotherapy remains open-ended and without definition of goals or a termination date, then the diffuseness of the therapeutic process expands the client's perception (conscious and unconscious) of the time available for the "work" of therapy to occur. Both therapist and client may become more passive, and less involved, and in many instances this results in unilateral termination from psychotherapy by the client. One effect of this is erosion of the therapist's confidence, particularly if it occurs during training or if the therapist is inexperienced. It may also result in a negative therapeutic experience for the client that will impede future productive involvement in therapy or in other helping services that are needed.

CONCLUDING REMARKS

Creating and maintaining structure and focus in crisis intervention is necessary to use this model effectively. The goals for crisis intervention are by necessity limited. If the limited goals for crisis intervention are accepted, then defining the structure necessary for use of this model is easier. The primary goal of and the criterion for success for crisis intervention are restoration of the client to that level of functioning that existed before the onset of the crisis. Those gains made beyond stabilization and restoration of the client's usual homeostatic balance are a therapeutic bonus, and result in optimal crisis resolution that will reduce the probability of a future similar crisis.

Structure in crisis intervention must be instituted early for maximal helpfulness. Lemon and Goldstein (1978) point out that "lack of ambiguity in a highly structured time-limited arrangement, particularly when such an arrangement is made after one interview, is reassuring to most clients" (p. 591). Therapists often feel that this structuring is difficult or impossible because of incomplete information about the client early in the crisis intervention process. Although there is no specific time frame for creating structure, a clinical rule of thumb is to establish the structural parameters for intervention by no later than the end of the second therapy hour. The crisis therapist begins intervention quickly and proceeds on the basis of less than complete information, and initial formulations of the problem or relevant issues can be refined as additional information is gained (Lemon and Goldstein 1978). It is the capacity to quickly and accurately obtain and use material from crisis assessment to create structure and focus for the intervention process that is the mark of the seasoned crisis therapist.

Structure in crisis intervention is attractive to consumers in ways that permit more receptivity to involvement in a therapeutic process and to change. Defining problems, goals, time available, and strategies to attain goals in advance helps to define for the client (the consumer) what is being "purchased" from the therapist (Bellak and Small 1978). The therapist also becomes more accountable for the services being offered through this initial structuring process. This structure is reassuring to client-consumers who often are not interested in lengthy psychotherapy (Ewing 1978) and who may feel stigmatized by it.

Creating structural boundaries in psychotherapy, particularly in crisis intervention, has other benefits. For example, Cummings (1977) has produced evidence highly favorable to brief interventions with a clear focus. He found a surprisingly positive cost-effectiveness ratio for such interventions, not only in enhancing productive use of therapist time but also in reducing the incidence of later clinic visits by clients. In this respect, use of the crisis model reduces pressure on the clinic, and the client-consumers of clinic services benefit as well. Others who have examined the use of the crisis model have found that brief, structured interventions are not only effective (Katzenstein 1971) but are also favorably evaluated by clients even when there is early termination (Dorosin, Gibbs, and Kaplan 1976).

Kardener (1975) believes that many of the tenets of crisis theory and the methodologies of crisis intervention have been available for some time but have only recently become accepted as an effective therapeutic model and a treatment of choice. This may be due to the recent pressure to provide more helping services in the community. Growth in crisis intervention has paralleled the increasing prominence of community psychiatry and community psychology as emerging disciplines. Indeed, crisis intervention can be seen as a therapeutic model that has been derived from the principles of community mental health. It represents one significant interface between the principles of psychotherapy and the community mental health movement.

As a creative blend of present problem solving and proven principles of psychotherapy within a structured framework (Baldwin 1979b, 1980), the crisis model is attractive both to consumers who are not interested in long-term psychotherapy and to the hard-pressed professionals serving those consumers. However, there is still much to be learned about crisis intervention. Increasing numbers of clinicians of all persuasions are now using this model, and more research interest is focused on developing the constructs of crisis theory that determine effective clinical practice. The crisis model has helped to legitimize structure and focus in the intervention process and has proved the value of client-therapist contracting. The various roots of crisis theory and practice are now converging (Baldwin 1980), and the result is a more unified and internally consistent conceptual framework that will enhance teaching of this approach and use of it by mental health professionals.

REFERENCES

AGUILERA, D., and J. MESSICK, *Crisis Intervention: Theory and Methodology,* St. Louis: The C. V. Mosby Company, 1974.

APPELBAUM, S., "Parkinson's Law in Psychotherapy," *International Journal of Psychoanalytic Psychotherapy,* 4 (1975), 426–36.

BALDWIN, B., "Crisis Intervention in Professional Practice: Implications for Clinical Training," *American Journal of Osthopsychiatry,* 47 (1977), 659–70.

————, "A Paradigm for the Classification of Emotional Crises: Implications for Crisis Intervention," *American Journal of Orthopsychiatry,* 48 (1978), 538–51.

———, "Training in Crisis Intervention for Students in the Mental Health Professions," *Professional Psychology,* 10 (1979a), 161–67.

———, "Crisis Intervention: An Overview of Theory and Practice," *The Counseling Psychologist,* 8 (1979b), 43–52.

———, "Styles of Crisis Intervention: Toward a Convergent Model." *Professional Psychology,* 11 (1980), 113–20.

BELLAK, L., and L. SMALL, *Emergency Psychotherapy and Brief Psychotherapy.* New York: Grune & Stratton, Inc., 1978.

BUTCHER, J. and G. MAUDEL, "Crisis Intervention," in I. Weiner, ed., *Clinical Methods in Psychology.* New York: John Wiley & Sons, Inc., 1976.

CAPLAN, G., *Principles of Preventive Psychiatry.* New York: Basic Books, Inc., Publishers, 1964.

CAPLAN, G., and H. GREENBAUM, "Perspectives on Primary Prevention: A Review," *Archives of General Psychiatry,* 17 (1967), 331–46.

CUMMINGS, N., "Prolonged (Ideal) versus Short-Term (Realisitc) Psychotherapy," *Professional Psychology,* 8 (1977), 491–501.

DOROSIN, D., J. GIBBS, and L. KAPLAN, "Very Brief Interventions—A Pilot Evaluation," *Journal of the American College Health Association,* 24 (1976) 191–94.

EWING, C., *Crisis Intervention as Psychotherapy.* New York: Oxford University Press, 1978.

GOLAN, N., "When Is a Client in Crisis?" *Social Casework,* 50 (1969), 389–94.

HOFFMAN, K., and M. REMMEL, "Uncovering the Precipitant in Crisis Intervention," *Social Casework,* 56 (1975), 259–67.

KARDENER, S., A Methodologic Approach to Crisis Therapy," *American Journal of Psychotherapy,* 29 (1975), 4–13.

KATZENSTEIN, C., "The Effectiveness of Crisis Therapy." Ph.D. disseration, University of Chicago, Chicago, 1971.

KORNER, I., "Crisis Reduction and the Psychological Consultant," in G. Specter and W. Claiborn, eds., *Crisis Intervention.* New York: Behavioral Publications, 1973.

LEMON, E., and S. GOLDSTEIN, "The Use of Time Limits in Planned Brief Casework," *Social Casework,* 59 (1978), 588–96.

LEVINSON, H., "Termination of Psychotherapy: Some Salient Issues," *Social Casework,* 58 (1977), 480–89.

MONTGOMERY, A., and D. MONTGOMERY, "Contractual Psychotherapy: Guidelines and Strategies for Change," *Psychotherapy: Theory, Research and Practice,* 12 (1975), 348–52.

NELSON, Z., and D. MOWRY, "Contracting in Crisis Intervention," *Community Mental Health Journal,* 12 (1976), 37–44.

RAPOPORT, L., "The State of Crisis: Some Theoretical Considerations," *The Social Service Review,* 36 (1962), 211–17.

SILVERMAN, W., "Planning for Crisis Intervention with Community Mental Health Concepts," *Psychotherapy: Theory, Research and Practice,* 14 (1977), 293–97.

STUART, M., and K. MACKEY, "Defining the Differences between Crisis Intervention and Short-Term Therapy," *Hospital and Community Psychiatry,* 28 (1977), 527–29.

WALLACE, M., and W. MORLEY, "Teaching Crisis Intervention," *American Journal of Nursing,* 70 (1970), 1484–87.

WOLKON, G., "Crisis Theory, the Application for Treatment, and Dependency," *Comprehensive Psychiatry,* 13 (1972), 459–64.

4

THE ASSESSMENT
OF EMOTIONAL CRISES

Crisis intervention and other forms of brief therapy have recently become a treatment of choice for many clients.[1] However, there remains a significant lag between the need for well-trained professional crisis therapists and training programs that systematically and comprehensively teach this model (Baldwin 1977). Special skills are needed for crisis intervention, and without these skills the effectiveness of the crisis model is compromised. In training students in the mental health professions in crisis intervention, the skills required for the use of this model must be integrated with the clinical skills needed for psychotherapy in general (Baldwin 1977, 1979a).

Several areas of difficulty are encountered by those learning to use this model. One major problem area is crisis assessment, which differs from more traditional diagnostic and evaluation procedures. Crises must be assessed accurately and quickly with issues defined and a structure created for the resolution process if the impact of this model is to be optimized (Baldwin 1979c). Emotional crises are time-limited events (Caplan 1964), and extended evaluation of the client before therapeutic intervention may cause the

[1]This chapter, through page 91, is expanded from B. A. Baldwin, "A Paradigm for the Assessment of Emotional Crises Derived from Crisis Theory." Presented at the XVII Interamerican Congress of Psychology, Lima, Peru, July 1979.

opportunity for rapid growth and adaptive learning created by the crisis to be lost.

In crisis therapy, the question is not whether an emotional crisis will be resolved. The crisis *will* be resolved in a reasonably short period of time, usually in an average of four to six weeks. The real question is whether the crisis will be resolved in an adaptive fashion that results in enhanced maturity and stable functioning or in a maladaptive way that increases client vulnerability to future crises. When using the crisis model, the therapist must proceed with the intervention on the basis of less than complete information about the client. As Morley, Messick, and Aguilera (1967) state, "Material not directly related to the client's crisis has no place in an intervention of this kind" (p. 537). Yet, information that is obtained must be accurate and well conceptualized to provide the foundation for negotiating a time and goal contract with the client for the intervention and resolution process (Baldwin 1979c; Nelson and Mowry 1976).

Every crisis involves an individual responding to a stressor within a particular psychosocial context. By structuring crisis assessment to emphasize the individual in a stressful situation, the interaction of that person's coping responses and the situational stressor become the focus that is established for the client. The message to the client must be clear: "There is a problem you are encountering that is solvable, and it is central in importance." This is in lieu of the message: "You have problems and you need psychotherapy."

Crisis assessment requires this shift in emphasis when interviewing the client. In the assessment interview in crisis therapy (or in any other type of therapy), the therapist's style and emphasis create expectations for the therapeutic relationship and the change process that follows. Many clients become discouraged when their presenting problems are not addressed early. Particularly distressing to them is therapist concern about past problems rather than about current difficulties. The emphasis in crisis assessment is on the "here and now" problem, and this is attractive to many client-consumers. However, although crisis assessment is very present-oriented and limited, it does not neglect or deny the psychodynamic implications of the crisis situation.

Crisis assessment is a most difficult aspect of the crisis model to master. It is also the first postural shift the therapist must make to use this model effectively. Rapid assessment is threatening to inexperienced therapists because of the need to quickly grasp the situation, the issues, and the emotional meaning of that situation for the client. The crisis assessment model helps to structure this process, and it becomes an integrated part of the framework defined by crisis theory. As a result, crisis assessment "fits" with the remainder of crisis theory rather than existing as a nebulous but troublesome gap in the practice of crisis therapy.

CHARACTERISTICS OF CRISIS ASSESSMENT

As a fundamental skill that the crisis therapist must bring to crisis intervention, crisis assessment differs in several significant ways from more traditional psychodiagnostic and evaluation procedures. In fact, some mental health professionals feel that such comprehensive evaluations are counter-productive to the effective use of the crisis model. They state:

> In considering assessment in crisis therapy, it is first helpful to distinguish assessment from diagnosis. Formal psychiatric diagnosis is not particularly useful in crisis therapy and may in fact be detrimental in that it may orient the therapist toward seeing and planning for chronic pathology and blind him to important and manageable critical events. Although a reaction to crisis is often seen as indicative of the person's pre-stressed personality, evidence from studies that have attempted to predict the outcome of a stress situation solely on the basis of personality have tended to disconfirm this belief. [Butcher and Maudel 1976, P. 618]

Stuart and Mackey (1977) assume that "person plus stress yields reaction" (p. 527) is a model on which to define crisis intervention in contrast to short-term (and by extension, longer-term) therapy. These same elements can also be used to distinguish crisis assessment from the emphasis in diagnostic evaluations. All emotional crises involve interaction between a client vulnerability and a problem situation (Baldwin 1979b). The locus of the stress may be primarily external (environmentally determined) or internal (intrapsychically determined). Regardless of the locus of the stress, the focus in crisis assessment is on the interaction of the person in a situation and not on the client character structure or personality organization as in diagnostic procedures nor on accumulating historical information as is characteristic of intake evaluations.

More specifically, there are several dimensions of difference between crisis assessment and other types of diagnostic and evaluation procedures.

Crisis Assessment Is Present-Oriented

In crisis assessment, the present stressor and the client's reaction to that stressor are paramount, and there is no movement away from this emphasis during the course of crisis intervention. This does not imply that crisis intervention ignores antecedents. In fact, many crises have a precipitant (Hoffman and Remmel 1975) that is an unresolved conflict or trauma reactivated by a current event. However, psychodynamic issues are responded to only in terms of their influence on and impairment of adaptive resolution of the present crisis. These reactivated issues are often resolved or partially resolved as the client is helped to modify coping responses to the present stressor. Helping to resolve these underlying issues within the framework of helping the client to deal with the present is a basic strategy for crisis intervention that helps to reduce client vulnerability and consequently to reduce the probability of future similar crises.

Crisis Assessment Is Selective

Both crisis assessment and crisis intervention are focused and therefore limited in scope. The information needed for crisis assessment is selective, and it must necessarily be accurate and "on target" to be effective (Morley, Messick, and Aguilera 1967). If necessary, initial formulations of the problem and the goals for crisis intervention can be modified (Lemon and Goldstein 1978), but the crisis therapist must define as accurately as possible a starting point for the crisis intervention process during crisis assessment. It is very easy for therapists to explore the client's past or the psychodynamics of the problem and thereby neglect the problem itself, or to explore other client problems not related to the present crisis. It is the therapist's responsibility to quickly and selectively focus the crisis assessment process and prevent diffusion of either assessment or intervention away from the present stressor being experienced by the client.

Crisis Intervention Has an
Interpersonal Orientation

Longer-term psychotherapy and the more complete evaluations on which it is based tend to be intrapsychic in orientation. It is characteristic in crisis assessment to focus on the interpersonal dimensions of a problem situation experienced by a client, and on the client's coping responses to that situation. Emotional crises always are interpersonal events. There are always significant others involved in the crisis (Baldwin 1979b), and detecting and understanding the involvement of these others (past or present) are key aspects of crisis assessment. Since crisis resolution is determined more by the influence of psychosocial factors than by past experience or by character structure (Paul 1966), it becomes essential to understand these interpersonal dimensions in depth.

Crisis Assessment
Is a Collaborative Process

In the conduct of crisis assessment, therapist and client work together to define and agree on the problem, the relevant issues, and the coping responses (both adaptive and maladaptive) that are being used in that crisis situation. Therapist and client together may direct energy to the mobilization of both internal (personal) and external (environmental) resources. There may be an educational process that is integrated with the assessment procedure. These assessment tasks (Baldwin 1979c) all involve the client and therapist in a working relationship that communicates the action orientation and problem-solving focus of the crisis model. This approach to assessment also helps to create a therapeutic alliance in which responsibility for change remains with the client. Many novice crisis therapists fail to communicate these dimensions of the crisis intervention process early and as a result may encourage transferences and/or dependency that complicates crisis resolution and that is antithetical to the use of this model (Wallace and Morley 1970). The crisis assessment process is the first opportunity to directly and indirectly communicate the expectations for the crisis intervention and resolution process, and the seasoned crisis therapist uses it.

Crisis Assessment
Is a Therapeutic Intervention

To a greater extent than in other evaluation procedures, crisis assessment is used not only to understand the client's crisis but also to intervene in the crisis and prepare the client for crisis resolution. In crisis assessment, therapist and client create a conceptual structure for understanding and defining the crisis. This process of conceptualizing and organizing the client's crisis experience helps define the crisis as a solvable problem with a clear origin. It reduces the confusion, perceptual distortions, and the dysphoric affect that often characterize clients in crisis. Such cognitive restructuring (Rapoport 1962) also helps the client to mobilize available problem-solving skills and adaptive coping responses. Crisis assessment as an initial therapeutic intervention cannot be underestimated in its impact on the client. However, this opportunity can be missed if the assessment focuses on the past, on psychodynamics, or on nonrelated client problems. A clear focus and a conceptual structure created through a collaborative crisis assessment often restore to the client a sense of optimism and consequent involvement in the therapeutic process.

A MODEL FOR CRISIS ASSESSMENT

Crisis assessment involves five primary component parts that together create an in-depth understanding of the crisis. Each of these components of crisis assessment is discussed below along with a rationale relating it to the tenets of crisis theory. See also Table 4-1 for a summary of this model.

Assessment of the Precipitating Event

Crisis theory is based on the interaction of an individual and a stressful situation. Understanding and working with the "person in the situation" is the emphasis in crisis therapy and the starting point for crisis assessment. The precipitating event as the manifest origin of the client's crisis provides clues for latent determinants and ultimately helps to define the course of crisis intervention and resolution.

Understanding in detail the precipitating event that resulted in a failure to cope and an emotional crisis is a necessary part of crisis assessment. This

Table 4-1

A Model for the Assessment of Emotional Crises

Assessment of the Precipitating Event
   a. The time and place of the precipitating event.
   b. The interpersonal dimensions of the problem situation.
   c. The affective reaction to the precipitating event.
   d. The client's psychological request of the therapist.
Assessing the Psychodynamic Issues in the Crisis
   a. An event directly analogous to a past unresolved conflict or trauma.
   b. An event that activates anticipatory fear of experiencing a past trauma or conflict again.
Assessment of Present Coping Responses
   a. Examining client gains through use of maladaptive coping responses.
   b. Defining alternative, more adaptive coping responses.
   c. Risk analysis of adaptive coping responses.
Assessment of Client's Precrisis Functioning
   a. Client's usual repertoire of coping behaviors.
   b. Emotional style and communication skills.
   c. Existing social support system.
   d. Personal vulnerabilities.
   e. Self-report personality description.
Related Areas of Client Assessment
   a. Suicide assessment.
   b. Drugs currently used (prescription, street drugs, OTC).
   c. Recent medical history.
   d. Recent psychiatric history.
   e. Mental status.

---

*OTC = Over-the-counter drugs.

information helps to structure and focus the intervention process. However, Knoepfler (1967), discussing the search for precipitating events by trainees learning the technique of short-term therapy, finds that this aspect of assessment is easily neglected or is not thoroughly explored. It only becomes an area of emphasis after intensive training and supervision.

It also cannot be assumed that the client is aware of or understands the relationship of the precipitating event to the emotional crisis, and creating this understanding may be an important aspect of helping the client organize the crisis experience. Harris, Kalis, and Freeman (1963) emphasize that

> restoration of equilibrium is facilitated by understanding the precipitating stress—stress that is not conscious at the point of application. While the events evoking conflict are remembered by the patient, they may not be reported, at least immediately, and are often not specifically connected with the subjective distress. To establish such connections is the primary task of the therapeutic transaction. Asked why he comes now, the patient cites long-standing difficulties, vaguely refers to the build-up of tension, or offers other rationalized explanations. It seems that if he could really answer the question, he would be better able to cope with his distress and achieve a new psychic equilibrium. [P. 467]

Several aspects of the precipitating event warrant close scrutiny and exploration by the crisis therapist.

Defining the Time and Place of the Precipitating Event

Sometimes clients easily define the time and place of the event that precipitated the crisis. However, this is not always the case, and in many instances the client has not defined the event that evolved into the crisis nor its emotional meaning. Defining the event and placing it into the framework of the client's recent experience is essential in crisis assessment. Sometimes the event is quite subtle and is difficult to detect even by the skilled therapist. However, there is always a situational trigger for the crisis that when conceptualized is helpful to both client and therapist in understanding the crisis.

For clients with little or no psychological-mindedness or capacity for insight, defining the time and place of the precipitating event may be difficult. However, with such clients, examining emotional cause and effect relationships can be very helpful and often is part of the psychological education that becomes part of the crisis assessment process. At other times, the precipitating event will not be evident even with close scrutiny of the client's recent past. In such instances, the course of crisis intervention is initiated on the basis of available information, and it is not uncommon that the precipitating event becomes clearer during the course of crisis resolution.

Understanding the Interpersonal
Dimensions of the Problem
Situation

It is extremely important for the crisis therapist to assess not only the time and place of the precipitating event but also the interpersonal parameters of the situation as well. It is a corollary of crisis theory that all crises are interpersonal and involve significant others in a direct, indirect, or symbolic way (Baldwin 1979b). Sometimes significant others from the past are involved in the present crisis because conflicts or traumas associated with them are reactivated by a present situation. Or sometimes an examination of the interpersonal dimensions of the current problem may lead to definition of others not directly involved but certainly part of the present crisis and essential for its resolution.

Kalis et al. (1961) also believe that crises involve an interaction of present events and past or present conflicts. These authors have conceptualized five general types of events that produce failure to cope, and all have interpersonal components: (1) object loss or threat of object loss, or the lack of opportunity to restore lost objects, (2) a bind with previous sources of help, (3) a dormant conflict is reactivated when another individual experiences a problem analogous to that unresolved issue, (4) a surge of unmanageable impulses, and (5) a threat to current adjustment.

Strickler and LaSor (1970) define the interpersonal dimension of emotional crises in terms of an actual or potential loss to the client. They believe that all crises result from loss in one of three areas: (1) loss of self-esteem, (2) loss of sex-role mastery, or (3) loss of nurturing. Although they speculate that one type of loss is usually dominant in any given crisis, in some instances, elements of all three are present. It is defending against such losses, or attempting to replace them, that determines many maladaptive coping responses to problem situations and precipitates the crisis.

The Affective Reaction
to the Precipitating Event

Reacting to the precipitating event, the client experiences disruption of homeostatic balance. This disruption is characterized by a rise of unpleasant or dysphoric affect that intensifies with time because there are no effective coping responses available to reduce it. The longer this situation (i.e., the crisis) continues, the more intense this disruptive affect becomes and the more incapable the client becomes in retaining perspective of the situation, defining viable courses of action, and mobilizing problem-solving or coping skills. It is frequently very helpful early in the crisis assessment process to encourage the client to express such affect and thereby defuse (at least temporarily) some of the intensity of the crisis (Butcher and Maudel 1976).

However, the nature of the dysphoria being experienced by the client is also important in crisis assessment. It helps to determine whether any emergency measures must be taken to insure client welfare. The client may be experiencing guilt, anger, anxiety, or depression, or may have already decompensated. The nature of client stress is diagnostic, and often reflects a particular type of vulnerability that has been instrumental in producing the crisis. A description of the affective experience of the crisis, in the client's own words, is also helpful in detecting the underlying issues or the precipitant of the crisis (Hoffman and Remmel 1975). These descriptions often are related in slang or cultural-specific ways the therapist may find useful later.

Defining the Client's Psychological Request of the Therapist

In crisis intervention, the client seeks the help of the therapist with often implicit expectations for the helping process. The nature of the help that the client seeks (i.e., the psychological request) may be directly or indirectly communicated, and may be healthy or quite regressive in nature. Assessing this request, always present in a client contact, is of importance in understanding the crisis and the client's response to a particular stressful situation and in planning an appropriate intervention process.

Lazare et al. (1972) have also found that "diagnosing" the client's request in the helping contact is clinically important. They believe that if this request is not accurately understood and acknowledged early in the assessment process, there is a much higher dropout rate from therapy. The therapist, in acknowledging the client's request, must make a decision about whether to grant it. If the therapeutic decision is not to grant this request, this becomes an area of negotiation and part of the assessment transaction between therapist and client. These authors have developed a structure for assessing client requests that is presented below in modified form.

a. *Request for Support.* Clients frequently request support from the therapist, but support may take a number of forms: control (please take over), reality contact (help me know I am real), succorance (take care of me), personal contact (always be there), confession (take away my guilt), and ventilation (let me get it off my chest).

b. *Request for Therapy.* In those clients who are directly or indirectly requesting therapy, two different types of requests are encountered: clarification (help me put things in perspective) and intrapsychic (help me deal with my past).

c. *Request for an Authority Figure.* Several types of requests are indicated when clients seek an authority figure: medical (I need a physician), administrative (I need your legal power), social (do it for me), advice (tell me what to do), and education (teach me what I need to know).

d. *Other Requests.* Sometimes clients make requests outside of these major areas, two of which are not uncommon: community triage (tell me where I can get what I need) and nothing (I want nothing).

These authors (Lazare et al. 1972) have noticed that there is often a hierarchy of client requests. If the initial request of the client is defined and responded to effectively, there is a shift that is progressive (i.e., from sicker to healthier for that client). On the other hand, failure to respond to the client's request may lead to subtle negotiations over regressive requests that move from healthier to sicker for that client. How the therapist handles the initial client request, even when presented quite indirectly, is often influential in determining the outcome of crisis intervention.

Assessing the Psychodynamic Issues
in the Crisis

Many emotional crises are determined, at least in part, by unresolved conflicts or traumas from the past that are reactivated or brought again to awareness by a particular event. The psychodynamic component of the crisis, the precipitant (Hoffman and Remmel 1975), is frequently instrumental in producing a failure to cope and impedes adaptive crisis resolution unless addressed as part of the crisis intervention process.

Although not all crises have psychodynamic determinants, most do involve antecedent factors reactivated by the precipitating event. When this is the case, the client experiences an emotional overreaction that is often surprising in its intensity. The precipitating event has activated a dormant vulnerability of the client, and the intensity of the affect produced is often overwhelming and confusing. When this occurs, usual coping behaviors become inoperable, and the client may use coping responses that are more oriented toward ego-protection than toward mastery of the situation (Silverman 1977).

It is the task of the crisis therapist, when a precipitant is detected, to help the client to respond adaptively to the present situation while using the situation to simultaneously address and work through the reactivated conflicts and traumas from the past. Harris, Kalis, and Freeman (1973) believe that identification of the precipitating event is only the first step. Their emphasis is on ". . . the working through and resolution of the conflict derivatives involved in the stressful disruption. [Their] hypothesis is that such exploration and working through facilitate the establishment of a new adaptive balance" (p. 466). When this is accomplished as part of the crisis intervention process, the client is less vulnerable, and future similar situations will not result in an emotional crisis.

Perhaps the most significant preventive function of crisis intervention lies in working through the precipitant of the crisis while helping the client to respond more adaptively to a present stressor. It is working with the precipitant of the crisis within the context of a present-oriented problem-solving approach that distinguishes the professional clinician from the paraprofessional, and the experienced crisis therapist from the novice. By missing the underlying determinants of the crisis, an opportunity is lost to help the client to remove a personal vulnerability that may be reactivated again in the future.

Hoffman and Remmel (1975) have defined these underlying but reactivated determinants of a crisis in the following way:

> The precipitant is the thought or feeling aroused by the precipitating event. Although related to the precipitating event, it is distinct from it and more highly repressed. It is the pain connected with the earlier unresolved conflict, and it is precisely this experience which compels the client to pick up the telephone to call for help. [P. 260]

Detecting and working through the precipitant is perhaps the most challenging aspect of crisis intervention. It requires all the skills of the well-trained psychotherapist. The precipitant may be activated in two basic ways: (1) by an experience that is somehow *directly analogous* to a past conflict or trauma, or (2) by an event that activates *anticipatory fear* of experiencing a past trauma again. When the latter is the case, coping responses are mobilized to avoid anticipated pain and to provide protection of the self.

There are a number of ways that the crisis therapist can explore the crisis situation for clues to the precipitant. Some of these strategies are the following:

1. Defining similarities between current client affect and affect recalled from past painful experiences.
2. Exploring situational similarities between the present experience and past experiences that remain painful and unresolved.
3. Detecting specific types of interactions that remind the client of past pain.
4. Determining the time of onset of the crisis and exploring for a precipitant in the form of an anniversary reaction.
5. Defining the worst possible outcome of the present situation and relating it to painful experiences from the past.

6. Scrutinizing the client's present coping maneuvers for possible secondary gains and linking these to past unresolved issues.

7. Reviewing the client's past for models for maladaptive coping behaviors and for identification with that model.

8. Examining the present problem within the context of the client's fear of being similar to a significant other with whom there is an ambivalent relationship.

9. Exploring with the client any dreams or nightmares that occurred in close proximity to the precipitating event for significant links of past to present.

10. Inquiring of the client whether there have been recent memories, feelings, or thoughts that have emerged unexplained into consciousness.

Understanding the precipitant is important in crisis assessment, and therapist inquiry in this area is essential. However, developing insight is not the therapy, and in some instances the precipitant, although operational in determining and preventing resolution of the crisis, may not be detected during crisis assessment. However, as Appelbaum (1975) has pointed out, often modification of behavior (in crisis intervention, modification of coping responses) results in the ability to define and conceptualize the antecedents of the crisis quite clearly! In sum, when the precipitant cannot be defined in the crisis assessment process, using the basic strategy of crisis intervention by helping to modify responses to a present stressor often reveals the precipitant.

Assessment of Present Coping Responses

When an emotionally hazardous situation has evolved into an emotional crisis, there has been a failure to cope. Assessing the coping behaviors the client is using in response to a present stressor leads to more complete understanding of the crisis. It also helps to differentiate adaptive from maladaptive coping responses for the client and to differentially reinforce them. Assessing the client's present coping strategies also provides an opportunity to psychologically educate the client about emotional maturity and the differences between adaptive and maladaptive coping responses (Baldwin 1979c).

Coping mechanisms encompass an incredibly wide range of human behavior. They can be simple or complex, direct or indirect, cognitively based or affectively oriented, manipulative or nonmanipulative, active or passive, intrapsychic or interpersonal, verbal or nonverbal. Coping responses occur at the fully conscious, the preconscious, and the unconscious levels of awareness (Perlman 1975). At the unconscious level, coping behaviors are synonymous with the ego-defense mechanisms. Unfortunately, graduate training programs emphasize ego defenses and working with them within the context of long-term psychotherapy in lieu of emphasis on the conscious and preconscious coping behaviors that are more the province of the crisis therapist.

It is a basic task of the crisis therapist to assess the client's coping responses at all levels. However, the thrust of crisis therapy centers on definition and modification of coping responses at the preconscious or fully conscious levels. In some respects, a major goal of effective crisis intervention is to bring coping behaviors operating at the preconscious level (i.e., just beyond awareness) to the conscious level and then to modify them. This involves defining and conceptualizing the implications of these responses in a collaborative process with the client. Frequently, discussion of the differences between adaptive and maladaptive coping responses becomes part of this aspect of crisis assessment. The crisis therapist reinforces and encourages adaptive client coping responses but discourages use of those responses that are maladaptive or otherwise inappropriate.

Once the client's present coping behaviors in response to the stressor have been conceptualized, a functional analysis of any maladaptive coping responses being used is initiated as part of crisis assessment. This process is very helpful in more fully understanding the crisis and the sources of client resistance to modifying maladaptive coping responses, and ultimately in defining the precipitant of the crisis. This functional analysis is also an important aspect of client education and is often part of crisis assessment. There are several steps in this analysis.

Examining Client Gains through
Use of Maladaptive Coping Responses

The functional analysis of coping responses begins with an examination of what the client psychologically obtains and avoids through use of these responses. The client, through use of maladaptive responses, usually avoids personal responsibility and gains a modicum of (at least temporary) security or safety. However, these gains are not directed toward healthy resolution of the problem situation. Typically, there are other payoffs from the use of maladaptive coping behaviors. For example, clients may obtain revenge, nurturance, attention, control, or temporary stress reduction through use of maladaptive coping. In addition, clients may avoid confrontation, anger, loss, or feelings of failure through use of these same behaviors. It is frequently helpful, once maladaptive coping responses have been defined, to specifically discuss with the client the psychological gains that use of these mechanisms bring.

Defining Alternative, More
Adaptive Coping Responses

The second step in the functional analysis is defining with the client more adaptive coping responses to the crisis situation. Clients often have at least some idea of "what needs to be done" to resolve the crisis situation, but they may need help from the therapist to conceptualize these responses clearly and to develop a sound rationale for their use (i.e., to define why more adaptive responses are more helpful than maladaptive ones). Sometimes, with clients who have little or no psychological-mindedness, the therapist must take the initiative to define more adaptive responses to a problem situation. Conceptualizing and developing a rationale for more adaptive coping behaviors is an important part of helping the client learn more about emotional maturity in general and about more adaptive ways to respond in a given problem situation in particular.

Risk Analysis of Adaptive
Coping Responses

Once adaptive responses have been defined, the central question becomes: "Why is this client not using these responses?" For some the answer is simple: "They have not thought of them, or they had no rationale for such responses." For many others, however, the use of adaptive coping responses involves psychological risk. It is the inability to directly accept these risks that determines the maladaptive responses on one hand, and that produces resistance to their modification on the other. Examining the risks, and by implication the fears of the client, frequently leads to definition of the precipitant of the crisis.

There are two types of risks that clients fear in "giving up" maladaptive responses: internal (or intrapsychic) risks and external (or interpersonal) risks. Either or both types of risks may be operational in any given crisis. The crisis situation, and the client's responses to that situation, must be explored in terms of both types of risks. Often, these risks may be similar to what is being avoided through the use of maladaptive coping responses, but the risks may also involve differences. By defining the risks, the therapist and client gain a deeper understanding of the subjective meaning of the crisis to the client and the basis for client resistance to change, when present. Understanding these aspects of the use of maladaptive responses is essential in planning effective interventions that encompass present problem solving blended with therapeutic response to client resistance and to the dynamics of the precipitant of the crisis.

Assessment of Client's
Precrisis Functioning

It is necessary in crisis assessment to understand the client's psychological functioning in the period just before the crisis occurred. Such assessment provides a base line against which to evaluate the impact of the crisis on the client. In addition, this base line becomes the criterion against which successful crisis resolution (i.e., restoration of the client's precrisis level of functioning) is determined.

The level of adjustment of the client before the crisis is important in evaluating the crisis itself. By determining the normal or usual functioning of the client, valuable clues about relevant issues and about the psychodynamic determinants of the crisis are often obtained. Although a complete or formal history is not part of crisis assessment, the client's psychological functioning on a variety of interpersonal dimensions in the precrisis period (i.e., in the six months prior to the crisis) is important. This six-month period becomes the framework against which the crisis is evaluated.

In some ways, the particular dimensions on which the client's precrisis functioning is assessed vary with the clinical population and the individual client. However, several themes are important in this assessment, and each is related to understanding more completely the "why" of the crisis.

The Client's Usual Repertoire
of Coping Behaviors

The range and quality of the client's usual coping responses are important parts of assessing the client's precrisis functioning. Some clients have only a single coping behavior in response to stress (e.g., to attack or to withdraw). Others have developed a range of coping responses that are selectively used in different situations. In addition to the range of coping behaviors the client typically has available, the therapist must also gain a sense of the maturity of these responses. In some clients, there are many coping behaviors available, but these may be neurotic, regressive, or otherwise maladaptive. It cannot be assumed that because the client uses a variety of coping behaviors that these are healthy.

In this assessment, it is often productive to inquire of the client how particular situations are dealt with. For example, the clinician may directly ask what the client's responses are to anger, to disappointment, to loss, or to failure. The client's responses help to elaborate the range and adaptiveness of coping behaviors usually used, but in addition they also provide insight into the client's awareness of or conscious use of these coping mechanisms. Are these mechanisms primarily operating at the preconscious level of awareness, or is the client selectively using them in response to the requirements of particular situations? This knowledge helps the therapist become more aware of the impact of the crisis on the client's usual mode of functioning, and it also helps the therapist to begin formulating a tentative intervention strategy.

The Client's Emotional Style and Communication Skills

The client's general level of emotional awareness is important to understand when assessing an emotional crisis. Some clients are aware of and experience easily a full range of emotions and their emotional life is very rich. Yet, for others, there may be limited awareness of emotions in general, or selective blocking from awareness of specific emotions. For example, for some clients in crisis, it is not uncommon to find there is a lack of emotional awareness of anger, even when warranted. Instead there is only the experience of depression. Therefore, assessing the client's general emotional awareness and specific emotional blocks is often of value in understanding an emotional crisis.

On the other hand, it is also important to assess how the client deals with emotion interpersonally. This is the client's emotional style, and it may vary considerably from client to client. For example, some clients may be extremely expressive emotionally, to the point of being volatile and losing emotional control under certain circumstances. At the other extreme are those who characteristically "bottle up" their emotions and do not express them except in very limited ways, if at all. Others may use a very intellectual style of response to emotions. Understanding this usual emotional style of the client helps to put the crisis situation in perspective. This assessment also provides the crisis therapist with clues regarding the ability of the client to relate emotional responses to particular events (i.e., the client's psychological-mindedness).

The Client's Existing Social Support System

The client's "connections" to others and the nature of these relationships are important aspects of the client's precrisis functioning. The most basic dimension of the client's social support system is the number of relationships that the client has formed. In addition, the depth of these relationships is also useful information to obtain. Some clients may have many acquaintances but no real friends to count on. Others may be very gregarious and have formed many and deep relationships. Assessing these relationships helps the therapist to determine on whom the client can count for support during the crisis intervention and resolution process.

It is also helpful to explore the client's social skills and level of social initiative. Can this client form new relationships and take the first step in socially relating to others? Or is this a client who is withdrawn and who relies on others for social involvement (i.e., to provide invitations, social activities, etc.)? Another related factor is the time the client spends alone, and whether that time alone is by choice or by default. Some clients need alone time, and they create time for this each day. Others, particularly those with poor social skills, spend time alone because they have no one to relate to. As a result, they become quite lonely and depressed because of their social isolation. The client's social support system is often directly or indirectly related to the crisis situation and can either help or hinder adaptive crisis resolution.

The Client's Personal Vulnerabilities

Everyone has emotional vulnerabilities. In certain situations, a client may exhibit emotional overreaction and the inability to respond maturely and appropriately. For most individuals, such situations occur infrequently or are of minor importance. However, for some individuals there are areas of vulnerability that have a significant influence on their adjustment and on their ability to cope with the vicissitudes of life effectively. To understand the nature of the client's vulnerabilities is frequently of great help in understanding the issues involved in an emotional crisis.

Although it is "normal" to have some areas of vulnerability, it is usually in these same areas that effective coping behaviors have not been fully developed. As a result, individuals are prone to experience crises related to an area of weak or absent coping responses. Asking the client to define those situations that cause difficulty coping or where emotional overreactions are likely to occur is helpful in assessing precrisis functioning. These situations often involve issues that are also inherent in the event that precipitated the emotional crisis and that may be related to the psychodynamic determinants of the crisis as well (i.e., the precipitant).

The Client's Self-Report
Personality Description

A last area of precrisis functioning to be assessed is the client's self-image. This self-report may be defensive or disparaging, or it may reflect a balanced awareness of personal strengths and weaknesses. For a variety of reasons, individuals are more aware of their negative qualities and weaknesses than of their assets and strengths. The adjectives used in self-descriptions by clients are often quite helpful in gaining an understanding of the clients' ego-strengths, as well as a perception of their personal deficits that may be involved in the crisis.

There are several ways that a self-description can be obtained from the client. For example, the client may simply be asked to describe himself or herself using a very open-ended question. Or the client may be asked to provide a self-description through the eyes of significant others (e.g., a friend, spouse, parent, etc.). Sometimes it is appropriate to ask about very specific aspects that the therapist feels may be contributing to the crisis (e.g., body image, masculine/feminine identity, parental role, etc.). This description should be directed toward the client's self-image before the crisis. This provides another dimension of contrast to the client's self-concept during the crisis. Not infrequently, from such a description the therapist can help define personal strengths of the client that can be mobilized to aid in crisis resolution.

Related Areas of Client Assessment

To gain additional information about the etiology of an emotional crisis and to insure adequate client care, several areas of inquiry are part of *every* crisis assessment. Although not directly derived from crisis theory, these aspects of crisis assessment are part of the therapist's responsibility to understand and to use in making therapeutic decisions.

Among the most important of the related areas of client assessment that must be addressed during the crisis assessment process are the following.

Suicide Assessment

Every client in crisis is experiencing emotional turmoil and painful disequilibrium. The crisis therapist must inquire (of *every* crisis client) about suicidal ideation, plans, and history of previous attempts/gestures. Clients usually do not volunteer this information, but they readily respond to questions when directly asked. When suicidal ideation or plans are detected, other factors related to increased suicidal risk (Hodge 1975; Slaby, Lieb, and Tarcredi 1975) must also be assessed. When significant risk is determined, appropriate action is taken as part of the crisis intervention process. The therapist assumes responsibility for decision making when the client cannot. Interventions may include a no-suicide contract (Drye, Goulding, and Goulding 1973), admission to an inpatient unit, or mobilization of support from other persons or from appropriate community resources.

Drugs Currently Used

The client's pattern of drug use and the nature of the drugs being used are important in crisis assessment. This information provides clues regarding the client's coping responses to stress, life style, and general level of functioning. Prescribed medications, street drugs, and over-the-counter medications must all be reviewed. It is not infrequent that symptoms experienced by clients in crisis are produced or aggravated by drugs the client is currently using. When the drugs being used by the client are unknown, particularly prescription drugs, it is often helpful to review information about possible side effects in the *Physician's Desk Reference*. Other references are available for street drugs and over-the-counter medications.

Recent Medical History

The client's medical history for at least the six months preceding the emotional crisis should also be an area addressed during crisis assessment. Recent illnesses or traumas may have weakened the client's ability to cope. In addition, it is not uncommon for illnesses or hospitalization to reactivate significant issues that produce or contribute to an emotional crisis. Sometimes, symptoms from a previous trauma resurface unexpectedly to produce a crisis. This is frequently seen in rape victims or in those involved in natural disasters where symptoms dissipate but reappear later.

Recent Psychiatric History

In crisis assessment, it is often productive to inquire about recent contacts with mental health facilities or professionals, as well as with alternate services. The nature of the problems that prompted contact with those services is important, and discussing these contacts also provides clues about the client's past use of therapy, general attitudes toward mental health professionals, and issues that may be involved in the present crisis situation. At times, clients will contact crisis therapists because of a crisis in their on-going therapy (Skodol, Kass, and Charles 1979), and these crises can be discussed within the context of the continuing therapeutic process.

Mental Status

The mental status of any crisis client should be assessed either informally or formally as needed. Often, clients presenting in crisis clinics or emergency services are in acute distress, and a mental status examination is necessary to assess level of functioning and to make appropriate decisions for treatment. Although not all clients require a formal mental status examination, the crisis therapist must be skilled in its use and must be able to apply it more informally in less acute crises within the general context of crisis assessment.

CONCLUDING REMARKS

Because of the time-limited nature of most emotional crises, a rapid and accurate assessment is required to create a foundation for the crisis intervention process. This assessment necessitates an active therapeutic posture and engagement of the client in a collaborative problem-solving endeavor. Because of these requirements, effective use of the crisis intervention model requires a crisis assessment paradigm derived from the tenets of crisis theory. This prevents much of the disparity that occurs when clinicians attempt to use the crisis approach but begin "assessing" the crisis situation using the techniques and procedures characteristic of more traditional diagnostic evaluations.

Yet, the skills of the well-trained clinician are necessary for the conduct of crisis therapy, and by extension for the assessment of emotional crises. Crisis intervention and crisis assessment emphasize the present, but the client's past experiences are not neglected. However, past experiences are pursued only selectively and only with the justification that they are related to and help to determine the present crisis. The ability of the clinician to screen information rapidly, and to separate the relevant from the tangential, is a function of both clinical training and experience in psychotherapy. In crisis assessment, the clinician must "know where to look" for the dynamics and issues of the crisis and must know how to conceptualize those issues quickly. This is one reason why crisis therapy requires previous experience and advanced levels of training. Novice therapists find crisis therapy anxiety-provoking and frustrating, and this is no less true of the requirements for rapid and accurate crisis assessment.

Crisis assessment (and by extension the crisis model) is often made difficult or impossible because of the structure of many mental health service delivery systems. Frequently, there is an intake process that is separated from therapy, and it is often done by different clinicians. Clients may be placed on waiting lists, or a great deal of time is spent obtaining voluminous historical data before treatment can be started. These methods reflect administrative mandates for records but are antithetical to crisis assessment and the use of the crisis model. It is not uncommon for such clients to feel that their immediate problem is neglected and that they are bogged down in "red tape" dealing with the clinic bureaucracy.

However, this clash between the administrative structures of many clinical facilities and the requirements of the crisis model is not unresolvable. Clinics that are adopting the crisis model as a primary treatment modality find that adapting their service delivery structure to this approach is not difficult. This approach also helps clinics to optimize the opportunity provided by client crises to learn, to make adaptive changes in response to stress, and (ultimately) to prevent future crises. Emotional crises dealt with early and effectively reduce the need for longer-term therapy and also reduce the need for later clinic visits. There is more and more recognition of this fact in mental health facilities, and this is one reason why the use of the crisis model is not only increasingly accepted but is emerging as a major treatment of choice in this decade.

For the clinician, the use of a crisis assessment model derived directly from the principles of crisis theory makes the practice of crisis intervention easier. In the past, lack of an assessment paradigm has been a major deficit in the framework for the practice of crisis therapy. Many of the gaps in crisis theory are now being closed as the concepts on which this approach is based are modified and expanded. It remains to be seen whether crisis intervention will become an important part of the "third revolution" in mental health (Ewing 1978), after the advent of psychoanalysis and the discovery of psychotropic drugs. However, it is fair to say that crisis intervention has earned an important place as an innovative model for providing needed services in the community. It will continue to be influential not only in the practice of psychotherapy but also in determining the structure of mental health service delivery systems.

REFERENCES

APPELBAUM, S. A., "Parkinson's Law in Psychotherapy," *International Journal of Psychoanalytic Psychotherapy*, 4 (1975), 426–36.

BALDWIN, B. A., "Crisis Intervention in Professional Practice: Implications for Clinical Training," *American Journal of Orthopsychiatry*, 47 (1977) 659–70.

_____, "Training in Crisis Intervention for Students in the Mental Health Professions," *Professional Psychology*, 10, 1979a, 161–67.

_____, "Crisis Intervention: An Overview of Theory and Practice," *The Counseling Psychologist*, 8 (1979b), 43–52.

_____, "Crisis Intervention, Parkinson's Law and Structure in Psychotherapy." Paper presented at the XVII Interamerican Congress of Psychology, Lima, Peru, July 1979c.

BUTCHER, J. N. and G. R. MAUDEL, "Crisis Intervention," I. Weiner, ed., in *Clinical Methods in Psychology,* New York: John Wiley & Sons, Inc., 1976.

CAPLAN, G., *Principles of Preventive Psychiatry.* New York: Basic Books, Inc., Publishers, 1964.

DRYE, R. C., R. L. GOULDING, and M. E. GOULDING, "No-Suicide Decisions: Patient Monitoring of Suicidal Risk," *American Journal of Psychiatry,* 130 (1973), 171–74.

EWING, C., *Crisis Intervention as Psychotherapy.* New York: Oxford University Press, 1978.

HARRIS, M. R., B. L. KALIS, and E. H. FREEMAN, "Precipitating Stress: An Approach to Brief Therapy," *American Journal of Psychotherapy,* 17 (1963), 465–71.

HODGE, J. R., "How to Recognize a Suicidal Patient," *Medical Times,* 103 (1975), 119–20.

HOFFMAN, K. L., and M. L. REMMEL, "Uncovering the Precipitant in Crisis Intervention," *Social Casework,* 56 (1975), 259–67.

KALIS, B. L., R. M. HARRIS, A. R. PRESTWOOD, and E. H. FREEMAN, "Precipitating Stress as a Focus in Psychotherapy," *Archives of General Psychiatry,* 5 (1961), 219–28.

KNOEPFLER, P. T., "The Search for Precipitating Events by Trainees in the Mental Health Field," *Journal of the American College Health Association,* 15 (1967), 357–60.

LAZARE, A., F. COHEN, A. M. JACOBSON, M. W. WILLIAMS, R. J. MIGNONE, and S. ZISOOK, "The Walk-In Patient as a 'Customer': A Key Dimension in Evaluation and Treatment," *American Journal of Orthopsychiatry,* 42 (1972), 872–83.

LEMON, E., and S. GOLDSTEIN, "The Use of Time Limits in Planned Brief Casework," *Social Casework,* 59 (1978), 588–96.

MORLEY, W. E., J. M. MESSICK, and D. C. AGUILERA, "Crises: Paradigms of Intervention," *Journal of Psychiatric Nursing,* 5 (1967) 531–44.

NELSON, Z., and D. MOWRY, "Contracting in Crisis Intervention," *Community Mental Health Journal,* 12 (1976), 37–44.

PAUL, L., "Crisis Intervention," *Mental Hygiene,* 50 (1966), 141–45.

PERLMAN, H. H., "In Quest of Coping," *Social Casework,* 56 (1975), 213–25.

RAPOPORT, L., "The State of Crisis: Some Theoretical Considerations," *The Social Service Review,* 36 (1962), 211–17.

SILVERMAN, W., "Planning for Crisis Intervention with Community Mental Health Concepts," *Psychotherapy: Theory, Research and Practice,* 14 (1977), 293–97.

SKODOL, A. E., F. KASS, and E. CHARLES, "Crisis in Psychotherapy: Principles of Emergency Consultation and Intervention." *American Journal of Orthopsychiatry,* 49 (1979), 585–597.

SLABY, A. E., J. LIEB, and L. R. TARCREDI, *Handbook of Psychiatric Emergencies.* New York: Medical Exam Publishing Company, 1975.

STRICKLER, M., and B. LASOR, "The Concept of Loss in Crisis Intervention," *Mental Hygiene,* 54 (1970), 301–5.

STUART, M. R., and K. J. MACKEY, "Defining the Differences between Crisis Intervention and Short-Term Therapy," *Hospital and Community Psychiatry,* 28 (1977), 527–29.

WALLACE, M. A., and W. E. MORLEY, "Teaching Crisis Intervention," *American Journal of Nursing,* 70 (1970), 1484–87.

5

THERAPIST ADAPTATION
TO THE STRUCTURE
OF THE CRISIS MODEL

Crisis intervention is defined by a system of constructs that creates boundaries and focus for a problem-oriented therapeutic intervention. It is essentially a structural framework within which the work of therapeutic change is conducted. Throughout its rather short history, crisis intervention has been consistently associated with innovation in therapeutic approach and service delivery. It has been adapted to a range of clinical services, client needs, and therapeutic orientations. At the present time, with an increasing need for brief therapy models, this trend is not only continuing but accelerating. The constructs of crisis theory are the base around which therapists must adapt clinical services to insure effective crisis intervention.

However, a major neglected area in the literature on crisis theory and practice is the process of adapting various clinical services and therapeutic orientations to this model. This adaptation process is an integral part of the ultimate effectiveness of a crisis-oriented clinical service. Crisis intervention is not a system of psychotherapy by itself (Baldwin 1977). Rather, it provides the framework within which clinical services are organized and provided. Because of this characteristic, crisis intervention as a therapeutic model is very flexible and can easily be adapted to different problems or clinical settings. Kardener (1975), discussing therapist adoption of the crisis model, had this point in mind when he stated:

> The range of techniques in achieving the initial goal (of crisis intervention) encompasses all of the known and usual modalities from environmental

manipulation, family, drug, behavior conditioning, or hypnotherapies to psychodynamically oriented psychotherapy, to name but a few. Regardless of the modality utilized, all therapeutic intervention techniques are designed to facilitate meaningful change. [P. 8]

Frequently, it is the therapist's recognition of the need for and the capacity to adapt to the structural limitations of the crisis model that determines how well client needs are met and, in the end, client satisfaction. The clinician working within or designing a crisis-oriented service must succeed in this adaptation process by integrating the crisis approach and the clinical services to be rendered. Failure in this endeavor may seriously compromise the effectiveness of the service and, ultimately, reduce community acceptance of such services.

There are several aspects of this adaptation process that the clinician must be sensitive to and must work toward integrating with the tenets of the crisis model. Any or all of these facets of adaptation may have to be addressed in any given crisis service depending on its structure and thrust. The three primary components of adaptation are: (1) adapting the clinician's preferred therapeutic orientation to this model, (2) adapting a particular therapeutic modality to the crisis approach, and (3) adapting the crisis model to the needs of a particular clinical population or a specific type of client problem.

It is the purpose here to highlight these types of adaptation to the crisis model to help clinicians effect such modifications as necessary in their personal approach to therapy or in the organization of a clinical service to make it maximally effective within the constraints of the crisis model. Provided are descriptions of each of the three basic types of adaptation in clinical services that have been successful. These services reflect the experience and expertise of the clinicians in blending the parameters of the crisis model with their particular style of helping. Optimally, these descriptions will provide clinicians with the understanding needed to prevent basic mistakes, mistakes that frequently create problems in crisis services that can often be traced to ineffective adaptation to the crisis model.

ADAPTING TO A PARTICULAR
THERAPEUTIC ORIENTATION

Because crisis theory primarily defines a conceptual framework within which the clinician's preferred orientation to therapy is used, it should come as no surprise that there are effective crisis therapists of many theoretical persuasions now using this approach. However, for effectiveness the crisis therapist must be well trained and experienced as a clinician prior to adopting the crisis model. Sound clinical training is the substratum on which modification of a personal orientation to therapy is based. The crisis therapist must have a repertoire of clinical skills, an understanding of the process of therapy, and a sense of self as a therapist before the adaptation to the framework for crisis therapy can be effected.

Contrary to initial impressions, the practice of crisis intervention is challenging and difficult. It requires all the skills of a well-trained therapist plus the skills necessary to use the crisis model. Experience in training crisis therapists has demonstrated that this form of therapy is most easily learned at an advanced stage of professional training and after there has been closely supervised experience in longer-term psychotherapy (Baldwin 1979). Premature exposure to this rather intense and fast-paced form of therapy is anxiety-provoking and often creates barriers to professional growth instead of facilitating it.

One of the corollaries of crisis theory is that the intense stress of an emotional crisis facilitates a disproportionate measure of growth and learning in a short period of time if effective help is available to the client. For the clinician learning crisis therapy the same holds true: The intensity of crisis therapy can facilitate a disproportionate measure of growth and maturation as a mental health professional if there is readiness for this experience and help in using it for such growth. Poor timing for training in this approach and ineffective or lack of proper training and supervision in the adaptation of a personal therapeutic style to the structure of this model can account for many of the failures of crisis therapists.

Whether during graduate training or during in-service training while in practice, the clinician seeking to use the crisis model must confront a number of issues. Kapp and Weiss (1975), discussing training for crisis therapists, found that

> the specific skills that our trainees seem to acquire . . . include diagnostic skills, the ability to establish rapport quickly, the ability to conceptualize and implement a plan of action, and familiarity with a wide array of techniques. [P. 344]

Knowledge of these skills and the ability to apply them creatively in a relatively brief therapeutic relationship with clients require that the crisis therapist be well trained at both the theoretical and applied levels of crisis intervention.

Relating a particular therapeutic orientation and the skills that are part of that orientation to the crisis model is necessary for the effective practice of this approach. The psychoanalytically oriented crisis therapist does not practice a pure form of psychoanalytic psychotherapy when engaged in crisis intervention; rather, it is a modified form of psychoanalytic therapy. The same is true of any of the various orientations to psychotherapy. The following article illustrates how a hypnotic orientation to therapy has been integrated with the crisis model to provide an effective intervention style. The process of adapting any therapeutic orientation to the crisis model is more or less the same and requires therapist skill in *both* a preferred therapeutic orientation and in the theory and practice of crisis intervention.

Crisis Intervention and Enhancement of Adaptive Coping Using Hypnosis[1]

Mental health professionals schooled in different therapeutic orientations have successfully adapted their personal therapeutic styles to the crisis intervention framework. Hypnosis is useful in and compatible with crisis intervention as it: (a) helps clients to attain a relaxed milieu for therapy that counters many of the negative effects of the crisis state, (b) potentiates the effects of many therapeutic techniques associated with various therapeutic orientations, and (c) provides additional techniques unique to hypnosis that are useful in facilitating adaptive crisis resolution.

Because the emotional disequilibrium of the crisis state impairs adaptive coping, effective intervention is more difficult unless the dysphoric affect is brought under control. Relaxation training as an active coping skill (Goldfried and Trier 1974) is particularly suited to the crisis model. Hypnosis provides a structure within which the client learns a powerful form of relaxation that may be critical to the intervention process and eventual crisis resolution. Such training is also instrumental in helping to reestablish a client's sense of control that enhances taking positive steps toward crisis resolution.

Further, characteristics inherent to the hypnotic state often potentiate the effectiveness of techniques associated with a range of therapeutic orientations. Several qualities of the hypnotic state (Hilgard 1965) that enhance the effects of nonhypnotic techniques used during crisis intervention are as follows.

Redistribution of Attention

During hypnosis, the client is able to focus attention and concentrate more fully. This quality of hypnosis counters distortion of the stressful situation that often exacerbates emotional crises. Focusing aids the problem-solving emphasis in crisis intervention and helps the client to more objectively approach a specific problem.

[1]This section, through page 100, by Bruce A Baldwin. Originally published in the *American Journal of Clinical Hypnosis,* 21(1978), 38–44, under the same title. Reprinted by permission of the *American Journal of Clinical Hypnosis.* Copyright 1978.

Increased Availability
of Memories from the Past

Crisis intervention entails determining the precipitant of the crisis with origins in the past. During hypnosis, the availability of memories helps in formulating the precipitant and in bringing critical insights that relate past to present. These dynamic aspects of a present crisis also help in understanding how maladaptive responses to particular stresses originated.

Heightened Ability for Fantasy
Production and Role-Behavior

Many therapeutic techniques, especially those that are behaviorally oriented, require the client to role-play or to experience novel situations in fantasy. These techniques are based on the client experiencing self in different ways with modified reinforcement contingencies. Hypnosis may enhance the vividness of fantasy productions and the depth of client involvement in fantasy experience. Positive outcomes experienced in fantasy productions often enhance skills necessary for crisis resolution and build the confidence needed to confront a stressful situation adaptively.

Increased Suggestibility

During hypnosis, the client becomes more susceptible to suggestions that may facilitate adaptive crisis resolution. General suggestions such as those used in hypnotic ego-strengthening (Hartland 1971) are useful in helping the client to establish a sense of control by mobilizing internal resources and decreasing dysphoric affect. More specific suggestions such as those given to help the client relax on a given cue are also very helpful during the course of crisis intervention.

Creativity Is Enhanced

Within a hypnotic state, the boundaries that define thought patterns during consciousness (i.e., those of convergent thinking) that are constricted or distorted by the crisis state are relaxed. The client becomes better able to perceive the crisis "problem" from a more constructive perspective and can creatively define and evaluate alternative modes of action to resolve the stress.

Frequently, these characteristics of the hypnotic state are useful in potentiating the effects of techniques associated with different therapeutic orientations used during crisis therapy. For example, the Gestalt "double chair" technique[2] may be enhanced by increased client capacity for role playing during hypnosis. Similarly, developing insight, a psychoanalytic technique, may be facilitated by the increased availability of memories when hypnosis is used. Behavioral techniques (i.e., systematic desensitization) may be more effective when hypnosis is part of crisis therapy because of greater client capacity for fantasy production. In addition, other techniques developed specifically for use with hypnosis are not only helpful in crisis intervention, but greatly increase the repertoire of available intervention techniques when the crisis therapist is hypnosis-skilled.

Case Examples

In the three case vignettes presented [below], goals developed with the client for crisis intervention included a combination of the following (Baldwin 1976): (a) *decisions* that the client needed help in making, (b) *feelings* that the client needed help in becoming more aware of or resolving, (c) *insights/dynamic relationships* the client needed help in becoming more aware of or understanding, and (d) *tasks* that the client needed help in carrying out effectively. During crisis therapy, each hour included discussion of the crisis situation and any psychodynamic issues involved, and use of hypnotic interventions to catalyze the crisis resolution process.

Case #1

Precipitating Event: A student pianist panicked before an important recital and the panic prevented him from performing. He became excessively fearful of a recurrence and developed severe anticipatory anxiety that further impaired his performing ability.

Precipitant: This student was older than his peers and felt unrealistic demands to excel that had been strongly reinforced in the past by his parents. Professors, because of his age and ability, further reinforced these expectations and produced a growing fear of "failure" and of disappointing others that culminated in a panic reaction before a recital.

Crisis Intervention: After crisis assessment, he was taught hypnotic relaxation. Hypnotic ego-strengthening suggestions (Hartland 1971) were used to help him feel more in control, relaxed and better able to counter anticipatory anxiety about performing in a weekly practice group. Auto-hypnosis was

---

[2]"Double chair" refers to a flexible Gestalt technique in which the client responds to a significant other person (not present) or a part of the self imagined to be in an empty chair. This technique is used to enhance self-awareness and to resolve interpersonal or intrapsychic conflict.

learned to help create a relaxed and positive state (using relaxation imagery) prior to each performance. Each day he hypnotically relaxed and gave himself ego-strengthening suggestions to reinforce confidence about his musical abilities.

Discussion in therapy focused on the precipitant of the crisis and the origins of his fears of not meeting his and others' expectations. As these conflicts were identified in the present crisis situation, hypnotic intervention that stressed positive behavior rehearsal was initiated using imagery obtained from the client. Auto-hypnotic relaxation continued on a daily basis during this process.

As the client began to experience more success in his playing, use of paradoxical imagery (Frankl 1975) was introduced into the therapy. This imagery, enhanced through hypnosis, helped him work through his fear of failure and of disappointing others. The imagery centered on a very flamboyant failure in an important musical performance. He was instructed to exaggerate this failure and to publicize it widely to disappoint others (and himself) even more profoundly. This client was soon able to resume playing confidently and well during performances. Both client and therapist felt that there was a significantly decreased chance of future crises of this type occurring after the crisis intervention process.

Case #2

Precipitating Event: A young woman, just before college graduation, became depressed and anxious due to mounting fears that she would not be admitted to graduate school. These feelings were exacerbated by a rejection notice from one university that seemed to confirm her fears.

Precipitant: A negative body image and generally poor feelings about herself as a woman, retained since adolescence when she was quite overweight, led this client to place disproportionate emphasis on academic achievement to maintain self-esteem. When this source of self-validation was threatened by possible rejections from graduate schools, the result was depression and anxiety. These presenting symptoms were associated with a need to keep interpersonal distance from most of her peers whom she feared would not accept her if she was more open.

Crisis Intervention: After gaining initial understanding of this client's present crisis situation and the precipitant, she was trained in hypnotic relaxation. Regression techniques were used to help her to reexperience particular events during her early adolescence (and the affect associated with these events) that had created insecurity about herself as a young woman and her negative body image in particular. Much of this affect had been kept from awareness through use of intellectual defenses.

Hypnotic imagery enabled her to contrast her present physical self with her previously developed negative body image. Through this comparison process, she brought her body image "up-to-date." Her compensatory need to excel academically as a means to validate herself was easily established and conceptualized as the precipitant of her crisis.

Hynotically enhanced behavior rehearsal combined with ego-strengthening suggestions (Hartland 1971) helped to build more positive feelings about herself as a woman. She soon began to accept *in vivo* interpersonal risks of rejection (her greatest fear) by allowing others to know her more fully as a woman. Concurrently, she reduced her reliance on narrowly defined sources of self-validation (i.e., through academic achievement). Her growing positive feelings about herself as a woman permitted her to tolerate academic disappointment (although this remained difficult) as her crisis was adaptively resolved.

Case #3

Precipitating Event: A young man was referred by a physician who saw him shortly after his first sexual encounter. He had failed to ejaculate and this greatly increased his concern about his masculinity. He had never been able to ejaculate during masturbation (although occasionally ejaculation occurred during sleep). He became very anxious about his sexual ability and the effect this problem might have on future relationships with women.

Precipitant: With minimal and distorted information about sexual functioning obtained directly and indirectly from his parents, this client developed many ambivalent attitudes about his sexuality. This ambivalence created anxiety about sexual expression and a need to highly control his sexual responses.

Crisis Intervention: Initial therapeutic intervention focused on providing factual information to this client about human sexuality (both male *and* female), including psychological factors that influence sexual functioning. He was taught hypnotic relaxation and was given general ego-strengthening suggestions using Hartland's (1971) approach. This helped reduce the anxiety generated by his failure to function sexually that exacerbated pre-existing doubts about his sexual adequacy.

Using hypnotic regression techniques, this client was helped to reexperience particular interactions with his parents that had generated discomfort with sexuality in general and insecurity about his own adequacy in particular.

This client was not highly psychologically minded and awareness of the precipitant of his crisis came with difficulty. Many of the sexuality related messages from his parents were quite indirect but nontheless influential in shaping his sexual attitudes. Defining and conceptualizing more clearly the conflicts and doubts about his sexuality led to better understanding of the origins of his ejaculatory incompetence.

The client was taught auto-hypnotic relaxation to further reduce sex-related anxiety. Auto-erotic imagery was developed and integrated with hypnotic behavior rehearsal to permit him to relax while responding to sexual stimuli. Given permission and instruction to masturbate at home using these techniques, he soon began to ejaculate during masturbation easily and naturally as he became desensitized to sexual stimuli. A referral was made for further therapy to resolve other aspects of this client's interpersonal problems.

Discussion

In the literature on hypnosis, case examples in which hypnotic techniques were successfully used in short-term treatment (i.e., within the limits of the crisis intervention framework), focus is primarily on symptom reduction or removal rather than on facilitating adaptive coping and creative problem solving. Crisis theory as a reference framework within which hypnotically enhanced therapy is carried out seems to have been neglected.

It is the structure defined by crisis theory rather than the techniques per se that defines the crisis therapist whether hypnosis is used or not. Moss (1967) aptly summarized the stance of the crisis therapist (or hypno-therapist) when using this model:

> It is recognized that current problem situations may reactivate past unresolved conflict areas; however, treatment does not involve extended psychoarcheological explorations, nor is it concerned with intrapsychic manifestations to the exclusion of immediate, meaningful, real life problems. [P. 257]

In one relevant study (Moss et al. 1965), experienced therapists who used hypnosis in their clinical work were compared to others who did not. It was found that those using hypnosis were more active during therapy, were more supportive of clients, were environmental-manipulative and manifested a more flexible approach to the treatment of client problems. These qualities are necessary for effective crisis intervention, and are found in experienced crisis therapists. While not all emotional crises are equally amenable to the crisis approach (Baldwin 1978), the hypnosis-skilled crisis therapist has available an important dimension of intervention in brief therapy emphasizing adaptive coping and creative problem solving.

ADAPTATION TO A PARTICULAR
THERAPEUTIC MODE

Another important aspect of adaptation to the crisis model occurs when there are structural "givens" that are part of a clinical service delivery system to which crisis therapy must be adjusted. When this occurs, the crisis model must be adjusted to these parameters while retaining its essence. In many crisis services, special uses of this model have been developed by adapting it to various therapeutic modes of helping that are often innovative or nontraditional. These programs demonstrate the viability and flexibility of the crisis model; they bring needed innovation to existing concepts of service delivery on one hand and put helping services within reach of often neglected segments of the community on the other.

There are several variants of the "givens" created by a particular mode of therapy that affect how the crisis model is adapted. The first variation is when the mode of helping is basically a particular role (or part of a role) of a clinician or other helping individual. In this case, it is the structure of the primary role that determines how helping relationships are structured and limited. One emerging example of this is the police officer or the police social worker trained in crisis intervention to handle family disputes (Driscoll, Meyer, and Schauie 1973; Reid 1974). In this adaptation of the crisis model, intervention is made *in situ* in highly charged and dangerous domestic situations.

A second variation occurs when a facility and/or its service delivery system impose limitations on the helping process. Perhaps the most easily recognized example of this type of adaptation occurs when crisis intervention is used in emergency rooms (Bartolucci and Drayer 1973) or in walk-in services. One visit is the norm for intervention and disposition, and follow-up by the same clinicians is often very difficult or impossible. Further, a growing number of outpatient facilities are adopting the crisis model but are imposing severe limitations on the number of visits permitted each client. With an emotional crisis lasting an average of four to six weeks, imposing a maximum of three to four visits (or sometimes less!) not only requires adaptation of the crisis model but also limits the ability of the therapist to help clients fully resolve crises. In one service with a rather long waiting time (unfortunately very common!), one enterprising crisis therapist created a short-term crisis-oriented group for those on the waiting list (McGee and Larsen 1967).

As a third variation, it is often necessary to integrate use of the crisis model with a specific therapeutic modality. Here it is the form of the helping modality that determines how the crisis model is adapted. A frequently used helping modality, deeply rooted in the origins of crisis theory and practice, is telephone crisis intervention. The telephone has certain helping and limiting characteristics as a therapeutic mode (Lester 1974) to which the crisis therapist must adapt when involved in this type of crisis intervention. The success of clinicians and paraprofessionals to adapt basic tenets of the crisis model is attested to by the continuing viability of community crisis services or "hot/lines" using the telephone as a basic means of helping.

Another emeging therapeutic mode that is being integrated with crisis intervention is the use of various group formats. In the past, some crisis intervention was done in heterogeneous, problem-oriented groups with some degree of success (Morley and Brown 1969; Strickler and Allgeyer 1967). A second and more recent trend is to integrate principles of crisis intervention with time-limited and highly structured groups with a specific theme on which the participants focus (Drum and Knott 1977). This structured learning group format with a combination education/intervention/prevention focus is becoming increasingly popular among clinicians and clients alike. This type of group format is extremely flexible and "how to" descriptions and protocols of structured learning groups as responses to particular types of problems are now appearing in the literature (for example, see Granvold and Welch 1979).

Still another group format to which the crisis model is being adapted is the peer support and self-help groups that have deep roots in American tradition (Dumont 1974). In these groups, individuals experiencing similar crises meet to support one another, to work through feelings, and to develop more adaptive and mature ways to cope. These groups have been found helpful with individuals experiencing a wide range of problems and typically are unstructured except for time limitations. Usually there is professional leadership, but it is kept low key and members are guided into helping one another.

Caplan (1964) has noted that the quality of the emotional support present and the availability of task-oriented assistance provided by a social network are often critical dimensions of helping in mental health. For special problems, this support and assistance are provided by the self-help, peer-oriented support group. As described below, a group of this type was organized to aid victims of incestuous relationships. These "silent victims" often find it very difficult to obtain effective assistance because of their reluctance and because of lack of professionals, facilities, or programs especially oriented to the problems of this type of client. Therefore, the peer self-help group is one format that is helpful to such individuals.

A Peer-Oriented Support/Intervention Group for Victims of Incest[3]

Intervention groups using the peer support model as a modality for response to crises of various kinds have met with success and are increasing. Such groups have been helpful to those who are single parents, victims of child or

---

[3]This section by Hollis Wheeler. Section ends on p. 109.

adolescent sexual abuse, battered wives, homosexuals, runaway youth, alcoholics, and with many other types of problems as well. The peer support model of crisis intervention provides the client with acceptance and understanding when other social support systems and/or facilities to help with problems are inaccessible or (in some instances) nonexistent. In a peer group setting, it is easier to neutralize the stigma associated with some problems, and the opportunity to openly discuss experiences with others with similar problems in a controlled and nonjudgmental atmosphere is the foundation for change.

A peer support group consists of three to twelve (ideally five to seven) clients who share a problem and who meet regularly for the purpose of aiding one another to resolve that problem (or problems) and to learn to cope more adaptively. Most often, groups using this model meet for a set number of times so that the point of closure is known in advance. To be effective, these groups must be organized by a clinician who is familiar with the tenets of crisis intervention, experienced in small group work, and familiar with the issues involved in the particular problem that is the focus for the group.

One type of peer support/intervention group now emerging involves (usually young) adults who were sexually abused as children. This type of group is helpful to its participants because they have experienced traumas that carry a social stigma and few services have been designed to respond specifically to this type of problem. It is a problem that may affect self-esteem, general adjustment, and relationships for many years. Fortunately, those who have been victims of incestuous relationships and who develop the "silent victim syndrome" (Burgess and Holmstrom 1978) are now finding more services available and more professional attention focused on this type of problem. The format for organizing and developing a peer support/intervention group for victims of incest that has proven successful is described below.

Organizational Considerations

The organizational mechanics for a peer support/intervention group of this type are not difficult. The following are guidelines found helpful in organizing and implementing a group for clients who share in common previous sexual abuse in the form of incestuous relationships.

Publicity.   A minimum of two weeks before the group is to begin, and preferably three to four weeks beforehand, publicity (i.e., newspaper ads or radio spots) can be arranged. Two weeks are usually needed for potential clients to carefully weigh the decision to join and to muster the courage to make contact. Publicity should stress confidentiality and should inform women that they can call in anonymously for more information if they desire. In addition, posters can be placed in public locations around the community such as grocery stores, laundromats, schools/colleges, and other places where people will see them. Local mental health facilities and professionals, another source of referrals, can also be informed of the group and its emphasis.

Location.   Optimally, meetings should be arranged in a warm, comfortable, and private setting. It may be a house, school, church, YWCA, women's club, or any public or private facility that is in a more or less central location. The location for meetings is determined before the first meeting so group time and energy are not dissipated on this issue. Arrangements for refreshments are also helpful.

Screening.   A screening contact before the start of the group is helpful in several ways. It provides an occasion to create expectations for the group, a chance for the clinician to become acquainted with potential group members, and an opportunity to screen out those who are not ready for such an experience or who are otherwise inappropriate. Screening can be done over the telephone, but it is more effectively done in person. For those who are not ready for this type of helping experience, a referral is often necessary and appropriate. At times, a recommendation to obtain brief individual counseling as preparation for such a group is helpful and frequently welcomed.

Referrals.   Before beginning the group, the clinician should identify and make contact with all available referral resources in the area. These may include specific professionals as well as facilities or programs that are sensitive to this type of problem and the issues involved. The aware family physician can be extremely helpful here, (Boekelheide 1978). Sometimes a specific referral network is available as in western Massachusetts where there is an Incest Consultation Network. Contact with referral resources is also helpful for members who need additional work after the group has terminated its sessions.

Developing Guidelines

For effective functioning, a support/intervention group requires guidelines to structure and provide boundaries for the helping process. Among necessary guidelines are the following.

Closing Membership.   At the first meeting, a cutoff date for accepting new members is decided on. Members are encouraged to arrive on time and to minimize interruptions during the group time (e.g., telephone or messages). It is also helpful to obtain members' home telephone numbers (if they are agreeable) in order to relate changes in schedules, problems, etc. In the group, first names may be used if more informality (or anonymity!) is desired by participants.

Outside Contacts.   Another helpful guideline for the group to consider is that there be no discussion of other group members outside the group. This depends on self-monitoring for enforcement but makes participants more comfortable. Group members who meet outside the group should be particularly cautioned against discussing the group or its members. This is helpful to avoid cliques or alliances and helps insure that if an issue needs to be raised, it is done in the group.

Confidentiality.   The group may decide on specific confidentiality guidelines as these are extremely important in this type of group. Participants should be permitted to retain as much anonymity about their identities within the group as is comfortable. A decision about any record-keeping or observers/ supervisors for clinicians-in-training must also be made.

Time Limits for Meetings.   It is easy to run over the time limit for meetings once issues, feelings, and experiences suppressed for years begin to emerge. However, it is helpful to close the meeting on time whenever possible. This prevents participants from becoming physically and emotionally exhausted from the interaction. Members find it helpful if they are left with the desire to meet again and continue the following week. However, issues being discussed must be brought to a reasonable point of closure before the meeting is adjourned to prevent members from feeling they have been left hanging.

Possible Crises.   It is not uncommon for one or more group members to experience an emotional crisis during the course of a support/intervention group of this type. The clinician may elect to give his/her phone number to members with instructions to call if anyone becomes extremely distressed during the week. The release of long-suppressed memories and feelings often overwhelms capacity to cope and produces an emotional overload and consequent crisis. The clinician must be sensitive to this possibility and must take preventive measures by giving the group members specific instructions on what to do if and when this occurs.

Termination.   A termination date for the group is always established at the onset. As the termination date approaches, the clinician reminds the group of this fact so that members are able to prepare themselves for separation. Termination issues are anticipated and dealt with with the guidance of the clinician. It is possible, but not always advisable, to extend the group meetings if there is a strong sentiment to do so within the group membership.

Group Structure

Group members must decide on the basic dimension of structure; that is, the group must decide on a structured or unstructured format. As a general rule, as the size of the group increases the need for structure also increases.

Structure can be imposed in many ways and can be negotiated by the clinician with the group. One example of a structured format is allotting each member a specific length of time to talk, with members more or less taking turns during the course of the meeting. Conversely, an unstructured alternative is to ask all members to make sure they do not use excessive time for discussion and to encourage all members to participate and become involved. It is axiomatic that in an unstructured format, the clinician and the group must more closely monitor the process.

The clinician may seek to establish an unobtrusive group leadership role so that after the first two or three meetings the group is able to guide itself. In the peer-oriented support/intervention group, beneficial effects accrue from interactions among members, and the clinician may function only as a low-key facilitator who steps in when the group "gets stuck" or off the track or when a problem becomes manifest. Sometimes the role of "facilitator," with the clinician present, can be rotated from one group member to another week by week if participants decide on that format.

Disclosure of personal experiences has not been made a prerequisite for this type of group membership. However, individual members are gently and supportively encouraged to disclose as early in the group as they are willing but without pressure to disclose prematurely. After initial apprehension, one group member usually breaks the ice, and once trusting relationships develop among group members, initial apprehension may evolve into a desire to share with the group. Generally, details of incestuous acts are the most difficult to discuss, and many women do not provide much specificity here. It is more important to share and discuss the feelings generated by these experiences than the acts themselves.

An alternative format that has met with success has been described by Onsley (1978), whereby a detailed account of the incestuous relationship(s) is encouraged at the initial meeting. This disclosure permits instant cohesion of the group, although it does create great self-consciousness and apprehension. Onsley reports asking specific questions in a gentle way (e.g., "Was there any oral sex involved?") as though she was taking a history. Members report that although this is anxiety provoking, it is nevertheless worthwhile because a high level of group support develops quickly and all have shared their similar experiences, which helps initiate meaningful group interaction. These groups meet for five weeks with one follow-up meeting two months later.

One interesting variation in this type of group is to develop a group action project when the group meetings are about half over. Such a project serves two primary purposes: (1) it helps bring closure to the group by producing some product at its ending that all have been part of, and (2) it helps group members begin turning outward and to their futures after focusing inward during the group. One group decided to be interviewed by a journalist who submitted the resulting article about the group to a magazine for publication. Another group met periodically following the regular group meetings to discuss and write about their relationships with their mothers. Yet another possibility is for group members, with the help of the clinician, to initiate another group for others with similar problems.

Small Group Dynamics and Interventions

As the group begins, group members can be asked to define their hopes or expectations for the group. Questions not previously covered by the clinician in the introductory remarks can be answered. It should be explicitly stated that each member's role includes supporting others in the group as well as working on personal concerns for emotional growth.

Although group members know in advance that the theme for the support/intervention group is sexual abuse and/or assault in an incestuous relationship, some individuals may remain apprehensive and reserved about discussing their experiences. If the clinician has been a victim, she may become a role model by disclosing some of her background, experiences, and growth. Or, if one member is willing to take the initiative to disclose, this can encourage others to relate their experiences. Still another option is to show the film *Incest: The Victim Nobody Believes* (Motorola Teleprograms, Inc.) as a means to begin group interaction and disclosure. This film portrays an excellent twenty-minute conversation by three adult victims of childhood incest/abuse.

In creating expectations for the group members, some apprehension can be allayed by assuring all members that: (1) the group will take seriously and accept all they have to say, (2) the group wants to help and to hear what members have to say, and (3) the experience of sharing is therapeutic, particularly when that sharing is with others who have had more or less similar experiences. Once group disclosure and discussion of feelings begin in earnest, members invariably find they have a lot in common. One member commented:

> I was really bummed out after the first meeting. I was hoping there was someone else who had a mother who was weird. But by halfway through the group, I was finding out that things weren't really that different—that there were things in other people's situations that I was resonating with. That was really a lot of what I had wanted to find out.

Another way to build confidence and rapport among group members is to spend some time focusing on the strength and courage all have demonstrated simply by deciding to join the group and attend the first meeting. It is also helpful to comment on the strength it takes to cope with a problem such as theirs entirely alone for a long period of time, and to congratulate them on taking a constructive new step to work out this problem in conjunction with others who have had the same type of experience.

It is often useful to close each meeting with a few minutes devoted to "debriefing." This helps clients to make an emotional transition back to their private lives and the real world outside. Someone may be asked to summarize what has been discussed in the meeting. In one group, one member asked everyone present to join hands, and she reinforced everyone for something that had been accomplished as she went around the circle. These closure techniques may be substituted for "debriefing" in many instances, and members also find they build greater group cohesion as an added benefit.

Related Considerations. Several other points are salient for group members and the clinician must be aware of and responsive to them. Because of the difficulty in breaking the silence about past incestuous experiences, group members may experience an increase in anxiety as the group meeting time draws closer each week. This is a normal response and to be expected, but it may create concern (and avoidance!) in group members if they are not sensitized to this possibility in advance.

Further, members have typically been coping for years with their feelings and memories, and the group interaction may upset a stable, but perhaps not entirely adaptive, pattern of coping. For some participants, dealing with these issues in the group may cause relationships with important other people to change. Often key interpersonal relationships become more tenuous as deep feelings are dealt with and then change for the better. Members again can be sensitized to this possibility and can be advised to talk about such an eventuality with those they are close to.

The clinician must also anticipate, with the strong feelings involved in incest victims, that emotional outbursts may occur in the group. Often seen is strong anger, crying, or even self-destructive behaviors. The clinician can handle these situations directly within the group but must be aware that they may also occur outside the group after feelings such as these have been "opened up" following perhaps years of suppression or denial. A plan for handling such emergencies must be discussed with the group members so they will know whom to call and how to obtain help when needed.

As the group draws to a close, at least some members may desire (or need) to continue in some form of helping relationship. It is at this point that referral resources are very helpful. A knowledge of local services, programs, or helping resources can help to facilitate referrals. In some cases, the clinician can provide names or the mechanics of making contacts, and in others he/she may become actively involved in facilitating a referral quickly. Handling referrals is an important but easily neglected aspect of the clinician's functioning in a support/intervention group of this type, but it is also an area of responsibility that is critical for some women to fully resolve their feelings.

Discussion

Incest is a form of sexual abuse and trauma with many emotional consequences that is still underreported. It occurs in all geographic areas, social classes, and races. It is stigmatizing to the women who are victims, and too often the victims protect those who abused them while suffering silently and coping the best they can. It is only recently that professional attention has turned to treatment of this problem, one that is more common than previously recognized. The support-intervention group is one modality that is helpful to these women because it is peer oriented and dissipates that sense of aloneness so often encountered in such cases. As a form of crisis intervention, the support/intervention group is innovative and flexible with many therapeutic possibilities and great potential for alleviating problems and strengthening adaptive coping.

ADAPTATION TO PARTICULAR CLIENT PROBLEMS

Sometimes the crisis model must be adapted to the particular needs of clients who experience specific types of crises or who share certain characteristics as a population-at-risk. Here, the needs of clients determine the parameters of the adaptation process to insure that the crisis approach can effectively meet these needs. In the past, many crisis services became specialized to meet particular community needs or as responses to certain client populations. More recently, the crisis model has been used as a treatment of choice in general outpatient clinics. However, innovations in adapting the crisis model to specific clinical populations and/or to particular client problems continue today and are providing us with ever-increasing knowledge about crisis theory and intervention.

It is the task of the crisis therapist working in any "specialized" crisis clinic not only to adapt a personal therapeutic orientation to the framework of this approach, but also to adapt his/her practice to the parameters of the specialized services being provided. The poor or disadvantaged, those confined to nursing homes, and single parents in the community are segments of the population in general that represent special risks, and crisis services must be tailored to meet their particular needs. Battered women, those experiencing a sudden death in the family, or individuals adjusting to separation/divorce are further examples of specific types of problems to which the crisis model must be adjusted and that form the basis for organizing a specialized crisis service.

Therapists in specialized crisis clinics must be acquainted with the general dimensions and dynamics of a particular type of crisis at the generic level. Jacobson, Strickler, and Morley (1968) find this knowledge very helpful and state that "for each (type of) crisis, such as bereavement, birth of premature children, divorce, or so on, there are certain identifiable patterns, some of which result in adaptive and others in maladaptive outcome" (p. 340). Understanding a particular type of crisis at the generic level is complemented by clinician awareness of the individual and unique characteristics of a given crisis. Although a clinical service may be organized around generic understanding of particular types of crises, the clinician's training insures that ideosyncratic qualities of a particular crisis are also taken into account during crisis assessment and in defining goals for the intervention process.

Adaptation of this type also requires the crisis therapist to tailor the *interventions* to both the generic and the unique aspects of a specific type of crisis. Generally, however, as Jacobson, Strickler, and Morley (1968) state, in a service of this type, intervention "consists of specific measures designed to be effective for the target group as a whole" (p. 340). Yet this level of response will not be effective unless individual variations in the dynamics and course of a particular type of crisis are also incorporated into the crisis intervention and resolution process.

When the crisis approach is modified to meet the needs of particular types of clients or specific types of crises, it is the framework for the crisis approach that determines the structural boundaries for the therapeutic process. But, it is also the particular characteristics of a specific type of crisis that determine conceptual understanding of that therapeutic process and the type of interventions required. In the following description, two clinicians relate how they have adapted the crisis model to a type of crisis that is increasingly encountered and that has many generic qualities: the problem pregnancy. Here clinicial services have been organized within the context of the crisis model to meet the needs of the women experiencing this particular type of crisis. These women represent a clinical population-at-risk, and a crisis service has been organized to meet their particular needs.

Problem Pregnancy Counseling as Crisis Intervention[4]

As unexpected pregnancy may represent a major life crisis with the potential for enhancing personal growth or causing later problems. Women faced with an unplanned pregnancy experience a range of confusing feelings, both positive and negative. Predominant feelings are guilt and depression (Gispert 1976), frequently mixed with satisfaction that conception has occurred. These feelings are in conflict and increase the difficulty in making and integrating a decision about the pregnancy. Problem pregnancy counseling in a college

---

[4]This section, through p. 118, by Sharon K. Meginnis and Janet Urman.

mental health setting is an increasingly encountered form of crisis intervention. Most women in this population elect abortion following the crisis counseling process, and this description of a clinical service for these women consequently emphasizes pregnancy termination.

It is clear that the framework and goals of crisis intervention are applicable to problem pregnancy counseling. Within the brief time available for crisis intervention, goals for the resolution process include some combination of the following (Baldwin 1976): (1) *feelings* that must be recognized and worked through, (2) *insights and understandings* that must be brought to awareness, (3) *decisions* that must be faced and made, and (4) *tasks* that must be carried out by the client. All of these factors are part of problem pregnancy counseling not only to ensure adaptive crisis resolution but to enhance maturity and to prevent future similar crises.

Making a decision about a problem pregnancy is essential to crisis resolution and is the issue around which much of the counseling is organized. This process has been referred to as "decision counseling" aimed at fostering a "high quality" decision (Bracken 1977). The individuals concerned must consider the many factors involved in a problem pregnancy and their consequences or implications, both long-term and short-term, and then decide on the most feasible course of action.

Conflicts must be faced, insights developed, and deeper understanding created during the process of decison making and implementation. Any deficiency in the problem pregnancy resolution process may undermine comfort with the decision later. It is the task of the problem pregnancy counselor, operating within the constraints of the crisis model, to help each woman to make a sound decision that will not create later problems.

Goals of Pregnancy Counseling

The primary function of the pregnancy counselor is to be available, nonjudgmental, and supportive to a woman in crisis and to facilitate a sound decision about the pregnancy. The counselor should remain objective and make no attempt to influence the woman's decision, but instead should establish a helping relationship that enables the client to move toward assuming control of the situation. A counselor must resolve personal feelings about premarital sexuality, pregnancy, abortion, and birth and must also believe in a woman's right and responsibility to make her own decision.

More specifically, the problem pregnancy counselor strives to:

1. Explore the social, emotional, and medical ramifications of the pregnancy with each client.
2. Help each client mobilize her resources to cope with the problem.
3. Clarify values and value conflicts with regard to sexual behavior,

and with each client consider alternative courses of action and the feelings associated with each one.

4. Discuss with the client all alternatives and arrive at and implement a decision that can be accepted.

5. Explore the social, emotional, and medical aspects of her decision.

6. Inform each client about available resources.

7. Clarify physiological and contraceptive issues, and refer the client for contraceptive counseling as appropriate.

8. Anticipate unresolved conflicts and refer the client for ongoing counseling or therapy as indicated.

9. Provide follow-up to insure resolution of the crisis.

It should be noted that although these issues are presented separately, most are interrelated. The flow and focus of each interview will depend on those issues most pertinent and conflict-laden for a particular woman. Because pregnancy termination is the alternative of choice in most college women, emphasis in the following discussion is directed to that decision.

Important Areas to Be Addressed in Problem Pregnancy Counseling

Marital Status.   A woman's marital status is ascertained at the outset. If her partner is present and willing, he will be seen as well. However, it is advised that a woman, married or not, be seen alone sometime during the counseling process to give her an opportunity to raise those issues she may not have shared with her partner (e.g., previous abortions, questionable paternity, etc.) as well as any other fears, misgivings, or desires not openly aired with him.

Factual Data.   Early in counseling it is necessary to determine specific information about the pregnancy. This includes: (a) first date of last menstrual period, (b) results of the pregnancy test, and (c) results of the pelvic examination. The purpose is to confirm that these facts correspond and that there *is* an intrauterine pregnancy. Although these procedures are often routinely done before the woman begins counseling, the wise counselor will review the findings to rule out or understand any discrepancies. Errors do happen, and those caught early save time, money, and considerable anguish for the woman involved.

Emotional Ramifications of the Pregnancy.   Although much of the focus of discussing an unwanted pregnancy is on what to do about it, it is important not to ignore feelings about the pregnancy. The unwanted pregnancy presents a significant stress, which may be accompanied by positive as well as negative feelings. For a woman experiencing her first pregnancy, this represents confirmation of fertility, and she may express delight with the knowledge that "my body works." This pleasure seems confusing to the woman who, without any ambivalence, intends to abort. A typical statement heard is, "It was so crazy. I knew I was having the abortion on Friday, but I kept eating healthy foods all week." Acknowledging the ambivalence provides an opportunity to express both aspects of the woman's feelings and leads to increased understanding of her conflict.

In addition to healthy positive reactions, there may be "less healthy" positive feelings associated with the pregnancy. For example, some may see pregnancy as a means to a better relationship with the partner, or may see the pregnancy as a test of his commitment, a way to increase his sense of responsibility or a vehicle for making the relationship more permanent. In addition, the potential child may be seen as an opportunity to have someone to love or to love her or as an end to loneliness. Sometimes a pregnancy represents a mechanism or rationale for attention, increased self-esteem, or a greater sense of importance or purpose. By identifying the source of these feelings, they can be examined more realistically to assess if the pregnancy and child are in fact what is desired or whether they represent a means to an end that may be achieved by alternative and healthier means. By understanding her own motivations, a woman is freed to have more control over herself, her choices, and her life.

Self-Esteem.   Exploring a woman's feelings about herself can provide a valuable corrective experience. Some women have grown up believing pregnancy outside of wedlock only happens to "others" or to "girls from the wrong side of the tracks." These individuals are shocked by the fact that they are now pregnant. This may call their self-concept into question (e.g., "Am I that kind of person?"), and loss of self-esteem may be a consequence. It is important to help a woman recognize these issues, gain a more appropriate perspective, and work through the feelings produced by such perceptions.

Family History.   It is helpful to obtain a selected family history, focusing on key relationships, especially the mother–daughter one, to identify sources of conflict or pathology that may be related to the unplanned pregnancy or that may inhibit a decision for resolution. Some family influences commonly found to contribute to unplanned pregnancies include: overidentifying with the mother and the mothering role; being, or perceiving herself to be, of central importance in the mother's life, thus using the pregnancy to give the mother a child so that the daughter may leave the family; the marriage or pregnancy of a sibling that raises issues of competition for and/or rebellion against parents (Gispert 1976).

Family values and expectations about premarital sexual behavior, contraceptive use, and abortion provide the context in which the woman's views have been formed. Understanding her family views as they are similar to or differ from the woman's own can serve to reduce conflict. Likewise, similar events in the family history, such as a premarital pregnancy in a sibling, an abortion by another member of the family, or an adoption of a family member, can serve to influence a woman's reaction to her situation. It is important to foster an understanding of the relationships among these events, the feelings about the pregnancy, and the intended disposition.

Psychiatric History. Any previous contacts with mental health professionals should be noted with particular focus on whether there has been a history of emotional difficulties, depression, or recent loss because these problems may be reactivated by an unexpected pregnancy. Exploring how a woman has responded to other crises in her life, to whom she has turned for support, and how well she has coped provide information helpful in assessing how she will cope with this crisis, as well as indicate the level of intervention required during counseling.

Sexual History. Specific aspects of a woman's sexual history are often relevant to the crisis and resolution of an unplanned pregnancy. Among these aspects are family upbringing, contraceptive use, acceptance of sexual activity, previous sexual traumas, and previous pregnancy. It is helpful to clarify the attitudes incorporated from family and society, particularly via the mother, about menstruation, sexual development, childbearing, and "being a woman." These understandings may be very helpful for both client and counselor. A woman with a constricted or negative attitude about sex or menstruation often carries a sense of shame and need for secrecy. On the other hand, a woman with a positive perception of her body and its functioning is usually more open to discussing her feelings, particularly the sadness and sense of loss that usually accompanies pregnancy termination.

Support System. A woman's support system should be explored to determine who has been told about the pregnancy and why. It is important for the client to understand clearly reasons for her sharing the news with a partner, friends, or family and what is potentially gained or lost by doing so. The goal is not to encourage or discourage sharing with others, but to explore the motivations involved. For those women who refuse to tell their partner, it may be an indication of a nonexistent or tenuous relationship. It is the woman who chooses to communicate with no one and seeks to deal with the crisis entirely on her own that causes most concern. Often this is an indication of high levels of guilt or shame with possible detrimental consequences if these feelings are not acknowledged and worked through in counseling. Of similar concern is the woman who broadcasts to everyone the news of her pregnancy, seeking support and sanction indiscriminately from others.

Decision Making in Problem
Pregnancy Counseling

A critical aspect of counseling is promoting active and effective decision making. Janis and Mann (1977) note that maladaptive behaviors frequently result from defective emergency decision making. Bracken (1977) emphasizes the difficulty involved in the decision to terminate a pregnancy because of the high levels of stress associated with this decision. The most common defect in problem pregnancy decision making is a blind rush into a decision to abort without consideration of other alternatives or of the emotional ramifications of that decision. A major goal of the counselor is to slow down the decision process and to encourage active, careful, and comprehensive consideration of all relevant factors before a decision is made. In this way, a woman is able to arrive at a well-thought-through decision with acknowledgement of the feelings involved and the reasons for the decision that is eventually made. The counselor assesses the woman's usual style of decision making and compares it with the manner in which the current decision is approached.

It is helpful to discuss with these clients all the available alternatives: abortion, adoption, single parenthood, and married parenthood, and to have each woman define the advantages and disadvantages of each option and the positive and negative short-term *and* long-term consequences of each. Women who do not address the crisis of pregnancy with this active decision making process are more likely to question their decision later on. It is the counselor's role to discourage these women from avoiding difficult or painful conflicts because these will remain issues and may surface later (sometimes in unexpected circumstances) and at that time will be more difficult to resolve.

Janis and Mann (1977) have provided a list of criteria a problem pregnancy counselor can use to assess the quality of a woman's decision:

1. Has the client thoroughly canvassed a wide range of *alternative courses of action?*

2. Has the client surveyed the *full range of objectives to be fulfilled* and the values implicated by the choice?

3. Has the client carefully weighed whatever she knows about the *costs or drawbacks* and the *risks of negative consequences as well as the positive consequences that could flow from each alternative?*

4. Has the client intensively searched for *new information* relevant to further evaluation of the possible alternatives?

5. Has the client correctly *assimilated* and taken into account any *new information* or expert judgment to which she is exposed, even when the information or judgment does not support the course of action she initially prefers?

6. Has the client *reexamined the positive and negative consequences of*

all known alternatives, including those originally regarded as unacceptable, before making a final choice?

7. Has the client *made detailed provisions for implementing* or executing the chosen course of action, with special attention to *contingency plans* that might be required if various risks were to materialize?

Abortion Considerations

Many women are certain that a present pregnancy is undesired and that it would interfere significantly with their plans for the future, and they are able to state this without ambivalence. However, when they explore thoughts and feelings with regard to abortion, confusion may emerge. For most women, some degree of ambivalence is considered normal. However, for those who talk about abortions as "killing Johnny's baby," or "committing a mortal sin" or state that "I'll never be able to live with myself" but are still planning to abort, it is imperative to focus on how these conflicts will be resolved should abortion be the chosen alternative.

Although these statements sound dramatic, they are not uncommon. The counselor also should pay attention to the terms a woman uses as labels or synonyms for the contents of the uterus (e.g., potential for life, our child, fetus, my baby, chromosomes) and for the procedure (e.g., termination, killing, murder, removal, taking a life). These words are indicators of potential conflict.

Some women feel a sense of urgency to make a decision immediately, wanting to "get it over with," with the fantasy that all unpleasantness, ambivalence, and uncomfortable feelings will terminate with an abortion. Supportive counseling provides an opportunity to temper the process to enable identification and resolution of these feelings at the appropriate time, rather than leaving issues unresolved.

Procedure

In addition to the emotional factors attendant on the decision to abort, many women express anxieties about the physical procedure. Some fear it as an unwanted invasion of their bodies; for others it represents a dreaded or feared medical procedure comparable to previous negative medical experiences. Many acknowledge fear of the unknown and fear of pain. Reducing, although not minimizing, these anxieties helps to clarify the factors directly relevant to the decision.

Once the decision has been made and related thoughts and feelings explored, the counselor's role shifts to that of information giver. In order to apprise those who choose abortion as fully as possible of all that is involved, the counselor must explain the appropriate procedure in detail.

It is helpful to provide a detailed description of the environment (clinic, procedure room, etc.) in which the abortion procedure will take place. In explaining the procedure, one should discuss the experience step by step, drawing on a woman's experience with the pelvic exam as a basis of comparison. A description of the abortion procedure should include visual examples of instruments used, their function, and their probable physical impact on the body, making comparisons to menstrual cramping in order to explain the uncomfortable feelings she will experience.

Women need to be informed of the range of short-term postabortion reactions (bleeding, cramping) and should be given the warning signals for infection or for incomplete procedures (fever, severe bleeding, and/or cramping). Guidance is given on the care of the body, observations for infection, use of tampons, resumption of intercourse, the need for a two-week follow-up medical exam, contraceptive considerations, and possible effects on the relationship with one's partner. In addition to the physical experience of the procedure, it is helpful to anticipate with the woman possible emotional reactions, specifically relief, sadness, loss, and whatever else may be relevant to each *individual.*

Postabortion

Women should be encouraged to keep a postabortion follow-up appointment with the pregnancy counselor. This provides them with an opportunity to relate their experiences and to share their thoughts and feelings. Usually a feeling of relief is dominant at this point, but a sense of sadness and loss may be evident also. The counseling may well refer back to issues that had been identified earlier as potential pitfalls. Adaptive coping responses should be reinforced.

The counselor can also engage in anticipatory guidance (Caplan 1964) to help a woman prepare for future occasions that may trigger waves of feelings (e.g., the pregnancy of a friend or family member, ads for diapers and baby foods, the presence of an infant or pregnant woman). By anticipating such potentially troublesome stimuli before their occurrence, the counselor can assist a client in preparing a response, and thereby reduce the negative impact on her.

Women frequently find it helpful to discuss the effects of this experience on their relationships, paying particular attention to the unresolved conflicts that may have been uncovered or provoked by this crisis. For other couples this may have been a strengthening experience that was successfully shared together.

The counselor needs to be attuned to any indication of regret, remorse, or depression, or an inability to cope with negative feelings, and several follow-up sessions may be necessary to help resolve these reactions. In those few cases where severe or ongoing emotional turmoil is noted, the counselor must be prepared to refer the woman to a therapist for continuing work.

Discussion

The woman who benefits from effective problem pregnancy counseling typically emerges from the crisis with less anxiety, less guilt, and less depression than those who do not. The detailed information she is given during the process fosters the reduction of fear and anxiety and strengthens a sense of self-control. Through careful exploration of all related issues, this woman achieves a degree of self-understanding not possible for the woman who does not receive counseling. This enhanced self-awareness and understanding, as well as the adaptive coping mechanisms used, serve to provide this individual with tools for preventing future similar crises and for preventing maladaptive responses to other stressful situations.

For most women, the opportunity to talk openly and honestly about their sexual activity, their relationships, their pregnancy, and their thoughts and feelings about abortion is a unique experience with the potential to enhance self-esteem and reduce negative associations or emotionally unhealthy responses to such a situation. Problem pregnancy counseling is an ideal forum for the practice of crisis intervention. For most women, an unexpected pregnancy does create a crisis, which, like most crises, can be resolved in adaptive or maladaptive ways. To the extent that the problem pregnancy counseling helps to resolve the crisis in the direction of enhanced self-awareness, maturity, and personal responsibility, the possibility of postabortion problems is reduced. Further, such intervention helps to prevent future similar crises because this crisis is used as a vehicle to strengthen coping and develop self-awareness, and to identify and work through underlying issues that are often determinants of such a crisis.

CONCLUDING REMARKS

In summary, the ability of the crisis therapist in adapting the crisis model to a personal therapeutic orientation, a specific therapeutic model, and/or to particular problems or clinical populations-at-risk in large measure determines the effectiveness of the services provided. In all of these aspects of the adaptation process, there are specific skills inherent to crisis intervention that the crisis therapist must be familiar with and skilled in using. These skills are not only necessary for effective crisis intervention but also define the parameters of the adaptation process. At the risk of being a bit redundant, an overview of the basic skills necessary for the effective practice of crisis intervention (Baldwin 1977, 1979) follows. These same skills are also the basis for adapting this model to various clinical contexts.

Basic Skills Needed for Crisis Intervention[5]

Setting Limits on Therapeutic Contacts

Many clinicians initially experience difficulty learning to negotiate time limits for crisis therapy directly and explicitly with their clients. This aspect of crisis intervention contrasts markedly with the less overt structure of longer-term therapy where the client is understood to leave when "well" and the termination date is not usually agreed upon early in the therapeutic process. It is necessary to set time boundaries for crisis therapy in order to formulate goals that can reasonably be attained within these limits.

Negotiating Specific Achievable Goals

Defining achievable goals is a complementary and necessary area of expertise for the crisis therapist who must help clients focus on specific and realistic (albeit limited) foci for the crisis intervention and resolution process. Limiting and defining specific goals are an essential part of the focal stance of the crisis therapist as is consensually formulating and conceptualizing with the client a statement of the "problem" from which the goals are then derived.

Focusing the Intervention on the Present Stress

The aim in crisis intervention is to help the client respond adaptively to a present stressor, a stressor that by definition the client is unable to cope with maturely alone. Learning to maintain a specific and relevant emphasis related to the precipitating stress is difficult but essential for the use of this model. Although conflicts from the past are often determinants of emotional crisis, the focus remains on the present problem situation, which can become a vehicle to work through and resolve underlying conflicts. When this occurs, the client attains a more adaptive level of functioning and removes an underlying vulnerability that prevents future similar crises.

Accepting Appropriate Outcomes

The general goal of crisis intervention and resolution is to help the client experiencing an emotional crisis to reestablish a level of adaptive functioning at at least the precrisis level in the shortest period of time and at the least

[5]This section, through page 121, is reprinted with permission from B.A. Baldwin, "Crisis Intervention in Professional Practice: Implications for Clinical Training," *American Journal of Orthopsychiatry,* 47 (1977), 659–670. Copyright 1977 by the American Orthopsychiatric Association, Inc.

psychic cost. This goal, the criterion for success in crisis therapy, contrasts with the therapeutic emphasis of longer-term therapy where resolution of deeply rooted or pervasive conflicts over an extended period of time and helping the client to progress toward optimal possible functioning are therapeutic goals.

Becoming More Practical
as a Therapist

Crisis intervention requires not only a focused and present-oriented approach but also a therapeutic strategy that is helpful at a practical and concrete level. Hitchcock (1973) has aptly stated that "the umbrella over all crisis intervention is the problem-solving process" (p. 1388). Promoting personal growth and adaptive adjustment in clients in a limited period of time necessitates not only effective use of general clinical skills but also familiarity with practical problem-solving techniques and (in appropriate circumstances) direct advice or helpful suggestions.

Attaining Skill
in Rapid Assessment

Crisis clients frequently present with a broad spectrum of problems, differing levels of mental health and adjustment, and varied backgrounds. One important part of rapid assessment with such varied clients is learning to sift relevant from irrelevant information and to formulate a concise statement of the problem from which therapeutic goals and a strategy to attain those goals are derived. With little time available for in-depth evaluation, the crisis therapist must quickly assess the situation and reach a relative depth of understanding so that an effective intervention can be planned and implemented.

Becoming More Direct
But Not Directive

Using the crisis model requires the clinician to become more direct and to adopt a more active role with the client than in longer-term therapy where a slower pace and a more passive therapeutic posture are often the norm. To make this shift necessitates a modification of style that can be initially stressful if there is apprehension about an active and cooperative therapeutic process or insecurity about therapeutic skills. A common difficulty is that becoming more direct and actively engaging the client is confused with becoming more directive with consequent overcontrol, inappropriate advice giving, and otherwise unnecessarily mandating the client's actions.

Managing Difficult Clients

Crisis therapists frequently encounter clients who are difficult to treat because they are management problems. Among those who present challenges to the crisis therapist are those who have decompensated, clients prone to act out under stress, clients with minimal suicidal or aggressive impulse control, and various types of very manipulative clients. Making appropriate and effective therapeutic responses to these types of clients is at once difficult and most essential for the effective crisis therapist. It requires therapeutic maturity, clinical skill, and sound judgment to manage such difficult clients and to create a context for growth within a short-term therapeutic framework.

Developing Termination Skills

Because of the time-limited nature of crisis intervention, termination skills are an important part of the crisis therapist's repertoire. The dynamics of separation (e.g., transference, dependency, manipulation, anger, loss, etc.) are all manifested in crisis clients even though the therapeutic process has been quite brief. The crisis therapist must be prepared to respond in growth-enhancing ways to these issues, but must also be willing to "let go" of clients after the goals of crisis therapy have been attained even though other noncrisis related problems remain.

Facilitating Appropriate Referrals

After the goals of crisis intervention have been attained, some crisis clients will require additional helping services. The crisis therapist must be familiar with available community resources of a therapeutic nature (e.g., inpatient facilities, day care, group therapy, etc.) as well as other helping agencies whose services clients may need (e.g., legal services, health department, housing authority, etc.). The crisis therapist must know the mechanics of referral to a broad spectrum of agencies in the community and must have the skills necessary to create client acceptance of such referrals. For many clients, crisis intervention is a first contact with therapy, and the helpfulness of this relationship greatly influences follow-through to other agencies following crisis therapy.

REFERENCES

BALDWIN, B. A., "*Crisis Assessment.*" Unpublished outlines, 1976.
———, "Crisis Intervention in Professional Practice: Implications for Clinical Training," *American Journal of Orthopsychiatry,* 47 (1977), 659–70.

————, A Paradigm for the Classification of Emotional Crises: Implications for Crisis Intervention," *American Journal of Orthopsychiatry,* 48 (1978), 538–51.

————, "Training in Crisis Intervention for Students in the Mental Health Professions," *Professional Psychology,* 10 (1979), 161–65.

BARTOLUCCI, G., and C. S. DRAYER, "An Overview of Crisis Intervention in the Emergency Rooms of General Hospitals," *American Journal of Psychiatry,* 130 (1973), 953–59.

BOEKELHEIDE, P. D., "Incest and the Family Physician," *Journal of Family Practice,* 6 (1978) 87–90.

BRACKEN, M. B., "Psychosomatic aspects of abortion: Implications for counseling," *Journal of Reproductive Medicine,* 19 (1977), 265–72.

BURGESS, A. W., and L. L. HOLMSTROM, *Rape: Crisis and Recovery.* Bowie, Md: Robert J. Brady Co., 1978.

CAPLAN, G., *Principles of Preventive Psychiatry.* New York: Basic Books, Inc., Publishers, 1964.

————, *Support Systems and Community Mental Health.* New York: Behavioral Publications, 1974.

DRISCOLL, J. J., R. G. MEYER, and C. F. SCHANIE, "Training Police in Family Crisis Intervention," *Journal of Applied Behavioral Science,* 9 (1973), 62–82.

DRUM, D., and J. E. KNOTT, *Structured Groups for Facilitating Develment: Acquiring Life Skills, Resolving Life Themes, and Making Life Transitions.* New York: Human Sciences Press, 1977.

DUMONT, M. P., "Self-Help Treatment Programs," *American Journal of Psychiatry,* 131 (1974), 631–35.

FRANKL, V. E., "Paradoxical Intention and Dereflection," *Psychotherapy: Theory, Research and Practice,* 12 (1975), 226–36.

GISPERT, M., "Psychological Aspects of Abortion," *North Carolina Journal of Mental Health,* 7 (1976), 76–95.

GOLDFRIED, M. R., and C. S. TRIER, "Effectiveness of Relaxation as an Active Coping Skill," *Journal of Abnormal Psychology,* 83 (1974), 348–55.

GRANVOLD, D. K., and G. J. WELCH, "Structured, Short-Term Group Treatment of Post-Divorce Adjustment," *International Journal of Group Psychotherapy,* 3 (1979), 347–58.

HARTLAND, J., "Further Observations on the Use of 'Ego-Strengthening' Techniques," *American Journal of Clinical Hypnosis,* 14 (1971), 1–8.

HILGARD, E. S., *Hypnotic Susceptibility.* New York: Harcourt Brace Jovanovich, Inc., 1965.

HITCHCOCK, J., "Crisis Intervention: The Pebble in the Pool," *American Journal of Nursing,* 73 (1973), 1388–90.

JACOBSON, G. F., M. STRICKLER, and W. E. MORLEY, "Generic and Individual Approaches to Crisis Intervention," *American Journal of Public Health,* 58 (1968), 338–43.

JANIS, T. L., and L. MANN, "Emergency Decision Making: A Theoretical Analysis of Responses to Disaster Warnings," *Journal of Human Stress,* 3 (1977) 35–48.

KAPP, R. A., and S. D. WEISS, "An Interdisciplinary, Crisis-Oriented Graduate Training Program within a Student Health Service Mental Health Clinic," *Journal of the American College Health Association,* 23 (1975), 340–44.

KARDENER, S. H., "A Methodologic Approach to Crisis Therapy," *American Journal of Psychotherapy,* 29 (1975), 4–13.

LESTER, D., "The Unique Qualities of Telephone Therapy," *Psychotherapy: Theory, Research and Practice,* 11 (1974), 219–21.

MCGEE, T. F., and V. B. LARSEN, "An Approach to Waiting List Therapy Groups," *American Journal of Orthopsychiatry,* 37 (1967), 594–97.

MORLEY, W. E., and V. B. BROWN, "The Crisis-Intervention Group: A Natural Mating or a Marriage of Convenience?" *Psychotherapy: Theory, Research and Practice,* 6 (1969), 30–36.

MOSS, C. S., "Brief Crisis-Oriented Hypnotherapy," in J. E. Gorden, ed., *Handbook of Clinical and Experimental Hypnosis.* New York: Macmillan Publishing Co., Inc., 1967.

MOSS, C. S., G. RIGGEN, L. COYNE, and W. BISHOP, "Some Correlates of the Use (or Disuse) of Hypnosis by Experienced Psychologist-Therapists," *International Journal of Clinical and Experimental Hypnosis,* 13 (1965), 39–50.

ONSLEY, N., personal communication, 1978.

REID, T. A., "Training Suburban Police in the Management of Social Interaction Disturbances," *Crisis Intervention,* 6, No. 3 (1975), 2–12.

STRICKLER, M., and J. ALLGEYER, "The Crisis Group: A New Application of Crisis Theory," *Social Work,* 12 (1967), 28–32.

II

TYPOLOGY
OF CRISES

The second part of the book expands into separate chapters the six major classes of crises that frequently come to the attention of clinicians: These are dispositional crises, transitional life crises, traumatic stress crises, developmental life crises, crises reflecting psychopathology, and psychiatric emergencies. For illustration and application, examples from the various types of crises are included in the relevant chapter along with the general crisis intervention strategy. The traditional crises situations will not be discussed since many are more adequately covered in other publications. Rather, we have selected crises illustrations that we believe are surfacing as key crisis areas for attention. Clinicians who are currently working within these areas have written the material.

6

CLASS 1: DISPOSITIONAL CRISES

A dispositional crisis (Butcher and Maudel 1976) may be defined as the distress resulting from a current problematic situation confronting the client. The problem is well defined by the client. The clinician responds to the client in ways peripheral to the therapeutic role in that the intervention is not primarily directed at the emotional level. Rather, the approach may be to provide educational information, make a referral to a specific agency or discipline, or provide administrative leverage to the situation.

A dispositional crisis is a problematic situation confronting the client with a sense of immediacy. For example, a family member reveals the stress caused to the family as the result of an alcoholic family member. Providing information to the client about local treatment options such as Al-Anon and other groups is a type of intervention in a dispositional crisis. In another example, a college student discusses the disruption caused to his study needs because of an untenable living situation in a residence hall. The crisis clinician may grant this student administrative release to seek a new dormatory environment. And in a third example, a young man reports an episode of impotence while very intoxicated. The clinician may provide psychological education to the client about situational causes of impotence as an intervention for this dispositional crisis.

The following preventive service model for children will be discussed as an example of implementation of Class I crises.

PREVENTIVE SERVICES
FOR CHILDREN: A MODEL[1]

The need for providing primary prevention and care in the area of mental health for children has long been recognized in the professional literature as well as in clinical practice. Various approaches to this concern have included the development of school psychology programs, prenatal classes in child care, and, recently, the Department of Health, Education and Welfare's Forward Plan for Health for 1978–82 redirected training funds of the National Institute of Mental Health to increase the number of primary health care workers. The current emphasis in primary health care is on prevention and health maintenance, including psychosocial as well as physical needs (Tuma and Schwartz 1978). Taking into account the psychosocial needs of children is felt to impact on concerns regarding child abuse, child neglect, mental retardation, and learning difficulties as well as the child's emotional adjustment. To provide this comprehensive care would seem to require the development of liaison programs between the primary health care provider and the mental health professional (Schroeder 1979).

A model for this liaison between the pediatrician (who is most often the primary health care provider for children) and professionals trained in dealing with the development and management of children was started at the University of North Carolina in Chapel Hill in 1973. Staff from the University's Division for Disorders of Development and Learning joined together with Senior, Sheaffer, Conley, and Christian, a private practice group of pediatricians who serve over 10,000 children, to provide preventive education and crisis intervention to parents in the community (Schroeder, Goolsby, and Stangler 1975). This collaborative effort involves offering services to families as well as training for graduate- and postgraduate-level students from nursing, psychology, social work, and medicine. The services for parents include evening education groups in child development and management, a telephone service, and regular hours to schedule appointments with the professional staff. All the services take place in the pediatrician's office and are advertised through the local newspaper, the Welcome Wagon community group, notification in the pediatrician's billing system, and by word of mouth. Anyone in the community may use the

[1]This section, through page 137, is written by Carolyn S. Schroeder, Gary B. Mesibov, Judith Eastman, and Elaine Goolsby. The authors would like to thank Marva Price, Becky Conover, and Blan Minton for their continued work on this service. As always, we are indebted to Drs. Senior, Sheaffer, Conley, and Christian, the pediatricians, who have been models in collaboration and support of the services. The parents' continued use of the services and their willingness to take time and thought to answer our many follow-up questions are greatly appreciated. The preparation of this paper was supported by Maternal and Child Health Service Project No. 916, and Grant HD-03110 from the National Institute of Health.

services, and a physician's referral is not necessary. Because of the training component of the project, there is no charge for any of the services.

Parent Education Groups

The general format of the parent education groups includes three one and one-half hour weekly sessions each month with two sessions focusing on a specific age group and one session focusing on a topic that would cut across the concern of several age groups or all age groups. The age groups covered are: 0–3 months, 3–6 months, 6–12 months, 12–18 months, 18–30 months, 30 months–4 years, 4–5 years, 6–7 years, 8–9 years, 10 years, 11–12 years, and adolescents. The first two sessions include a 30–45-minute review of normal child development in the cognitive, motor, language, social, and emotional areas and an introduction to how children learn. Following this brief presentation, the group leader encourages group problem solving for the parents' questions on child behavior management and development. The leader attempts to facilitate the problem-solving process by presenting a perspective on the child's development and how this fits into learning new skills and tasks. The topics of the third session each month are based on subjects that parents frequently ask, for example, toilet training, discipline, and sibling rivalry. These meetings include an opportunity for the parents to define what they want to teach their children on these subjects, and the group leader then discusses the skills needed and the developmental level required to learn these skills. There is also a general discussion on how to solve the specific problems children and parents have in these areas. The emphasis in all of the education classes is on positive action that parents can take to help their children grow and develop most effectively. The principles underlying learning and development are stressed rather than simple solutions or answers to parents' questions. The mean number of parents attending these sessions over the past seven years is 10–12 a session with occasionally as few as 4 and as many as 30. Parents' evaluation is requested at the end of each session with the parents consistently rating the emphasis on the child's development and how this fits into behavior management as being the most effective part of the sessions.

Call-In/Come-In Services

The call-in service consists of a telephone service in the pediatric office, which is available two hours per week for parents to make direct calls to the project staff. Come-in appointments allow for a more in-depth discussion of a concern and are available for four hours each week. Parents can arrange these appointments through the office receptionist without first using the call-in service. The staff answering the call-in service telephone calls may also decide that a problem should be discussed face to face with the parents and may request that a parent make a come-in appointment. Situations that might warrant this recommendation would be calls that last for more than fifteen minutes, or when parents repeatedly call about the same problem, or when a problem is out of the particular staff member's area of expertise, or when the tone of the parents' discussion is alarming.

The emphasis of the call-in/come-in services is to answer parents' questions on child development and management when a concern initially arises. Given this preventive approach, ongoing treatment is usually not part of the service. However, if a parent contacts the staff three or more times about a particular problem, then the question of referral is discussed with the parent; or if the child is a patient of the pediatric practice, referral is also discussed with the child's primary physician. On questions of developmental delays, screening instruments such as the Denver Developmental Test or the Alpern-Boll are used to determine if a referral for more extensive evaluation is indicated. A project staff person and the physician then together provide this information to the parents.

Program Evaluation

From the inception of this preventive services project for children, program evaluation was seen as an important component. Evaluation has been done on the types of concerns and problems parents bring to the service, the age and sex of the children that the parents are concerned about, and the effectiveness of the suggestions offered by the staff. Program evaluation has been done through a mail questionnaire (Eastman 1974) or through a telephone follow-up to parents six months to a year after they have used the call-in/come-in services (Mesibov 1977; Schroeder 1979). It is recognized that these methods of evaluating effectiveness have many pitfalls, but other methods are limited because of the brief contact with parents and the limited opportunity for direct behavioral observations.

At the time of each call or come-in appointment, a log is made with the name and age of the child, the primary presenting problem, the length of the contact, and the name of the staff member handling the contact. In addition to this information, individual records of each client are kept using an abbreviated problem-oriented model and include the nature of the presenting problem or concern, a listing of the parents' specific questions, and the staff member's suggested plan of action for each question. Parents are asked at the end of each appointment if they could be contacted in six months to a year to evaluate the effectiveness of the staff's suggestions and to find out how things are going in general. In the past seven years, only a few parents have refused this request for follow-up.

The types of concerns parents bring to the service have been categorized into 22 categories (Mesibov, Schroeder, and Wesson 1977). Independent raters have classified a random sample of 100 records on two separate occasions, giving interrater reliability coefficients of .84 and .80 (Schroeder 1979). Table 6-1 lists the categories of concern and gives the percentage of calls for each category for the years 1973–1976, 1977–1978, and 1978–1979. The categories are generally self-explanatory, but those needing some clarification are as follows:

(a) *Negative behaviors* refer to behaviors directed at parents such as noncompliance, oppositional, having tantrums, demanding, and whining.

(b) *Toileting* refers to toilet training, enuresis, and encopresis.

Table 6-1

Call-In/Come-In Services:
Percentage of Concerns According to Problem

Problem	1973–1976 (n=672 concerns)	1977–1978 (n=277 concerns)	1978–1979 (n=248 concerns)
Negative behaviors	15	14	18
Toileting	13	7	7
Developmental delays	11	6	3
School problems	11	7	8
Sleeping problems	10	8	8
Personality or emotional problems	8	18	8
Sibling/peer problems	8	8	8
Divorce/separation problems	6	6	11
Infant management	2	1	2
Family problems or concerns	3	5	6
Sex-related issues or problems	2	4	<1
Food/eating problems	1	1	—
Specific fears	2	1	2
Specific bad habits	1	3	1
Parents' negative feelings toward child	2	1	3
Physical complaints	1	4	<1
Parents' concerns regarding school	1	3	3
Adoption/foster/ guardianship	1	<1	<1
Moving	1	<1	2
Miscellaneous	<1	<1	<1
Death	<1	<1	2
Guidance of talented child	<1	<1	<1

Table 6-1 illustrates the percentage of concerns according to problems reported by parents through the call-in/come-in services between the years 1973 and 1979.

(c) *Personality or emotional problems* refer to lack of self-control, lack of motivation, failure to assume responsibility, lying, stealing, and excessive dependency.

(d) *Sibling/peer problems* refer to not sharing, aggression, and rivalry.

(e) *Family problems* refer to parents disagreeing on discipline, the mother feeling isolated, parents arguing, and child abuse.

It is clear from the wide variety of problems parents brought to these services that the staff should have a sound background in child development and the management of children's problems in order to effectively help the parents. The staff and students of this project are fortunate to be part of a clinic with twelve health-related disciplines that can be easily tapped for specific information outside a staff member's area of expertise. For example, questions on how much a child should be eating could best be answered by input from nutritionists, and questions on the effects of thumb sucking on teeth are best answered with some input from a pedodontist.

The staff's ability to deal quickly and effectively with a variety of issues has increased over the years, but the complexity of the questions and concerns parents bring to the service remains a challenge. The increase in the number of questions on the effects of divorce, separation, and custody issues from 6 percent in 1973–1976 and 1977–1978 to 11 percent in 1978–1979 seems to reflect the national increase in divorce and separation. Concerns in this area include questions on how and when to tell children about a separation, visitation schedules, changing children's names to that of a new stepfather without adoption, the sudden and intense changes in a child's behavior, and the effects of parents dating and "live-ins" on children. The change in custody practices also involves questions about the effects of joint custody on children. The professionals involved in answering these questions need understanding of children's needs as well as skill in working with the hostility felt and projected by parents about each other. Helping a parent to see how his/her anger affects a child's relationship with the other parent is as important as setting up the most desirable living arrangements for a child. Also, considerable skill is needed to assess a child's understanding of what is happening so that reasonable decisions about the child's involvement in any agreement can be made (Mesibov, Schroeder, and Wesson 1977). The staff have found themselves on a number of occasions being asked to go to court to present their views on the effect of certain living or visitation arrangements on children.

The data on the type and frequency of parental concerns presented in Table 6–1 point out not only the training needs for a staff providing these services to parents but also the areas in which professionals should provide a wider range of preventive services in the community. It is recognized that each community is unique and that the generality of the findings is restricted by the middle socioeconomic class using the service and by the private pediatric office setting in which the service is offered. The data-based model, however, on which this service is operated should be generalizable to any setting or population.

Examples of attempts to use the information parents bring to the service to find more effective ways of meeting their needs can be seen in the categories of toilet training, developmental delays, and, most recently, negative behaviors. The significiant decrease in calls and come-in appointments on concerns regarding toileting (13 percent in 1973–1976 to 7 percent 1977–1978 and 1978–1979) could be, in part, the result of an evening parent group meeting on toilet training begun in 1977. The last class was attended by 35 parents, and a request was made to hold similar classes several times a year. In addition to toilet-training problems, the 1973–1976 records included a number of children who were encopretic. A closer look at the individual records showed that a large percentage of the calls on this problem occurred in September and October with children age six who attended one of two elementary schools. A quick investigation at the two schools discovered bathrooms with no toilet paper, little privacy, and rules limiting available times to use the bathroom. This situation for a child who is going to school for the first time can be quite upsetting. The result seemed to be a refusal by the child to use the school's bathroom facilities for bowel movements and then to lose control later in the day. When the bathroom problems were discussed with the school administration and the appropriate changes were made, the number of encopretic six-year-olds in the fall of each year dropped dramatically!

The concerns over developmental delays were most often (46 percent) about preschool children (Mesibov, Schroeder, and Wesson 1977). These concerns centered on motor, cognitive, social, and language development. This information led to the establishment of routine screening in the pediatric office for three-year-olds with the Denver Developmental Screening Test. By offering the screening session, parents were able to get direct feedback on how their child was developing, and some parents no longer seemed to need the intermediary step of the call-in/come-in services. The drop of concerns in this area from 11 percent in 1973–1976 to 6 percent in 1977–1978 and to 3 percent in 1978–1979 is felt, in part, to be due to this additional service; yet, it is recognized that other factors such as the pediatricians answering more questions in this area or evening parent groups could also account for some of the decrease.

The consistently high number of concerns about negative behavior and the increase in these concerns to 18 percent of all the concerns brought to the project in 1978–1979 are disconcerting. Not only did more parents have concerns, but the concerns crossed all age levels. The majority of concerns in this area are with children six years and younger, but there are a fair percentage (25–30 percent) of concerns about older children. In the 1977–1978 follow-up, parents indicated that the staff's specific intervention suggestions were very effective, but that they (the parents) continued to have problems with negative behavior. When the parents were asked if they had any additional concerns or problems, 66 percent reported an average of 7.4 additional problem categories including sibling/peer problems, specific bad habits, and the parent feeling negative toward the child.

These findings prompted the staff to attempt an early intervention program with these "negative" children and their parents (Milar and Schroeder 1979). Now when a parent contacts the service with a primary complaint of negative behavior, particularly with a preschooler, the staff try to determine if the presenting problem is specific to one situation such as bedtime or if the negative behavior occurs across many situations and is an indicator of more serious problems in the parent-child interaction. If there is concern about the parent-child interaction, the staff will tell the parent about the early intervention program. Parents have been quick to enter into this program. The focus of the program is to increase positive parent-child interactions as well as to teach parents how to make and follow through on commands to their children. The goal of the individual one-hour-a-week six-week program is not only to intervene in the current negative interactions but also to prevent subsequent behavioral problems. Following these children over the next several years will allow the project to say more about the long-term effectiveness of the program.

An interesting and rather confusing finding was the abrupt increase in concerns about emotional/personality problems from 8 percent for 1973–1976 to 18 percent for 1977–1978. One hypothesis was that the parents, in general, had increased confidence in the services offered and, therefore, brought these more difficult problems to the staff's attention. It was also noted that during 1977–1978 the town's mental health services for children essentially collapsed, and it was hypothesized that more parents were using this special project because there was not another public service alternative. The drop in the number of calls and come-in's for these problems in 1978–1979 back to 8 percent coincided with the reestablishment of the children's services at the Mental Health Center.

Mesibov, Schroeder, and Wesson (1977) examined the 1973–1976 data by age and sex. More calls were made about children under five years of age (63 percent) than for older children, but the number of calls on older children has increased slightly over the years. Interestingly, a number of teenage girls have elected to use this special service to discuss family problems and personal concerns. The project had significantly more calls on boys (60 percent) in the areas of toileting, developmental delays, school problems, and personality/emotional problems. These overall sex diffences should come as no surprise to clinicians who have worked with children.

The effectiveness of the staff services has been evaluated by Eastman (1974), Mesibov (1977) and Schroeder (1979). Eastman did a mail questionnaire study of the first 100 parents who used the call-in/come-in services and found 95 percent of the parents viewed the suggestions given to them as very helpful. Eighty-two percent of the parents reported that the problem they had identified was either greatly improved or gone. Since the initial study, phone follow-ups have been made six months to a year after the original call, and parents are asked to evaluate the effectiveness of specific suggestions on a 1-to-5 scale, with 1 being not effective and 5 being very effective. Confidence in the staff has been consistently high with an averaged 4-to-5 rating on the 5-point scale. This high confidence rating is true even for parents who have not found specific suggestions very effective. Parents found staff suggestions to be effective in the following areas: (1) focusing on their child's positive behavior and minimizing attention on negative behavior, (2) learning how to use alternative methods of punishment, (3) receiving information on what to expect at a certain age, (4) being reassured that what they were doing was appropriate, and (5) hearing about how children learn and being able to apply that to teaching such things as truthfulness, compliance, etc. Parents across all categories have liked hearing "what to expect" at various ages. Finding out that other children experience similar problems (something that grandparents, relatives, and friends often share) was, in general, viewed as very supportive and helpful. The follow-up methods used are limited, but they do provide guidelines on effective intervention strategies for this type of parent service (Mesibov 1977; Schroeder 1979). The staff initially had great concern about the viability of offering help to parents over the telephone, for an average time of fifteen minutes, but the follow-up data give assurance that what they (the staff) are doing is both feasible and helpful. The implications for the use of this service model for Class 1 dispositional crises are strong and should be explored and developed.

Assessment Guidelines for Call-In/Come-In Interventions

The interaction between the parent and professional during the call-in or come-in time is complex, particularly in view of the time limit of the contact and the lack of previous information that the clinician has available. The order of gathering the information is not as important as the awareness of the type of information that helps analyze childhood problems and facilitates response to the parents' question(s). For example, the affect with which the parents describe the problem should always be a major consideration in responses made by the staff (i.e., Are the parents angry, depressed, desperate, frantic, etc.?). The following set of guidelines was developed to aid staff and students in working on the call-in service (Schroeder 1977). The guidelines are also applicable to come-in appointments that allow a longer period of time to assess the problem.

1. Initially listen to the parent describe the problem and note the affect used in this description. At this point, it is important to give verbal feedback to the parent's feelings, such as: "It sounds like it is difficult to be home with two preschoolers." It is important that you do not immediately jump to conclusions regarding the problem and its treatment. Gather information during this time regarding: (a) how long the problem has occurred; (b) number of siblings and ages; (c) parents in terms of whether they both work, are they divorced or separated, how much time they spend with the children. Usually, you do not have to ask for this information, but if the parent does not tell you, then be certain to ask.

2. Next, try to specify the problem(s) in objective concrete language. You can do this by simply reflecting what the parent has said: "The problem is that your child is three years old and you are wondering if it's time to start toilet training?" Or you might have to ask for clarification of the problem: "It sounds like you are concerned about your five-year-old's temper tantrums, as well as the different ways you and your husband are handling these tantrums?" It is very important that the problem(s) be clearly stated in this stage. The greatest difficulty in answering questions comes at this point when the staff members assume that the parent's concern is clear to them as well as to the parent.

3. Gather specific information about the problem(s). If there are several distinct problems, you might want to focus on a major one ("major" being determined by the parent's view rather than yours). Ask leading questions to gather information in the following areas:

   a. *Antecedents of the problem.* What seems to set off the problem? When does it occur? Where does it occur? A major question you want to keep in mind is, What role does the *environment* play in this problem? For example, a very active child might be overactive in an open or unstructured classroom, yet do fine in a structured classroom. A two-year-old in a house full of antiques is more likely to present management problems than in a house with few restrictions. Clues pertaining to *physical* antecedents should also be explored. For example, consider the child who is five years old and suddenly is wetting during the day. Has she been sick? What is happening just before she wets? Does she scratch herself, etc.?

   b. *Consequences of the problem.* What do the parents do? How does the child react? What effect does the problem have on the larger environment—family, school, neighborhood? What effect do the problems have on the child?

   c. *Developmental aspects of the problem.* Is the child at an age where these problems are likely to occur? Is the child delayed in an area? Is the child precocious? Are the parents expecting too much or too little?

4. You now should have some idea about the problem(s) or at least some hypothesis as to what areas need further exploration. For example:

    a. Is the problem environmentally based?

    b. Is the problem a developmental problem?

    c. Is the problem a physical problem?

    d. Do the consequences need to be changed?

5. Share your ideas with the parents and make your suggestions based on your hypothesis as to the nature of the problem. If you are uncertain, suggest a come-in appointment or a physical examination if you think the problem is in that area.

6. Suggested Interventions for Specific Problems:

    a. If a referral to another agency is made, give the parents the specific information such as a phone number or person to contact. If you are concerned about follow-through, then ask if you could make the call for them.

    b. Be sure to provide appropriate emotional feedback during the conversation; for example: "A child crying all night is upsetting." Or: "I can understand how difficult it is to change sheets every day."

    c. If you have a call on which you cannot get closure, you can either make a come-in appointment for the parents or indicate that you will discuss it with other members of the staff and have someone call them back.

    d. If you make a referral, be certain to let the child's primary physician in the pediatric office know about this. However, this is not necessary if the child is not a patient in the practice.

    e. If you feel the case is an emergency, discuss it with the primary physician and make an immediate plan of action.

SUMMARY

The preventive services for children model presented here demonstrates the feasibility of handling many parental concerns on child management and development by brief phone or face-to-face contacts. The scope of preventive services available to children and their families can be broadened by collaboration with pediatricians, who are the primary child-care providers. The data gathered from the call-in/come-in services provided information on the various types of concerns parents have and on effective intervention methods to meet those concerns. The services provided by this project were able to be carried out by the staff and students from several disciplines, including psychology, social work, and nursing, all of whom had had training in child-development and child-management techniques.

REFERENCES

BUTCHER, J., and G. MAUDEL, "Crisis Intervention," *Clinical Methods in Psychology,* I. Weiner, ed. New York: John Wiley & Sons, Inc., 1976.

EASTMAN, J., "An Evaluation of a Pediatric Call-In Service: A Challenge to Preventive Social Work." Master's thesis, University of North Carolina at Chapel Hill, 1974.

MESIBOV, G. B., "Effectiveness of Several Intervention Strategies with Some Common Child-Rearing Problems." Paper presented at the meeting of the American Psychological Association, San Francisco, 1977.

MESIBOV, G. B., C. S. SCHROEDER, and L. WESSON, "Parental Concerns about Their Children," *Journal of Pediatric Psychology,* 2 (1977), 13–17.

MILAR, C., and C. S. SCHROEDER, "Prevention-Oriented Model for Early Intervention in Maladaptive Mother/Child Dyads." Paper presented at the meeting of the American Psychological Association, New York, 1979.

SCHROEDER, C. S., "Assessment Guidelines for Come-In/Call-In Interventions." Manuscript, University of North Carolina at Chapel Hill, 1977.

———, "Psychologists in a Private Pediatric Practice," *Journal of Pediatric Psychology,* 4 (1979), 5–18.

SCHROEDER, C. S., E. GOOLSBY, and S. STANGLER, "Preventive Services in a Private Pediatric Practice," *Journal of Clinical Child Psychology,* 4 (1975), 32–33.

TUMA, J. M., and S. SCHWARTZ, "Emerging Roles of the Psychologist and the Primary Health Care Provider," *Journal of Clinical Child Psychology,* 7 (1978), 2–4.

7

CLASS 2:
CRISES INVOLVING
LIFE TRANSITIONS

Transitional life crises reflect upsetting, but usually normative, life situations over which the client may or may not have substantial control. The client may seek assistance at varying stages during a particular life transition. Help may be sought prior to, during, or after the life transition has taken place. The clinician responds to the client utilizing his or her therapeutic skills, and the intervention is directed to the emotional level.

Most examples of transitional crises include a change in role status. For example, becoming a parent adds a new role to existing role responsibilities. Mid-life career changes or returning to work also adds a new role component, or alters an existing role identity. The transitional phases of marital separation and/or divorce move an individual from one role back to a former role or nonmarital status. Developing a chronic illness or experiencing mutilating surgery involves a change in body image as well as a possible role change.

This chapter will discuss three types of transitional crises that have been prepared by clinicians working with specific client populations. These crises include: (1) infertility, (2) women returning to work, and (3) the therapeutic/legal forces involved in divorce.

INFERTILITY[1]

Infertility represents a barrier to biologic parenthood and in this regard complicates the transitional crisis of parenthood. Infertility is emotionally stressful, financially expensive, psychologically threatening, and often physically painful. It is all the more stressful because it is rarely *expected*.

A life issue involved in understanding the multidimensional aspects of infertility is that of generativity. Erik Erikson (1950), who developed the life cycle concept, describes generativity as "primarily the concern of establishing and guiding the next generation" (p. 267). The failure to achieve generativity leads to a state Erikson calls stagnation, or personal impoverishment. An aspect of biologic generativity is that all institutions—the family, schools, churches, and government—safeguard and reinforce this behavior as desirable and codify the ethics of generative succession. Therefore, failure to biologically reproduce may be seen as the failure to achieve an important developmental goal. Unsuccessful achievement of this life stage denies a person progression to the final and most adult state of all, that of ego integrity (whose antithesis is despair). Whether or not the theory of Erikson is accepted, it is clear that infertility represents a complication to parenthood that can be defined in crisis terms.

Concept of Infertility

Physicians define infertility as the inability to conceive a pregnancy after one year of sexual relations without contraception or the inability to carry pregnancy to a live birth. A couple should not be bound by an imposed definition of infertility. They have the right to be considered "infertile" whenever they begin to feel that they are, especially if they are over 30 years of age or if either has had a fertility-related event or disease (such as endometriosis or pelvic inflammatory disease in women or orchitis or varicocele in men, or venereal disease in either). It is also possible that single people may want to have their fertility status evaluated. For those who care greatly about having biological children, this is a reasonable request.

Infertility is frequently subdivided into primary infertility, which occurs without history or previous conception, and secondary infertility, which may occur after one or more successful pregnancies. The reasons for secondary infertility are many of the same as those for primary infertility. Each pregnancy is unique and tells nothing about the potential for a future pregnancy.

[1]This section, through p. 158, reprinted with permission from Barbara Eck Menning, *Infertilty: A Guide for the Childless Couple* (Englewood Cliffs, N.J.: Prentice-Hall, Inc., 1977), pp. 105–124.

It is estimated that 15 percent of the population of childbearing age in America is infertile at any given time. The three basic causes of infertility break down almost equally: male factor 35 percent, female factor 35 percent, and combined factor 30 percent. The general public is greatly misinformed about infertility and generally considers it a female disorder. This is why both the woman and the man must be studied in a work-up, or else the results will not be complete. The following case example illustrates this situation.

> Don was a successful business man of 28 when he married. He and his wife Jane used birth control for two years while they established a comfortable home. Jane conceived the month after birth control was stopped. Unexpectedly, at eleven weeks of gestation, June experienced bleeding and cramping. She was hospitalized and lost the pregnancy. Following this episode, pregnancy did not occur again. After one and one-half years the couple sought medical advice. June was worked up thoroughly and found to be normal. The doctor suggested that she quit her teaching position and try to "relax." After another year, the couple decided to seek another medical opinion. This doctor insisted that Don be examined as well as his wife. A semen analysis revealed a normal spern count but very low motility. Medical treatment did not improve the condition. At this point Don and June have sought counseling prior to considering artificial insemination.

Even though the infertility rate is high—involving over 8½ million people in this country—the successful "cure rate," referring to those who achieve a pregnancy and live birth, is increasing steadily. Research and technology developed within the last five years have dramatically improved the diagnostic tools and treatment available to a physician. This new technology has been made possible, in part, by pressure on the medical profession to come up with better results, for adoption, once the easy alternative to biological parenthood, is no longer readily available. A competent specialist in infertility now cures between 50 and 60 percent of his or her patients. This is an optimistic note and should encourage infertile couples to pursue diagnosis and treatment. However, the rigorous tests and treatments now available are not without their psychic cost. It is possible that when couples submit to this regimen and do *not* become pregnant, they may arrive at the end in a state of emotional, physical, and financial exhaustion.

Infertility appears to be increasing in the population. There are many speculations as to why this might be so. Certainly, some sociological trends, such as delaying marriage and childbearing into the years after 30 and the prolonged use of birth control (particularly the pill and interuterine devices), might be partially responsible. Venereal disease is reaching epidemic levels in some parts of the country. If allowed to go untreated, it is a major threat to both male and female infertility. Some doctors believe that the new abortion legislation and the resultant high abortion rate are beginning to be reflected in the infertility rate. It is possible that abortions performed under less than ideal conditions may be a source of subsequent infection and may result in infertility. It is also true that more accurate reporting and recording of health conditions will reflect a higher infertility rate.

Psychological Components of Infertility

There are many complex feelings about infertility. People confronting such a diagnosis find that they experience varying feeling states. Not all people feel emotional pain of equal intensity, but most can express feelings and emotions which are particularly difficult to bear.

Surprise

The first feeling, although temporary and superficial, is one of surprise. Most people generally assume that they are fertile. And one cannot, obviously, know if one is fertile until one attempts to become pregnant. Many infertile couples give histories of using birth control for many years. It is not until the couple try to conceive a child that the problem becomes conscious and reality based. Then they find the decision was not theirs to make.

Denial

"This can't happen to me!" How often these words are spoken for a variety of crises that can and do happen to all of us. Denial serves a purpose. It is true that as a defense mechanism it does not work for long, but it allows the body and mind to adjust at their own pace to events that might otherwise be overwhelming. This is often true in a sudden diagnosis of absolute infertility, as in azoospermia or unexpected hysterectomy. Denial often comes into play at the time of miscarriage or stillbirth. The loss is too enormous and sudden to endure. It needs to be processed slowly until it can be absorbed.

Isolation

As the awareness of infertility grows on a couple, a feeling of isolation and loneliness often occurs. This is a personal and inherently sexual problem. It is not easy to talk about. Family and friends usually keep an embarrassed distance from the subject or else they offer platitudes, misinformation, or gratuitous psychiatric advice. "Relax!" "Take a second honeymoon!" If the wife works, "Quit!" If she is staying at home, "Get a job." Little wonder that a couple may keep their feelings very much to themselves. In the process, they may lean so heavily upon each other that marital stress results. The following is one such example.

> Betty had a therapeutic abortion at age twenty for a premarital pregnancy. She married another man two years later and used birth control for a year while she finished a graduate course. When she failed to conceive after being off birth control for six months, Betty became very anxious and sought medical care. Her husband was found to be normal, but Betty had moderate adhesions of both Fallopian tubes. She underwent tuboplasty which appeared to improve her situation. Still no pregnancy resulted. Betty's anxiety over her infertility increased, and she found herself unable to work (which involved small children). Her relationship with her husband deteriorated into frequent fights and talk of divorce. Betty sought therapy as a last resort. She felt almost immediate improvement when she was helped to express unresolved feelings about her abortion. As she experienced and acknowledged feelings of guilt and grief, she found her present infertility more bearable. She and her husband have reconciled and Betty has resumed her work. They are seriously considering remaining childfree.

Another form of isolation comes as the couple attempt to protect themselves from social gatherings and events they know will be painful. It is very common for infertile couples to become highly sensitized to pregnant people and to baby announcements and christenings, yet it may be seen as socially mandatory to applaud the announcement of a pregnancy, to ask to hold the new baby, to buy gifts and send congratulatory cards. The social amenities become excruciatingly painful.

> My dearest friend got pregnant and asked me to be godmother when the baby was born. I cried when I got home—for me. I wanted it to be *me* having the baby. I was jealous. . . . I'd tried harder, waited longer. I deserved it so much! Then I thought—Am I so small and selfish that I've lost the ability to love and be happy for people I care so much about? Oh God, what's happened to me!

Sometimes the infertile couple will radically change their life style to avoid the painful memories of other's fertility. This may lead either partner to quit a job that involves children, move from a neighborhood filled with children to an area without children, and cut off ties with married friends who have children. The isolation may become extreme, until it feels as if there is no one else in the world who has ever been infertile, and, conversely, as if fertility is everywhere.

I remember going to the market one night and being assaulted by the fertile world. At the bubblegum machines, a mother was helping her toddler put a penny in the slot. A bit further down the aisle I was passed by a woman balancing a quart of milk and four containers of yogurt on her protruding belly. At the bakery one woman shouted across the buns to a young man, "Was it a boy or a girl?" It is an unwritten law that what you want most seems to elude you but not anyone else. The gnawing desire to become pregnant is accentuated by every young or expectant mother you see. And take my word for it—they are everywhere.

Anger

When a couple enter a diagnosis and attempted treatment of infertility, they surrender much control of their bodies and destinies to the care of the physician who treats them. Even in the best of medical relationships, the feelings of helplessness are extreme. At this point anger is often displayed. The anger is often very rational—focused at real and correctly perceived insults, such as pressure from families to "produce" or the pain and stress of various tests or treatments. Such anger may be irrational—displaced on targets such as the physician or the adoption agency, but it is really a result of the abject helplessness that the couple feel.

One of the best ways to release the anger without detriment to oneself or to others is through therapy or a support group, such as RESOLVE. RESOLVE is a support group designed to aid infertile couples. This forum provides the opportunities for people to discuss decisions that might seem relatively simple to other couples. For example, should they live in an apartment or buy a house? Can they justify owning a house with no children? Should they take a new job offer if it means leaving their infertility specialist? Should they spend their money now or save for the future? Should the man take a business trip during his wife's fertile time? Decisions to continue education or change careers are particularly hard for the woman who does not know, when, if ever, she may get pregnant. All aspects of life become complicated and the result is the predictable—anger.

Guilt and Unworthiness

It is logical for people to try to make a cause-and-effect relationship between infertility and something they have done (or not done) in life. All people can think of something to feel guilty about if they review their lives thoroughly. Infertile people frequently decide they are not achieving a pregnancy because they are in some way unworthy. Pregnancy is being withheld as a punishment. Some common guilt-producing events are premarital sex, an abortion, the use of birth control, venereal disease, a previous divorce, masturbation, and any unusual sex practices.

Once the guilty act is acknowledged, the infertile person goes through a stage of bargaining or atoning, with Fate or God, so that the guilty act may be forgiven and the punishment ended.

> Giving blood is painful for me; the veins collapse and go into spasms and sometimes it takes ten or fifteen minutes of probing to get a sample. But in the months after my diagnosis, when blood was being drawn regularly to double check FSH levels, I welcomed the pain. The longer it took to find a vein, the more it hurt, the bigger the black and blue mark, the better! I bargained constantly with Fate: a year of my life, ten years, my right arm, anything, in exchange for a pregnancy. It seemed there was no amount of pain I wouldn't undergo gladly in exchange for a body that could make a baby. Maybe that's what fertility rites and ritual sacrifice are all about. I am an educated woman of the twentieth century, but emotionally I guess I'm not much different from my cave-dwelling ancestors. Rationally, I don't believe in their gods—but still I bargained with them, offering sacrifical blood samples.

When the prayers, sacrifices, and atonements of the infertile person go unheeded, more anger is often experienced at the injustice of the way fertility is dispensed. On the one hand are seen abortions, abandoned and battered children, people saying they wish they had never had their children; on the other hand, the people who long for a child. Anger is felt toward God or Life or Fate that such injustice can exist.

> I began to volunteer in the local Children's Hospital. I loved holding the infants and mothering them and cuddling them. It tore my heart up to see the kids without visitors for the whole time I was there. I once again felt there was no justice in the world. Here I am filled with love and caring for strangers. Their own parents cannot even find the time to visit.

This theme can be extended to the point where a person feels there is no point in working toward excellence or worthiness in anything. Jobs, education, even marriage can suffer the consequences if a person decides there is no point in trying to be worthy any longer. Indulgence in self-destructive measures such as drugs, excessive alcohol, and total apathy may result. Most often the feelings of guilt and unworthiness are more happily resolved by the acceptance that humankind does not control all aspects of one's life, and that worthiness and fertility are not related.

> I got to the point where I realized that pregnancy is not the reward for worthiness. Worthiness is its own reward.

Grief

When it is diagnosed that pregnancy will be impossible for the couple, the necessary and unavoidable feeling which must be experienced is *grief.* To deny or repress this feeling will prolong the resolution process indefinitely. The grief is for the loss of a life goal, the loss of fertility, the loss of potential children, and the loss of the pregnancy experience itself.

> Death is a lot of things. The end of the Jones family and the Jones name. It dies with us, because of me. My husband is the last of the male children in his family. Death before life . . . before we even knew our child, because he never existed. The hardest part of this death is the fact it is the death of a dream. There are no solid memories, no pictures, no things to remember. You can't remember your child's blond hair or brown eyes, or his favorite toys or the way he laughed. Or the way it felt to be pregnant with him. He never existed.

It is a strange and puzzling kind of grief. The rituals society has for death pertain to actual losses, not potential losses. There is no funeral, no wake, no burial, no grave to lay flowers on; and family and friends may never know. The couple often grieve alone.

Standing Alone

The literature often talks of an "infertile couple," but when the final word is given, unless it is a combined biophysiological problem, one person stands alone for a time and realizes he or she is the person with the infertility problem and that he or she is denying the marriage partner genetic children. The infertile partner may entertain fears or fantasies that the fertile partner will leave, or worse, stay and be secretly hostile and condemning. There may be a period of turmoil in which the infertile partner behaves erratically and attempts to prod the other partner into revealing the perceived negative feelings. This "begging the question" usually culminates in an admission by the fertile partner that they are *both* hurt and disappointed by the turn of events. This simple disclosure seems to lay the blame and guilt away and allows the couple to get on with the business of living.

> He was so loyal, so accepting, so totally loving, that I could not believe I was seeing his true reaction. I had dreams of his divorcing me or coming home to tell me he had gotten another woman pregnant. There followed a time when I drank excessively and behaved outrageously. I picked on him, I clobbered him with every physical and social defect I could find in him. We now, laughingly, refer to these as my "Virginia Woolf routines." Anyway, one night I finally got him to cry and made him admit that I had

let him down by not bearing him children—and that he was actually sad that he would never see his own genetic children. He let me know I had put him through hell to get to the point of this admission. He had not wanted to hurt me, he said. I told him I could live far easier with his sadness and disappointment than all that love. It was a definite turning point in our ability to accept what had happened to us.

Sexuality

There are few health conditions as threatening to one's sexuality as infertility. A man who is infertile seems to suffer keenly in his concept of masculinity or virility. This is especially true when the problem is a low or absent sperm count. The process of being "counted or scored" is intensely disturbing and threatening to many men. Men also react with similar feelings when the problem is related to inability in deposition of sperm because of anatomical abnormalities, impotence, or premature ejaculation. When the problem is of low motility or blockage in the transport of sperm, the man may accept his problem with more equanimity. Such problems are usually acquired and have no congenital or psychogenic origin. More important, they leave the highly charged issue of sperm production and ability to perform intercourse intact.

Women are also affected by infertility in their sense of sexuality. If the woman had a traditional upbringing, she may have defined her entire sexuality, or even her entire identity, around childbearing. When this is denied to her, she must reexamine her concept of sexuality and attempt to redefine it around the fact that childbearing will not occur. It is important for her to see that she is neither defective nor impaired nor less than whole because she does not complete this one potential. Infertile women are often able to learn this important lesson when they talk with women who have no desire to bear children, women who chose to remain celibate, and women past the childbearing age who are self-actualizing.

Women, more than men, seem to mourn the loss of the childbearing experience per se. Many women specifically grieve over the inability to see their bodies grow and change with pregnancy and to successfully master the labor and delivery of a child. These events are often highly idealized and may be the subject of dreams or fantasies. It is particularly true of women who have lost pregnancies through spontaneous or induced abortion that successful mastery of pregnancy and childbirth is important. Men, however, seem to mourn the loss of the child itself, and they often focus on aspects of the genetic heritage which is ended.

Surgical removal of any or all of the organs of reproduction may precipitate a double-edged grief process. The person needs to grieve the loss of the organ and regain an intact body image, as well as to grieve the loss of potential childbearing. Also the issue of sexuality and the loss of the body organ must be addressed. The trade-off in these cases is usually that the surgery has been done to halt some life-threatening or incapacitating condition and that the individual may usually find comfort in the reality of improved general health.

Assessing the Precipitant Event

A diagnosis of infertility may occur suddenly, as in the case where a hysterectomy occurs for life-saving reasons, or may take many months of diagnostic testing. When did the person learn of his or her infertility? How did the fertile partner react? How were they told about the diagnosis? How much education did they receive? What was the emotional reaction by each person?

Assessing the Precipitant of the Crisis: Motivations for Parenthood

There are two important assessment areas related to the precipitant of the crisis: (1) the individual's motivations for parenthood, and (2) the individual's motivations for a pregnancy.

Parenthood as a Way to Conform to Societal Pressures

The pressure on society for fertility is strong and parenthood is a way to conform to societal pressures. Societal norms play a great part in the life goals people set for themselves. Society safeguards and reinforces all behavior relating to procreation and childbearing.

Very large families are still seen by many as an accomplishment, even in this time of world population. Conversely, those who do not bear children, whether by choice or by accident or other factors, are often prodded and provoked into revealing why they are not conforming to society's demands that families should generate families.

Parenthood as a "Rite of Passage" to Adulthood

In her excellent book, *The Growth and Development of Mothers,* Angela Barron McBride (1973) includes a chapter on why women (and men) have babies. She states:

> Having a child may mean that you are finally emancipated from you own parents. Once I was pregnant I expected them to see me as an equal,

mature, no more their "flighty kid." Having the baby is a rite of transition. For a woman to be considered "grown up" in much of American Society, she has to have children. If she wants people to listen to her as a responsible person, she has to be able to show her credentials—Tom, Ann, Billy, Wendy, and so forth. [P. 17].

There is much truth in this statement. Many segments of society see a woman's education and work as something to do "until your babies come," and going back to work while children are young is still a subject which raises great social discussion. The Woman's Movement has been a vital force in legitimizing education and career as important aspects of any woman's credentials.

Parenthood as a "Reliving" of One's Own Childhood

In many couples there is a strong desire to bear and rear children in order to reexperience their own childhood through adult eyes. How often we hear poems and songs of the innocence and spontaneity of little children! The adult who witnesses such magic moments as a child running naked through the sprinkler, celebrating a first birthday party, or tracking an ant in the grass for half an hour remembers his or her own youth and is filled with nostalgia. If a person had a sad or impoverished childhood, he often desires to live vicariously through the child and give him all that his parents never did. Most people experience a "mixed bag" of good and bad as children and see parenthood as a way to relive that time, perhaps correcting a few of the wrongs and just as possibly slighting a child in other areas. The person who truly desires a child as an extension of himself is setting up a dangerous situation for the child, who must then be responsible not only for his own life but for his parent's life as well.

Parenthood as a Desire to Compete with One's Own Parents

In psychoanalytic theory much is made of wanting to bear children in order to compete with the like-sex parent. The man who produces a child is saying to his father, "See, I'm virile too." The woman is saying to her mother, "I'm a complete woman, like you." To have a smaller family may be a subtle way of saying, "See, we are smart about birth control and are not going to breed irresponsibly." To have a large family may be a way of saying, "We can handle *more* responsibility." It is no doubt true that people wish to bear and rear children as a way of showing their parents they can. In cases where parents have been loved and admired, it is possible that the motivation is emulation rather than competition.

Parenthood as Role Fulfillment

The present generation in their childbearing years still has its roots very much in traditional upbringing. The impact of feminism and antisexism regarding roles will not be felt for another full generation. Most young adults, no matter how liberal, still define themselves in stereotyped male and female roles. The man expects to play his major roles as impregnator of the woman, nurturer of the pregnant woman, and then provider for the young child or children. Provision mainly means bringing home a paycheck, and maybe some recreation time and occasional baby-tending on the side. The woman is much more involved in needing parenthood as role fulfillment. She may have formed her whole identity around the expectation that one day she would marry and bear children.

Parenthood for Its Own Sake

Some people wish to bear and rear children because they actually like children. It has become almost fashionable to protest and despair over the rigors of child rearing, as attested to by many current books by disenchanted mothers. However, some people genuinely still like children and that is their motivation.

Motivations for Wanting a Pregnancy

It is interesting that among couples some are very *child* oriented and some are very *pregnancy* oriented. Most people express desire for *both* the pregnancy and the end result, the child. Common motivations for wanting a pregnancy are as follows.

Desire to Experience the Bodily
Changes of Pregnancy

This feeling is natually more profound in women than in their partners. There may be intense curiosity about what it would feel like to carry a baby inside, to feel its kicks, to swell and grow, and finally to give birth. This state of pregnancy is often highly idealized, seen as an almost holy state, not the very real state of stretch marks, hemorrhoids, and heartburn it may be. Emphasis is placed on feelings of "glowing" and "blooming." When a woman says she wants a pregnancy to feel complete, she is actually saying she wants to experience the total performance her body might be capable of giving. Her partner may wish to experience these feelings vicariously through her, as men are more actively involved in pregnancy, labor, and delivery than ever before.

Men often say they feel proud and virile in the presence of their pregnant mate. Women often feel "sexy"—pregnancy is a statement to the world that they are sexually attractive.

Desire for Genetic Continuity

"He's a chip off the old block!" Many people have great curiosity and pride about what their combined genetic material may produce. If the outcome is a handsome and bright child, they may bask in the glory of what they have made. If the outcome is a sickly and dull child, well . . . there is always someone else on the family tree to blame for that. The situation may become extremely loaded when there is a long line of succession in a family line or one last male child to continue the family name. Then not just the pregnancy but the sex of the child becomes vital. Women can be divorced in some cultures for failing to bear a son.

Pregnancy as Proof of Virility

In some cultures there is a great deal of machismo attached to keeping a woman constantly pregnant. In our culture, where discussion of sex is more explicit, people have other, more effective ways to allude to the success and frequency of their sex lives. In actual fact, pregnancy has a negative effect on the frequency and quality of sexual relations.

Pregnancy as a Narcissistic State

The love a woman has for herself (narcissism) may be invested in the fetus, and pregnancy may be experienced as an end in itself, not as a means to an end. In cases of neurotic narcissism, the woman desires not the child, but only the cherished state of pregnancy. Many women will confide that they feel special and pampered while in a pregnant state. The following quote describes some normally narcissistic thoughts.

> I do not ever want to stop being pregnant. My body enjoys a speeded-up metabolism. My pores have closed up, and my complexion is really rosy. I like to rest my hand on the jumping mound. I like to pat my stomach. I feel arrogant and wanton. . . . I am now too pregnant for sex. I feel virginal, precious. I am initiated into the sisterhood. . . . Who would ever have thought my whims would be accorded such importance. . . . This is the first time in my life I've ever felt delicate or fragile. I never want to stop feeling precious. [McBride 1973, p. 25]

Pregnancy as Recapitulation
of a Previous Pregnancy

For a woman who has lost pregnancies either by therapeutic or spontaneous abortion, the successful mastery of another pregnancy and labor and delivery may be very important. The following quote by an infertile woman captures this issue.

> I had an abortion when I was twenty. Who would have ever thought I would be infertile! I had a miscarriage early in my marriage and actually felt relieved though I grieved. I said, "That's God getting back at me. Now the score is even." But other problems developed and finally I learned I would never be able to conceive again. In my mind I kept going back to that first pregnancy and trying to play it out—but it is like a stuck record. I needed a successful pregnancy to finish what was interrupted. . . .

Desire to Breastfeed

An aspect of pregnancy not to be overlooked is that it allows a woman to breastfeed her child. For an increasing number of young women in America, breastfeeding is enjoying a resurgence as a valued and healthful practice. Loss of the pregnancy experience also means loss of the breastfeeding experience. There are cases on record of women successfully nursing adopted children, but this is rare and involves some unusual heroics. It also requires adoption of an infant under six weeks of age.

> My worst despair came over thoughts about breastfeeding—an experience I had always wanted. I bought a print of Picasso's mother and child and became very bitter at the thought I might not be able to duplicate that scene myself. Now that I have had a successful pregnancy I know I was right—breastfeeding was an important and beautiful experience for me.

Assessing Present Coping
Responses: Common Feelings
about Infertility

The couple facing a block in a life goal they value greatly—having children—are thrown into a situation that their usual coping strategies cannot manage or solve. A period of emotional disequilibrium follows, and it is this state that is called a crisis. . . . The outcome can be one of three possibilities: the couple may emerge as stable as they were previous to the crisis; the couple may emerge with increased strength and emotional insight; or the couple may regress to a less stable level of functioning. It is for this reason that a state of crisis should be taken very seriously, as mental health itself may ride on the outcome.

The couple in crisis are particularly vulnerable and can be gravely hurt by the indifference among their family, friends, and peers, lay psychiatric advice or platitudes. The man and the woman often have little help to give each other, as they are both in a state of turmoil.

There are many complex feelings connected with infertility. Some of them are actual and rational, based on the very real and difficult events of testing, treatment, and decisions about alternatives. Other feelings are more irrational, based in part on myths or superstitions and on childlike magical thinking about cause and effect. Whatever their origins, the feelings of infertility deserve to be studied in depth, both for the sake of the couple who may feel no one else has ever felt the way they do and for the sake of professionals who attempt to help them and find themselves unable to understand.

Self-Image

Self-image (also called body image) is the concept people have about their bodies—both the visible exterior and the invisible interior. One of the most common words used to describe self-image in infertile persons is *defective*. A defect exists; something is not functioning as it should. The defect is invisible, carried within. Nevertheless, the infertile person often wears the defect as if it were external and apparent to all. Some say it would be easier if the problem were visible so that others would understand the feelings.

For the person who brings to infertility a very poor and negative self-image, the situation tends to confirm and compound the feeling that "my body can't do anything right." The person who has a positive self-image and much confidence may be confronted with the first situation in which his or her body has failed to perform, and this situation leads to great frustration. For people who place a great deal of emphasis on physical beauty, a schism may develop between external and internal image.

> I have always been told I was pretty. I like the way I look, and I feel confident in social situations. After my pelvic surgery the doctor told me he had never seen a worse mess of adhesions in his life. He said it looked like a little kid had gotten loose with a pot of glue and stuck everything together. I am ugly on the inside and pretty on the outside. I would gladly have the reverse if it would make me a baby.

For the person who feels very stigmatized by infertility, contact with other infertile people can be very helpful. One woman who was deeply shaken in her own self-image entered her first meeting of a RESOLVE support group and exclaimed, "My God, you're all so *normal* looking!"

Sexual Identity

The concept most likely to be threatented by infertility is *sexuality*. The connection of sexuality to childbearing and impregnating is so strong that it may take a great deal of effort to understand that the infertile person still possesses sexuality. The fertile partner is often at a loss about how to help the infertile partner see that he or she is still a sexual being. Those who feel very threatened in their sexual identity may try unusual measures to recover their "lost" sexuality.

For several years after my hysterectomy I went through what I call my "Happy Hooker" phase. I felt like a eunuch inside, but, by God, I still had a great bosom and I went all out to prove it—tight knit tops, deep-cut dresses, you can imagine for yourself. It sure turned the guys in the office on. All the gals hated me. Then one day I took a look at myself in the washroom mirror and thought, "Here I am, a happily married woman of thirty acting like Zelda, the street walker." I decided it was time to clean up my act.

When I found out that the sperm count was so low that treatment was hopeless, I began seeing other women. I picked them up in bars, through my work, whatever I found. It felt good to have sex with anyone who didn't know my problem.

There is, unfortunately, no easy cure for those who feel childbearing or impregnating are vital to sexuality. They generally realize after a time that self-depreciating measures such as those mentioned not only are *not* helpful but are also destructive to self-esteem.

Self-Esteem

Self-esteem can be defined as pride in oneself. What happens to self-esteem when a person experiences infertility? Predictably, those who have healthy self-esteem and take pride in themselves will feel normal feelings and see the situation as something external and unfortunate that is happening to them. Those who have poor self-esteem often view the situation as something they must have caused by their unworthiness, and great guilt and efforts at atoning are experienced.

I could never do anything to please my parents. . . . I think that is one reason infertility hurt so much. I thought at the very *least* I would be

able to successfully marry and have a couple of kids. . . . I searched my
mind. . . . Why was I so bad that I was being punished?

Successful resolution of infertility should allow a person to regain a feeling of
being a fully functioning sexual person, a person whose self-image (however
good or bad) is at least not made *worse* by the realization of infertility, and
whose self-esteem is able to rise above this setback in plans and focus on other
areas of worth and pride.

Depression

The feeling of depression can be seen in two distinctly different
mechanisms in infertility. Pathological depression is a smokescreen behind
which some much more powerful and frightening feelings lurk. Inability to
address anger, guilt, or grief can lead to repression of these natural and
necessary feelings. A chronic depression can ensue that may continue
indefinitely until the real feelings are acknowledged.

Normal depression is a real and legitimate state of sadness, despair,
lethargy, and vague symptoms of distress. It is a natural part of moving from
anger and rage to the acceptance that a loss has occured and that grief is
imminent. When infertility is marked by an end point, such as final knowledge
that pregnancy will never occur, depression gives way to grief. One might
describe the depression stage as a sort of "doomed" feeling and a subdued,
pregrief state.

Grief

When a final diagnosis is reached that pregnancy will be impossible for a
couple, or if a couple truly gives up the quest for pregnancy of their own
volition, the feeling that is necessary and unavoidable is grief. The grief is for
the loss of a life goal, the loss of fertility, the loss of potential children, and the
loss of the pregnancy experience itself.

The first stage of normal grief is usually *shock and disbelief.* This is
analogous to denial and allows the couple to absorb the loss gradually so they
will not feel overwhelmed. As infertility usually unfolds in gradual fashion,
when the diagnosis is nearing the couple may have some notion that a loss is
coming. Shock is most often seen in the couple who experience a sudden,
unpredictable, and final event.

> We found out about my infertility almost by accident, long before we
> actually considered starting a family. It came in one blow, one sentence
> from the doctor—no uncertainty, no use for more tests, nothing more to

be said. In a way we were strangely cheated. We never had a chance to make the happy decision, "Let's have a baby." My fertile years were over before they began. The loss was somehow unreal, confusing, because it was a loss not of something concrete, but of something potential. When my father died suddenly in the night, twenty years ago, I remember that for months afterwards his death seemed unreal. I'd wake up every morning thinking: "Nothing has happened. I dreamed the whole thing. I'll go to my parents' room and find them both there." I experienced the same confusion with my infertility. It was like a bad dream. Nothing had changed in my everyday life: No one had died, no one was sick, everyone looked the same. *Yet everything had changed.*

The second stage of grief is actual *suffering*—experiencing the painful feelings of sadness and emptiness. This stage is often accompanied by weeping and sobbing and the physical symptoms of loss of appetite, exhaustion, choking or tightness in the throat, and sighing. The feelings of loss are reviewed over and over, often in waves of alternate active and passive states. This "grief work" progresses, and the acute stage of suffering will usually pass within several weeks to several months.

Finally the third stage of grief, *recovery,* begins. Signs that the grieving couple have successfully freed themselves from ties to the lost object begin to be seen. The couple wish again to establish relationships and new interests; they try to function as they did before the loss; and they show renewed ability to experience pleasure, diversion, and satisfaction. Grief, of course, may be reactivated from time to time, as the couple have reminders of their loss. But the suffering is never as acute again. Anniversaries of losses, holiday times, and family get-togethers are often difficult times. In infertility, birth announcements, christenings, and even ads on television for baby products may reawaken the loss.

The maladaptive coping responses may be due to the failure to grieve. There are a number of very understandable and logical deterrents to normal grieving in infertility that the clinician should assess.

1. There may be no recognized loss. A very real barrier to grieving occurs when the couple do not recognize the losses they have experienced. As has been mentioned, it is often the loss of a potential, not an actual, object. Friends and family are frequently not aware of the infertility problem at all, and hence they do not rally to give support. Loss in miscarriage or stillbirth, although tragic, is more conducive to normal grief work, as it is the loss of an actual child, and the family and friends are more often aware and able to be of support.

2. There may be a "socially unspeakable" loss. Some losses may be so unspeakable that those members in the social support system of the grieving couple cannot be of any help. Both male and female infertility are laden with

sexual overtones and guilty feelings, and it is possible that people—even those directly involved—just cannot bring themselves to talk about the loss.

3. There may be uncertainty over the loss. In cases where infertility is not absolute, there is an uncertainty over whether there has, in fact, been a loss. Some people have likened it to the feeling of having a loved one missing in action in war. Possible loss is not actual loss. Both the couple and their family and friends do not know how to deal with the uncertainty.

4. There may be social negation of the loss. There are some events, including infertility, that may be socially negated as a loss. Other examples of situations include abortion, the giving up of a child for adoption, and hysterectomy. In all these cases even though the loss is known, there is the expectation that the event should be kept secret and the person involved should not inconvenience others with discussion of a distasteful event. There may even be punitive remarks. Another form of social negation occurs if people disallow the feelings of loss by comparing infertility to a more serious health problem, for example, saying, "It's not as if you had cancer!" Those who do not value children or parenting may negate the loss by saying, "You're better off without children," or, "You don't know how lucky you are."

5. There may be an absence of a social support system. Because the grief work of infertility is intense and painful, there may be great reluctance to give in to it in the absence of family or friends who can give comfort. We are increasingly a society without roots—30 percent of our population moves every year. We are increasingly nuclear families. Loved ones may be far away when the need to grieve arises.

Assessment of Precrisis Functioning

The clinician needs to review the client's repertoire of learned coping behaviors as well as the client's emotional style and communication skills. Who is available to the client in terms of social network? Is the couple able to disclose the infertility diagnosis to their family? Can their family be supportive to them? What impact has the diagnosis had to their self-esteem and sexuality? Do they report any disruption in sexual activities?

In addition, the clinician should assess for depression and suicide potential. What drugs are being used and has there been any recent medical history or psychiatric difficulties?

SUMMARY

A diagnosis of unresolved feelings of infertility may be made if the person has experienced a block in the usual resolution process. Most frequently, the blockage occurs in terms of the feelings of denial, anger and rage, and/or guilt and unworthiness. Frequently all the couple need to facilitate their grief is: (1) permission to grieve, (2) understanding that a loss of great magnitude has taken place and that grief is *normal,* (3) a social support system to comfort them as they grieve, (4) awareness that grief runs a predictable course and that it ends and recovery will ensue, and (5) a milieu that is supportive, empathetic, nonjudgmental, and caring.

Successful resolution is characterized by a return of basic faith and optimism and a desire to turn energy previously caught up in infertility problems into new endeavors. The couple accept the block in their life plans and find a way around it. The decision is made to do something alternative, such as to adopt a child or to try donor insemination or to remain childfree. Not only do they discuss the alternative, but may become ready to act on it with confidence and optimism. People who have successfully resolved their infertility feelings can usually talk of their crisis without weeping or becoming angry. There is more a sense of "sweet sadness" than the former bitterness.

MOTHERS RETURNING TO WORK[2]

Although this section is concerned with the effects on the female of reconciling two major life roles—paid work and motherhood—it would be a mistake to assume that these statuses have always existed as separate entities. In historical terms, such role segregation is very new indeed, and it comes as something of a surprise to realize that throughout most of society, for many centuries, men and women have performed similar tasks, undifferentiated either as to sex or as to location.

All this changed, of course, with the Industrial Revolution. Specialization and division of labor were not just concepts specific to the assemblyline; they permeated society—neatly compartmentalizing roles that had once been seen as integral and severing statuses such as family and occupation, parent and child, male and female. Along with the separation of roles, sifting downward from the privileged classes, came an ideology; that is, the natural (morally correct) place for a woman is in the home, raising her (now viable) children. This thesis could obviously not have preceded role differentiation, but, once elaborated, it became institutionalized, until by the present century it was accepted as fact.

It is interesting that at this point, a scant half century later, we are witnessing a reversal of role differentiation and instead see a growing trend toward the integration of roles. This trend appears to be true both for the female, who is tentatively trying to combine work with homemaking, and for the male, who seems increasingly invested in family as well as in occupation.

---

[2]This section was written by Jessica Segrè.

For the woman, a number of factors have been cited as "changing the basic (!) structure of woman's relationship to work" (Ginzberg and Yohalem 1966, p. 2), including lightened homemaking tasks, reliable birth control methods, the impetus of both World Wars in catapulting women into the labor market, and, more recently, the advent of the Feminist Movement.

As with any large-scale transition in normative behavior, there exists a group of people who get caught in the middle. These are liable to be individuals who not only are socialized to a now archaic set of values, thus experiencing cultural discontinuity with the introduction of new mores, but who also perceive the possibility of personal change.

Those who are currently middle-aged are just such a cohort. And there exists an extensive body of research illustrating the effects of the early socialization process on this generation of mid-life females. Primarily these females have been found, both by their own admission and by others' observation, to be more passive and less outwardly aggressive than males. Females have also been found to be more submissive to those whom they see as holding power, and to perceive themselves as more anxious than males. Further, although there does not seem to be a sex difference in the motivation to achieve, males appear to be stimulated to perform by a competitive environment; females do not (Kagan and Moss 1962; Maccoby and Jacklin 1974; Mischel 1970).

The portrayal of the "unambivalently feminine" adolescent of the mid-fifties appears consistent with this picture of her childhood characteristics. Douvan and Adelson (1966) describe her as having a compliant, dependent relationship with her parents; favoring internalization of conflict rather than expression of hostility; gaining self-esteem through playing a nurturant role; and being uninterested in competitive achievement. Her focus, which appears as a clear synthesis of this self-sacrificing passive stance, is on a lifetime of giving herself to others, primarily as wife and mother. Although recent research has failed to support many of these findings as applicable to a newer generation of females (Maccoby and Jacklin 1974), the group of middle-aged women with whom this section is concerned were not only socialized during this past era but also appear to have adopted the primary goals of marriage and motherhood.

As other authors (Nye and Hoffman 1963) have noted, however, there is a crucial need for more detailed research and information on the relation between women and work. For example, although there have been many studies comparing working and nonworking women, the treatment of employment as a dichotomous variable (one is either "in" or "out" of the labor force) has made it impossible to factor out issues, problems, personality characteristics, etc., that may be specific to entrance or exit from the labor force at a particular point in the life cycle. Further, the detailed studies that do exist have tended to focus on highly successful, career-committed professionals, who doubtfully represent even the middle-class population (Birnbaum 1971; Ohlbaum 1971).

Writers, concluding from the studies just cited that middle-aged career women are consistently "happier" than housewives, have been unanimous in their advice to the latter: "Go to work" (Birnbaum 1971; Ohlbaum 1971). However, the fact that successful professional mothers esteem themselves more highly than their stay-at-home sisters does not necessarily mean that *starting* a career in mid-life will have the same effect. For example, if a woman feels a loss of self-competence as her mothering role decreases, does the assumption of another role really address this lack and result in better feelings about herself? Or it is possible that the woman who attempts suddenly, in mid-life, to add an unfamiliar role may in fact be subject to greater distress?

Although returning to work will be treated as a transitional crisis in a woman's life, it is clear from the above summary, that both society and the individual woman are simultaneously in transition, and that each of these processes importantly affects the other. This section will first address briefly two alternative life styles: The housewife and the working woman; next, the transitional position of the returnee will be addressed; and finally, a model for facilitating crisis resolution will be presented, based on strategies that have been found to help the woman through this transitional period.

Alternate Life Styles

The Housewife

It should be made clear that, as Jessie Bernard (1973) reminds us, virtually *all* married women are housewives, and therefore in this subsection we will be dealing only with those who do not additionally hold jobs outside the home.

Housewife or *homemaker* appear to be terms in such general usage that it is not always felt necessary to define them. Further, a major difficulty in definition has been isolating the component of house*work,* implying, as it does, a connection with the occupational world. Although some authors simply delineate the tasks incumbent upon a marital relationship—allocating them to either one partner or the other, usually in a highly sex-related division of labor (Blood and Wolfe 1960), other writers have suggested that it is the kind of work that a woman does that defines her status, and that the appropriate dichotomy is not between male and female work but between the sites of "home market" and "labor market" (Orden and Bradburn 1968).

A definition of *housewife* that appears to reconcile some of the above confusion has been suggested by Oakley (1976):

> The synthesis of "house" and "wife" in a single term establishes the connections between womanhood, marriage and the dwelling place of

family groups. The role of housewife is a family role; it is a feminine role, yet it is also a work role. [P. 1]

This formulation seems to stress both the expressive and the instrumental aspects of the housewife status. It also appears to support Rossi's (1968) assertion that task and support functions are present within each position—be it husband, wife, etc.—rather than accepting the Parsonian view that these characteristics must be conceived of dichotomously, and that within the family these are represented by proto-typical sex-linked behaviors (Parsons 1951).

In view of the seeming disparities inherent in the role, it is surprising to note that the results of two decades of research on the woman-as-housewife reveal amazingly consistent findings (Douvan and Adelson 1966; Sheehy 1976). Although a number of typologies have been put forward, suggesting that it is possible to differentiate among housewives according to their primary-role focus—e.g., housework, husband, family—it would appear that the differences are largely a factor of age, education, and life cycle, and that for the middle-class woman with children at home, the most salient status remains that of mother (Lopata 1972).

In fact, for that same educated, middle-class housewife, the nurturant role seems to encompass a degree of commitment that is striking both in its breadth and its intensity. For example, numerous studies have seemed to show that the housewife-mother is willing—indeed eager—to relinquish a portion of her ego in the service of merging a part of her own self with that of her child. This is felt to enable her to "live through" her offspring, thus sharing in its aspirations and achievements, while also delaying individuation on the part of the child (Birnbaum 1971; Friedan 1974).

Turning now to the homemaker's perceptions of herself within her other roles, two major findings appear to emerge: (1) with respect to her status as housewife, she feels lonely and isolated; and (2) in terms of her marital and more general sex-role-status, her position may be characterized as highly traditional.

Bernard, in *The Future of Marriage* (1973), has summarized previous authors in describing the role of housewife as an unwitting occupation, entered into automatically at marriage, of menial status and no future promise. Oakley (1976), in a study of 40 suburban London homemakers, found that the low status of the role was consistently stressed, as was the monotony, task fragmentation, and isolation of the position.

Marital and sex roles were examined together in Birnbaum's (1971) comparison study of middle-class/middle-aged homemakers and professionals. She found that not only did the housewives come from traditional middle-class backgrounds themselves—characterized by successful fathers, nonworking mothers, and an emphasis on stereotypic feminine values—but that as adults the housewives appeared to subscribe to a similar viewpoint. In terms of marriage, they saw themselves as acquiescent and submissive to their husbands' justifiably dominant position, and they adhered to a rigid sex-role division of family tasks. Appropriately, they had married men of high professional status, whom they perceived as concurring in their traditional ideology.

Several studies also included measures of self-concept, or self-esteem, with a depressingly repetitive quality to the results: housewives, when compared with working women, were found to be less happy, more discouraged, and more self-doubting, even in those areas such as marriage and motherhood, that are the most important to them (Birnbaum 1971; Ohlbaum 1971). Terms such as *alienated, frustrated, guilty,* and *socially insecure* crop up with alarming frequency, and one looks in vain for a single piece of recent research that pictures the housewife role in other than negative terms.

The Working Mother

According to the U.S. Department of Labor 1975, as of April 1974, 45 percent of the noninstitutionalized female population over the age of 16 were in the labor force. Women comprised 39 percent of the total workers, as compared to 33 percent in 1960, and 29 percent in 1950. Patterns of female labor force participation have changed dramatically since 1940, when the highest proportion of women worked prior to marriage, after which a decline ensued and continued over the course of the life cycle. By 1960 the age distribution of women workers was bimodal, with the first peak continuing in the early years, but a second and even higher point evident in the 45–55 year range. In 1974 the early 20's were again the peak years for labor force participation, with 61 percent of all women in that age bracket working; but now the rates for the most fertile childbearing years, 25–34, showed the sharpest increase. For women college graduates whose husbands earned more than $10,000 in 1974, the proportions of working wives were as follows: 68 percent with no children under 18, 60 percent with children 6–17, and 39 percent with children under 6 years (U.S. Department of Labor 1975; 1976).

In terms of occupation, there has been little overall change in the distribution of women workers during the last fifteen years. In both 1960 and 1970 more than 50 percent of employed women were working in clerical, operative, or service positions, and even in the professional and technical fields where women are heavily represented, they tend to fall at the lower-status end of each category (e.g., elementary and secondary school rather than college teachers). Marital status appears to have little effect on the distribution of female occupations, and the small differences noted are felt to be primarily a factor of age (U.S. Bureau of the Census 1970; U.S. Department of Labor 1975).

From the point of view of their own life cycle, it would appear that, for most women, attachment to the labor force undergoes a phasing in-and-out process, determined primarily by maternal status. A second, and more recent pattern of female work attachment is that of the career-committed mother. This term is generally used to refer to a person who, despite marriage and a family, has maintained continuous ties to an occupation, which is also particularly satisfying to her. The occupation is usually assumed to be a high status or professional one, and to have involved extensive training and experience (Birnbaum 1971; Holmstrom 1972).

In terms of roles, it is evident from the studies of middle-class, educated, working mothers that in opting to add a status (work), they have in no sense subtracted another one (housewife). Although most research shows that husbands of employed wives do more of the actual housework and the women themselves do less (Blood 1963; Hoffman 1963), the responsibility for running and organizing the home and its occupants remains with the wife (Poloma and Garland 1971).

A second echo of traditional sex-role ideology lies in the pattern of dominance within the marriage relation. Even among the most highly trained and professionally successsful dual-career couples, there appears to be a tendency for the wife to accede to her husband (Birnbaum 1971; Holmstrom 1972).

These examples, however, appear to represent the last vestiges of a traditional perspective. In the main, studies of working mothers, when compared to housewives of similar middle-class status, consistently show the working mothers to be more liberal and self- and achievement-oriented in terms of sex roles, and more independent, assertive, and self-assured in their personality makeup. As opposed to homemakers, for whom maternity was seen as a focal status, professional mothers seem to be equally involved in both interpersonal and achievement roles. Further, affiliative and achievement needs appear to be clearly distinguished from each other, and there is no evidence that the working woman attempts to submerge her identity in order to succeed through either her husband or her children. Indeed, her career provides an independent avenue for achievement motivation; and although she remains constantly aware of the strains inherent in combining her various roles, she sees these difficulties as problems to be solved—by flexibility, by mutual task-sharing, by an ordering of priorities—rather than as immutable impediments to her chosen life style (Birnbaum 1971; Fogarty, Rappoport, and Rappoport 1971; Holmstrom 1972; Ohlbaum 1971).

It is not surprising, given this picture of the self-confident, well-integrated career mother, that studies have also shown that this woman esteems herself more highly and feels generally more satisfied with life than her housewife counterpart (Birnbaum 1971; Ohlbaum 1971). Further, an important component of self-concept for the employed woman is in the area of work itself, and here the research has been unanimous in presenting the middle-class, educated, working mother as extremely contented in her professional role (Holmstrom 1972).

The Transitional Position: The Returnee

Despite a notable lack of studies, there has been no dearth of opinions as to whether women should or should not return to work, or as to when. As far back as 1946, Komarovsky (1972) was writing of the conflict for college women of simultaneously facing "feminine" and "modern" (achievement) roles; but, in general, the postwar period, with its idealization of the housewife, intimated dire consequences for all involved should a mother withdraw even part of her emotional commitment from her family (Bowlby 1965). As late as 1969, Blood stated that, "if a husband's income is adequate, few wives work unless they are dissatisfied with their marriage" (p. 229).

Bardwick (1972) has assumed a middle-of-the-road tack. Although she states categorically that women who are not motivated to achieve the traditional nurturing roles of wife and mother may be considered pathological, she feels that independent achievement needs are probably also a component of the self-concept of middle-class, educated women. Such needs, however, become ascendant only after affiliative roles have been successfully enacted. Thus, Bardwick is seen as a supporter of the current discontinuous pattern of female labor force participation.

Other writers, notably Rossi (1972) and Bailey (1974), have taken a strongly opposing view. They suggest that a woman who resorts to part-time and/or intermittent work as a solution to the marriage-job dilemma risks jeopardizing her career. This can occur either due to a "blunting" of ambitions as the realities of raising a family sink in, or due to the difficulty inherent in reorienting one's role and value system, despite the best intentions, after a long period of time.

Further, aside from self-doubts concerning long-unused skills and the ability to function within a vocational setting, some authors have suggested a number of difficulties of societal origin facing the woman-returnee. In the first place, as Ginzberg (1975) points out, there has been a change in the economy over the past several decades, leading to decreased federal support for education and research and a lower demand for skilled labor. At the same time, there has been an increase in the supply of educated personnel, resulting in a situation in which job qualifications have risen tremendously—leaving the "educated" woman of fifteen years ago in a much less favorable position. Second, Leavitt (1976), among others, notes that this generation of middle-aged adults has been caught in the midst of a cultural shift. Aspirations have been raised, and new attitudes have been formed; but old ways of thinking and doing have not necessarily been replaced, frequently resulting in confusion and ambivalence. Last, in a rather blatant condemnation of exactly the need-fulfillment sequence that Bardwick espoused as necessary to female maturity, Sheehy (1976) has written:

> An unforgivable disservice was done to women who were promised pie in the sky later if they were good little role fillers now, meaning for fifteen or twenty years. . . . It is not hard to imagine why some of the angriest middle-aged women around today were the intellectual girls of the 1940s. [P. 217]

The variable of reentry was addressed by the author (Segrè 1978), in a recent study of 136 middle-class, middle-aged, college-educated mothers. Comparisons were made between three groups: part-time returnees, full-time returnees, and full-time homemakers, with the women in both working groups having been full-time homemakers themselves for an average of nine and one-half years before reentry. The great majority of women in *all* groups had been educated in the traditional women's professions (teaching, nursing, etc.), with only two women having eventually pursued professional degrees.

Results indicated that, on the whole, the part-timers were leading the most satisfying lives, whereas both the homemakers and the full-time workers were experiencing some dysphoria, albeit for different reasons. The fact that the part-timers appeared to be happier seemed the result of two factors: (1) their recognition of and attendance to the important motivators in their lives; and (2) their feelings, unlike those in either group, that they themselves had clearly *chosen* their current position.

It was striking that the early motivators, which the women shared in common, including the needs for conformity, compliance, dependency, and order, remained salient—again for all women—at mid-life. It was only the part-timers, however, who consciously based their decisions on these factors, carefully balancing their roles as wives, mothers, and employees. They neither denied the importance of incipient needs, such as the homemakers did when they disparaged paid work; nor did they ignore the importance of once-crucial needs, such as the full-time returnees did when they disparaged their marriages.

Of the three groups, the full-timers had the least happy marriages. This condition seemed inextricably linked to the feeling that they had not freely chosen to return to work, although many, nonetheless, enjoyed their jobs. They subscribed to the thesis, as did all the women, that full-time paid work is a before-and-after-appendage to one's major life role of wife/mother. They resented having been "forced" to reenter ahead of schedule (i.e., when they still had young children), and they faulted their husbands for having let them down. It is interesting to note that although there was no difference in socioeconomic status among groups (all being middle-class), the full-timers' husbands had experienced more past job *disruptions,* which had, in turn, influenced the wives to seek employment. Therefore, although the women had found jobs, they had neither forgotten nor forgiven, and they continued to yearn for a bygone day when they could still "depend" on their husbands.

Part-timers, on the other hand, not only had the happiest marriages, but also, unlike the full-timers, they did not perceive work as having made any real changes in family functioning: for themselves, their husbands, or their children. Paid work was most frequently undertaken for social reasons, again unlike the full-timers, who returned overwhelmingly due to financial "necessity." The importance of the need to balance roles was illustrated most strikingly in the area of job choice. Part-timers were not only willing to reject good positions that did not fit in with their clearly defined parameters (of time, distance, etc.), but were also quite willing to take jobs that they themselves perceived as marginally interesting.

As Leavitt (1976) predicted, confusion and ambivalence resulting from the cultural shift in attitudes toward women's roles were much in evidence, particularly among the homemakers and the full-time workers. The former displayed a strong need to defend themselves against perceived societal criticism of their position—a status that, as they frequently reiterated, was reversed only a decade previously. Full-timers were also confused, however. Although results corroborated past studies (Fogarty, Rappoport, and Rappoport 1971; Ohlbaum 1971), in showing these women to be more self- and achievement-oriented and less dependent on either their husbands or their kids for self-satisfactions, these factors were not associated with either increased self-esteem or greater overall happiness. This was apparently due to the continuing ambivalence with regard to the path they had taken, as best exemplified by their conflicts concerning work.

It would appear that the characteristics of the entire sample—working and nonworking women alike—are clearly reflective of the kind of traditional socialization outlined at the beginning of this section. Not only were all these women similarly enculturated but they had each spent long years at home enacting and reinforcing the traditional role. It is clear then that any change, such as returning to work, must not only be undertaken slowly but that *as a totality* it is crucial to these women to feel that their lives are running smoothly. It is with these factors in mind that we turn now to a discussion of intervention strategies.

Model for Intervention and Crisis Management

This subsection will focus on helping the middle-aged, middle-class woman who is still currently engaged in both marital and maternal roles to make the difficult transition between home and work. Although many of the same factors are pertinent to both the older woman, no longer involved in caring for young children, and the widow or divorcée, no longer enacting the marital role, the situation of the wife–mother–employee is the most complex in terms of role interaction and remains the modal life style for women. Specific management and intervention strategies will be discussed using the model for assessing emotional crises presented in Chapter 4.

As a general principle, it is crucial that the woman anticipating a return to work or school be helped to view the process as one of gradual change over which she has a reasonable degree of control each step of the way. Although women very commonly experience a sense of urgency at this point in their lives, once they have finally decided to "do" something, precipitous change and consequent disappointment may confirm their worst fears and may either complicate or even terminate the process of change. On the other hand, it is equally important for the counselor to stress that any single decision need not be a permanent one. Thus, if a carefully considered move proves to be a mistake, it is not then conceptualized as an immutable failure. The latter point may seem obvious until it is remembered that in all probability the client has enacted only one role for most of her adult life, frequently tolerating a great deal of stress, which has been perceived as inherent to the position. The client is therefore less likely to think in terms of "justifiable" changes, and is more liable to accept once again feeling trapped, albeit in a different role.

It is also important for the clinician to become familiar with the educational and the employment opportunities in the area. Although it is obviously neither necessary nor feasible to have a detailed knowledge of every profession, it is possible to gain a general understanding and also to be aware of the more specific resources available (libraries, employment centers, etc.). Since a move into the occupational world involves a combination of both personal and situational factors, it is crucial that neither the client nor the clinician confuse the two, particularly by attributing economic realities to intrapsychic conflicts.

Parameters of the Decision Itself

As in all crises, the first step toward resolution involves a detailed assessment of the precipitating event, in this case the decision to enter the labor market. Both the reasons for initiating and the circumstances surrounding this decision must be considered, with the counselor addressing not only the usual question, "Why now?" but also the variant, "Why necessarily now?" Referring to Chapter 4 and to the author's study (Segrè 1978), the following factors seem pertinent.

Timing of the Decision.   Timing was seen as perhaps *the* most critical factor in determining the success of a woman's return to work. Those women who felt that they had been able to *choose* the time, according to their own enculturated and internalized schedule, were clearly more contented. The major factor impeding free choice was the perceived financial necessity, with conflicts compounded in cases where the woman also had a preschool child. Thus, when the counselor unearths a perceived coercive element to the woman's decision, a number of techniques may be employed: (1) The woman's perception of "financial necessity" should be carefully assessed. Frequently the client will realize that she has overreacted to a temporary financial setback and that, for her, waiting might be the wiser choice. (2) Alternately, the clinician, but not the client, will come to the same realization, in which case a more thorough investigation of the reasons behind the client's reaction may be in order. (3) If it is clear that money per se is a real issue, as to whether or not the woman feels psychologically "ready" to work, then it is important for the clinician to explore and clarify motivations, implications, etc., with both husband and wife together. It is not surprising to find that the husband is often entirely unaware of the wife's smouldering resentment, hidden beneath an agreeable, solicitous exterior. Nor is the wife sufficiently attuned to the husband's feelings—of failure, incompetence, and so on—while responding instead to the outward signal: money.

Interpersonal Aspects of the Decision.   Because the traditional mother has occupied such a pivotal position within the family constellation, any change in her status must be accompanied by a reclarification of her relationship to all those around her. This is best done by meeting with the entire family. It is helpful to elicit first any expectations, fears, etc., of the impending change, and then to attempt to draw up a mutually satisfactory contract specifying the new distribution of roles and responsibilities.

Contracts will usually begin with such concrete issues as dividing home-care tasks and chauffeuring duties. However, it is incumbent upon the counselor to point out that this task redistribution also represents a redistribution of support functions, thus addressing everyone's (often un-spoken) fear that the mother's return to work will spell the end to the cohesive family unit. One issue that is not as crucial to the middle-aged woman as to the younger woman is the question of child care, since the middle-aged woman's youngest child is usually of at least school age and older siblings may take turns as babysitters.

The couple's relationship is the most critical and sensitive area to be explored. Results of the author's study (Segrè 1978) seemed to indicate that marital satisfaction was high only when the mother's work in no way interfered with her traditional marital role. Therefore, if a woman is willing and able to limit her commitment to part-time employment, no problems may ensue. If, however, she contemplates full-time work, or even possibly a "career" rather than a "job," a detailed exploration of anticipated changes in the couple's relationship is in order.

One of the most productive approaches for the counselor to take is to help the couple to redefine the meaning of *change*—which is frequently seen as *only* a pejorative term, implying a negative judgment on all that has occurred before. If, instead, change can be viewed from a developmental perspective—that is, not only is it inevitable but it also provides opportunities for new and exciting growth, then some of the couple's fears may be allayed.

Affective Reaction to the Decision.   A woman's emotional responses to reentering the labor market run the gamut from excited and exhilarated to scared, guilty, and depressed. In fact, she frequently feels guilty *because* she's happy and excited, and conversely, her exhilaration may serve to hide her fears and uncertainties. Further, because this is a transitional period, her emotional reactions tend to be quite labile, and since her moods are still very dependent on those around her, they (her emotions) may also shift in response to these relevant others ups and downs.

Clearly, one of the clinician's major goals is to help the client to function, eventually, on a more even keel. In order to accomplish this, it has been found helpful to distinguish three possible sources of affective reactions: (1) factors relating to the job itself, (2) factors relating to family functioning, and (3) factors relating to the woman's internalized value system. Reactions stemming from each of these sources need to be addressed differently, even though they may look superficially alike. Of course, a woman may experience the same affect for more than one reason, in which case both motivations need to be explored. In general, job-related factors (fear, lack of self-confidence, etc.) may be dealt with directly, using verbal, behavioral, and/or group techniques, and are the easiest to address. Family-related issues, such as guilt over "abandoning" one's children or anger toward one's husband for refusing to renegotiate roles, have to be resolved within the context of the family itself, as outlined above. The most difficult issues, however, are those that have been precipitated by the societal transition in attitudes toward women's roles, leaving the woman confused and ambivalent both about her position and about her long-held values. For these questions, support groups have been found to be particularly appropriate and effective, since they help the woman to place her feelings in a cultural perspective rather than seeing them as idiosyncrasies that she alone must shoulder and resolve.

Underlying Conflicts Related to the Decision.   The most frequent conflicts either activated or reactivated by a woman's decision to return to work are those having to do with autonomy, dependency, separation, loss, competence, sex-role status, and aging. The typical middle-aged woman of this era has virtually never functioned on her own, having shifted dependence from father to husband at marriage. Therefore any move toward autonomy at mid-life is going to be accompanied by enormous anticipatory anxiety, since the last time such a step was initiated, at marriage, it resulted not in independence, but rather a new dependent position. The fact that this prior independent move was only partially completed (away from one dependency; toward another), has two important implications for later similar steps: (1) the woman has been deprived of the concrete experience of learning to manage by herself; and (2) even more importantly, she has never really had to cope with the anxiety generated by such a possible step, since the internal conflict was originally removed (when she married), rather than "worked through."

Conflicts around loss are extremely important in middle age. While this may be due partly to having not fully grieved previous separations and deaths, the primary reason would seem to be the sheer numbers of significant losses that a woman experiences at this time. She is facing the loss of her own youth, and usually the impending loss of her aging parents. She is also—crucially—dealing simultaneously with the loss of her most salient status—maternity, and of the self-esteem that that role has engendered throughout her adult life. It is therefore not surprising that a step such as going back to work, which concretizes these losses, is going to reactivate the trauma with which the losses were originally associated.

It is of course important for the client to understand the similarities between present and past conflicts, and to see where resolution has been aborted, or distorted, previously. It is also important, however, for the counselor to stress that such issues are still resolvable, and that the decision to go back to work has in fact presented a unique opportunity to address a number of these problem areas.

Coping Responses

One of the most striking differences between the homemakers and the working women in this study (Segrè 1978) was in the area of defensive functioning. Although all women showed strong needs for approval and support, these factors were so crucial to the housewives that they were frequently unwilling to acknowledge *any* problem areas in their lives. This pervasive use of denial (since, of course, they were no more immune to problems than the rest of us) was accompanied by another, equally nonfunctional, coping mechanism—rigidity, in terms of both thought and action. It is clear that these kinds of defenses have served to protect women from having to face either themselves or their issues realistically. It is also obvious, in terms of the primitivity, the duration, and the tenacity of the defenses, that it would be a therapeutic error to attack them head on. On the other hand, it is impressive that the working women, themselves housewives for an average of four years previously, were able to admit and address problems on a functional and realistic basis. It is also felt that the woman who is already in the process of making a decision about returning to work is one step ahead of the housewife who is still prone to disparage achievement needs.

Therefore, using this stepwise process as a paradigm, and bearing in mind that the more adaptive mechanisms of flexibility and practicality must be seen as worthwhile (i.e., self-esteeming) alternatives, groups have been formed, composed of women at varying stages of reentry, who can then serve as concrete models as well as supportive figures.

SUMMARY

This section has outlined some of the issues and strategies pertinent to dealing with a woman's mid-life transition from the home to the working world. The focus has been on the present event: the decision itself and its implications both for the client and for the therapeutic process. It goes without saying that the counselor must also assess the client's general psychological functioning to determine whether more severe pathology is present. It is also clear that techniques will differ slightly according to the point in the decision-making process at which the client is seen. One other factor that has been addressed only by implication is the importance of clarifying the client's actual request, whether it be for support, information, catharsis, etc.

Despite the fact that returning to work has been embraced by society as a panacea to the mid-life crisis, this drastic role change, in and of itself, can precipitate a crisis for the long-time homemaker. However, if both the woman and her family are enabled to acknowledge, clarify, and formulate strategies to deal with changes and conflicts, it is felt that this transition can be made both successfully and happily—for all concerned.

DIVORCE: A LEGAL-THERAPEUTIC PERSPECTIVE[3]

The disruptive elements in separation and divorce have been well documented in the literature. Many of the unhappy results of the divorce process may be avoided if the therapeutic potential in the process is recognized by lawyers. This can be accomplished by lawyers either acquiring therapeutic training and skills themselves or by teaming up with a crisis clinician. Either approach will make the divorce less of the nightmare it sometimes is.

The lawyer who initiates an action for dissolution of a marriage does so knowing that the results are rarely satisfying—for either the attorney or the client.

The anger and pain that cause one spouse to seek a divorce often intensify during the divorce process. Many clients find that their painful

[3]This section was written by Joseph L. Steinberg and is reprinted with permission from J. L. Steinberg, "The Therapeutic Potential of the Divorce Process," *American Bar Association Journal,* 62 (May 1976), pp. 617–20.

positions deteriorate even more during the legal action as pressures mount and postures harden. The final judgment of the court too often results in a parceling out of pain to assure each former spouse a share of fiscal pressures, wounded pride, and vengeful dreams.

Because these pains frequently persist long after judgment, court calendars are clogged with the fallout. Contempt actions and motions to modify alimony, support, custody, or visiting rights have become a major judicial function. Each of these postdivorce actions or motions is tumultuous testimony to the failure of the parties to resolve the basic issues equitably. Each is an angry attempt to change the balance of the judicial scale.

Given the adversary nature of our legal system, some of the unhappy results are understandable. But given its flexibility, many of the unhappy results are avoidable.

Therapeutic Divorce Is Possible

Therapeutic divorce, in which couples use the legal process to accommodate their differences rather than magnify them, is possible. Personal growth, in which couples mourn the death of their marriage rather than intensify their bitter emotional relationship, is possible. Negotiations that result in an appreciation of the other spouse's needs and a tempering of demands is possible. The goal is to achieve divorce of emotions while seeking the legal divorce.

If attorneys will approach the divorce as therapeutic agents as well as legal counselors, the pain may lead to growth rather than destruction. If they will counsel their clients to be agents for resolution rather than warriors for victory, their clients will achieve more. If they will use their skills to dissipate angers rather than intensify them, more clients will complete the dissolution process with satisfaction.

These salutary results are not easily achieved, but they require no more effort than the typically contentious *pendente lite* hearing or the traditionally pugnacious contested divorce.

The world of psychotherapy has much to offer the legal profession. Like the attorney, the therapist deals with people in stress and with resolution of problems that disrupt the lives of his clients. Unlike the attorney, however, the therapist looks to the people in pain to resolve their own problems and rarely represents one of the parties in an attempt to conquer the other.

A combination of legal knowledge and therapeutic insights could transform the divorce process and alter the lives of the families drawn into its orbit. There are two basic paths the divorce attorney can follow to achieve therapeutic results.

Psychotherapeutic Training
May Be Acquired

One path is for lawyers personally to gain training in psychotherapeutic techniques in order to sharpen their existing counseling skills. Neighboring colleges and universities offer courses in therapeutic skills. The wide growth of private therapy training centers makes it probable that there is a reputable center nearby. Many hospitals have training programs in their mental health clinics. I am in my second year of training as a family therapist in Connecticut's Bristol Hospital.

Whatever source of training a lawyer turns to, be assured that most therapists are genuinely pleased to welcome lawyers into their field. The enthusiasm of the staff at Bristol Hospital has made me feel like a welcome participant.

Most mental health practitioners are acutely aware of the key role attorneys play in the major traumatic experiences of their clients' lives. They see the attorney's ability to intervene with skill both legally and therapeutically during times of major stress as a means of minimizing both the client's trauma and the therapist's caseload.

Mental health practitioners also welcome the opportunity to expose lawyers to the mental health field in the hope that the two professions may then find a basis for cooperatively serving the many clients who need both disciplines.

I serve as a volunteer in the inpatient psychiatric service of Hartford Hospital. In more than half its beds, there are patients who have divorce-related ills as a significant part of their problems. Some of those patients might have been less traumatized had the divorce process been handled by therapeutically oriented attorneys.

Creating an Attorney-Therapist
Team

The second path to therapeutic results in divorce cases is for the attorney to work with a therapist in an attorney-therapist team in order to expand the attorney's counseling insights.

Consider the initial divorce interview. "I want a divorce" is a universal cry with myriad meanings. For some clients it means "I'm scared," or "I'm angry," or "I'm hurt." To others it means "He's stronger than I am, and I want to use you as a club to increase my power while we continue to argue," or "She threatened me and used the word divorce. I'll be damned if I want her to get in the first blow." For some it means what it says, "I want a divorce."

A therapeutically inclined attorney recognizes the latent ambiguity and listens for clues to the reluctance that lies just beneath the surface. A substantial percentage of potential divorce clients are truly eager to have their reluctance exposed and their uncertainty clarified.

Unless the attorney is experienced in therapeutic techniques and is willing to schedule a series of conferences to resolve the client's uncertainty, the client should first be referred to the sensitive probing of a therapist. Until the issue has been explored and his uncertainty has been resolved, the divorce attorney has no clear role. By working closely with a consulting therapist, after securing the necessary releases, attorneys not only gain a clearer understanding of their client's intent than they could get by their own efforts, but they also often gain a clearer understanding of the client's negotiation priorities as well.

Teaming with a therapist often increases an awareness of those settlement terms that the attorney may otherwise overlook. The most important negotiation issues are often the most subtle.

The therapist's office also serves as a place where the rage that interferes with a constructive divorce can be released. A client in therapeutic counseling is less likely to assume the kind of negotiation postures that escalate the marital differences into deadly combat.

The client in therapeutic counseling is more likely to bury the marriage, accept its death, and move out into the future without constantly turning back angrily to relive the past. Put in very practical terms, the client in therapeutic counseling is less likely to become a source of motions to modify.

Perhaps the most attractive bonus available to the attorney who uses therapeutic techniques or who works as a team with a therapist is the increased ability to satisfy the client. It is not uncommon for attorneys to find that many clients whose marriages they have helped to dissolve go elsewhere for their later legal needs. However skilled they might have been in procuring the earlier divorce, their lack of perception of the psychological issues has resulted in dissatisfaction. The role the attorneys played in the adversary process, in which bitterness clouded the client's life after the divorce, is another source of client dissatisfaction.

Principles of Constructive Dissolutions

There are four basic principles that enable divorce attorneys to help their clients toward constructive dissolutions. If those principles are adopted and followed to their logical conclusion, many more divorce clients will find themselves able to deal with the needs of all the people affected by the divorce: husband, wife, children, grandparents, and friends. Bitter divorces, propelled by vindictiveness, can do damage to a wide range of people both within the marriage and on its perimeter.

1. The Parties Must Establish Reasonable Communication

The first principle is based on the conviction that no matter what the cause of the breakdown of the marriage, it is vitally important for both parties to be on the best possible terms during the dissolution of the marriage. People who talk to each other are rarely as vengeful as those who have no contact and are not as likely to circulate defamatory stories, to use children as weapons, to empty joint bank accounts surreptitiously, or to lie during negotiations. People who talk to each other have taken the first essential step toward finding a constructive path to the dissolution of their marriage.

The same intimate understanding of the spouse that enables one mate to prod the other into a rage with as few as four carefully chosen words can be used to engage that mate in relaxed conversation. Communication at the time of divorce often degenerates into an exchange of invectives and inneundoes. An attorney's office is the ideal place to introduce cooling reality into the heated atmosphere. With the therapeutic attorney's urging, with an exploration of what approaches might be most fruitful, and with a careful explanation of the pragmatic benefits that often result, clients can be encouraged to follow this constructive behavior.

Because reasonable communication during dissolution is so uncommon, and so difficult to achieve when the parties are left to their own devices, it generally happens only when someone with therapeutic insights makes an issue of its benefits. Once one of the parties accepts the concept, the other generally follows the lead.

2. The Divorce Is the Client's, Not the Attorney's

The second principle arises because the attorney has dealt with many divorces and because the client is generally new to the courtroom. The client, therefore, often expects the attorney to take charge. The attorney is asked to decide whether to issue the writ; to decide whether to ask for alimony; to decide how much support to seek; to decide what the visiting rights should be.

Only the clients should make those decisions. Only they can possibly know what decisions will meet their needs and can make choices that will wear well for them in the years after divorce. The attorney's and the client's values cannot possibly be so similar as to permit the attorney to make appropriate judgments on behalf of the client.

To permit clients to depend on attorneys' judgments about their life is to reinforce the most destructive self-image arising from a broken marriage: "I am a failure. I cannot succeed." It fosters dependence. If counsel make the decisions, they prevent their clients from developing confidence in their ability to handle their own lives after divorce. Once the judge pounds the gavel, the attorney will most likely disappear from the scene. It is vital that clients be encouraged to assume independence as early in the process as possible.

3. Spouses Should Negotiate the Terms of Their Divorce Directly with Each Other Whenever Possible

The third principle holds that once the client has thought through the issues and has come to a series of decisions, the attorney should stand aside and urge that the negotiations be held directly with the other spouse—without counsel present. If one attorney undertakes to negotiate on behalf of a client, the negotiations must then necessarily be conducted through the other spouse's attorney. This increases the participants to four and multiplies the opportunities for misinterpretation.

If you remember the party game called "Telephone," you know how garbled the simplest messages can become as they pass around the circle. In the emotionally charged atmosphere of a divorce, one client's impassioned self-concern is often heard as an infuriating demand as it passes from ear to mouth among four people.

Too often, if attorneys undertake negotiations, their values creep in to replace the clients'. It is a subtle but almost inevitable process during the instinctive give-and-take of the negotiation process. One spouse is far more capable of communicating with the other than the attorneys, who are strangers to the family, unaware of the subtleties of its rhythms and values, and more likely to err.

Unfortunately, experience may show that some clients are simply overwhelmed by the presence of their mate or by the patterns they have established in their marriage. They need the protection of an attorney so as not to be consumed in the negotiation or communication process. In these cases, counsel must play the traditional role of advocate in the adversary system.

4. Clients Must Be Realistic in Assessing Their Positions

Finally, before deciding what position to assume in the negotiations, clients must consider the realities of their own needs, the realities of their spouse's needs, and the realities of the courtroom.

First, consider the client's needs and the client's abilities to meet those needs. Encourage the client to get past the initial anger and pain and those early outrageous positions: "I want every nickel he owns," or "I don't want her to get one red cent. And I want the kids."

Getting past those heavy emotions requires the attorney to take the time to listen to the painful gropings and the angry postures. When some of that anger has been aired and some of the pain has been released, the therapeutic attorney can help the client isolate the needs and the client's abilities to meet them. Those needs and abilities can then be discussed and evaluated realistically and reasonably. The attorney can question the appropriateness and sincerity of the client's positions. The attorney can offer countersuggestions, ideas that the client might not have thought of. But as the attorney challenges and expands the client's thought process, it is essential that the ultimate decisions still be left to the client.

An attorney who accepts a client's unrealistic position, for whatever reason, increases the probability of angry and protracted negotiations as well as the probability of the client's ultimate disappointment. It is far better to raise the issue of realistic positions at an early stage, before the client's position has hardened. The pain of facing reality increases as the process lengthens.

An attorney who assumes an adversary stance and encourages a client to assume unrealistic positions increases the probability of client dissatisfaction. Clients who are urged to make realistic appraisals often respond with sincerity. They are looking for the rules of the contest and respond well to leadership.

Second, consider the needs and abilities of the other spouse. Encourage clients to abandon their adversary position, to analyze their spouse's position with impartiality and compassion, and to apply the same standards to their spouse's position as the clients did to their own: the same generosity in analyzing needs and the same reality in assessing the ability to meet those needs.

When clients overreach in this area, it is as self-destructive as when they overreach in analyzing their own position.

Third, consider the realities of the courtroom. If the attorney has been able to lead the client to reasonable appraisals of both party's positions and then explains the probable judgment of the court based on those appraisals, the client generally reaches a negotiation position realistic enough to enable the attorney and the legal system to satisfy the client's desires.

The happy result of following this process is that the client's moderation often becomes contagious. Both husband and wife tend to accept moderate positions when one of them has the strength to take the first step.

Benefits Are Not Dependent
on Reciprocity

There are major benefits to this series of therapeutic approaches, benefits that apply even if the other spouse remains a hardened, angry adversary.

First, a reasonable position is a powerful one from which to face an adversary. Judges and other courtroom personnel are so accustomed to unreasonable extremes, they become supportive and almost grateful for a client's moderation. If you establish the therapeutic approach as a policy and constantly enter the courtroom representing reasonable positions, the cumulative effect soon earns you and your clients a presumption of moderation and an advantage. Your past history becomes a reassuring clue to the judge who is attempting to choose between two opposing positions. As opposing counsel learn that your position will be a consistently reasonable one, they will work to modify their client's extremes, if only to avoid appearing unreasonable to the court.

Second, your client will emerge from the process better prepared to face life after divorce. It would be far better if the other spouse were to reciprocate, but even if the benefits are unilateral, and therefore short of perfection, they remain substantial.

Finally, and perhaps most satisfying, the therapeutic approach is a much more pleasant way for an attorney to practice family law. It is less debilitating. Because it dissipates anger, the attorney can accurately represent the client's position without adopting the raging emotional extremes so often witnessed and so often destructive of attorney's digestive tracts.

It is more rewarding. It gives one a sense of serving the whole client, of being a healer as well as a warrior.

It is more selective. As the therapeutic approach becomes instinctive, the attorney learns to sense those prospective clients whose attitudes are rigid and inflamed. In a burst of enlightened self-interest, the therapeutic attorney learns to insist that such destructively programed people seek other counsel.

The unique advantage of the therapeutic divorce is that is it self-policing. There is no separation agreement or judgment decree, however artfully drafted, that does not permit mischief. If either of the parties is determined, checks will be mailed late or children will be in the bathtub rather than at the front door when the time for a visit comes.

A combination of legal knowledge and therapeutic insights could transform the divorce process and alter the lives of the families drawn into its orbit.

In summary, at the primary or educational level, people concerned with the dissolution of marriages can do a number of things to prevent crises:

1. Educate the professional and lay community to understand that divorces need not be an adversarial process. Help them to know that the courtroom is the least appropriate arena for resolution of divorce disputes. These issues can be resolved in mediation and negotiation far more quickly, less expensively, and with greater personal satisfaction.

2. Encourage people to maintain communication between spouses. Preventative interaction is best accomplished with a third party trained in the skills of marital communication. Outreach programs by mental health centers should be encouraged.

3. Therapeutic intervention, when there is marital crisis, should not involve individual psychotherapy with isolated spouses. It is far more preferable to have the family seen by a family therapist.

With regard to secondary or therapeutic intervention in postdivorce crises, it is suggested that clients do best when they enter a counseling group and become aware that everyone passing through the divorce process has adjustment problems similar to their own. It is also essential to understand that divorce is not a legal problem but, rather, a people problem. Thus, the courts cannot give appropriate redress to the emotional distress that divorce precipitates. Peace comes internally, not through lawyers. Continuing efforts to seek a balance that scales or extract vengence are doomed to failure. People in the postdivorce period who travel through their lives looking back at their ex-spouse through their rear-view mirrors are as married as they were before divorce. Hate is a powerful, enduring relationship.

GENERAL INTERVENTION STRATEGY IN TRANSITIONAL CRISES—ANTICIPATORY GUIDANCE

In responding to life transition crises, the first task of the crisis therapist is to develop with the client a full understanding of the changes that have or will take place and to explore the psychological implications of these changes. The basic intervention strategy for this type of crisis, once a supportive relationship and understanding of the situation have been developed, is use of anticipatory guidance to help the client define ways to cope effectively and adaptively with the changes that the transition will bring (Caplan 1959).

Anticipatory guidance is a technique that is the cornerstone of crisis intervention when responding to crises involving normative life events and when the individual has some modicum of precrisis psychological and emotional adjustment. This technique is defined as helping the individual in crisis to anticipate certain internal or external events and to prepare for these events in a healthy and adaptive way. It is reassuring for the client to anticipate and to have time to prepare for the impact of change by planning and mobilizing effective coping strategies in advance. Such planning can enhance the likelihood of adaptive emotional adjustment to the change or transition. For example, Lindemann (1944) has spoken of the beneficial effects of anticipatory grief, and it has been demonstrated that, in cases of bereavement, forewarning of death has a positive influence on subsequent adjustment of spouses (Carey 1977; Glick 1974). In contrast, adjustment to a sudden death in the family is more difficult and is psychologically hazardous, and there is increased probability of later adjustment problems (Wiseman 1975).

A variety of group programs have been developed to aid individuals facing life transitions to anticipate and adaptively adjust to change. In recent years, there has been a trend among such groups to emphasize not only adaptive adjustment but also development of support within the group. Such groups include premarital counseling groups, Parents without Partners, and the Lamaze prechildbirth groups for couples. The importance of transition-focused crisis intervention has been receiving greater atttention in community mental health work.

REFERENCES

BAILEY, L., "Family Constraints on Women's Roles," in R. B. Kundsin, ed., *Women and Success: The Anatomy of Achievement.* New York: William Morrow & Co., Inc., 1974.

BARDWICK, J. M., *Readings on the Psychology of Women.* New York: Harper & Row, Publishers, Inc., 1972.

BERNARD, JESSIE, *The Future of Marriage.* New York: Bantam Books, Inc., 1973.

BIRNBAUM, J., "Life Patterns, Personality Style and Self-Esteem in Gifted Family-Oriented and Career-Committed Women." Doctoral dissertation, Ann Arbor, Mich.: University of Michigan, 1971.

BLOOD, R. O., "The Husband-Wife Relationship," in F. I. Nye and L. W. Hoffman, eds., *The Employed Mother in America.* Chicago, Ill.: Rand McNally Publishing Co., 1963.

———, *Marriage.* New York: The Free Press, 1969.

BLOOD, R. O., and D. M. WOLFE, *Husbands and Wives: The Dynamics of Married Living.* New York: The Free Press, 1960.

BOWLBY, J., *Child Care and the Growth of Love.* New York: Penguin Books, 1965.

CAPLAN, GERALD, "Practical Steps for the Family Physician in the Prevention of Emotional Disorders," *Journal of the American Medical Association,* 170 (1959), 1497–1506.

CAREY, R., "The Widowed: A Year Later," *Journal of Counseling Psychology,* 24 (1977), 125–31.

DOUVAN, E., and J. ADELSON, *The Adolescent Experience.* New York: John Wiley & Sons, Inc., 1966.

ERIKSON, ERIC H., *Identity: Youth and Crisis.* New York: W. W. Norton & Co., Inc., 1968.

FOGARTY, M. P., R. RAPPOPORT, and R. N. RAPPOPORT, *Career, Sex and Family.* London: George Allen & Unwin Ltd., 1971.

FRIEDAN, B., *The Feminine Mystique.* New York: W. W. Norton & Co., 1974.

GINSBERG, E., *The Manpower Connection.* Cambridge, Mass.: Harvard University Press, 1975.

GINZBERG, E., and A. M. YOHALEM, *Educated American Women: Self-Portraits.* New York: Columbia University Press, 1966.

GLICK, I., R. WEISS, and C. PARKES, *The First Year of Bereavement.* New York: John Wiley & Sons, Inc., 1974.

HOFFMAN, D., and M. REMMEL, "Uncovering the Precipitant in Crisis Intervention," *Social Casework,* 56 (1975), 259–67.

HOLMSTROM, LYNDA LYTLE, *The Two-Career Family.* Cambridge, Mass.: Schenkman Publishing Co., Inc., 1972.

KAGEN, J., and H. MOSS, *From Birth to Maturity.* New York: John Wiley & Sons, Inc., 1962.

KOMAROVSKY, M., "Cultural Contradictions and Sex Roles," in J. M. Bardwick, ed., *Readings on the Psychology of Women.* New York: Harper & Row, Publishers, Inc., 1972.

LEAVITT, H. J., "Comment II," in M. Blaxmall and B. Reagan, eds., *Women and the Workplace.* Chicago: The University of Chicago Press, 1976.

LINDEMANN, ERIC, "Symptomatology and Management of Acute Grief," *American Journal of Psychiatry,* 101 (September 1944), 141–48.

LOPATA, H. Z., *Occupation: Housewife.* London: Oxford University Press, 1972.

MACCOBY, E. E., and C. N. JACKLIN, *The Psychology of Sex Differences.* Stanford, Calif.: Stanford University Press, 1974.

MCBRIDE, ANGELA BARRON, *The Growth and Development of Mothers.* New York: Harper & Row, Publishers, Inc., 1973.

MISCHEL, W., "Sex-Typing and Socialization," in P. H. Mussen, ed., *Carmichael's Manual of Child Psychology,* 3rd ed. New York: John Wiley & Sons, Inc., 1970.

NYE, F. I., and L. W. HOFFMAN, *The Employed Mother in America.* Chicago: Rand McNally Publishing Company, 1963.

OAKLEY, A., *Woman's Work.* New York: Vintage Books, 1976.

OHLBAUM, J., "Self-Concept, Value Characteristics and Self-Actualization of Professional and Non-Professional Women." Doctoral dissertation, San Diego, Calif.: U.S. International University, 1971.

ORDEN, S. R., and N. M. BRADBURN, "Dimensions of Marital Happiness," *American Journal of Sociology,* 73 (1968), 715–31.

PARSONS, TALCOTT, *The Social System.* Glencoe, Ill.: Free Press, 1951.

POLOMA, M., and T. N., GARLAND, "Jobs or Careers?" in A. Michel, ed., *Family Issues of Employed Women in Europe and America.* London: E. J. Brill, 1971.

ROSSI, A. S., "Transition to Parenthood," *Journal of Marriage and the Family,* 30 (1968), 26–39.

————, "The Roots of Ambivalence in American Women," in J. M. Bardwick (ed.), *Readings on the Psychology of Women.* New York: Harper & Row, 1972.

SEGRÈ, J., "Self-Concept and Depression: Mothers Returning to Work or Remaining at Home." Doctoral dissertation, Boston University, 1978.

SHEEHY, G., *Predictable Crises of Adult Life.* New York: E. P. Dutton & Co., Inc., 1976.

U.S. Bureau of the Census, *1970 Census of Population,* 1 (1970).

U.S. Department of Labor, Women's Bureau, *1975 Handbook on Women Workers,* Bulletin 297. Washington, D.C., 1975.

U.S. Department of Labor, Women's Bureau. *Mature Women Workers: A Profile.* Washington, D.C., 1976.

WISEMAN, R., "Crisis Theory and the Process of Divorce," *Social Casework,* 56 (1975), 205–12.

8

CLASS 3:
CRISES RESULTING
FROM TRAUMATIC STRESS

Traumatic stress crises are emotional crises precipitated by externally imposed stressors or situations that are unexpected and uncontrolled. These crises are emotionally overwhelming to those persons directly involved. The problem is clearly identified by the client. Psychological assistance may be sought immediately following the impact of the stressful event, or there may be a time delay. The clinician responds to the client by utilizing acute crisis intervention techniques.

Examples of traumatic stress crises include situations that cause sudden and unexpected disruption. The sudden or untimely death of a family member or spouse triggers an immediate grief reaction. The sudden loss of job or status disrupts an individual's life plans and/or career. A person learns of a diagnosis involving terminal illness. Natural disasters involving floods, earthquakes, blizzards, or drought create severe stress. Acts of human aggression such as war produces war combat stress; and crimes of rape, assault, and murder set into a motion a series of psychological responses for the victim and his or her family.

This chapter provides illustrations for four types of traumatic stress crises: coping with the dying child, mental health intervention after a natural disaster, treating the victims of rape trauma, and understanding the real problems of war combat stress.

THE DYING CHILD:
A FAMILY CRISIS[1]

A mother awakened at night to the faint cry of her six-year-old son who was terminally ill. She went immediately to his side to comfort him. As she responded, he asked, "Will it be long now?" she whispered, "No, it won't be long anymore, "and she carried him to her bed where he lay between her and his father. Together the family fell asleep. When the parents awoke a couple of hours later, they found that their son had died quietly in his sleep.

A major life crisis to confront a family is the knowledge that a child is dying. For example, there is now no known way to reverse the course of childhood cancer in its final stage. What options do families have to cope with this type of crisis? How do parents cope with this difficult experience if they chose to have the child die at home?

This section will discuss intervention aimed at relieving the stress on the family when one of its members is stricken with a life-threatening disease. Specifically, the example used will be of families who have a child with cancer. Three separate time periods will be discussed. First, the diagnosis and treatment; second, the child's dying and death at home; and finally, the family after the child has died. Although the examples will be drawn from the authors' work with childhood cancer, many of the principles apply to other chronic and acute diseases. Childhood cancer is a particularly relevant example in its own right since it is a source of a great deal of stress on family and individual functioning for extended periods of time, i.e., years. Also, at least for younger children, interventions are, out of practical necessity, generally of a family rather than individual nature. Therefore the problems are approached through the parents or through the family as a whole.

Diagnosis and Treatment

The impact of childhood cancer on the family is multidimensional. Hopkins (1973) points out that although the impact of the diagnosis of any life-threatening illness is generally overwhelming, the threat to a family of the loss of a child through disease is a crisis that can totally disrupt family functioning. Obviously the child with the disease and attendant poor prognosis faces a dire crisis. However, in some cases it is the parents who suffer as much or more psychological stress than the patient does. With the improvement in medical treatment, some children may be long-term survivors, and parents and family will face major problems. One mother described the terrible conflicts that occurred between her husband and herself and the opposite behaviors of each (wife becoming angry; husband becoming quiet). The stress increased each time their daughter was hospitalized. The wife miscorrectly thought her

[1]This section, through p. 192, is written by Ida M. Martinson and Gordon D. Armstrong.

husband viewed her behavior as "crazy." The husband revealed that they had never talked about their separate feelings about their child and her illness.

When a child is diagnosed as having cancer, a number of medical, psychological, economic, and logistical problems are precipitated. The previously ongoing family structure, whatever its makeup, becomes taxed and often changes in response to the crisis.

Once a final diagnosis of one or another form of cancer has been made, treatment including hospitalization generally begins immediately. In many parts of the country, cancer treatment is concentrated geographically in scattered, highly sophisticated facilities. This means that the family will be physically separated. The child is out of the home, and in many cases, is hundreds of miles from home. Subsystems within the family structure must either adapt to this change or in many cases must cease to function for a time. For example, at the time of the child's biggest crisis to date, he or she is away from siblings who may not even be allowed to visit; and logistic problems will affect the amount of support the child can draw from previous interaction with a parent, especially the mother. A parent must also disrupt other family functioning in order to spend large amounts of time with the child. In the case of those who live far away from the cancer facility, the mother may have to move to the city where the child is being treated, while the father and other children remain at home. This disruption occurs to a lesser extent even when the family lives near the treatment center. The mother will still spend many hours at the hospital. Thus a potential source of support for parents at this time, i.e., each other, is disrupted. And siblings of the patient will also have less attention from their parents. In attempting to assist the family at the time of diagnosis, it is important that health care and other professionals be aware of the immediate problems the family faces at diagnosis.

All too often the focus may be on the child's medical treatment only. Although this is, of course, the primary concern at the time, the emotional impact on the child, the parents, and, to a lesser extent, on the other siblings cannot be overlooked.

Often the child cannot understand or is not told about the seriousness of the disease. Thus his or her concern is about the immediate problems of being in a new and frightening environment and being subjected to the pain and discomfort of treatment. Nurses and other professionals can establish a relationship with the patient that communicates friendship as well as providing for the patient's physical comfort. At the same time it must be kept in mind that the child's old systems, e.g., his relationship with his mother (and father) should be disrupted as little as possible. To this end, the mother can be encouraged to care for her child in the hospital just as she was the primary care provider in the child's life before the disease developed. It may be inconvenient to the hospital staff to have parents around, and the help they provide may at times generate as much work for the staff as it saves. However, the psychological benefits, not just the manifest values, must be considered.

Returning to the parents at the time of diagnosis, there is great potential for intervention. Friedman et al. (1963) point to the problem of communicating information about the child's disease to the parents. Upon first hearing the diagnosis, parents experience a feeling of "shock" or of being "stunned." It may take several days before the meaning of the diagnosis is fully felt. At the same time there is much to do and much to be communicated to the parents.

The child's oncologist will spend time with the parents, but his or her primary time commitment centers around the child's actual cancer treatment. Thus it is helpful if a nurse can fill the role of information provider as well as that of emotional support giver to the parents. The nurse can answer most questions about the disease, and should spend the extra time necessary to insure that the parents actually do understand what is happening to their child. At the same time, the nurse can start to build a relationship, either three-way with both parents, or two-way between the mother and the nurse, that will be helpful during future treatment and hospitalizations. This entails much that has nothing to do with the child's treatment. For example, the nurse may help the parents find a place to eat or stay overnight. In this role the nurse is helping the parents deal with mundane problems so that they can direct their energies to helping each other and their child deal with the situation. When exposed to the new environment of the hospital and its rules and procedures at a time of grave crisis, the family very much needs to establish contact with someone who is interwoven into the system. The nurse is a prime candidate for this. He or she is familiar with the disease, the treatment, and the hospital. The nurse can also be a liaison with the physician if the latter is not available. Above all, the nurse can be an understanding person who can show concern for the child and parents.

The important thing to remember about the days following the time of diagnosis is that the family structure is disrupted physically with the child's hospitalization, and at the same time the ability of old subsystems to function is threatened by the psychological shock experienced by the parents. The child has the disease, but the parents and other siblings, as well as the child with cancer, all face a crisis.

Following the child's initial treatment, assuming it is effective, will come a period of months or years when the disease is under control and the family can return to its normal functioning. There is no immediate crisis, but a shift in family structure often takes place. Benoliel (1972) points to the newly protected position the child with cancer often is put in. The child is treated differently from other siblings, being given a favorite and sheltered position. The parents show concern for the child and may restrict some of his or her activities. The child may be allowed unnecessarily to miss school or may be forbidden to engage in some sports or play activities with peers. A parent, especially the mother, may even become the child's principal playmate and entertainer. This may in turn disrupt the mother–father substructure.

Interventions at this time may take the form of informal or organized interaction with other parents who have children with cancer. There is a strong need for parents to communicate with others in similar situations. They will talk with other parents in the hospital or in outpatient clinic halls and waiting rooms. They may wish to join a parent support group, which may be led by any of numerous different types of professionals, including nurses as well as lay people. Such support groups (Martinson and Jorgens 1976) can provide emotional support, practical advice, medical information, and a sense of commonality as the parents realize that their situation is not unique. This serves to move the families back to their normal form of functioning. The group also helps the parents prepare for what is probably coming, i.e., the eventual death of their child.

Candlelighters is a national foundation composed of lay people, predominantly parents of children who have or have had cancer. These individuals are attempting to meet the needs of parents in such situations. Recently a group was organized within the Twin City metropolitan area in Minnesota with help from the service committee of the Minnesota Division of the American Cancer Society. The increased strength from such a system may well be a major factor in the stability of a family unit.

The Child's Dying
and Death at Home

The second great crisis, i.e., the child's dying and death, is particularly poignant. There comes a time in the course of the disease of most childhood cancer patients when cure-oriented treatments are no longer effective. The treatments may be continued, or the child may be given only comfort treatment; but in either case it is a time when the participants realize that the probability of death within weeks is very high. For such children and their families, it is the arrival of a time they have dreaded since diagnosis. Over the course of the disease the family may have adapted to the condition including the incorporation of health professionals and other parents into their everyday lives. Now with the child dying, the latent crisis is made manifest. Although these individuals may have previously accepted the prospect of death on a cognitive level, the realization that death is imminent now hits them on an affective level.

There is much that health professionals can do to help the family during this crisis, but it is also a time when the medical system as it typically functions is strangely inappropriate. That is, medicine, nursing, and hospitals are geared toward curing and the restoration of health. A dying person does not fit well into this system. There are some notable exceptions in the form of palliative care units, hospices, and home care. The first two of these are still primarily for adults. But the third approach, home care, has been shown to be both feasible and desirable for children dying of cancer. Its success, however, has rested on changes in the relationships between health care professionals and the family as well as changes among the health professionals (Martinson et al. 1978b).

The success of home care at this time of family crisis rests on the fact that it provides a minimum of disruption of family structure so that existing coping mechanisms may work. The home care nurse acts as a source of emotional support to the parents and to a lesser extent to the child. With home care the parents are the child's primary care givers, with the nurse coordinating the care and the physician serving as a consultant. The health care professionals help the parents help their child in their own home. Thus, rather than dying in an institution surrounded by strangers, the child dies in a secure environment surrounded by the rest of the family. The child's friends may also visit at times. One mother told how her daughter had her tenth birthday six days before she died. Her 22 classmates made a cake and brought it to her home to help celebrate her birthday.

Since the parents are the primary care givers, they are active participants, not spectators, in the child's final days. The home care program provides that the parents can do as much as they wish in providing their child's care. They cannot control the eventual outcome of death, but they can play a part in keeping the child comfortable and secure.

Seligman (1975) stresses the adverse effects of helplessness. It is physically and psychologically debilitating to be in a situation in which one can neither control nor predict what will happen. Family members may have developed a hostility toward the hospital staff who are the very people working so hard to help their child. Some of this hostility can be understood in the context of helplessness. The parents are reacting to the stress of being in a critical situation in which they are unable to take effective action. It is their child who is sick; it is they who do not know what will happen; it is others, i.e., the doctors and nurses, who control the events.

Use of Control in Home Care Intervention

The use of control is very important in home care intervention. Two types of control have specific usefulness in home care with a dying child: These are (1) parental control and (2) limiting the uncertainty.

There are two aspects to parental control—the "perceived" and the "actual." Both aspects must be considered at all times. For example, in one case, the child's parents actually had excellent control of the family and patient situation, but at first they believed that their management was inadequate. The mother said, "I knew Eric wanted to be at home, but I was by no means all that confident that we were enterprising enough to handle it."

In helping parents to gain and maintain control, it is best for the nurse to avoid giving direct care to the child during the home visit. If the child needs mouth care, for example, the nurse should give an explanation of how it should be done and then let the parent do it. For the nurse to be the "expert" and perform such care would undermine the parents' confidence in their ability to perform these basic skills.

But it is also important for the parents to know that professional support is available. Crucial to this is the encouragement given to the parents to call at any time, day or night, when they need help or advice, even if it means a home visit at inconvenient times. All families have said afterwards that the freedom to call was essential to their ability to manage home care for their child. And they did make use of this opportunity, calling sometimes at 3 or 4 A.M.

In the cognitive domain, support is offered by preparing the parents for various complications that might occur, such as hemorrhage, infection, or coma. For example, the parents are told that the child may hemorrhage; therefore, a good supply of towels should be on hand so that the child does not see the accumulation of blood. Many of these complications never occur, but preparation of the parents can help avoid increased anxiety on their part. Parents were asked directly, "Do you remember when I told you there may be hemorrhaging? What are your feelings now? Would you have preferred that I had never mentioned it?" All replied that they were grateful for being prepared for the eventuality. It made them aware of their important role in the control of the situation, and if these things had occurred, they would not have become panic-stricken.

The second intervention is limiting the uncertainty. For example, one 3 A.M. an anxious mother telephoned the nurse to report that her child's leg had become cold. The nurse knew that leukemia cells can cause a temporary block in a blood vessel, thus reducing circulation; but the obstruction often moves and circulation is reestablished. The nurse explained to the parent the possibilities—the leg might become even colder before returning to normal, or the cold would continue, leading to complications. One sign of trouble would be color change. The parent was asked to keep in touch with the nurse regarding any change. Because the parent previously had no idea of what to expect, the complete uncertainty was now somewhat limited.

In another instance the parents telephoned the nurse at midnight. Their child was bleeding from the gums. What should they do? The nurse explained measures to control such hemorrhaging. She also said that the situation might return to normal without emergency intervention. Another time a child's jaw became locked, and the parents called to ask what might follow. Although the nurse did not communicate her own anxious feelings, especially the implications of possible hemorrhaging or vomiting, she explained the possibilities, including that the jaw might relax again very soon—which it did.

When informing parents of the possibilities, it is extremely important to choose words carefully, because the images that terminology conjures in the minds of the lay person are often different from those intended. For example, one nurse in attempting to reassure a mother said, "When you can no longer manage, your child can go to the hospital." The mother then asked, "When will I know the time has come that I am no longer able to manage?" This mother understood the nurse to mean, "At some point, your child will have to be hospitalized." What the nurse meant was simply that the option of hospitalization remains open to the end.

A further benefit of the home environment is that the parents' logistic problems entailed in running a household and comforting a child in the hospital are solved. With home care, it is the concern of the nurse that needed medications, supplies, and equipment are brought to the patient rather than the other way around.

While the child is receiving home care, the parents may request help from the nurse whenever they wish it. With home care as well as in the hospital, the nurse is in a position to interact with the family as an understanding and reassuring person as well as a provider of technical nursing care.

Death of the Child at Home

A wide variability exists among families in their practices immediately following the death of a child in the home. There is a lesson to be drawn from this that applies to hospital deaths as well. Rigid culturally defined patterns of behavior for the time period immediately after the death of the child seem not to exist. That is, there is apparently not sufficient precedent or knowledge of precedent to dictate what should occur. Specifically, when allowed to do whatever they wish, some families will, after a short period of time, allow the nurse to do any necessary washing to changing of clothing of the child's body and then leave it covered. This follows the model of what occurs in the hospital. However, other families have held the child's body or, in the case of babies, have passed it from one family member to another for an extended period of time. Others have bathed and clothed the child's body by themselves. Some have taken the body to the mortuary in their arms in the family car. They were not required to do any of these things; rather they were alllowed to do what they wished. Such practices shocked some of the nurses and may not be tolerated in hospitals. To the family members who were doing these things, however, they appeared to be normal and natural and provided a meaningful experience for them.

The nurse at this time can assist the family by notifying the physician, mortuary, and others as necessary. This allows the family members to grieve without unwanted interruption. The nurse may mourn with them or comfort them; however, just as often he or she will withdraw to another room and allow the family members to grieve in privacy as a family unit.

One young patient asked her family to pray with her, and they all came and stood around the bed and prayed. They opened her birthday presents and she thanked each one for the presents. She drank some water. There was no longer a strong grip in her hands. The father held the child's hand. He later said, "She just went to sleep. There was no suffering. We wouldn't have been with her if she had been in the hospital. It's much better than dying in the hospital." They were surprised she died so quietly.

Coping with the Loss

The third and final time of crisis for the family occurs in the months following the death as the family grieves their loss and adapts their family structure and activities to the new situation.

This is a time generally overlooked by the health care professionals involved before the death. Although there is usually some contact by involved doctors and nurses immediately after the death, this contact typically does not continue. Also the survivors do not seek it out because the original cause, i.e., the deceased's illness, no longer exists. Engel (1961) presented stimulating arguments that he has updated (1977) examining the role of health professionals in the grieving process. He presents a very holistic view of physical, mental, and social problems that bring grieving within the pervue of health professionals.

As part of home care, nurses can continue contact with the families. Not only did they attend the funeral but telephoned and visited the family in the months after the child's death. The families have appreciated this. At the time of death many comforters come forward. However after the funeral, families are typically isolated. The stress of the child's dying makes family members susceptible to the formation of a rapid and strong bond with the home care nurse. It seems reasonable that this bond not be immediately broken. That is, doctors and nurses in the hospital or home have been with these people at times of great stress. Now in their grieving the families may be without the very people they had come to turn to in those times of stress.

Following the death of the child, there are innumerable aspects to consider. One sibling who spoke about home care for his brother who died said: "Let's put it this way. A child feels more secure at home. He doesn't feel as if he is banned from something."

Parents of a child who had died said they did not, themselves, find the last few days stressful compared to the difficulties they had suffered during the last eight years.

SUMMARY

In summary, we have presented a model of intervention that concerns the family as a whole not the one member being treated. It involves an interaction of personal and medical aspects of approach to the participants. The roles of nursing at diagnosis, and treatment, during dying and death, and following death have been outlined. For much of this time span, it is possible that one individual nurse could fill many of the functions, e.g., the hospital primary nurse who later becomes the home care nurse. Implementation of these suggested practices in some cases involves a modification or expansion of more traditional approaches to care.

MENTAL HEALTH INTERVENTION
AFTER A NATURAL DISASTER[2]

Managua, the capital of Nicaragua, was destroyed by a natural disaster the night of 22–23 December 1972. Eighty percent of the physical structures in the city, all its hospitals, and all its fire stations were leveled by the three violent earthquake tremors. Fires raged for days; streets were impassable; communication with outside world was severed. Almost eveyone suffered some loss: either the death of a family member or friend, destruction of property, or loss of employment. The death toll was estimated at 10,000 with another 20,000 severely injured. Some 300,000 of the capital's 400,000 residents were dislocated by the catastrophe.

This paper reports the planning and development of a mental health program to assist victims suffering from psychological consequences of the earthquake. Specifically, this article reveals the work of a group of North American volunteers who cooperated with Nicaraguan mental health professionals in the definition of the mental health problem faced by the refugees, the design and implementation of an assessment of need, and the development of a mental health plan to service these identified needs. Finally, this article discusses the implications of this experience for postdisaster mental health intervention.

Mental Health Reactions

The literature on disaster reports a variety of psychological problems at the impact and postimpact phases. At the moment of the disaster, people may act stunned, confused, and disoriented, often in a state of shock. These reactions may last for minutes, hours, or even days.

In the postimpact phase, the victim comes face-to-face with daily life in

[2]This section, through p. 203, is written by Frederick L. Ahearn, Jr. and Simeon Rizo Castellon and is adapted from a paper presented at the First International Conference on Mass Casualty Management in Israel, September 18, 1978.

an environment that has been radically changed by the calamity. Some individuals are affected with a tormenting memory of the disaster, forever fearing its recurrence (Fritz and Williams 1957). It is common for these people to wish to talk about or ventilate their feelings, but others may react with helplessness, underactivity, dazed apathy, or mute, motionless behavior (McGonagle 1964).

Postimpact reactions that may last for the remainder of a person's life include behavioral symptoms of anxiety, fatigue states, psychotic episodes, recurrent catastrophic dreaming, and depressive reactions. These behaviors have been labeled as "traumatic syndrome" or "posttraumatic neurosis." Victims may also experience insomnia, digestive upsets, nervousness, and other such results of nervous tension.

In recent studies of the 1972 Buffalo Creek, West Virginia, flood (another example of a natural disaster) this postimpact phase has been conceptualized in terms of a "second disaster," which refers to the resulting social and community disorganization. In other words, psychiatric impairment may result not from the disaster itself but rather from the inability to cope with one's new social reality. In the case of the Buffalo Creek flood, victims presented a variety of emotional problems such as serious depressive reactions, paralyzing fear, terrible nightmares, and a profound sense of guilt for having lived when loved ones died (Lifton and Olson 1976).

Mental health professionals have usually maintained that natural disasters will produce or influence psychological reactions. Although this is a controversial issue, there is sufficient evidence to suggest that the emotional implications following a catastrophe may be great. Mental health experts feel that the trauma of a natural disaster and its subsequent social consequences produce extraordinary stress for the victim who may or may not be able to cope. One's ability to cope seems to be associated with a number of factors; these are diagrammed in Fig. 8-1.

At the moment of the calamity, the individual may or may not have had prior stress; may or may not have had successful prior coping behavior; or may or may not have had previous disaster experience. The type and duration of the disaster, the degrees of loss, the victim's role, and his coping skills and support system will determine his behavioral outcome. Some individuals, after a brief period of disorientation, will adapt; others will not. This stress, produced at the moment of the catastrophe, is indicated in Fig. 8-1 as "S_1." Some time later, the victim will have to confront his new social reality, such as relocation, loss of a loved one, unemployment, or destruction of familiar places, and this may also be a producer of stress. For victims, this is another source of stress that alone or in combination with the stress of the disaster impact may bring about maladaptive behavior. This stress is noted as "S_2." Finally, it is conceivable that some individuals, not victims of the disaster, may be exposed to the stress of the postimpact phase and, thereby, react with emotional problems noted as "S_3." In any case, a person's ability to adapt is correlated with the degree of stress, his coping skills, and his formal

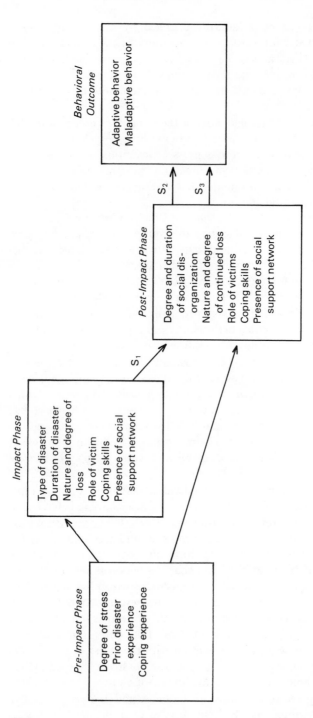

Key: Stress $_1$: Produced solely by the disaster itself
Stress $_2$: Caused by the disaster as well as the subsequent community disorganization
Stress $_3$: The result of community disorganization

Figure 8-1. Paradigm of Influences on Disaster-Related Behavior.

and informal support system (see Fig. 8–1).

In summary, the mental health professionals who planned the Managua project assumed that victims would be vulnerable to disaster-related stress and would present a range of psychological problems. They believed that mental health intervention after a natural catastrophe was an essential and integral part of the overall reconstruction effort. What follows, then, is the planning process in the design and implementation of mental health services for the victims of the Managua earthquake.

Organization of U.S. Mental Health Teams

The organization of the three North American teams was quite accidental. Two mental health professionals, one from Washington, D.C., and the other from Massachusetts, independently called the International Desk of the U.S. National Institute of Mental Health (NIMH) to suggest the idea of a program to aid the Managuan victims. These two individuals believed that emotional consequences, often overlooked, are a common result of natural disasters. One of these individuals and an official representative of NIMH visited Managua several weeks after the catastrophe and obtained cooperation from Nicaraguan officials and mental health professionals for the North American participation. The agreed-upon goal was to assess the emotional consequences of the earthquake and to design appropriate services to resolve the problem.

NIMH took the leadership in organizing the three teams, each with four to five persons, to serve as volunteers in Managua. Fourteen professionals, including psychiatrists, psychologists, psychiatric social workers, and nurses, plus a social planner, were selected from hundreds of volunteers. All except one were of Hispanic background. Financing of the teams came from three sources of funds: (1) NIMH—for travel within the United States; (2) the Nicaraguan government—for travel from Miami to Managua and two vehicles for use by the teams; (3) the Nicaraguan Relief Fund (a U.S. group that had raised money after the earthquake)—for living expenses in Managua.

The first U.S. team arrived April 1, 1973, four months after the calamity, and the last group left Managua the first week of August 1973. Involvement of the U.S. teams totalled seventeen weeks.

Need Assessment

Given the assumption that natural disasters produce socioemotional consequences, it was necessary to gather additional information to specify the types and degree of emotional problems that the Managuan victims were experiencing. Essential to this task was an assessment of need, the development of a profile of affected population groups, extrapolation of the size of the problem, and, last, an inventory of existing resources. This process was initiated so that the teams could have a clear idea of the emotional problems of specific groups of victims as well as a notion of what resources were available to bring to the resolution of the problem. This informational step would directly influence the type of plan that would be devised.

Social problems and social needs are defined differently by different societies. For example, certain behavioral responses that are perfectly acceptable in some societies would be classified as deviant within other societal contexts. A problem or need in one country may not be the same in another. Because these definitions depend on the interaction of societal norms and values, traditions, culture, standards, and current practice, outside consultants must be extremely sensitive to these differences in defining social problems and social needs.

When the first North American team arrived in April 1973, it was concerned about gathering enough data so that it could make a reasonable assessment of the emotional problems of the earthquake population. However, before this, it was necessary to secure the official and unofficial legitimation and sanction to carry out its work. The team met with the Managuan president's wife, various ministers of government agencies, the local psychiatric association, and workers at the National Psychiatric Hospital. It was able to gain the official support of the government as well as the unofficial informal cooperation of mental health professionals. With this support secured, the team began the needs assessment of the disaster victims.

Several techniques were used to obtain information about the emotional responses of victims. A first step was long discussions with Nicaraguan mental health professionals who had some experience in dealing with the problem. A second step was a careful review of case records of patients admitted to the inpatient and outpatient services of the National Psychiatric Hospital. The third step was the setting up of various makeshift mental health clinics in the disaster area. These clinics, which operated for a month, provided the team with a sample of cases not known to the psychiatric hospital.

Information from each of these steps was carefully processed and analyzed so that specific problem areas and population groups could be identified. For instance, it was found that most emotional problems were of the neurotic variety. Phobias, depression, anxiety, and hysteria were the most common behavioral expressions. It was discovered that three population groups were most affected: young children, young mothers, and the elderly. Children up to twelve years old were found to be especially vulnerable to a variety of fears, phobias, behavioral and school problems. It was common to see a young child who would not sleep in his own room or who refused to be separated from his mother. Young women, especially mothers, were another identified group in need. Their problems were usually linked to losses (death, property, or income) resulting from the earthquake or related to their inability to adjust to their new reality. Their symptoms were usually physical complaints such as headaches and various aches and pains or emotional reactions such as crying, insomnia, and the inability to eat. Last, it was discovered that older adults were particularly impacted by the disaster. This probably was related to one or both of the following factors. Many of these individuals had lived through the 1931 earthquake that had completely destroyed Managua, and they no longer had the energy and motivation to begin life over again after having twice lost everything. Their symptoms were similar to those listed above but usually were expressions of profound despair and depression.

The team attempted to ascertain the size of the groups expressing emotional problems, but it was impossible to do this with any precision. It was commonly assumed that possibly 15 percent of the 400,000 residents of Managua, or 60,000, might be demonstrating symptoms. In any case, the problem seemed much larger than any possible program to resolve it.

The team also initiated a study of existing resources. Through discussion with agency directors, it learned the range of services provided and the type of service strategies employed. In mental health, it discovered that only limited services were available. These included inpatient and outpatient services at the National Psychiatric Hospital, a private clinic dealing with problems of drug abuse and alcoholism, and about fifteen psychiatrists and a few psychologists with private practice. For disaster victims, there were a variety of social service programs, but none had a mental health component.

Mental Health Plan

In order to design any program, a thorough understanding of the elements within a plan is essential. One such guide is a consideration of four key steps for developing a plan. These are:

1. Functional requisites.
2. Technological requisites.
3. Efficiency requisites.
4. Systemic requisites.

The first step, functional requisites, is the identification and listing of the specific activities and/or services of the plan. For example, what service does the plan purport to offer? The second step involves the technological requirements of the plan, which include the material and staff needs for the purpose of carrying out program activities. For instance, one must consider space and facilities, the type and number of staff, needed equipment, materials, and furniture. The third step in plan design is that of the efficiency requisites. This includes a design for the type of administration, accounting, information, and evaluation systems, the mechanism of service integration, and the method of supervision. Finally, a planner must tie the service plan to other existing services through agreements, board representation, or contracts. These factors address the systemic requirements of the plan, the fourth step.

Upon completion of the needs assessment, the first North American mental health team turned its attention to the formation of a committee of Nicaraguan mental health professionals to assist in setting program goals, to consider alternatives, and to develop a mental health plan for the earthquake victims. Representatives of the psychiatric association, the National Psychiatric Hospital, and the Ministries of Public Health, Social Security, and Social Services participated in the planning process. Using the planning framework mentioned above, the plan may be described as follows.

Functional Requisites

It was decided that the population to be served would include any victim with an emotional problem, but special attention was to be given children, young mothers, and the elderly. Specific activities planned were aggressive outreach services to locate potential clients; provision of consultation and orientation to school teachers, priests, and other agency personnel; and diagnostic and treatment services on an outpatient basis. The latter included psychiatric examinations, psychological testing, individual crisis intervention, and group treatment services.

Technological Requisites

Resources necessary to carry out the activities of the plan were personnel, facilities, materials, and equipment. The committee decided to use interdisciplinary mental health teams, each of which would include a psychiatric nurse, a social worker, and a psychologist. Given financial resources and funding possibilities, it was concluded that ten teams would be created. In addition, the committee proposed to hire a project director, a psychiatric consultant, and several secretaries.

The plan also suggested ten separate facilities. In most cases these facilities were a room or two in an existing school, public health clinic, or small building. Each facility required desks, chairs, and files, plus appropriate supplies such as psychological testing equipment, intake and treatment forms, writing materials, and several vehicles for transportation.

Efficiency Requisites

In making the mental health plan, a number of crucial issues had to be decided. These were:

Auspices, sponsorship, and administration of program.

Centralization versus decentralization.

Length of program.

Form of accountability.

Nature of program supervision.

The program was to be decentralized so that services would be close to the disaster victims. It was concluded that the governing body for the program would be representatives of the three Ministries—Public Health, Social Security, and Social Services. The project director, who would report regularly to this board of directors, was responsible for the overall operation of the project. A team leader, selected by and responsible to the program director, was in charge of the day-to-day team activities.

Supervision was to be provided on a weekly basis by the psychiatric consultant and the project director. In addition, the North American volunteers would provide training and seminars in treatment modalities. Finally, a system of accountability required that each team keep statistics on the number of clients served, their personal characteristics, and their psychiatric diagnoses. A combined report would be presented monthly to the board of directors by the project director.

Systemic Requisites

The scope of the mental health project was considered by the planning committee. Since little was known about how long emotional consequences would persist, a project of six-months duration was planned to serve victims in and around Managua.

Agreements with other agencies were necessary. These agreements concerned the provision of personnel, space, and a few jeeps by the Ministries of Public Health, Social Security, and Social Services. Also, referral arrangements were made with the National Psychiatric Hospital, schools, and disaster relief agencies. A public education program through the media was designed to gain support for the project.

Implementation

As the first North American team was returning to the United States, the plan requesting an additional $50,000 was submitted to Caritas, an International Catholic Relief Organization. The second U.S. team arrived on May 1, 1973, to continue the work of the first team, but an event that almost destroyed the project occurred.

A member of the first team spoke to the Nicaraguan press as he was leaving the country. Apparently, this person criticized the reconstruction efforts of the Nicaraguan government, in general, and specifically cited what he believed to be oppressive tactics of the government. His comments made front-page headlines in Managua. The next day his comments were repeated to the *New York Times,* which also featured the story on the front page. The reaction of the Nicaraguans was predictable and quick. The government, which was negotiating reconstruction loans from the World Bank, decided to sever its support for the mental health project, and the psychiatric representative to the project was removed by his superior. Other Nicaraguans became understandably guarded in their dealings with the North Americans.

The second team had to deal with the sudden loss of government sanction for the project. All its activities were thus focused on rebuilding confidence in the project and reestablishing communication linkages necessary for support. The president's wife refused to see the team and withdrew all formal recognition of the plan. However, after weeks of work, other agencies and individuals decided to continue with the mental health program. A new representative, a young dynamic psychiatrist, was appointed by the Ministry of Public Health. This representative quickly won the necessary assurances and support to enable the project to continue. In all, the second team had spent a month undoing the harm of the two press releases. As the second team left for the United States on June 1, 1973, it received word that the project had been funded for $50,000 by Caritas. The project was back on track.

The third U.S. team was responsible for the implementation of the mental health plan. Its activities included the procurement and hiring of staff, establishment of site location and facilities for the ten mental health teams, training of staff, project administration, supervision, development of an information system, and establishment of links to other programs and services. The month of June 1973 was spent in obtaining staff and locating sites and facilities, plus the design and implementation of an intensive training program. The program began on July 1, 1973.

To begin with, it was necessary to recruit the mental health workers for the project. The Ministry of Social Services provided ten psychiatric nurses, and the Ministry of Public Health donated a psychiatric consultant. With the Caritas funding, the Nicaraguan project director, a psychologist, and ten social workers and ten psychologists were employed. The two Ministries of Social Services and Public Health donated facilities, equipment, and transportation (cars and chauffeurs).

The training program for the project workers had three goals: first, to achieve an understanding of the types of emotional problems usually presented by disaster victims; second, to review and master concepts and techniques of crisis intervention, group counseling, outreach activity, and community organization; and third, to provide training seminars designed so that each of the ten mental health teams would develop an esprit de corps and begin to divide work tasks.

Location of the ten facilities was in the disaster area. Three were situated within refugee camps; four were in public health facilities; two in other affected areas—not refugee camps; and one was placed in the National Psychiatric Hospital. Accessibility of mental health service was deemed a key criterion in the planning of facility location.

The administration of the program was carefully detailed. The most experienced team member was designated team leader, and he directed the day-to-day activities of the group. This individual had the authority to make assignments, supervise staff, and assist in setting work priorities. In addition, the team leader was responsible to the project director for the operation of the mental health team.

A uniform information system was created that included a case record form and a statistical fact sheet. The former was used only by the worker for case notes, whereas the latter was completed and sent to the project director. The statistical information provided the necessary data to evaluate the progress of each team and was used in preparing reports for the various ministries and for Caritas. The evaluation and accountability functions were taken quite seriously.

Each team varied in its approach to mental health intervention, but all included similar activities differing only in the degree of emphasis. Individual crisis counseling, chemotherapy, and group counseling were common strategies for adults. Forms of group counseling and play therapy were preferred modes in treating children. It was discovered early that disaster victims do not consider themselves mental health patients. They believe, and rightly so, that they are normal people who have had an extraordinary experience. The net result was that few people came on their own initiative to the mental health facility. This required major blocks of staff time to seek out potential clients and to do crisis intervention under a variety of nontraditional circumstances. It was not uncommon that workers would go door to door, or would visit bars, churches, schools, and public gathering places in search of victims with emotional problems. Aggressive outreach is necessary for the success of any mental health program for disaster victims.

Contacts with community agencies and public relations were additional key activities of the mental health teams. Considerable time was spent in sensitizing schoolteachers, priests, and other agency workers as to the potential emotional reactions of Managuans. The contacts became important sources of referral. For example, some schools identified children with problems, and treatment groups were organized within the schools. A centralized public relations campaign was instituted to publicize the services as well as to convey the message that certain symptoms such as anxiety, sleeplessness, or minor depression were common reactions to disaster loss. Managuans were pictured as heroes who should not be ashamed of their feelings. If necessary, a trained staff was available to talk with them.

Conclusion and Discussion

This section suggests a careful and detailed approach to the planning of a mental health service for victims of a natural catastrophe. A number of essential steps must be included in the planning process. These steps are sanction and support, understanding the cultural definition of health and illness, a needs assessment of the problem and those affected by it, a serious consideration of alternative approaches, and a well-defined plan of action. The mental health plan should detail the requirements of function, technology, efficiency, and systemic linkage. And, finally, the implementation of the project requires careful attention to staff training and to the design of the administrative and information structures, plus the creation of evaluation and accountability mechanisms.

The Managua mental health project lasted six months, that is, from July 1, 1973 to December 31, 1973. During that time the ten mental health teams had seen over 7000 patients, the vast majority of whom had problems of social adjustment with presenting symptoms of anxiety, depression, phobias, and hysteria.

Anyone considering a similar project for disaster victims should keep in mind the following issues. Outside experts or consultants need official sanction as well as much informal support. Also, the staff of disaster programs are likely to be disaster victims themselves and are subject not only to the tensions and "burnout syndrome" of the job but also to the stress of their own problems. Another key issue is financing such a program. To seek donations of personnel, equipment, facilities, and money from a variety of agencies is always a difficult task, one that requires sensitive attention until the last day of the project.

There is usually concern over what will happen to clients once the project has ended. Can the existing mental health system absorb these new clients? Usually not. In Managua, four of the ten teams were continued; the others were terminated. The teams that continued to operate were those attached to the public health clinics. This raises two interesting points. First, a mental health program for disaster victims cannot be independent of other community services. It would appear that program success is directly related to the degree of integration of mental health with other programs. This was the case in Managua with the four teams and the public health clinics. The other noteworthy point is that the psychiatric supervisor donated by the Ministry of Public Health was a respected professional who strongly advocated the integration of these teams within the broad framework of public health. Without his leadership, these teams would have also been terminated at the end of the project's funding.

Finally, it is essential that data from mental health projects be reported so that others may understand the nature of emotional stress experienced by disaster victims and the interventive strategies employed to deal with these mental health problems. Now, as there is a growing awareness that disasters produce psychological problems, there is an emphasis on mental health intervention with aggressive outreach and short-term crisis treatment.

Mental health for disaster victims, even in the poorest countries, is not the luxury it may seem but rather a necessary service for citizens suffering from the consequences of a natural calamity. Mental health planning in the wake of disasters, then, is an essential component of relief and reconstruction efforts.

VICTIMS OF RAPE TRAUMA[3]

Rape continues to affect the lives of thousands of people each year. The FBI *Uniform Crime Reports* indicate an increase of reported cases of rape with 121 percent increase noted between 1961 and 1970. The estimates in 1976 were that there were 56,730 reported cases in this country (FBI 1976). And it is a well-known fact that the number of reported rapes is significantly less than the number actually being committed. Thus, we are dealing with a social problem that generally goes undisclosed and unreported to professional health groups.

The laws defining rape differ from state to state, but generally include three elements: forced sexual activity, lack of victim's consent, and actual or threatened harm. Rape is an interpersonal act involving affective, verbal, and behavioral exchange between the persons involved. In most forcible sexual situations, the behavior exchange between rapist and victim consists of the offender accomplishing sexual penetration and the victim retaining her or his life.

The sexual assault of children, adolescents, and adults should be of concern to all mental health clinicians. The trauma suffered by the victim during the assault, immediately after the assault, and in the days and weeks to follow has physical, psychological, social, and legal implications. Clinicians who provide crisis intervention to rape victims can increase their sensitivity and expertise for this type of traumatic crisis by understanding some of the

[3]The following material on rape is based on a series of articles by Ann Wolbert Burgess and Lynda Lytle Holmstrom. See references list at end of chapter.

issues involved in rape behavior. The discussion that follows will focus on some of the key elements regarding linguistic strategies used by rapists to control the victim, coping behavior of victims to the rape, and crisis intervention techniques.

Gaining Access: Initial Control of the Victim[4]

The rapist's first goal is a pragmatic one. He must obtain a victim and get her sufficiently under his control so that he can then rape her. There are two main styles of attack among reported rapes that we have called "blitz" and "confidence" (Burgess and Holmstrom 1979a). The blitz rape is a sudden attack in which the rapist confronts the victim and there is no preliminary interaction or warning. The emphasis is on physically based strategies. For example, the rapist may grab a woman walking on the street and shove her into a car. His physical action may be reinforced by verbal means. In the confidence rape, the emphasis is on linguistically based strategies. The rapist gains access by winning the confidence of the victim and then betraying it. His "line" may be supplemented by physically maneuvering the victim into a position or place from which it is difficult to escape.

Two main styles of linguistic strategies occur at the point in time when the rapist is trying to obtain a victim. One is that of threats and orders, the other the confidence line.

Threats and Orders

The linguistic strategies of threats and orders can occur in either blitz or confidence styles of attack. In the blitz, they support the rapist's quick physical action and may appear very early in the interaction. In the confidence style they do not surface until after the victim's confidence has been attained and betrayed. The switch to threats and orders may happen quickly or it may occur after extensive conversation.

The threats and orders, in either style of attack, typically tell the victim to cooperate or be hurt or killed. Victims report being told "If you resist, you're a dead woman," "I'll kill you if you don't do it," and "Do what I say or your kids will get it." Threats to harm or embarrass help to gain the submission of the victim. They also set the mood of the encounter—that of its being a frightening experience for most victims.

[4]This section, through page 208, reprinted with permission from L. L. Holmstrom and A. W. Burgess, "Rapists' Talk: Linguistic Strategies to Control the Victim," *Deviant Behavior 1* (1) 1979: 101–125.

The Confidence Line

The confidence-line strategy can be used with victims known to the rapist or with strangers. If he already knows the victim, his conversation builds on this existing relationship. If the victim is a stranger, he uses a conversation to gain trust. His talk creates an image of normalcy and everyday experience that belies what is to follow.

The confidence rapist has the task of maneuvering the victim to where he wants her or maneuvering himself to where she is (e.g., in the front door of her home). To accomplish such maneuvers, rapists trade on social conventions and everyday activities and expectations. Rapists *offer assistance* ("Do you want a ride home?" and "I'll go with you to [find your husband]—I know where he hangs out."); *request assistance* ("Honey, can we use your phone?" and "I need a ride home."); *promise social activities* ("Want to come to my place and talk and listen to the stereo?" "Let's go over to the building— we can play pool."); *promise information* ("I want to tell you something." "I have information about your TV sets [that were stolen yesterday]."); *promise material items such as alcohol or drugs* ("We'll go to the house to get the papers [to roll the marijuana]."); *promise the possibility of employment and discuss business transactions* ("I need someone to do some line drawings."); *request her company while completing a task* ("Why don't you come on up while I put the groceries away?" "Come with me while I get my coat."); *refer to someone she knows or who might be there* ("I want to talk to you . . . about your 'brother's situation.'"); and *trade on social pleasantries and niceties* ("I'm leaving town, I want to say goodbye."). Sometimes the rapist's accomplice provides the con line. For example, one victim was persuaded to go to a house by two girls who said "We know a good place to go—there'll be a party."

The con lines of the rapists almost always sounded very ordinary. Their everyday quality is what makes them so effective. They sound credible at the time and do not arouse victims' suspicions.

Raping: Sexual Control of the Victim

Contemporary researchers stress the violent nature of rape and see it as expressing power, conquest, aggression, anger, degradation, hatred, and contempt. Rapists' goals on the social-psychological, motivational level are to demonstrate their power over the victim and to vent their anger at the victim. Sexuality is a component, but not the dominant factor. (See Chapter 11 for further discussion.) The rapist's power and anger may be directed at the individual victim, at the male perceived to own her, or at the group she is perceived to represent. Rapists' goals in pair and group rape may also include impressing their fellow-rapists. Linguistic strategies are one type of means used to achieve these goals.

Threats

Threats may continue throughout the rape. The threats may escalate from those that seem designed primarily to gain the physical control of the victim to threats primarily to torment and terrify the victim.

Orders

Orders may occur not only before but during the rape. They serve various functions. On the pragmatic level, orders often get the victim to do what the rapists wants. On the symbolic level, orders show both victim and rapist who has the power, who is in control. The rapist tells her to stop the behavior she is engaged in and do instead what he wants her to do.

The two most common types of orders are telling the victim to be quiet or unseen and telling the victim what to do sexually. Rapists tell victims "Shut up," "Be quiet," and "Keep your mouth shut." A quiet victim makes it easier to escape detection, as well as demonstrating who is in charge. Sometimes orders are given to avoid being seen ("Turn off the light.").

There are other linguistic strategies used during the rape by the rapist. Inquiries and statement by rapists about the victim's "enjoyment" may occur. For victims who reply to such inquiries is the added dimension that they were forced to talk against their will. Most often, victims are coerced into saying they "enjoyed" what was one of the worst experiences of their lives.

Rapists' talk contributes to the humiliation of the victim by sexual put-downs, as well as by orders and dirty names. The rapist may blame the victim for his lack of sexual satisfaction or taunt the victim with accusations of sexual inadequacy. Rapists may also laugh at the victim ("You don't know how to do anything right.").

Rape is a violent act against the victim. But it can also be perceived as an act against another man's property. The target here is not so much the female victim but the other male to whom she is perceived to belong—traditionally her father or her husband. In such cases, the rapist talks about taking another man's woman or female child.

Rapists engage in information games. Their strategy of asking personal questions increases the victim's vulnerability. They seek details about the victim's biography, living arrangements, habits, and property. The victim does not necessarily provide the information. But even to be asked is upsetting. Furthermore, rapists sometimes do get victims to reveal information they would rather not. Rapists ask questions that make the victim more accessible to future attacks by asking for identifying information—their name, telephone number, address.

Departure—Control
Over the Victim's Squawking

After rape, the rapist must return to the pragmatic goal of departing safely. To increase his chances of safe departure, the rapist often engages in what Goffman (1952: pp. 455, 462) calls cooling the mark out. He tries to continue to maintain control so that the victim will not raise a squawk. As Goffman notes, there are many procedures for "cooling," including the use or threat of force. Rapists' conversation for dealing with the victim after the rape can be categorized into two general types: the tough approach and the soft-sell.

Tough Approach:
Threats and Orders.

Rape is a frightening event. The terror is reinforced by rapists' orders saying not to tell, not to go to the police. Threats frequently are made to injure or kill the victim if the rape is disclosed to others or reported to authorities ("Don't tell anyone or I'll kill you," "If you go to the police, we'll get you when we get out of prison.").

Soft-sell: Apologizing,
Safe Return, and Socializing

Rapists sometimes depart discussing themes that may appeal more to victims' sympathies. Some rapists apologize; others combine the tough and soft-sell depatures. In one case, the 62-year-old woman was asleep in her bed. The rapist stabbed her in the stomach, then put a blanket over her head and kept it there while raping her. He later said to her:

> You might have to have a stitch in that wound. Do you have any bandaides? . . . I feel bad after I do these things. I feel ashamed. I hate to use the knife, but I just have to do it. . . . Keep the blanket over your head for twenty minutes. I'm leaving quietly. If you take off the blanket, I'll finish you.

Another rapist, after the rape, showed the victim literature about Jesus.

Rapists, when departing, may focus on the victim's safe return home. They may offer to give her a ride or walk her back. They may point her in the correct direction. Conversation after the rape may also serve to normalize the interaction. Socializing makes it seem like nothing out of the ordinary has happened. In one case, after beating and raping a girl friend on a Saturday afternoon, the rapist talked and played cards with her. He threatened her and told her if she went to the police he would kill her. He also wanted her to go with him to a party that Saturday night. Such conversation and actions may not normalize the interaction for the victim, but it makes the victim's allegation of rape less credible to outsiders. The account she gives sounds to others more like a social occasion and less like a rape. The case just described went to court. The assailant was found guilty of assault and battery and of unnatural acts, but on the rape charge the court found no probable cause. He received a one-year suspended sentence.

Rape is a crime of violence and force. By definition it cannot occur unless the rapist actively plays an exploitation game. The linguistic strategies of the rapist are related to the power aspect of the interaction and need to receive careful attention by the clinician assessing the crisis impact on the victim.

Coping Behavior of the Rape Victim[5]

The immediate efforts people use to deal with highly stressful situations are an important assessment point for clinicians who see patients in acute crisis. These coping behaviors may be viewed as problem-solving attempts an individual makes when facing demands that are highly relevant to his/her safety and that tax adaptive resources. In order to understand the victim's crisis response to being raped, it seemed important to analyze the coping behavior of rape victims in terms of thoughts, feelings, and actions as they related to specific time phases of the attack.

Most of the victims in the study perceived the rape as a life-threatening experience. The minority who did not so perceive it still saw the rape as an acutely stressful, frightening, and degrading experience. For almost all victims, this attack was something far out of the ordinary that seriously taxed their adaptive resources.

Early Awareness of Danger: Before the Attack

Appraisal of the degree of danger, threat, or harm is a psychological process that intervenes between a stressful event and coping behavior. This early awareness may be cognitive, perceptual, or affective, and often the victim describes it as a "sixth sense" or a feeling of impending danger. The coping task at this phase is to react quickly to this warning.

In listening to rape victims describe the circumstances of the attack, some spontaneously reported cognitive or perceptual awareness of the potential danger they faced. They were not totally sure or clear regarding the

[5]This section, through page 215, reprinted with permission from A. W. Burgess and L. L. Holmstrom, "Coping Behavior of the Rape Victim," *American Journal of Psychiatry* 133, no. 4 (1976), 413–18.

nature of the danger, but they knew something was wrong. This vague, obscurely formulated consciousness of danger varied. Victims said they saw a strange man and either *thought* he might do harm, *wondered* why the man had been hanging around all evening, *remembered* seeing the man before, *looked* at the car that pulled up, *thought* it strange the apartment light did not go on, or *heard* a noise in the kitchen and went to investigate. This ability to react depended on the amount of time between the threat of attack and the attack, the type of attack, and the type of force or violence used.

A majority of victims used one or more strategies and a minority of victims were unable to use any strategies.

Cognitive Assessment.   Victims may cope by mentally assessing the situation to determine possible alternatives. e.g., they may think about how they can get away from the assailant's grasp or escape from a car or room safely, or they may worry that the man will panic and hurt them and plan how to keep calm.

Verbal Tactics.   The majority of the coping strategies were verbal: they included talking one's way out of the situation ("I tried to engage them in conversation such as asking where they went to school and why they were doing this"), stalling for time ("I tried to talk to him; tried to get him to come for coffee at a restaurant down the street"), reasoning with the assailant by trying to change his mind ("I'm a married woman"; "I'm a virgin"), trying to gain sympathy from the assailant ("Look at the trouble you're causing me"; "What will I do?"), using flattery ("You're an attractive man; surely you don't have to do this for sex"), bargaining with the assailant ("There's my TV, take it and go"), feigning illness ("I'm sick"), threatening the assailant ("My husband is due home"; "My kids are in the next room"; "A policemen lives in this building"), verbal aggression ("Get your hands off me"; "Don't touch me"; "What are you doing?"), changing the assailant's perception of the victim ("I talked to him like a mother"), joking and sarcasm (a woman awakes to see a man coming in her room saying, "I'm escaping from the police"; she says, "OK—I'll let you out the back door").

Physical Action.   Some victims took direct action aimed at preventing the attack by fleeing from the situation or fighting the assailant ("I tried to stab him with the broken glass." "I tried to push him back out of the apartment.").

Without Strategies

Some of the victims are unable to utilize any strategy in avoiding attack. The victim might be physically paralyzed and totally overpowered by the assailant. For example, several victims were in their beds sleeping when the assailant gained access to their apartment and attacked them ("It was around 3 A.M. . . . . I woke to feel someone jumping on me."). Or the victim could be walking down the street and suddenly be grabbed by one or two assailants. The use of a weapon often paralyzed the victim to inaction. The following example from a referral case illustrates early awareness of danger and physical paralysis.

> . . . Buzzer door rang. . . . I was expecting friends and opened my door . . .
> saw three men with a paper in one's hand. . . . I froze . . . paralyzed for a
> moment . . . something went through my head . . . shut the door but they
> pushed it back open . . . with the gun.

And in some cases, the victim would be totally stunned or surprised by the change in behavior of a man whom she knew as a friend, neighbor, or acquaintance and say, "He just grabbed me before I knew it."

Victims may be psychologically paralyzed either through their defensive structure ("When I realized what he was going to do, I blanked out. . . tried not to be aware of what was going on.") or because of the use of alcohol or drugs prior to the attack ("I had been drinking that evening."). Thoughts of death may paralyze a victim ("I thought he'd be the last person I'd see alive.").

Multiple Strategies

Victims may try a number of strategies. One victim who was successful in avoiding attack said:

> First I tried to calm him down; tried to talk softly to him and said, "OK,
> we be friends." Then I said my brother was due home any time. . . . I tried
> all I knew, verbal and physical. . . . I screamed and fought.

The brother did come home and the assailant left without raping the intended victim.

Another victim who tried several strategies was not successful with the three men who had forced her into a car as she waited for a bus after her evening classes at a local university. She tried verbal tactics ("My husband will be worried and probably call the police if I am not home."), but the assailants told her remarks such as that would "get me dead." The victim then became silent; later tried bargaining ("I offered them my money to let me go."); and finally decided to comply ("I decided the only way was to play it their way.").

In another case one sees the coping behavior or early awareness, an affective reaction of fear, cognitive assessment, and verbal tactics of joking.

> . . . I got a warning . . . saw two men at the end of my hall . . . got frightened
> . . . didn't know how they got there. They said they needed to use my
> phone. I tried to joke and said, "Who you trying to call, Red China?"

During the Attack:
Coping with the Rape

At the moment of the actual rape attack, it becomes crystal clear to the victim that forced sexual attack is nonescapable and that there is no point of return. The coping task during this phase is to survive the rape despite the many demands such as oral, vaginal, and anal penetration forced upon the victim. She also may be forced to have conversation with the assailant. Victim's coping behavior during the rape included cognitive strategies, affective response, verbal strategies, physical action, psychological defense, and physiological reaction.

Cognitive Strategies

Victims often cope by mentally focusing and directing their attention to some specific thought in the service of keeping their mind off the reality of the event and on their survival. Remaining calm was a strategy in which the victim specifically controlled herself mentally so as not to provoke additional violence. The victim might talk to herself as in the following case.

> I kept thinking . . . keep cool. He said he'd kill me. He hit me, he choked me, he could kill me. I said to myself, "You can handle anything; come on, you can do it." I decided not to fight him . . . he was holding my neck so tight. . . . I responded a little to him . . . that blew his mind that I acted as I did. It was very quick, thank God.

Memorizing details was a strategy that proved to have some payoff later. One referral victim said, "I focused on their faces and thought to myself, 'I'll see you guys in court if I get out of this alive.'" She did. Another victim said:

> I played detective . . . tried to observe everything like the tatoo on his arm, remarks he made, route of travel of the car, license of the car . . .

Recalling advice with people on the subject of rape is a strategy victim's report.

> I remember a conversation I had with my husband. He said if I was attacked not to resist if he wants sex.

> My husband said the guy could kill me or the children . . . but sex wouldn't kill me.

Another victim said:

> I remember talking with people about rape and they always said not to resist . . . that a female could be killed, beaten, or mutilated. I didn't want that to happen.

Memory of previous violent situations provides victims with alternatives to try ("I struggled a little . . . then remembered when I was twelve I fought a neighbor boy and got my nose broken."). Praying is used as a tactic to decrease stress and tension ("Wasn't listening to them but concentrating on praying that my friends who had keys to my apartment would come."). Concentrating on the assailant in terms of who he is and what has led to this attack is a strategy.

> I remember thinking that this person must have a home . . . must live somewhere . . . why would he do this on Mother's Day . . . I thought of the irony of it.

Compliance or going along with the assailant is a strategy used to "speed it up . . . get it over with." To many victims, the attack seemed interminable ("It went on and on and on.").

Verbal Strategies

Victims combined verbal and affective responses when reporting that they screamed and yelled. This tactic was twofold: to relieve tension and pressure as an involuntary response and to deter or prevent the assailant from his full intent. This tactic brought police to the scene in several cases, and very often the assailant was apprehended during the rape attack.

Several victims believed that talking with the assailant during the attack helped them avoid additional violence. The assailant may demand to know how the victim is "enjoying" the rape. One victim handled this situation as follows:

> He kept wanting to know if it felt good and I had to say yes to keep him happy. . . . He said, "I'm on drugs lady and I need money . . . fuck me good or I'll kill you . . . ." He needed to be reassured.

If the attack continues over a period of time, the victim may try verbal tactics to calm the assailant and thus avoid further demands ("I talked to calm him down. . . . I asked questions and he kept talking."). Sarcasm may be used as a coping strategy especially if that matches the victim's usual verbal style.

As he was molesting me he asked if I enjoyed it and I said, "Oh, sure, it is great." I decided to go along with him. He seemed to need reassurance.... I wasn't scared then. First thought he'd get his kicks and then it'd be all over . . . I'd be dead. I got faith that he wasn't going to harm me.

Some victims tried to gain control in the situation by scaring the assailant(s) ("You'll be in real trouble if you kill me," or "You'll be sorry . . . I'll get someone to kill you."). This strategy was partially successful in some cases.

Physical Action

Victims reported struggling and fighting with the assailant in the attempt to avoid penetration ("I struggled and tightened my muscles."). Or sometimes the victim struggles to a certain point ("I fought and struggled until I realized he was going to rape me. He wanted to rape me more than I could manage to resist."). Or the victim quickly discovers that her struggle and fighting are just what the assailant wants her to do ("The more I screamed and fought, the more excited he would get.").

Psychological Defenses

Defense mechanisms are another way victims cope with the overwhelming fear of attack. Defenses close the cognitive field and thus block out the unbearable feeling. Victims denied the attack ("I never thought it could happen."); experienced dissociative feelings ("I pinched myself to see if I was real."); suppressed the rape ("I am missing 10 minutes of my life."); and rationalized ("I felt sorry for him if this was the only way he knew how to get sex.").

One victim describes her reaction as follows.

I did not struggle because of the knife. All those things you read about or plan to do don't help. . . . I felt I was not going to get out alive. . . . I was resigned; I felt nothing, empty; felt this can't happen to me.

Physiological Response

Not all coping behavior is voluntary and conscious. Certainly some of the screaming and yelling is involuntary, and it was noted that victims reported physiological responses of choking, gagging, vomiting, feeling nauseated, pain, urinating, hyperventilating, and losing consciousness. One victim described an epileptic seizure.

Only thing I remember is getting the key into the lock to get into the building. Then I got warning signs to my seizure attacks . . . getting overheated and the ringing in my ears and that's all. When I regained consciousness I was in the hall by the door to the basement. I dragged myself out as I heard someone saying, "Who left their keys in the door?"

Another victim described how her involuntary reaction scared the assailant off after he raped her ("I felt faint, trembling and cold . . . I went limp. I think he got scared and thought I was out.").

After the Attack:
Escaping from the Assailant

The stressful situation is not over when the actual rape ends. The victim must alert others to her distress, escape from the assailant, or free herself from where she has been left. The coping task immediately following the rape is to be free or escape from the assailant.

Alerting Others

Victims are always hopeful that someone will come to their aid, and they may spend time concentrating on how to obtain help.

Bargaining for Freedom

Often, the victim must negotiate with the assailant through a bargaining process. The assailant sometimes apologizes and tries to gain sympathy and thus get the victim to promise not to tell, or he may give the victim orders or instructions ("I'll kill you if you tell or go to the police"; "Don't move from that position for 30 minutes"). During the bargaining process the victim may cope by remaining silent or agreeing to instructions. Some victims promised not to tell anyone or invented stories to preserve their lives: "I told him my girl friend had this happen and when she went to the police they didn't believe her. I told him I'd never go to the police."

Freeing Oneself

The victim may have to free herself from the situation—if she has been tied and gagged, she has to cope with physically freeing herself. Cognitive assessment of the situation and keeping calm will be most useful strategies to her, as was the situation in the following referral case: "I lay still for a moment . . . then realized that the faster I got myself untied, the faster I could get to the police and my friends . . . ankle ties . . . getting cramps in my legs . . . so I had to tell myself not to panic and I worked the wrist ties and ankle ties next. . . . "

Mastery, in terms of survival of the attack, may be verbalized by the victim as well as her family and friends when this stage has been managed successfully: "The worst is over . . . I got throught it . . . I am grateful to survive."

Escaping

There are two main ways in which victim and offender disengage from the assault. The offender can initiate or the victim can initiate some action to terminate the assault.

Assailant Initiates.   There are two variations of the offender disengaging. He either leaves on his own accord, or he orders, physically or verbally, the victim out of the situation. When the assailant leaves the scene, he may run because he is scared off by noises he hears, or other times he has completed the rape and leaves. In addition, the assailant may give instructions to the victim as to what to do after he leaves as another method of insuring his continuing control over the victim. One victim said:

> I heard the guys looking through the apartment. I lay there for about five minutes and then couldn't stand it any longer. They had threatened me and I didn't know if they were still in the apartment but I got up. I took off the blindfold and saw the door was open and knew they had walked right out of the apartment. I locked the door and got dressed. Then I went out and knocked on every door in the building till someone answered.

In another case, a victim emphasizes her thoughts and reactions about the rape as she is waiting for the assailant to leave:

> He told me to stay in the bathroom. I waited till I was sure he was gone. He must have come in the bedroom window as that is the only window in the apartment which leads to a fire escape. I live on the third floor back apartment. . . . I felt stunned and wondered if this all happened. I was amazed I was still alive. I passed out on the bathroom floor. I lost consciousness. . . . Then I woke up and I wondered if I had dreamt it. Then I realized I was on the floor and went into the bedroom and saw mud on the carpet. But I didn't want to seem like an idiot and call the police if nothing happened. I decided it had happened and to call them. I brushed my teeth. There was a bad taste in my mouth. I had my pajamas on and wondered if I should get dressed or what. I decided to wait in case they needed the clothes or anything. I wrapped a blanket around me and sat on the couch waiting for them. They came very fast.

Victims may be so stunned by the rape that they are not totally aware of what happens to the assailant. As one 25-year-old woman said:

> I know I didn't pass out, but suddenly I was aware that no one was there. Suddenly the guys were gone and I was lying in an alley naked from the waist down. I was scared shitless. I was crying. I ran nine blocks back to my apartment.

Once the assailant has left, the victim still has to seek assistance of some type. When the assailant leaves the scene first, the victim may use a variety of tactics as in the following case.

> After the man left, I crawled upstairs to the next apartment and tried to waken them but was unsuccessful. Then I went back, changed into shorts and a shirt and went across the street to neighbors.

In another type of disengagement, the assailant forces the victim out of the situation. The victim may be pushed from the car or taken to a bus stop or literally thrown out of the car. In a gang rape case, the victim reported there was discussion in the car over where to let the victim out. One place was rejected because the victim might recognize it. Finally she was pushed out of the car as it continued driving.

Victim Initiates. The victim herself may be able to escape from the assailant and seek assistance. Sometimes the victim leaves in a dangerous way such as jumping out of a car. Or victims will wait until circumstances are safer—such as the man falling asleep—to leave the scene ("After he went asleep, I got dressed and ran back to my place knocking on every door for help."). In such situations, bystander reaction is not always sympathetic, as one 40-year-old victim reported.

> I ran from the man who then took my car and handbag. I went knocking on three or four doors saying, "Someone please help me. Could someone please call the police." Finally two girls opened a door and said they had no phone but the woman upstairs did. I could go no further. I just stayed there and pretty soon the woman came who had the phone. She let me in and I called my husband.

Once the victim is free of the assailant, another decision point is reached. The victim now faces what to do next. What does happen to the victim once she or he is free of the assailant? How much control over the sequence of events immediately following freedom from the assailant does the victim have?

The first decision to be examined is whether or not the rape is disclosed to anyone. Does the fact of the rape become known to outsiders or does it remain silent within the victim?

Disclosure to Parental Family

An important assessment item in working with rape victims is whether they have disclosed the rape to anyone in their immediate family. An analysis of a Boston City Hospital sample of victims (Burgess and Holmstrom 1979b) revealed that the most common pattern of disclosure was for victims to tell selective family (42 percent). That is, the victim told either mother or father or a sibling but not all family members. The next most common pattern was for the victim to tell all family members (33 percent). The least common pattern (25 percent) was not to tell any family member.

Victims gave various reasons as to why they told family members. The most common theme was wanting to tell. Victims also felt it was expected behavior ("I do not hide anything from them."); that they were pressured to tell ("Police and friends encouraged me to call my father."); and in some situations the victim was overwhelmed with feelings and not able to control what she said or how she behaved after the rape ("I didn't want to tell anyone but was hysterical after it happened and had to tell—no getting around it.").

Family Response to the News

The news that a family member has been raped usually triggers an emotional reaction in the other family members. Each of the parents, as well as other members in the family—if they are told—may have a separate response. Three types of behavioral responses are usually noted: a consistently supportive stance, an intermittently supportive stance, and an unsupportive stance.

Supportive Stance.   Family members who are consistently supportive of a raped family member are able to show their positive regard and concern for the person. They do not blame the person for the rape nor the circumstances surrounding the situation. They are loyal to the family member, and they are usually open to medical and counseling services for the family member. Even if parents do not know what to say to their child, they do concrete things to show their concern. As one 18-year-old victim said:

> My mother felt really terrible. She is happy I'm alive. . . . She didn't know what to say or do. But both parents have been extra specially nice—giving me whatever I want. My mother cooks my favorite meals.

There are two ways in which family members can be helpful to victims. One way is to be verbally sympathetic; that is, the family members can express concern and understanding at hearing the news. A second way is that the family members can do specific things to provide support such as accompanying the victim to the hospital or police station. In one case the victim and her mother determined what family members would be told:

> Lots of relatives think I was beaten up. Mother and I agreed who in the family to tell and who not to tell.

Intermittent Support. There are some family members who are only able to give intermittent support. Often these people have some ambivalent feelings that create conflict and detract from their support at key times. For example, the parents may be ambivalent about their child in general, or they may be ambivalent over the circumstances of the rape and their child's role in it. Their ambivalence is seen in their comments and behavior. In one situation a victim went right from the hospital to her father's office to tell him of the rape. She said:

> He called me terrible names—a slut, a goddamned tramp . . . that it was my fault the way I had been living. He told me to get out. [How did you feel about that?] It didn't surprise me. Father is like that. Not new for him to scream like that. It is a typical reaction. Didn't upset me. Then I went home, and he had called my mother in the meantime and she had the minister at the house. [How did you feel about that?] Well, she wanted him to talk me into staying home. She thought I would want to take off again. . . . Then when my father came home that night, he had calmed down and he apologized and said he shouldn't have said that, that it wasn't my fault and he had just flown off the handle.

Unsupportive Stance. Some parents and family members are unable to provide any emotional support for the rape victim. This may be because the crisis is just one more in a list of multicrises the family or child has experienced. Thus the rape crisis blurs with all the other crises facing the parents and immobilizes their inability to respond in a helpful way. Or, the parents may be overwhelmed by their own individual situation and have no energy left for providing support—a depletion of parental emotions. These parents are usually under considerable stress themselves. The parents may also have strong biases regarding rape and may deny any significance to the event—the rape is not worthy of any attention—or they may blame the victim. Or the parents may not know how to be supportive and helpful to their child. One victim who had to tell her parents because the police kept calling and her parents wanted to know why said:

I wasn't going to tell my mother . . . she wouldn't be able to handle it. I did have to tell. . . . She said, "Oh." And she didn't want to know any of the details.

Reasons for Not Disclosing the Rape to the Family

There is pressure for victims to keep a rape secret as well as pressure to tell. Societal attitudes are strong forces to keep victims from reporting a rape. Thus, many victims are successful is not disclosing the rape to their family as well as to outsiders.

Victims gave various reasons for not telling family members of the rape. Some victims do not disclose in order to protect the family from upsetting news ("It would kill her to know. She'd be so hurt by it."). Some victims feel that disclosing would create a value conflict with the family. These victims feel their parents will not understand because of their attitudes about rape, their religious orientation, or the fact that the parents do not approve of the victim's life style and thus may blame the victim for the rape. In other situations of nondisclosure, victims feel telling their parents would restrict their independence and would also serve as a lesson-in-point for the parents to bring up later. These victims prefer to maintain their independence and handle the rape themselves. The victim may also not trust the family member to keep the news confidential. Other victims feel psychologically distant from their family or geographically distant and thus do not disclose.

Assessment of the Emotional Crisis of Rape

Assessing the Precipitant Event

The circumstances under which the rape occurred, the characteristics of the assailant, the interpersonal dimension, and the affective response to the rape all influence the victim's reaction to the rape. Thus it is important for the clinician to find out as much as possible about the details of the rape.

Circumstances. When and where was the victim approached? Why was she or he there? Where did the rape itself occur? Knowledge of the circumstances is useful in predicting the immediate reactions of the victim as well as the long-term reactions following the rape.

The Assailant. Who did it? Was he of the same race? Was he known to the victim? Was he a stranger? If there was more than one assailant, how many were there? Answers to these questions may determine the degree of distress of the victim in terms of whether the assailant was a stranger or not.

Conversation. What kind of conversation occurred prior to the rape between the victim and assailant? Did he try to "charm" her or help her? Did he threaten her? Did he make humiliating comments? Did he talk during the rape? What did she say back to the assailant? How many orders and threats were part of the talk? The type of conversation may help determine the type of rapist the victim encountered.

Sexual Details. What type of sex did the assailant demand (vaginal, oral, or anal)? What type of sex did he actually obtain from her? What other degrading acts did he perform, such as urinating on her or pulling her breasts? How did she react to what she was forced to do?

For many victims, the sexual aspects of the rape will be very distressing. It is generally the topic that a woman wishes to forget and not talk about. However, the sexual details are apt to be the ones that will keep recurring in her mind, and for the counseling process to be ongoing, the intensity of her reactions will need to be observed over time. The victim may have more difficulty with this aspect of the rape later, and discussion at this initial interview provides an indication of how she is psychologically affected by the issue.

Physical and Verbal Intimidation. Did the assailant have a weapon? Did he threaten the victim physically or verbally? What kind of violence did he inflict, such as slapping or striking? It is important to ask about threats and violence. Fear is one of the main reactions to the rape experience. It is also important to discuss not only the victim's fears at the time of the incident but also what thoughts she had.

Struggle. Did the victim struggle or not? How does she feel about this? It is important to find out not only how much she struggled but also how she feels about this action. At the time of the attack, many victims decide that it does not make sense to struggle to any extent. They do not see any hope of winning, and they think that strong resistance on their part will simply cause them to be brutalized even more. Nevertheless, later on it is a common reaction to wonder whether they should have struggled more.

Alcohol and Drug Use by Assailant or Victim. Does the victim think the assailant was under the influence of drugs or alcohol, and had she been using drugs or alcohol? Information obtained on drug and alcohol use can give additional insight into the situation. Such use on the part of the assailant may have made the attack more frightening.

Emotional Reaction. How did the victim feel emotionally at the time of the rape, and how does she feel now? What are the most painful parts to think about? Part of settling the crisis involves the woman's being able to put her feelings into perspective about the experience. Thus, in addition to the comments she volunteers throughout the interview about her emotional reactions, it is worthwhile to ask questions that focus directly on this point. As she talks about her feelings, she will achieve some control due to the fact that she is verbalizing them. Discussing her feelings over a period of time also helps her to gain perspective and distance to the experience.

Sexual Reaction. What does the sexual assault actually mean to her? Is this her first sexual experience, or what has been her normal sexual style? What are her feelings about sex? Has she been attacked or raped before? Has she ever been pressured to have sex such as with a family member or with a date? Rape is a violent act in which sex is the weapon. For most women, the act of rape significantly disrupts their normal sexual style. For the virgin and for the victim not recently sexually active, the rape may trigger doubts and fears of a future relationship with a man. For the sexually active woman, the rape may create immediate problems in dealing with her husband or lover. This issue of sexuality needs to be dealt with promptly in the crisis process. It is easier to talk with the woman right after the assault regarding her sexual style, and to say it is important to be sure she is able to resume her normal style. If the subject has been mentioned during the initial interview, the woman then finds it easier to talk later during the follow-up.

After the Attack and Seeking Help. Where did the victim go for help? Did she clean up or change clothes before seeking help? Whom did she talk with to help her decide what to do, and did she decide to seek help or was the decision made for her?

Encounter with Institutions. If the victim reported the rape to the police, what was her reaction to this experience? Did the police encourage or discourage her from taking it to court, and how did she feel she was treated by the police?

If the victim sought medical attention, how did she feel about being at the hospital or clinic? Did the gynecological examination upset her or any of the tests performed? Was she informed of the tests? What concerns her most as a result of the rape—possible pregnancy, venereal disease, or feelings about the rape?

Pressing Charges. Is the victim willing to press charges, and is she willing to cooperate with the police and testify in court? How does she feel about this, and what has been her previous experience with the criminal justice system?

Social Network. Who is in the victim's family, and which people are important to her? Who will she tell in her family? What friends are there at work or school, and which friends will she tell?

Assessing the Precipitant
of the Crisis—Prior Victimization

It is very important to determine if the victim has had a prior victimization. If she has, the current rape may trigger an unresolved conflict and may activate the fears of experiencing a past trauma. In analyzing factors influencing recovery from rape trauma with the Boston City Hospital sample, prior victimization was related to a longer recovery time. Prior victimization included not only attempted and completed rapes, but pressured sex such as incest, molesting, mugging, and witnessing of victimizing situations. In reviewing the dynamics of victims with prior victimization, the following clinical observations were made:

1. *The time interval between victimizations.* For victims raped a second time within a two-year period, the second rape represented a setback. The victim might comment on this setback in terms of relating to people ("I was just beginning to trust people again."), or she might talk in terms of anticipated trauma effects of the new rape.

2. *Victim's point in the life cycle.* The sexual assault may take on specific meaning to victims according to their stage of development in the life cycle.

3. *Similarity with prior victimization.* The current rape may remind the victim of similar characteristics in a prior victimization.

4. *Comparison with prior victimization.* The victim may well compare the current rape with a prior victimization. Sometimes the victim denies to herself that such a situation could ever happen again.

5. *Prior victimization as an unresolved issue for the victim.* Very often the victim has not disclosed the prior rape to anyone and has just kept the burden within herself. This behavior did not allow for the victimization to be discussed and settled as a major life event. From a clinical standpoint, an assessment needs to be made regarding the prior victimization to see if the victim has settled the issue or if the event is still unresolved. A victimization may be unresolved at the time of a subsequent victimization if the issue has not been discussed or if sufficient time has not passed for the psychological work to be completed. This latter point may be one reason why a brief time interval between victimizations may result in a longer length of time for recovery.

Assessing Present
Coping Responses

It is important to assess the adaptive and maladaptive coping responses of victims following a rape in order to measure any gains made or offer suggestions as to different coping strategies. The follow-up study of the

Boston City Hospital rape victim sample analyzed the adaptive and maladaptive responses to rape in terms of recovery over a 4–6 year period.

Adaptive responses identified by rape victims on follow-up as helpful to recovery included positive self-esteem and the use of defense mechanisms and specific actions. Positive self-esteem was noted in victims who made a statement reflecting acceptance and/or approval of either their behavior taken at the time of the rape or their approach to the rape situation. Defense mechanisms aiding recovery included the victims' explanation of some reason why the rape occurred, minimization of the terrorizing aspects of the rape, suppression of or employing cognitive control over their thoughts of the rape, and dramatization or repetition of their feelings about the rape. Also, increased action such as moving, changing residence, travel, changing telephone number, reading on the subject of rape, noting radio and television programs on rape, and assisting in rape crisis centers appeared to aid recovery.

Maladaptive Responses

Victims do not always cope with the anxiety of rape in adaptive ways. Some victims fail to cope with the stress of the rape and develop maladaptive responses. Almost one-quarter of the victims from the Boston City Hospital sample reported either making a suicide attempt and/or seriously abusing alcohol or drugs after the rape.

Several victims reported making suicidal attempts. Sometimes the suicidal behavior is present before the rape ("When I was raped, I was very suicidal. I had attempted it several times"). Suicidal behavior may be part of a prior history of affective illness ("The rape made me manic, then depressed . . . then I attempted suicide"). Or the suicidal behavior may be a response to the failure to renegotiate a partner relationship after the rape.

The reliance on drugs and alcohol as a coping tactic after rape was used by some victims ("After the rape I stayed constantly drunk. I hit rock bottom. I drank to pass out . . . not to think of how bad things had gotten").

Assessment of Precrisis
Functioning

A careful assessment of precrisis functioning includes identifying how many learned coping behaviors the victim had at her disposal to help meet the crisis. Emotional style can be assessed in terms of *expressed style*—the victim's demeanor showing the feelings she is currently having such as fear, crying, anger, etc.—and *controlled style*—the victim expressing no visual feelings but rather assuming a guarded demeanor. Communication skills are important to ascertain how easy it will be for the victim to talk about the rape as well as to connect thoughts and feelings to her behavior. Specific areas in which the victim is most vulnerable need to be identified such as the disclosure of the rape to specific people.

The social support system is essential to discuss with the victim. Some clinicians might suggest that victims should disclose a rape to their immediate family members in order to receive emotional support. On the contrary, the authors (Burgess and Holmstrom 1979b) recommend that the issue of disclosure be part of the crisis planning aimed to help the victim predict whether the family will be understanding and supportive or blaming. The steps counselors can take to counsel victims on the issue of self-disclosure include:

Reviewing information from the victim to help make a prediction specifically in terms of what the family's prior reaction to stressful news has been.

Have the victim predict the family reaction.

Weigh the advantages of telling with the disadvantages of not telling.

Support the victim's decision whichever side she wishes to take.

Request that the victim report back the family reaction if she does decide to tell.

Additional counseling will be needed if the family blamed the victim and was not supportive.

Related Areas of Victim
Assessment

Assessing for suicidal thoughts is important. Clinicians will see victims who are actively suicidal or those who have made previous suicide attempts and need to be evaluated in terms of their suicidal potential. Any person with a history of depression or suicide attempts who has been raped should be carefully reviewed for suicidal intent. The specific areas to assess include: intensity of the wish to die; presence of a psychosis; social network involvement such as the number of people with whom the victim has a good relationship; and assessment of current stress situations such as chronic illness, economic stress, recent loss of an important person, recent surgery, or childbirth.

There should be a careful review of all drugs currently used by the victim including prescription drugs as well as street drugs. A mental status examination should be conducted if indicated, as well as a medical and psychiatric history.

Victims do not always cope with the anxiety of rape in adaptive ways. The use of maladaptive responses to rape trauma are usually related to a longer recovery period. The use of drugs or alcohol and/or acting on suicidal thoughts will hinder recovery. Also, the chronic life stressors—life situations that have persisted over time and from which the victim has relatively little control—will hinder recovery. These stressors include economic stress, lack of social support; and preexisting psychological, physiological, or social problems (Burgess and Holmstrom 1979a).

SUMMARY

In summary, recovery from rape is complex and influenced by many factors. These factors include prior life stress, style of attack, relationship of victim and offender (and whether it is an inter- or intraracial rape), number of assailants, language used by the assailant, the amount of violence or the sexual acts demanded, and postrape factors of institutional response to the victim, social network response, and subsequent victimization. Clinicians should consider all these factors in assessing and identifying victims who are at high risk for slow recovery from rape and will remain vulnerable to many life stresses for a long time.

Victim trauma has been identified as a Class 3 crisis whereas the offender is represented in Class 6 crisis level. This differentiation is important because the etiology of the victim's trauma is the offender's pathology. Rape is more than an illegal act and more than an extreme of cultural role behavior. From a clinical point of view, it is important that rape be defined as a sexual deviation and that the *pathology* of the offender be recognized.

WAR COMBAT STRESS

The recent pioneering work of Charles R. Figley and members of the Consortium on Veteran Studies (Figley 1978) provides another illustration of Class 3 crisis: war combat. Since 1974 Figley and his associates have studied the postwar adjustment problems of Americans who fought in the war in Vietnam. The major theme of their research is that "the war is not over for thousands of men who served their country during the Vietnam war" (1978, p. xiii).

The Nature
of Combat Stress[6]

Vietnam, like other wars, thrust millions of men into combat, which cost human lives and caused psychological debilitations resulting from war-related experiences. Most of the men were young, and they were ill prepared for the overwhelmingly stressful experiences they faced almost constantly for months and years. Yet aside from some clinical observations from earlier wars (Hammond 1883), combat psychiatry in general and the diagnosis of various combat-related stress disorders in particular began with the First World War (Figley 1978).

Before the First World War, psychological casualties resulting from war were seen simply as a sign of weakness or as a lack of military discipline, or both. One of the earliest psychopathologies related to combat was believed to be a psychological manifestation of artillery fire—both sending and receiving. Soldiers diagnosed as "shellshocked" were believed to be suffering from some kind of brain damage resulting from the air blasts of high explosives, which left these men dazed and confused. The reported symptoms for this disorder were remarkably similar to what was later referred to as "war neuroses" during the Second World War: pseudoconfusion; hypochondriacal, phobic, or anxiety symptoms; catatoniclike stupor, irritability, depression, startle reaction to noises, somatic symptoms, gross tremors, restlessness, insomnia, and nightmares or repetitive battle dreams (Brill and Beebe 1955; Grinker and Spiegel 1945; Menninger 1948; Nefzger 1970: also cf. Figley 1978, p. xvi).

During and following the Second World War, various terms were adopted to describe these psychiatric casualties in addition to the combatant being diagnosed as "shellshocked" or suffering from "war neurosis." Early in that war, commanders referred to psychiatric casualties as "psychos" (short for implying psychopaths). Later the U.S. Army commander in Tunisia ordered that all psychiatric disorders in the combat zone—regardless of the manifestations and degree of severity—would be known as "exhaustion." This move, of course, appeared to be a tactic to disregard the mentally debilitating potential of battle for the sake of expediency. As a result, accurate estimates of the psychiatric casualties of that war are difficult, if not impossible, to establish. The situation has not improved substantially since that time. During the Korean War, the term "combat exhaustion" was used early in the war but was soon replaced by "combat fatigue"; yet the symptoms remained the same as they were for the World War I veterans diagnosed as "shellshocked."

[6]This section, through page 234, was written by Charles R. Figley.

The DSM II:
The Case of the
Missing Combat Stress Disorder

During the Korean War, the original *Diagnostic and Statistical Manual* (*DSM I*) was developed and promulgated (1952). This manual delineated, albeit inadequately, combat-related stress disorders within an extensive classification of *gross stress reactions* defined as "situations in which the individual . . . [had] . . . been exposed to severe physical demands or extreme emotional stress," including combat situations. This categorization was welcomed by the Veterans Administration whose psychiatric wards were packed with men suffering from the symptoms of combat-related stress.

During the Vietnam War, the second revision (*DSM II*) was promulgated (1968). Unfortunately and mysteriously the only category that discussed combat trauma was dropped and was apparently replaced with a vague category, [Transient] Adjustment Reactions of Adult Life. Combat-related stress is only mentioned (in *DSM II*) in the brief explication and illustration of the category Adult Adjustment Reactions, which reads: "Fear associated with military combat and manifested by trembling, running and hiding"(*DSM II,*), hardly an adequate description of such a complex and potentially debilitating disorder.

It is interesting that no war existed between the promulgation of the *DSM I* and the formative stages of the development of *DSM II,* although the Vietnam War was quickly beginning to heat up. As Figley (1978) observes: "It is not unreasonable to assume that combat-related stress reactions were ignored as war veterans of the Korean and the two World Wars were assimilated into mainstream America" (p. xvii).

The latest revision, *DSM III,* published in 1980, has corrected, at least in part, this oversight by including the category of Posttraumatic Stress Disorder, both Acute (308.30) and Chronic (309.81), filed away under the ubiquitous heading of "Reactive Disorders Not Elsewhere Classifed." This new categorization has already had a dramatic impact on the Veterans Administration's Board of Veterans Appeals (see their *Memorandum on Posttraumatic Disorders,* 1978) in their acknowledgment of postmilitary mental disorders associated with combat stress.

Briefly, this new category of Posttraumatic Stress Disorder in the *DSM III,* to Shatan, Haley, and Smith (1977), describes the same characteristic symptoms of reexperiencing the traumatic event either through flashbacks, dreams, or nightmares, or all three, which results in numbing of responsiveness to or involvement with the external world and a variety of other autonomic, dysphoric, or cognitive symptoms as noted earlier.

Special Circumstances
of Vietnam Combatants

In a recent address to the American Psychiatric Association, Figley (1979) presented a generic model of posttraumatic stress reactions. First, he suggested that like other life-threatening events, combat includes four major elements that make it highly traumatic: (1) a high degree of dangerousness, (2) a sense of helplessness in preventing death, (3) a sense of destruction and disruption—both in lives and property, and (4) a sense of loss. Moreover, the long-term emotional adjustment to combat follows four stages: (1) Recovery, (2) Avoidance, (3) Reconsideration, (4) Adjustment.

The Recovery stage is the first stage and covers the period immediately following the war, which is a transition period between the combat era with constant danger calling for violent, destructive behavior and the postcombat era with constant safety calling for nonviolent, constructive behavior. As Figley (1978; 1980) and others, especially Wilson (1977; 1978), have noted, Vietnam veterans, more than any other American war veteran, had very little time to recover from their war and were thrust back into mainstream America within days of leaving the combat zone. Moreover, unlike other veterans, they returned from Vietnam to the United States on commercial airlines not with those they fought with in their outfit but with those whose time was also up. Thus, the Recovery stage was marked by considerable guilt about leaving their friends in Vietnam to die. Left to deal with the memories of war on their own, they quickly progressed to the next stage of Avoidance.

As Figley (1979) notes, the Avoidance stage "is a refuge from the extremely stressful experiences of the emergency event [combat experiences]. Survivors in this stage attempt as best they can to avoid any and all reminders of the event" (p. 12). Most stay in this stage of adjustment until some triggering event occurs, which cues the original stressful combat experience. Often the cue is either simulation of the original physical environment (e.g., low-flying helicopter, movie about Vietnam) or an emotion experienced there (e.g., helplessness, revenge, sorrow, fear). As a result the ex-combatant reexperiences the war as described in the Posttraumatic Stress Disorder category of the *DSM III*. If these reactions result in some informed assistance, the ex-combatant enters the next stage of Reconsideration, in which, according to Figley (1979), he "reflects on what has happened to him during and subsequent to the emergency—which may have happened only a few weeks earlier or many, many years earlier" (p. 14). If the veteran is able to work through his experiences, coming to grips with the most stressful facets of his war experiences and reaching what Figley calls a "Healing Theory" (what happened, why, the results of it, and the probability of it happening again), the vet enters the final stage, Adjustment.

In addition to these difficulties for the nearly 3 million men and women who served in Vietnam, Figley (1979) has observed five characteristics that set Vietnam veterans apart from previous American war veterans.

1. Entering and Exiting Alone

For the most part, soldiers entered and left Vietnam as individuals, not in military units as they did in other wars. They may have been shipped to Vietnam with their fellow soldiers from boot camp, but they probably parted company when assigned to different units overseas. Soldiers left Vietnam when their rotation dates came up (twelve months for all branches of the military except for the Marines who had thirteen-month tours). Thus, the Vietnam soldier was forced—more than any other combatant in any other American war—to deal with stress on his own. This may be the reason why most Vietnam veterans have little interest in military reunions and seldom refer to their years in Vietnam as "the good old days."

2. Opposition at Home

Opposition at home was another unique characteristic of the Vietnam War. The size and scope of the antiwar demonstrations against the Vietnam War were unprecedented in U.S. history. Although early opposition was limited to the college campuses and was voiced by a relatively small percentage of Americans, lack of support for the war grew, causing considerable ambivalence among the troops in Vietnam who were not really certain why they were there anyway.

This opposition at home toward the war left many Vietnam veterans feeling that their country had betrayed them. The lack of support displayed by the majority of Americans may well explain why so many veterans have felt that their sacrifices were all for naught, and why so many would refuse to return to Vietnam under similar circumstances.

3. Nature of the War

Like Korea, Vietnam was a "contained conflict." To the U.S. infantry-man in the field this meant that the war was designed by politicians but was fought with the blood of young men and boys. Troops located in a base camp participated in "search and destroy" missions of limited duration, then returned to their base camp. Thus, combatants found themselves taking and retaking the same hill or hamlet five or ten times in one year. Moreover, conventional tactics were used to fight an unconventional enemy. Until late in the war, the United States was not prepared to fight a guerilla-type war, complete with booby-trapped children.

A paradigm developed that read: "Limited War + Limited Tour of Duty = Limited Commitment." For the most part, soldiers of other wars were assigned for the duration. This was not the case in Vietnam. One of the major occupations among the combatants in Vietnam, especially among the enlisted men, was survival—being able to take care of yourself until that "Big Freedom Bird" came to take you back home. Therefore, what emerged toward the end of the combatant's tour of duty was the "short-timers' attitude." As one of the veterans we interviewed stated:

> Protect your own ass as much as possible as long as possible. Nothing is worth getting blown away: not this war, not these people, and not some lieutenant bucking for captain's bars.

Certainly the fragging of NCOs and officers was a natural manifestation of the nature of the Vietnam War.

The limited war mentality for the soldier meant simply "surviving your time" and may account for why so many Vietnam veterans have so many hostile feelings toward the U.S. government and the military, why so many are skeptical about what war can accomplish, why so many are plagued with guilt feelings about having left their buddies in the rice paddies of 'Nam, and why so few share a sense of pride in their contributions to the war effort.

4. Military Psychiatry in Vietnam

Military psychiatry was the fourth unique characteristic. As noted in Figley's book *Stress Disorders among Vietnam Veterans* (1978), lower psychiatric casualty rates in Vietnam were inappropriate indices of successful mental health management, particularly when you consider the long-term consequences of combat-related stress. The military, however, took great pride in its achievements and pointed to several key factors that appeared to account for its "success." First, there were more well-trained mental health personnel deployed in Vietnam; second, service was based on a twelve-to-thirteen-month rotation system; and third, frequent opportunities were given for rest and recuperation. These three factors supposedly accounted for a low incidence of so-called combat fatigue. However, research studies (Figley 1978; Bourne 1970; Figley and Southerly 1980; Wilson 1980) conducted by Figley and colleagues in the Consortium have discovered two glaring flaws in this scenario. First, other factors than what the military suggested can account for the *reported* good mental health statistics of the combatants (e.g., an inordinate amount of drug use, especially pot, which masked both the perception of and the reaction to stress). Another factor and an interesting

"Catch-22" of the Vietnam War is the administrative discharges. These "bad paper" discharges were used by the military to rid themselves of "discipline problems." These "problems" often were closely associated with stress disorders. Thus, rather than receiving needed psychiatric treatment, the problem combatants were given an undesirable discharge without a trial or court martial and were shipped home to face discrimination for the rest of their lives. Another miscalculation by military medicine was the assumption that "time heals all wounds." The signs of mental health problems during the war were simply delayed for months or years following service in Vietnam. We now know that many more combatants were experiencing stress reactions in Vietnam than have been reported.

This lack of appreciation for the long-term consequences of the Vietnam War stress by professionals and the public can at least be associated with why so many Vietnam vets feel such a sense of discontinuity about the war and their role in it (i.e., reexperiencing the war as bits and pieces of memory without a sense of wholeness). For the purpose of this discussion, for example, it may account for why so many Vietnam veterans, as survivors, have and will continue to be stuck in either the Avoidance or Reconsideration stages by reexperiencing the events they could not or would not deal with during and immediately following the war.

5. The Brief Transition Phase

The brief transition phase between being in combat in Vietnam and being at home in the United States is, perhaps, the most critical characteristic that makes the war unique in American history. The time lapse was often less than 72 hours between what is known as the "foxhole and the front porch." This period was particularly short in contrast to World War I and II veterans who arrived back home weeks or months following combat.

The Homecoming: Peace Marches But No Victory Parades

Viewing the Vietnam veteran as a survivor of a Class 3 Traumatic Crisis provides an opportunity to contrast his treatment with the typical treatment afforded survivors of other disasters.

Typical Reactions to Disaster Survivors

Attention has been focused on the individual survivor's reactions to combat stress. What are typical reactions to natural disasters? Who tries to help after a dam breaks or a tornado or storm hits? Usually the entire

community—and communities and individuals contiguous to the disaster—
will rally support and assistance for the survivors. Literally hundreds of
outsiders representing various agencies pour into the stricken area. Insurance
companies, the Red Cross, Civil Defense, and the National Guard rush to the
scene within hours. Immediately, disaster relief teams begin to set up offices in
the area, as they have in other areas in other emergencies.

On a more personal level, moreover, survivors of natural disasters
receive warmth, understanding, and kindness from everyone—family, friends,
neighbors, and strangers. The survivors are granted concessions and consideration due to their terrible experiences, their losses, and their pain.

Typical Reactions
to the Vietnam Veteran

In contrast to the thousands of Americans who survived major natural
disasters and were treated with respect and care, the Vietnam veteran returned
home from combat ignored or hated or both. There were no victory parades
for the Vietnam veteran, only peace marches. In a recent segment of the
popular television drama series, "The Lou Grant Show" (January 1979), a
young Vietnam veteran relates a familiar story of his "welcome" home:

> Tuesday afternoon I was in a fire fight. Tuesday night I got orders,
> "Report back home." My tour in 'Nam was over. Wednesday I was on a
> helicopter, Thursday morning on a jet from Tokyo to San Francisco. And
> I was still in uniform, and I was still dirty from being on the line, and I still
> had the sound of incoming in my ears, and I come off the plane, walked . . .
> toward the airport building, and when I went to the door. There was a
> crowd of people waiting for friends, and a man stepped out and he said I
> was a "baby burner" and he spit on me. . . . And you know something?
> Nobody did nothing. They looked away. A man called me a "baby
> burner" and spit on me and they all looked away. *I didn't know where I
> was; maybe I still don't.*

Additional Causes for Veterans'
Slow Adjustment to Peace

Apart from their mistreatment upon return—as if that wasn't bad
enough—there are several other factors that may account for the slow
progress many Vietnam veterans have made through the five postdisaster
periods and why only a relatively small percentage of Vietnam veterans
have truly adjusted to their experiences.

1. Short Transition Period
(Foxhole to Front Porch Period)

The short transition period did not allow vets to prepare adequately for their civilian roles. Many were back on the streets with the dirt of Vietnam still under their fingernails. When they arrived back home, they were expected to get their life in order immediately. Did we expect the survivors of the Buffalo Creek flood to immediately get their life back in order?

2. Limited Access
to Fellow Combatants

The limited access to fellow combatants did not permit Vietnam veterans to compare notes on their experiences—like veterans of other wars did and like the survivors of natural disasters certainly did. 'Nam vets returned alone and were left alone to deal with their memories and experiences. Developing their own Healing Theory was obviously more difficult without the support of their fellow vets.

3. Condemnation or Apathy
from Non-Vietnam Vets

Condemnation from non-Vietnam veterans was, perhaps, the cruelest paradox of the war. Those who chose to enter the military during the war rather than going to jail or feign illness or leaving the country were called "losers" and "baby burners" upon return. Tell me who would dare say to a tornado victim: "You shouldn't have lived in that area anyway!" or "What are you complaining about? A lot of people had it worse than you!" or "How come you get special treatment, just because you were dumb enough to not have avoided it?" But they said these things to returning Vietnam veterans.

4. The Lack of Adequate
Government Programs Designed
to Help

Another factor was the lack of adequate government programs for Vietnam veterans, which illustrated the disdain of the American people. Drug and VD screening programs were initiated to protect the country against the addicted and unhealthy Vietnam vet. The GI Bill for Vietnam vets provided few benefits as compared to the benefits received by World War II veterans. There were no adequate programs to combat drug and alcohol abuse, unemployment, unfair incarceration, and mental health problems. And the situation has not improved today.

5. Stigma Perpetuated
by the Media

The stigma perpetuated by the media is another cruel twist. Several years ago a young disabled Vietnam veteran wrote a short article in *TV Guide*. In it he complained about the bad TV image of the Vietnam veteran:

> I am a Vietnam veteran, and if I acted according to what I have seen on television in the last six months or so, I should be harboring extreme psychopathic tendencies that prompt me to shoot up heroin with one hand while fashioning plastique explosives with the other as my war-and-drug-crazed mind flashes back to the rice paddy where I fragged my lieutenant. (Brewin 1975)

Television police inspectors such as Kojak and Steve McGarrat of "Hawaii 5-0" were scripted to follow similar "leads" in attempting to link violent crimes with Vietnam combat veterans.

Hollywood has done its share of malignment of the Vietnam vet. The movie *Coming Home* is the first one to accurately depict the postwar experiences of the Vietnam vet. Even so, one is left with the impression that a typical "reaction" to the experiences of combat is aggression, as illustrated by the excellent performance of Bruce Dern as a recently returned Marine Corps captain. Yet, from conversations with numerous Vietnam veterans, the most important and truthful scene was not Dern's violent episode with his wife; it was Jon Voight, playing a disabled American combat vet, when he spoke to a group of high-school boys about the waste of the Vietnam War.

SUMMARY

In summary, there is no doubt that the Vietnam War is unique in recent history in terms of its duration, the political and philosophical opposition at home, the unconventional nature of the fighting, and the racial, economic, and political climate existing in the country when the veterans returned home. In addition, this section focuses attention on combat-related stress as a Class 3 crisis emphasizing the psycho-social needs and realities of combatants.

GENERAL INTERVENTION STRATEGY
IN TRAUMATIC STRESS CRISES

In Class 3 crises, the individual usually has been functioning reasonably well prior to the precipitating stress. However, at a given point, unexpected, intense stress imposed by external sources renders available coping mechanisms at least temporarily inoperable. The situation is likely to be new to the client, who must rapidly learn appropriate means of coping.

Emotional crises resulting from sudden intense stress can be precipitated by a single traumatic event, or by a combination of events that occur in proximity. It is in crises with these characteristics that biopsychosocial losses to the client (Strickler and La Sor 1970), an important factor in any emotional crisis, are most in evidence. An additional defining characteristic of Class 3 crises is that the refractory period (i.e., the time between the impact of the precipitating stressor and the ability to mobilize coping behaviors) is maximized, and the client is likely to experience a period of emotional shock and psychological immobilization. The client is emotionally overwhelmed, is unable to bring learned coping behaviors into play, and faces a situation he or she has not had to confront previously. The result is psychological vulnerability to learning maladaptive coping processes. It is the primary task of the crisis clinician to provide support and to develop understanding of the impact of the situation, while helping the client to mobilize available adaptive coping behaviors or to learn new ways to cope with stress.

Anticipatory guidance is also effective in this type of crisis once the period of emotional shock and psychological paralysis has passed. Although the crisis may be of a generic type, the client has had no preparation, and anticipatory guidance can be initiated only after the fact. Generic patterns for crises resulting from traumatic stress have been defined in this chapter. These response patterns, as with generic patterns found in adjustment to anticipated life transitions, are helpful to crisis therapists in guiding the client through the crisis.

Further, it is in Class 3 (as contrasted to Class 2) crises that the intensity and suddenness of the stress may increase the likelihood that the client will come to the attention of the police, the clergy, or the medical community, and consequently will be referred for appropriate help. It should also be noted that, to respond effectively to Class 3 crises, skills beyond those of the clinician trained to intervene in generic crises may be required for a significant proportion of clients.

REFERENCES

American Psychiatric Association, *Diagnostic and Statistical Manual.* Washington, D.C., 1952.
_____, *Diagnostic and Statistical Manual of Mental Disorders,* Revision II. Washington, D.C., 1968.
_____, *Diagnostic and Statistical Manual of Mental Disorders,* Revision III. Washington, D.C., 1980.
BENOLIEL, J. Q., "The Concept of Care for a Child with Leukemia," *Nursing Forum,* 11 (1972), 194–204.

BOURNE, P. G., *Men, Stress, and Vietnam.* Boston: Little, Brown & Company, 1970.

BREWIN, R., "TV's Newest Villain: The Vietnam Veteran," *TV Guide* (Summer 1975), pp. 4–8.

BRILL, N. Q., and G. W. BEEBE, *A Follow-up Study of War Neuroses.* Veterans Administration, Medical Monograph, Washington, D.C.: USGP, 1955.

BURGESS, ANN W., and LYNDA LYTLE HOLMSTROM, "Rape Trauma Syndrome," *American Journal of Psychiatry,* 131 (1974), 981–86.

———, "Coping Behavior of the Rape Victim," *American Journal of Psychiatry,* 133 (1976), 413–17.

———, "Recovery from Rape and Prior Life Stress," *Research in Nursing and Health,* 1 (1978), 165–74.

———, *Rape: Crisis and Recovery.* Bowie, Md.: Robert J. Brady Co., 1979a.

———, "Rape: Disclosure to Parental Family," *Women & Health,* 4 (1979b), 255–68.

———, "Adaptive Strategies and Recovery from Rape," *American Journal of Psychiatry,* 136 (1979c), 1278–82.

ENGEL, GEORGE L., "Is Grief a Disease? A Challenge for Medical Research," *Psychosomatic Medicine,* 23 (1961), 18–22.

———, "The Need for a New Medical Model: A Challenge for Biomedicine," *Science,* 196 (1977), 129–36.

ERIKSON, K., *Everything in Its Path.* New York: Simon & Shuster, 1976.

Federal Bureau of Investigation, *Uniform Crime Reports.* Washington, D.C.: U.S. Government Printing Office, 1970.

———, Uniform Crime Reports. Washington, D.C.: U.S. Government Printing Office, 1976.

FIGLEY, C. R., ed., *Stress Disorders among Vietnam Veterans: Theory, Research and Treatment.* New York: Brunner/Mazel, Inc., 1978.

FIGLEY, C. R., "Combat as Disaster: Treating the Vietnam Veteran as a Survivor." Paper presented at the American Psychiatric Association, Chicago, May 1979.

FIGLEY, C. R., and S. LEVENTMAN, eds., *Strangers at Home: Vietnam Veterans Since the War.* New York: Praeger, 1980.

FIGLEY, C. R., and W. T. SOUTHERLY, "Psychosocial Adjustment of Recently Returned Veterans," in C. R. Figley and S. Leventman, eds., *Strangers at Home: Vietnam Veterans Since the War.* New York: Praeger Publishers, Inc., 1980.

FRIEDMAN, S. B., et al., "Behavioral Observations on Parents Anticipating the Death of a Child," *Pediatrics,* 32 (1963), 610–25.

FRITZ, C. E., and H. B. WILLIAMS, "The Human Being in Disaster," *American Academy of Political Science Annals,* 10 (1957), 26–41.

GOFFMAN, E. "On Cooling the Mark Out: Some Aspects of Adaptation to Failure," *Psychiatry* 15 (Nov. 1952), 451–63.

GRINKER, R. R., and J. P. SPIEGEL, *Men Under Stress.* Philadelphia: Blakiston, 1945.

HAMMOND, W. A., *A Treatise on Insanity in Its Medical Relations.* London: H. K. Lewis, 1883.

HEALY, R. J., *Emergency and Disaster Planning.* New York: John Wiley & Sons, Inc., 1969.

HOLMSTROM, LYNDA L., and ANN W. BURGESS, "Rapists' Talk: Linguistic Strategies to Control the Victim," *Deviant Behavior,* 1 (1979), 101–25.

HOPKINS, L. J., "A Basis for Nursing Care of the Terminally Ill Child and His Family," *Maternal-Child Nursing Journal,* 2 (1973), 93–100.

LAZARUS, R. S., J. R. AVERILL, and E. OPTON, Jr., "The Psychology of Coping: Issues of Research and Assessment," in *Coping and Adaptations,* eds. G. Coelho, D. Hamburg, and J. Adams. New York: Basic Books, Inc., Publishers, 1974, 249–315.

LIFTON, R. J., and E. OLSON, "The Human Meaning of Total Disaster: The Buffalo Creek Experience," *Psychiatry,* 39 (1976), 1–8.

MARTINSON, I. M., and L. JORGENS, "Report of a Parent Support Group," in I. M. Martinson, ed., *Home Care for the Dying Child.* Englewood Cliffs, N. J.: Prentice-Hall, Inc., 1976.

MCGONAGLE, L. C., "Psychological Aspects of a Disaster," *American Journal of Public Health,* 54 (1964), 638–43.

MENNINGER, W. C., *Psychiatry in a Troubled World.* New York: Macmillan Publishing Co., Inc., 1948.

NEFZGER, M. D., "Follow-Up Studies of World War II and Korean War Prisoners, Vol 1: Study Plan and Mortality Findings," *American Journal of Epidemiology,* 91 (1970), 12–128.

SELIGMAN, M. E. P., *Helplessness: On Depression, Development and Death.* San Francisco: W. H. Freeman & Company, Publishers, 1975.

SHATAN, C. F., S. HALEY, and J. SMITH, "Johnny Comes Marching Home: Combat Stress and DSM III." Paper presented at the annual meeting of the American Psychiatric Association, Toronto, May 1977.

STRICKLER, M., and B. LA SOR, "The Concept of Loss in Crisis Intervention," *Mental Hygiene,* 54 (1970), 301–5.

SUTHERLAND, SANDRA, and DONALD SCHERL, "Patterns of Response among Victims of Rape," *American Journal of Orthopsychiatry,* 503–11.

TYHURST, J. S., "Individual Reactions to Community Disaster: The Natural History of Psychiatric Phenomena," *American Journal of Psychiatry,* 107 (1951), 23–27.

Veterans Administration's Board of Veterans Appeals, *Memorandum*

No. 01-78-12, on Posttraumatic Disorders. Washington, D.C., August 18, 1979.

WALLACE, A. F. C., "Mazeway Disintegration: The Individual's Perception of Socio-Cultural Disorganization," *Human Organization* (1957), 16.

WILSON, J. P., "Identity, Ideology and Crisis: The Vietnam Veteran in Transition, Part II." Mimeographed, Cleveland State University, 1977.

———, "Conflicts, Stress, and Growth: The Effects of War on Psychosocial Development among Vietnam Veterans," in C. R. Figley and S. Leventman, eds., *Strangers at Home: Vietnam Veterans Since the War.* New York: Praeger Publishers, Inc., 1980.

9

CLASS 4: DEVELOPMENTAL CRISES

Developmental or maturational crises are emotional crises resulting from attempts to deal with an interpersonal situation reflecting a struggle with a deeper (but usually circumscribed) issue. These developmental life issues have not been psychologically resolved adaptively in the past and thus represent unsuccessful attempts to attain emotional maturity. Several factors may account for a failure to resolve a life issue. One factor is that the individual may have had to deal with a stressful event to the detriment of achieving maturation of the normative life issues. Another factor involves the confrontation of the reality that a life goal cannot be realized, and this causes stress on the normal coping patterns. The clinician's task is to identify the key developmental issues involved as well as the impact of the current stressor.

There are a wide range of general examples of developmental crises with focal issues involving dependency, value conflicts, sexual identity, capacity for emotional intimacy, responses to authority, or the ability to attain reasonable self-discipline. Other situations include trauma situations that have created lags in the person's developmental progress such as deprived or abusive parenting experiences.

This chapter discusses two dimensions of developmental life crises. The first example about detecting child abuse describes techniques for assessment of ongoing abuse that interrupts development. The second example, incest, describes the developmental lags that may occur as a result of the child having to deal with the abuse during its formative years.

CHILD ABUSE

Year of the Child

The past decade has seen a growing interest in studying and improving the quality of life for young people. It was the United Nations that designated 1979 as the International Year of the Child, calling it a year to expand efforts to provide positive advances in the health of children, and to establish a "framework for advocacy on behalf of children and for enhancing the awareness of the special needs of children." Each nation was to organize its own programs, and in the United States each state was left to its own devices.

Professional organizations have attempted to develop strategies for implementing the United Nations' declaration. The American Nurses Association held hearings in five major cities—Boston, Atlanta, Los Angeles, Chicago, and Washington, D.C.—and testimony was provided from a wide sector of citizens including nurses, physicians, mental health professionals, researchers, public health officials, law enforcement officers, parents, and young people.

The American Psychological Association devoted a special issue of its official journal, the *American Psychologist,* to the topic of children. The issue was entitled, "Psychology and Children: Current Research and Practice," and it included essays in observance of the International Year of the Child. Two messages become clear in reading the published reports: (1) Many states view themselves as child-oriented and child-loving. (2) There is increasing evidence that this is not necessarily a true reflection of the facts.

Current Statistics on Health Needs of Youths

Health statistics over a 50-year period clearly identify changes in the causes of morbidity and mortality in children ages 1–4 and 5–14 (see Table 9–1). Scientific advances in our knowledge of infectious diseases and gastrointestinal disorders have helped reduce major causes of morbidity and mortality. When compared to 1970 statistics, these rates are less than one-tenth of what they were in 1920. In contrast, accidents are now the leading cause of death among children in the 1–15 age range (see Table 9–2). Also, homicides are ranked fifth in both age groups.

Infectious diseases such as venereal disease—gonorrhea in particular—have reached epidemic proportions among young people. Childhood gonorrhea, infection of the throat, urethra, vagina, or rectum (often asymptomatic), according to physician Suzanne Sgroi (1977), is indicative that the child has been a victim of child sexual assault. In Massachusetts, teenagers now account for one in five of the 10,000 new cases of gonorrhea seen annually.

Although the birthrate in general is declining, teenage pregnancies have dramatically increased. The number of children born to girls under the age of fifteen has doubled since 1960. Married teenagers have the highest birthrate of all—twice that of married women in the 20–24 age bracket. And births to unmarried females have risen from 35 to 130 percent in the last quarter of the century (National Center for Health Statistics 1973).

Self-destructive behavior is increasing in both children and adolescents. Although statistics indicate that children complete only a small number of suicides in comparison with other age ranges of the population, suicide threats and attempts are frequent among children (Hatton, Valente, and Rink 1977). A second self-destructive area is the use of alcohol and/or drugs—a behavior that is also increasing in scope. A California study (American Nurses' Association 1979) found that among those adolescents in the study sample who committed suicide, 40–50 percent were abusing alcohol and/or drugs at the time of their death. And in a Delaware study (Kelleher 1979) of the suicides reported in 1975, more than one-third were alcohol-related among teenagers.

Accidents account for the highest number of fatalities to children. A totally unexplored area is the nature of nonaccidental deaths. For example,

Table 9-1

Leading Causes of Death in Children, Both Sexes,
1–4 Years of Age, 1920 and 1970

	1920			1970	
Rank	Cause	No. 100,000	Rank	Cause	No. 100,000
1	Influenza and pneumonia	283.7	1	Accidents	31.5
2	Diarrhea, enteritis, etc.	141.3	2	Congenital anomalies	9.7
3	Diphtheria	90.5	3	Influenza and pneumonia	7.6
4	Accidents	80.2	4	Malignant neoplasms	7.5
5	Whooping cough	57.7	5	Homicide	1.9
6	Measles	56.4	6	Meningitis	1.9
7	Tuberculosis, all forms	45.4	7	Diseases of the heart	1.7
8	Scarlet fever	23.2	8	Enteritis and diarrhea	1.4
9	Dysentery	12.8	9	Acute bronchitis and bronchiolitis	1.0
10	Diseases of the ear, nose, and throat	12.3	10	Meningococcal infections	1.0
	All causes	987.2		All causes	84.5

Source: Adapted from *Facts of Life and Death* (DHEW, National Center for Health Statistics, 1974), pp. 33–34.

the incidence of arson is increasing nationally (Federal Bureau of Investigation 1976). A relatively unexplored area in the literature is the physical abuse of children receiving nonaccidental burns. Ayoub and Pfeifer (1979) conducted a study of children admitted with burns to a medical center in Tulsa, Oklahoma. Twenty-six children with burns received child abuse consultation for a one-year period. Of these 26 children, 7 were accidental with extreme neglect, and 5 appeared to have been inflicted, suggesting a 46 percent child abuse problem with burns.

Child sexual assault—forced as well as pressured sexual situations between adults and children—is increasing with regard to reporting. In 1968 Vincent DeFrancis (1969) in a study with the American Humane Association estimated a yearly incidence of about 40 per million. The number of cases seen at the Santa Clara County Child Sexual Abuse program in California suggests that the true incidence could be as high as 800 to 1000 per million (Giarretto 1976). The National Center for Child Abuse and Neglect estimates that the current annual incidence of sexual abuse of children in the United States is between 60,000 and 100,000 cases per year. In Boston, a six-month study of reported cases of sexual abuse, as compared with other abuse and neglect cases, indicated 4.6 percent of the cases were sexual abuse. In a city the size

Table 9-2

Leading Causes of Death in Children, Both Sexes,
5-14 Years of Age, 1920 and 1970

1920			1970		
Rank	Cause	No. 100,000	Rank	Cause	No. 100,000
1	Influenza and pneumonia	45.1	1	Accidents	20.1
2	Accidents	44.3	2	Malignant neoplasms	6.0
3	Diphtheria	28.0	3	Congenital anomalies	1.6
4	Tuberculosis	22.4	4	Influenza and pneumonia	2.2
5	Diseases of the heart	21.8	5	Homicide	0.9
6	Typhoid fever	7.1	6	Diseases of the heart	0.8
7	Diarrhea, enteritis	4.1	7	Cerebrovascular diseases	0.7
8	Chronic and unspecified nephritis	3.5	8	All other neoplasms	0.4
9	Diabetes mellitus	3.5	9	Suicide	0.3
			10	Bronchitis, emphysema, and asthma	0.3
	All causes	263.9		All causes	41.3

Source: Adapted from *Facts of Life and Death* (DHEW, National Center for Health Statistics, 1974), pp. 33-34.

of Boston, it is estimated that about 40,000 children have been sexually victimized by incest before their sixteenth birthday (American Nurses Association 1979).

Sexual exploitation of children and youths involved in prostitution and pornography is harder to uncover due to the secrecy of the activity and the reluctance of the young people to turn to agencies for assistance. As Lloyd Martin, investigative officer in charge of the sexually exploited child unit in Los Angeles, testified at the American Nurses' Association, Kansas City, hearings:

> We go out and look for victims. We don't wait for them to come to us because they don't. They don't complain. . . . We have found that the children that are involved in these situations want out, but they don't know who to turn to. . . . To me a crime against a child has no equal. [1977]

Testimony presented at the House hearings (1977) on the sexual exploitation of children estimated that approximately 7 percent of the United States pornographic market involved sexual activity between children and adults. Among adults, writes psychologist Robert Geiser (1979), kiddie porn involves four groups: (1) those who are stimulated by it; (2) those who make a considerable profit from it; (3) those who find it turns their stomach; and (4) those who have never seen it. However, because no epidemiological data on the number of child victims involved or quantitative data on the operational methods used by adult offenders exist, the actual extent and nature of child pornography and youth prostitution are not known at this time.

Identifying Child Abuse[1]

Scope of the Problem

Child abuse is reaching alarming proportions. It is not known whether the incidences of child abuse are actually increasing or whether the increasing numbers of abuse being reported are due to better recognition and reporting of the abuse. Whichever the reason, the spiraling increases are indicative of a national problem. It can no longer be called only a health problem because it affects the other professions of education, criminal justice, and social sciences as well. In 1977 Fontana noted that while the incidence of child abuse and neglect was increasing rapidly in some communities in the United States the

---

[1]This section, through p. 258, on "Identifying Child Abuse" is written by Ellouise Ruth Sneed and is adapted from and reprinted with permission from *Child Abuse*, National Organization of Victim Assistance Monograph Series, Hattiesburg, Miss., 1980.

majority of our professionals were not willing to recognize the existence of such parental misbehavior.

Both Jordan (1978) and Gray et al. (1977) state that about 300,000 cases of child abuse are reported annually. Of these 300,000 abused children, at least 60,000 sustain significant injuries, 6000 suffer permanent brain damage, and 2000 die as a result of direct trauma or neglect. As of 1978, the number of child abuse cases in Florida had tripled over the past five years. In New York City between 1973 and 1976 the number of reported child abuse cases jumped from 18,000 to 30,000. New York City reports 83 children die each year from physical abuse. This is more than one child per week (Mundie 1977).

The repetition of child abuse adds yet another dimension to the scope of the problem. Table 9-3, "The Repetition of Child Abuse," identifies the investigator of the study, the year conducted, the size of the sample, and the percentage of repetition according to each investigator's research.

Table 9-3

The Repetition of Child Abuse

Investigator(s)	Year	Sample Size	% Repetition
Morse, Sahler, Friedman	1970	25	33-1/3
Friedman	1972	25	33-1/3
Johnson & Morse	1968	Not stated	20% of survivors
Skinner & Castle	1969	Not stated	60%

Source: Herrenkohl et al. 1979.

Herrenkohl and colleagues (1979), in conducting their study of child abuse repetition, broke the percentage of repetition down into the number of times, the type of abuse, and the number of abuses. Tables 9-4 and 9-5 summarize the percent and type of abuse.

The repetition of abuse is clearly seen as another angle of the child abuse problem. Until there is uniformity and complete reporting of any and all abuse, the total scope of the problem cannot be fully explored.

Defining Terms

There are many definitions of child abuse. These definitions may include or exclude neglect, physical harm, emotional abuse, sexual trauma, or battery. The term "battered child" had its origin at a seminar sponsored by the American Academy of Pediatrics in 1961. Kempe and Helfer (1972) view "the battered child" as one that encompasses the total spectrum of abuse. Their

Table 9-4

The Repetition of Types of Child Abuse

Sample Size: 260 Families
Years: 1967-1976

Type of Abuse	Percent of Repetition
Physical	54.1
Emotional	21.4
Sexual	29.6
Gross neglect	44.4

Source: Herrenkohl et al. 1979.

Table 9-5

Number of Recurrences

Sample Size: 260 Families
Years: 1967-1976

Number of Families	Number of Recurrences	%
82	2	66.8
71	2 to 5	53.1
24	6 to 10	8.3
39	> 10	5.4

Source: Herrenkohl et al. 1979.

definition of a battered child is "any child who received nonaccidental injury (or injuries) as a result of acts (or omissions) on the part of his parents or guardians" (p. xi).

In the Herrenkohl et al. study (1979), the following definitions for four types of child abuse are given:

1. Physical abuse is serious nonaccidental, physical harm to a child.
2. Emotional abuse is serious emotional harm to a child.
3. Sexual abuse is sexual activity with a child.
4. Gross neglect is nutritional or medical neglect that is immediately dangerous to the health of the child, and includes the "failure-to-thrive" syndrome.

Since there is no standard definition for the terms, each state or organization must develop their own definitions. The State of New York has defined the following terms as related to child abuse.

Definition of Terms Commonly
Used in Child Abuse Cases

(Based on Child Protective Services Act of New York State 1978) Abused Child means a child less than sixteen years of age whose parent or other person legally responsible for his care:

a. inflicts or allows to be inflicted upon such child physical injury by other than accidental means which causes or creates a substantial risk of death, or serious or protracted disfigurement, or protracted impairment of physical or emotional health or protracted loss or impairment of the functions of any bodily organ, or

b. creates or allows to be created a substantial risk of physical injury to such child by other than accidental means which would be likely to cause death or serious or protracted disfigurement, or protracted impairment of physical or emotional health or protracted loss or impairment of the function of any bodily organ, or

c. commits or allows to be committed, a sex offense against such child, as defined in the penal law, provided, however, that the corroboration requirements contained therein shall not apply to the proceedings under this article.

Maltreated Child includes a child under eighteen years of age,

a. defined as a neglected child by the Family Court Act,
   (1) whose physical, mental, or emotional condition has been impaired or is in imminent danger of becoming impaired as a result of the failure of his parent or other person legally responsible for his care to exercise a minimum degree of care:
       (a) in supplying the child with adequate food, clothing, shelter, or education in accordance with the provisions of part one of Article 65 of the Education Law (truancy) or medical, dental, optometrical or surgical care, although financially able to do so, or offered financial or other means to do so, or
       (b) in providing the child with proper supervision or guardianship, by unreasonably inflicting or allowing to be inflicted harm, or a substantial risk thereof, including the infliction of excessive corporal punishment; or by using drugs or a drug; or by using alcoholic beverages to the extent that he loses self-control of his actions; or by other acts of a similarly serious nature requiring the aid of the court, or
   (2) who has been abandoned by his parents or other person legally responsible for his care.

b. Who has had serious physical injury inflicted upon him by other than accidental means.

Physical Indicators of Abuse

The child victim of physical abuse may receive any number or type or combination of physical injuries. The following outline of physical indicators of child abuse was presented at a conference on "The Child in Crisis" by the Louisiana State University School of Nursing and Southeast Louisiana Medical Services Council (1979):

A. Bruises and welts that may be indicators of physical abuse:
   1. Bruises on any infant, especially facial bruises.
   2. Bruises on the posterior side of a child's body.
   3. Bruises in unusual patterns that might reflect the pattern of the instrument used, or human bite marks.
   4. Clustered bruises indicating repeated contact with a hand or instrument.
   5. Bruises in various stages of healing.
B. Burns that may indicate abuse:
   1. Immersion burns indicating dunking in a hot liquid ("stocking burns" on the arms or legs or "doughnut" shaped burns of the buttocks and genitalia).
   2. Cigarette burns.
   3. Rope burns that indicate confinement.
   4. Dry burns indicating that a child has been forced to sit upon a hot surface or has had a hot implement applied to the skin.
C. Lacerations and abrasions that may indicate abuse:
   1. Lacerations of the lip, eye, or any portion of an infant's face (e.g., tears in the gum tissue, which may have been caused by force feeding).
   2. Any laceration or abrasion to external genitalia.
D. Skeletal injuries that may indicate abuse:
   1. Metaphyseal or corner fractures of long bones—a kind of splintering at the end of the bone (these are caused by twisting or pulling).
   2. Epiphyseal separation—a separation of the growth center at the end of the bone from the rest of the shaft (caused by twisting or pulling).
   3. Periosteal elevation—a detachment of the periosteum from the shaft of the bone with associated hemorrhaging between the periosteum and the shaft (also caused by twisting or pulling).
   4. Spiral fractures—fractures that wrap or twist around the bone shaft (caused by twisting or pulling).

E. Head injuries:
   1. Absence of hair and/or hemorrhaging beneath the scalp due to vigorous hair pulling.
   2. Subdural hematomas—hemorrhaging beneath the outer covering of the brain (due to shaking or hitting).
   3. Retinal hemorrhages or detachments (due to shaking).
   4. Jaw and nasal fractures.
F. Internal injuries:
   1. Duodenal or jejunal hematomas—blood clots of the duodenum and jejunum (small intestine) (due to hitting or kicking in the midline of the abdomen).
   2. Rupture of the interior vena cava—the vein feeding blood from the abdomen and lower extremities (due to kicking or hitting).
   3. Peritonitis—inflammation of the lining of the abdominal cavity (due to a ruptured organ, including the vena cava).
G. Injuries considered to be indicators of abuse should be considered in light of:
   1. Inconsistent medical history.
   2. The developmental abilities of a child to injure itself.
   3. Other possible indicators of abuse.
H. Questions to ask in identifying indicators of abuse:
   1. Are bruises bilateral or are they found on only one surface (plane) of the body?
   2. Are bruises extensive—do they cover a large area of the body?
   3. Are there bruises of different ages—did various injuries occur at different times?
   4. Are there patterns caused by a particular instrument (e.g., a belt buckle, a wire, a straight edge, coat hanger, etc.)?
   5. Are injuries inconsistent with the explanation offered?
   6. Are injuries inconsistent with the child's age?
   7. Are the patterns of the injuries consistent with abuse (e.g., the shattered egg-shell pattern of skull fractures commonly found in children who have been thrown against a wall)?
   8. Are the patterns of the burns consistent with forced immersion in a hot liquid (e.g., is there a distinct boundary line where the burn stops—a "stocking burn," for example, or a "doughnut" pattern caused by forcibly holding a child's buttocks down in a tub of hot liquid)?
   9. Are the patterns consistent with a spattering by hot liquids?
   10. Are the patterns of the burns consistent with the explanation offered?
   11. Are there distinct patterns caused by a particular kind of implement (e.g., an electric iron, the grate of an electric heater, etc.) or instrument (e.g., circular cigarette burns, etc.)?

Legal Implications for Any
Suspected Child Abuse

Statements such as the United Nations' Bill of Rights for Children are lofty and morally persuasive. But moral persuasion alone is not enough to influence societies to prevent such abuse or to implement mechanisms for helping such children (Martin 1979). Additionally, education and legislation are necessary components for the child and the parents.

In arguing for the economics of child protection laws, Nelson (1979) reported that between 1963 and 1967 the American Humane Association, the Council of State American Medical Association, and the American Academy of Pediatrics all published guidelines for legislation or model statutes. Although state legislatures were then inundated with requests for child abuse legislation, only the Illinois law carried an appropriation.

With the state and organizational acts came federal legislation. Senator Walter Mondale (D-Minn.) chaired the subcommittee that authored the Child Abuse Prevention and Treatment Act (CAPTA) that became law on January 31, 1974. With the passage of this law the United States has a visible national commitment to recognize child abuse.

The courts not only provide immunity for the report of child abuse, but in some states prosecute those who fail to report. The following example reported by Dec (1978) is indicative of more and more of the feelings of the courts.

> A decision by the California Supreme Court in 1976, for example, gives a child who "allegedly exhibits the medical condition known as the battered child syndrome," the right to press suit against the hospital and treating medical personnel if the hospital releases the child to the parent's care (even though child abuse is suspected, but not reported) and the child is subsequently injured by the parent. This case should encourage reporting by hospitals and health care professionals, if for no other reason than for their own protection. [P. 26]

The Family's Right to Privacy

Although acts, laws, and decisions have been rendered for the rights of children, it must be remembered there is an international recognition of family privacy. This international recognition acknowledges the philosophical and legal components of the family unit. The United States recognizes the family's rights to privacy through the Fourth and Fifth Amendments of the Bill of Rights of the U. S. Constitution. The Fourth Amendment protects the family's privacy by prohibiting the search of the home or person and the seizure of effects without just cause. The Fifth Amendment was made famous by the *Miranda* warnings and serves to protect a family's privacy by prohibiting custodial questioning by law enforcement officials after the person has been deprived of his or her freedom in any way (Caulifield 1977). If a parent is questioned about child abuse in the presence of a police officer, *Miranda* warnings must be used. If the person (other than a parent) suspected of child abuse is questioned without a police officer present, the *Miranda* warning probably would not be needed (Caulifield 1977). Thus, it becomes "necessary for professionals in the field to set standards for investigations which recognize the concept of family privacy and protect it while still allowing for investigation and protection of children within the family" (Caulifield 1977, p. 166).

The Child's Right to Protection

With so many acts and resources spent on developing child abuse legislation, many individuals have come to view the legislative system as a panacea. Instead, it is a reactive system and a reactive process. In fact, only in the past several years has the child's interest in court been protected by an attorney. This attorney is known as the guardian. As of early 1979 only 26 states required the child's interest to be represented. The parents have an attorney and the state has an attorney, but the child has no one to represent his rights against child abuse in 24 states in America.

Resolution of a child abuse case follows three basic steps in all states. These steps are: (1) identification and reporting of the suspected victim, (2) investigation of the report to determine its validity, and (3) treatment for the child and his or her family. It is estimated that only about one-third of America's reported abused children are being investigated and resolutions made (Fraser 1979).

In protecting children, Solnit (1979, p. 196) identifies pitfalls to avoid as follows:

1. The ritualistic overuse of professional consultation and evaluation of individual children and their families, which wastes valuable time and resources and which changes the focus away from the least detrimental placement to diagnostic and therapeutic considerations, thus ignoring the need for a careful decision about placement to be made with respect for the child's time tolerances.

2. The criticism and derogation of life styles different from our own.

3. Our inability to shift ground when too much time passes or if conditions change during the process of assigning custody; and

4. Our ineffectiveness in avoiding placement of the child and using our resources to strengthen the family in order to protect continuity and in order to utilize the existing family as the least detrimental alternative for what is

available in the real reality. This pitfall leads us away from the prevention of unnecessary foster care, and toward the risk of neglect by the state through multiple foster placements.

A Tool for Screening
Elementary School Children

Gray et al. (1977) are utilizing tools to observe mothers during and after delivery to prevent child abuse; public health nurses have been trained statewide in Pennsylvania to identify possible child abuse in the child from birth to five years of age (Elmer, Bennett, and Sankey 1979); and Jones and Fox (1979) have identified the need for diagnosing child abuse in the schools. Drews (1972) believes that for the older child who is abused, the school may be his or her only recourse.

The following tool (Table 9-6) has been developed by Sneed for screening the school-aged child. Parts of it may be used jointly by the schoolteacher or the school nurse. The responsibility for obtaining subjective data rests primarily with the teacher. It must be remembered that for the teacher to recognize abuse, she/he must have had prior education in normative child development. Utilizing the information from the checklist provided in the Index of Suspicion (Table 9-6), the nurse completes the data collection with the physical assessment of the child, evaluates, makes a decision, and acts accordingly. If child abuse is detected or suspected, some type of referral is indicated as well as decisions for treatment of the child and for therapy or other arrangements for the parents.

Reporting Child Abuse

An assessment of the findings from the Index of Suspicion (Table 9-6) should be analyzed and synthesized in a nonjudgmental manner. If a case of child abuse is indicated by the presenting problems as related to the items included in the checklist, it is the responsibility of the nurse to report his/her suspicions of child abuse to the proper authorities, and to seek medical assistance for the child.

The suspicion should be reported to the school physician (if there is one), the school principal, and the child protection agency. Protective restraining orders can be obtained by hospital administrators, city courts, or other juvenile protective agencies if deemed necessary.

Parents must be contacted and referred to appropriate agencies for counseling and psychiatric evaluation. This usually is the responsibility of the child protection agency.

Protection of the child from further abuse will be the result of the nurse's

Table 9-6

Index of Suspicion:
Tool for Suspected Child Abuse
to be Used by a School Nurse Practitioner

Date _____

Place of Interview _____

Name of Interviewer _____

Ethnic Group _____

Age _____

Sex _____

Chief Complaint _____

I. SUBJECTIVE DATA

	Yes	No
A. Growth and Development		
1. Attentive in class	___	___
2. Excessive absences	___	___
3. Homework prepared	___	___
4. Finishes projects started	___	___
5. Works with others	___	___
6. Abides by school rules	___	___
7. Volunteers for play, groups	___	___
8. Bathroom habits appropriate	___	___
B. Physical Health/Appearance		
1. Neat and clean, well-groomed	___	___
2. Appropriately clothed for weather	___	___
3. Average weight and height	___	___
4. Coordinated for age and sex	___	___
5. Eats in cafeteria	___	___
6. Brings lunch	___	___
7. Often sleeps in class	___	___
8. Bruises, burns, scars, welts, sores on skin	___	___
9. Break, sprain and/or injury of limb occurring off school grounds	___	___
10. Has #9 occurred more than once in school year?	___	___

Table 9-6 *(continued)*

	Yes	No
C. Emotional Status (circle as appropriate in addition to checking yes and no)		
1. Alert, smiling, playful	——	——
2. Prone to tears, moods	——	——
3. Disruptive to others	——	——
4. Hostile, bully, explosive	——	——
5. Timid, slow speech, stutters	——	——
6. Edgy, withdrawn	——	——
7. Preoccupied, daydreamer, fantasizes	——	——
8. Defensive, secretive	——	——
D. Family/Home Environment		
1. One parent, two parents	——	——
2. Parents separated, divorced, second marriage	——	——
3. Natural home, foster, extended	——	——
4. Child signs own report card	——	——
5. Attends school activities	——	——
6. Do parents attend school activities? Which parent?	——	——
7. Any siblings	——	——
8. Is this a second or middle child?	——	——
9. Family is self-supporting	——	——
10. Child has money for recreation (candy, movie, etc.)	——	——

	Yes	No	Describe
II. OBJECTIVE DATA			
A. Growth and Development			
1. Height	——	——	
2. Weight	——	——	
3. Appropriate for age/sex	——	——	
4. Appears stated age	——	——	
5. Well-nourished	——	——	
6. Volunteers information readily	——	——	
B. Physical Health Assessment			
1. Head, face, neck			
a. Skull symmetrical	——	——	
b. Excoriated areas visible	——	——	

Table 9-6 *(continued)*

		Yes	No	Describe
c.	Bruises, lacerations, scars, burns, welts, scratches, lumps present	——	——	
d.	Is any area of #c in various stages of healing?	——	——	
e.	Hair character and distribution	——	——	
f.	Edema	——	——	
g.	Missing, jagged, or cracked teeth	——	——	
h.	Able to protrude tongue between teeth	——	——	
i.	Swollen lip	——	——	
j.	Asymmetry of nose	——	——	
k.	Periorbital edema of eyes	——	——	
l.	Scars/discoloration	——	——	
m.	Bruised/scarred external ears	——	——	
n.	Exudate of ear canal	——	——	
o.	Scar tissue of tympanic membrane	——	——	
p.	Discoloration of tympanic membrane	——	——	
q.	Range of motion			
	Mobility of neck	——	——	
	Mobility of dorsal spine	——	——	

2. Thorax

a.	Symmetry	——	——	
b.	Respiratory excursion	——	——	
c.	Retractions/bulging	——	——	
d.	Bruises, welts, scars in various stages of healing	——	——	

3. Abdomen

a.	Bruises, welts	——	——	
b.	Tenderness	——	——	
c.	Organ borders			
	spleen	——	——	
	liver	——	——	
	kidneys	——	——	

Table 9-6 *(continued)*

	Yes	No	Describe
d. Burns	——	——	
e. Scars	——	——	
f. a, b, d and e as to stage of healing	——	——	
g. reflexes			
upper	——	——	
lower	——	——	
4. Back, Upper, and Lower Extremities			
a. Nails dirty, broken, chewed, split, absent	——	——	
b. Edema	——	——	
c. Hematomas, lacerations, scars, burns, welts, scratches, tatooes	——	——	
d. Are any of #c in various stages of healing?	——	——	
e. Bone asymmetry	——	——	
f. Cast and/or other immobilizers present	——	——	
g. Gait/balance intact	——	——	
h. Range of motion			
shoulder	——	——	
elbow	——	——	
wrist, fingers	——	——	
hip	——	——	
knee	——	——	
ankle, toes	——	——	
spine	——	——	
i. Muscles			
tone	——	——	
strength	——	——	
symmetry	——	——	
j. Sensory			
paresthesia	——	——	
hyperesthesia	——	——	
k. Reflexes			
biceps	——	——	

Table 9-6 *(continued)*

	Yes	No	Describe
k. Reflexes (continued)			
triceps	——	——	
bracho-radialis	——	——	
patella	——	——	
Achilles	——	——	

C. Emotional/Mental Status

1. Mood is

	Yes	No	
flat	——	——	
fear	——	——	
apathetic	——	——	
hostile	——	——	
appropriate	——	——	

2. Oriented to

	Yes	No	
time	——	——	
place	——	——	
person	——	——	

3. Mental functioning

	Yes	No	
impaired	——	——	
appropriate for age and sex	——	——	

D. Family/Home Environment

	Yes	No	
1. Do you like yourself?	——	——	
2. Do you like to be touched, hugged, or kissed?	——	——	
3. What is your favorite hobby?	——	——	
4. What are your home chores?	——	——	
5. Who helps you with your homework?	——	——	
6. Do you like school?	——	——	
7. Do you like church?	——	——	
8. What do you do with your mother and daddy that you like best?	——	——	
9. Do you play with your brothers and sisters?	——	——	
10. What is the most fun with your brothers and sisters?	——	——	

Table 9-6 *(continued)*

III. EVALUATION AND ACTION

Index of suspicion in the following areas as determined by the data base: Stated in the child's own words.

A. History:

1. Delay in seeking help.

2. Relates story of injury that deviates from clinical findings.

3. Reluctance to give information.

4. Frequent visits to school nurse.

5. Repeated absences from school due to injury/illness.

6. Presenting complaint deviates from clinical findings.

7. Passing the blame for injury on to himself, siblings, friend, or relative.

B. Physical Exam:

1. Signs of general neglect, poor skin hygiene, malnutrition, withdrawal, irritability, passiveness, regressed personality.

2. Bruises, abrasions, burns, soft tissue swellings, hematomas, lesions in varying stages of healing, tenderness of abdomen.

3. Evidence of dislocation, fractures of the extremities, painful inspirations and expirations.

4. Expresses aggressive behavior or fear, helplessness, or apprehension during physical exam.

and/or teacher's careful assessment of the presenting facts. It is to be remembered that the nurse and/or the teacher are legally bound to notify the child protection agency. The reporting person is protected with immunity when reporting in good faith.

SUMMARY

In summary, child abuse is becoming a visible problem in the United States. However, clinicians are being caught unprepared to assess, diagnose, report, and treat the abused child and his or her family. This section presents an assessment guide to use when child abuse is suspected.

SILENT VICTIMS OF INCEST— PEER GROUP PROJECT[2]

Clearly, not all child abuse is reported at the time it is occurring. In fact, to calculate the hidden crime statistics, it is estimated that two out of three children keep their abuse silent. This silence means the children have continued living to adulthood without receiving any acknowledgment or verification of the abuse and without resolving psychologically any of their feelings about the abuse.

With the successful advance of the Women's Movement, the issue of rape has finally received proper recognition as an external traumatic crisis. However, the understanding of rape trauma has surfaced a second type of sexual trauma—incest. Slowly, more and more women have begun talking about sexual abuse by a family member. This abuse may have occurred 5, 10, 40 or more years ago. The question then became, What type of intervention could be useful to adults who had been abused in their childhood? In an acute crisis situation, the clinician seeks to resolve a current external crisis and return the individual as quickly as possible to the precrisis level of functioning. With an unresolved crisis situation, additional interventions are felt to be needed to assist the person who had already made some type of adaptive response to the crisis.

In working with silent incest victims, it was decided to test a peer support group model. A pilot project was designed and initiated to answer two questions: (1) Would adult women gather together and identify themselves as incest victims and join in a peer support group? and (2) if yes, What would they discuss in the group?

The project was successful in that women did respond positively to the request to start a peer group for incest victims. In fact, three groups met over a

[2]This section, through page 271, is written by Hollis Wheeler.

one-year period. From these group meetings, two major areas were addressed: the disclosure of unresolved feelings about the incest experience, and unresolved developmental issues.

Unresolved Feelings about Incest

Any peer support group composed of adult women who experienced childhood sexual exploitation by a family member is likely to surface several unresolved feelings of intense importance to all group members. The most common unresolved feelings that all women discussed included guilt and self-blame, and anger.

Guilt and Self-Blame

The negative self-image held by incest victims has been noted by clinicians in the literature. The feeling, identified so clearly by the adult women in the support groups, that contributes the most to the negative self-image appears to be guilt and self-blame. It was almost universally noted by the women that they hold themselves, at least to some degree, responsible for the sexual assault. This unresolved feeling was noted by the way in which they focused on how they, rather than the offender, contributed to the situation. Some women still believed that they had been completely responsible for their own abuse. The women did not necessarily see themselves as victims ("It freaked me out when you used the word 'victim.' I never thought of myself as a victim before."). One woman described her situation with her brother and the way in which he would turn the issue around to convince her that she had to participate in the sexual activity or he would tell their parents. The woman said:

> Like I was doing something I should be ashamed of. He had obviously psyched me out quite well. I was terrified that my parents would find out that such a horrible thing was going on. . . . I was five or six, and the logic there is fairly primitive, but I felt properly ashamed.

Another victim explained the pressure her father placed on her to cooperate and how this made her feel guilty.

> He told me I didn't have to do it, but yet I was brought up to be an obedient child and felt his strong pressure to do it. His "asking" me . . . fooled me for more than fifteen years into believing I was both a willing party, and that it was my fault that all this happened.

Family members who know the sexual abuse is occurring may further contribute to the child feeling guilty about the sexual activity. For example, some family members may hold the child responsible or take action with the child that might be more appropriate to be taken with the family member-offender. One woman remarked on her mother's reaction:

> My mom said to me, "How could your sister let him [father] do that?" She didn't know then that he had done it to me too. We were both only eleven years old.

Another woman described her mother's reaction to disclosure of the activity:

> When my mother found out, it was horrible. She sent me to my grandmother's for the summer. Why didn't she send him [father] instead?

Therefore a major function of group participation was for members to clarify the ways in which they felt at fault and the dynamics that led them to this position. The facilitator takes as given that a child has no responsibility for her own sexual exploitation, that even were it the case that she literally verbally or physically solicited sexual contact, the only proper course of action for the adult to follow would be, at minimum, to refuse such contact. An important goal of support group intervention has been reached if the adult victim comes to feel and believe that she has no responsibility for her victimization—if she learns to see herself as one who has been trespassed against, not the trespasser; as a victim, not an offender.

> We have an awful lot in common as far as our reactions to things go— feelings of anger, which we had turned toward ourselves, and self-hate. One of the advantages of the group has been learning to get that anger out and turn it toward the people to whom it belongs instead of toward ourselves.

It is not surprising to find that low self-esteem and poor self-image occur in people if they believe they are responsible for sexual activity that is taboo and stigmatized. A child learns how to regard herself from the way significant others regard her. In the case where a significant male adult uses a child sexually, she learns that that is her value. Particularly in a society with a double standard where women are degraded if they engage in sexual activity outside marriage, the child feels degraded at the developmental stages when her identity is forming, often by the very person who should be guiding her toward a healthy self-concept.

> I talked a lot at one meeting about my own poor body-image, and I think the other women felt the same thing. I know that's common among women, but I think it was probably exacerbated by our experiences.

You know what it does to your concept of yourself, your self-esteem and your feelings of being a worthwhile, worthy person. . . .You're used and abused, you learn at such a young age that that's part of your self-image . . . .

That it's right for you to have been degraded or humiliated, and you continue to put yourself in positions where that will happen.

Of course, my brother never knew our father was abusing me. Once a few years later he told me Dad had said to him, "Sometimes you think the only thing women are good for is sex." I'll never forget the feeling I had when he said that.

A goal of the support group intervention has been reached if members begin to feel better about themselves, if they begin to reassess friendships or love relationships in which abusive patterns are continued, and if they change or remove themselves from such relationships.

It is believed that 75 percent of prostitutes were once sexually exploited children. In relation to this, it is extremely common that the erotic fantasies of nonprostitute adult victims of child sex abuse/assault will include fantasies of being a prostitute. Since prostitution is one of the most socially degraded and stigmatized occupations (with the prostitute bearing far more stigma and legal penalties than her male clients), it seems clear that eroticism becomes (for child victims) tied to a negative self-identity of worthlessness:

A lot of my sexual fantasies take the form of prostitution fantasies. That's an incredibly painful way to think about yourself, but it indicates your self-identity.

Another woman described her fantasies:

In my erotic fantasies I'm either being forced, or I'm a prostitute. [How much do you get paid?] Twenty-five cents!

Through the peer support group, it was suggested that a member monitor over time the character of her fantasy life: How does she picture herself in fantasy situations? What type of fantasy roles does she assume? We all "talk to ourselves." Therefore the individual should monitor the imagined tone of voice, attitude toward self, appellations, etc. For example, she might notice she characteristically belittles herself, is angry at herself, feels guilty, etc. This may echo the predominant attitude taken toward her when she was a child.

Also indicative of low self-esteem, all members of all groups had had suicidal thoughts, which a minority had acted on. This is also an important topic for discussion, and if anyone in a group seems presently seriously inclined toward suicide, an immediate referral is certainly indicated.[3]

> Every one of us, and every one of the women in a film about child sexual abuse victims we've recently seen has had suicidal thoughts or feelings or been suicidal to some extent. Every one of the people in the group . . . even those who dropped out. Every one of them. I don't know how far that can be generalized, but . . .

Anger

As the group progresses, the women begin to identify the offender, not themselves, as the person responsible for the abuse. Concurrently there will undoubtedly be a growing anger or even rage at the offender. Even for those who enter the group angry at the offender, this feeling of anger is likely to increase. The women may heretofore have been angry at themselves if they were blaming themselves. Or they may have had a globalized anger at men in general, in which case it is most beneficial if this anger is focused on appropriate specific targets whom they can now identify as having offended against them in specific ways. They may need "permission" to be angry at the offender, and the group can function to legitimize this feeling of anger and the need to explore this anger.

> I'd like to go back to New York and find the guy and kill him, but I know I'd never be able to do that because it was eleven years ago. But I might be able to find the precinct chief who told me I was probably just crying rape because he was really my boyfriend and I was mad at him, and that I'd probably enjoyed it. I want to express my rage at the way he treated me.

> I want my father to die. I want him to die. I just wish he were dead.

> Someday I'm going to bring a lawsuit against my mother and her lover for what they did to me.

This anger may also extend to others who failed to protect the victim, or whom the victim perceives as having failed to protect her from the offender:

> My therapist said that I was angry at my mother for letting this happen to me.

[3]Although not a prostitute, Marilyn Monroe is a famous example of a woman who earned her living trading off her body as a super sex star. She was by self-report engaged in intercourse at the age of ten by an adult male, and she was subsequently a suicide.

It has been suggested by some mental health professionals that dredging up a repressed event and experiencing intense rage at the offender might not be in the best interests of the adult victim. However, the author's position here is consistent with that taken in contemporary Feminist Anger workshops. That position argues that it is not anger, per se, but what is done with the feeling that can be a problem. Anger used in a clear, direct way is an emotional tool that can be used in protection of the self. What is difficult is to activate change in ourselves and our world, and anger can be used as a positive energy for the activation of such change.

> My shrink said he thought it wasn't good for me to dredge up all this stuff again and go through this rage at my father. But I told him deep in my guts it felt healthy to be so angry, and now I wasn't angry at myself any more.

Women have a legitimate fear of expressing anger, of being called "angry women," in our society, because anger in women usually meets with strong disapproval. The feminist position is that anger at being abused, exploited, or assaulted is a reasonably healthy appropriate response.

One way for the group to get clarification on anger and other feelings is to go in a circle and ask each member to respond to the instructions: "Give your imagination free rein. If anything were possible, what would you like to see happen to the offender now?"

One woman who was sexually abused by her mother stated that she would like to get her mother to admit that she really did it. Another woman said she would like to confront the offender and hear him apologize for what he did to her. Writing a letter or a series of letters—which are not to be mailed—has also been suggested as an individual clarification or treatment technique, one that could be adapted for group use. It has been reported from some support groups that letters to family member offenders have actually been mailed.

It is difficult for some women to deal with their ambivalence toward the offender. Some women may want to resolve the abuse issue and continue some type of positive or ongoing relationship with the offender ("I want to believe my mother and father are good people."), whereas others may hate the offender. The action of severing all ties with the offender or "disowning" the offender has been reported. As one woman stated:

> I refer to him in conversation as my "ex-father." I had the post office return his mail unopened and marked "refused." I wrote him out of my will and I am not going to his funeral when he dies.

In such situations, the nature of relationships with other relatives may have to be negotiated. One woman stayed in touch with her stepsisters but told her stepmother that she would not see her until she divorced the father or until he died. Another woman stated her behavior in relationship to her parents:

> I never see my father any more. But now I can only see my mother when he is out of town on business. I don't think that's fair. I'm going to write to her and tell her I want her to meet me to be with *me*, not just when he's gone.

Unresolved Developmental Issues

Important factors influencing the unresolved issues included the length of the sexual abuse as well as the extent of the sexual activity and if physical assault was part of the abuse cycle. The unresolved developmental issues were: survival, trust/distrust, autonomy and control, power/dependency, and sexuality. These life issues are basic to the growth of all children. When there is interference, such as in child sexual abuse, the issues stay unresolved.

Survival

Some child victims may have been severely battered by one or both parents in addition to being sexually abused. The effects of beating and even torture interrelate with other issues, and victims should be supported in their discussion of this abuse.

> He used to take satisfaction in being able to kick accurately enough to *only* break a rib. . . . I am certain when they operated on my eye, they knew it was from battering. In all these years no doctor has ever asked me how my eye got to be this way.

Whether in response to sexual abuse or battering, much of the child's energy normally channelled into growth will be used up in self-protection and survival. Concentrating energy for such a basic need produces lags in development and behavioral styles that carry over into adulthood. Some specific behaviors typical of severely abused children include: inhibited verbal or crying response, extreme shyness, dependency, excessive self-control and concern for the needs of others, and fear of physical contact. The severely abused group member may discuss the ramifications in her adult life.

> I know the reason I keep my posture slumped over and my arms in front of me now is because my father used to threaten to cut off my breasts when I got big.

Trust/Distrust

A major unresolved developmental issue for all victims is the betrayal by the offender, and the ensuing distrust that may generalize from the offender to other groups such as all men or all people ("The ability to trust men is just shot."). Generalized distrust is problematic in the life of any individual, and a goal of the group can be to learn to discern whom it is reasonable to trust and to try to take the risk of trusting. If the group is experienced as trustworthy, that can be a first step in generalizing trust outward to other *selected* persons. As one woman said:

> I agree with what was said about not being able to accept sincere love from another person. I do a lot of testing of people that, intellectually, I know care about me. I'll test them anyway because it's too frightening to trust them. You think, "What if this person ends up taking advantage of me or using me?"

Some women find it more satisfactory to systematically eliminate men from part or all of their lives. This may be not only a sexual but also a socio-political choice as part of an integrated life structure.

> It can be hard to have a love relationship with a woman, too, but I would rather struggle for that relationship with a woman than with a man.

Autonomy and Control

Children who are abused by someone in a position of authority—as family members are—frequently fail to develop a sense of autonomy and control over their lives. The silence forced on children isolates them from each other. Frequently when the abuse comes to light, the child's experience is either rejected (as when she is blamed for her own exploitation) or disbelieved. These two societal responses function just as effectively to isolate the child as does a child's self-imposed silence. Given these responses, not only is it common for the child to blame herself, but it is not uncommon for her to actually doubt the reality that part of all of the abuse actually happened to her. This self-doubt negates any autonomy and control the child may be trying to exert developmentally. As a corrective experience, the existence of a support group is premised on disclosure; that is, disclosure in a supportive, nonchallenging atmosphere, where the belief of others can help the victim believe in herself and begin to take control of her life.

Members may or may not have ever disclosed their victimization before joining the group. If they have disclosed previously, discussion may help to clarify issues, and it may also encourage nondisclosing members to discuss painful issues. The following quotes illustrate the issue of disclosure and how the developmental issue of autonomy and control can be facilitated.

> I had never told anybody before I joined the group. There was always this feeling that people would think you were really strange and that you must be totally screwed up because of what happened. As it turned out, people were a little bit shocked—they were taken aback—but then they would just sort of shake their heads and feel anger.

> After I wrote that letter to [the offender, a family member], I was really scared of how my mother would react. But she was great; she came and visited me here and said she was glad I had done it.

As the victim begins to accrue positive experiences, she may grow dissatisfied with the silent role and assert more autonomy. Disclosures may snowball, and she may begin to touch the lives of other silent victims.

> I have had so much support—so much sympathy. Every time somebody tells me they hate my father, it makes me feel *so good!*

> I found that when someone would say to me, "Oh, yes, my sister was abused," or something like that, it made a big difference. The fact that you're not alone is just so important.

> The more I talk about it, even just among my circle of women friends—all of a sudden you find out that this woman you've known for seven years was abused, as a child, by her uncle; you find out that this woman you've known for four years has been raped twice as an adult.

However, it is also possible that the victim will find the reaction mixed or negative.

> When I told the man I was going out with, he was very supportive at first—he said it was a *shame* it had happened, and that his sister had told him the previous year about an employee of their father's who had molested her. But later when we stopped dating and I asked him why he didn't want to have a relationship with me, he said something about my "bad family data." It took me months to get over that, and I wouldn't tell my next boyfriend until a long time after I knew him.

Power/Dependency

The child victim, whether she is conscious of it or not, is extremely powerless and vulnerable to the pressure of an authority figure such as father or uncle, or to the brute force used by an older brother or neighborhood assailant. This may well leave her with unresolved issues of dominance/ dependency that may be transferred to her subsequent relationships. Her participation in the support group may provide a vehicle for her to gain a feeling that she is taking control of her life simply by the action it takes to attend the group. Furthermore, discussion by a member of issues of power, dominance, and dependency in her life, if it clarifies the dynamics of her previous victimization, may further the sense that she could not then, but now can, take control of her own life.

> I think this group has really helped me a lot, not only for all the companionship and support and caring and sharing and having people to talk with about my problem who will understand, because they've had similar experiences, but also I think I've gained a lot of confidence, just from being in the group. I'm able to do things I couldn't do before. Stuff like if I feel like crying in the middle of class, I can go into the bathroom and cry. Somehow I just had never realized that I could do that.

> We're now in positions where we *can* help ourselves. When the abuse took place, we weren't *able* to; we were children. We're learning and accepting that we're adults; now—we don't have to put up with that kind of behavior in any form. And *we can* do something about the feelings that we have; we're not just stuck with them.

> Looking back, I'm glad that I went through the whole experience of the group. It was very hard, emotionally—very draining—but I start feeling the strength coming from it now. And I think that will increase as time goes on. I can say, now, "I have a problem and I can do something about it." My family aways communicated to me that you don't admit you have problems, as though you don't have them if you don't admit you have them.

> I'd like to say the group's helped me with my school work, but I'm not sure it has! But it's definitely helped me feel less suicidal, which makes it easier to do school work.

Group experience may also provoke other actions in a victim's activities outside the group—where she actively takes control of her life, particularly insofar as she feels she can limit or eliminate further sexual victimization.

> Yesterday morning I sailed into the diner feeling strong and rested, and these three guys stared at my body from the counter, particularly my breasts—that "mentally undressing you" stare. I was in such a frame of mind, without a second's reflection I swept over to them and demanded in a loud, outraged voice everyone in the place could hear, "What are you guys staring at? Do I look funny or something? You don't have any right to look at me like that!" They were literally slack-jawed, all three of

them, speechless. I felt so great. I would never have done that a couple months ago.

I'm taking a martial art!

A technique used in one group to approach the vulnerability/power issue was to imagine other outcomes to the offender's initial attempt to gain sexual access to the victim—fantasizing outcomes more to the liking of the victim. After the members were familiar with each other's histories, one member went around the circle, constructing out loud a fantasy conclusion to the beginning of the real episode in the victim's past.

> Sylvia, let's say it's the first time your brother comes to your room and twists your arm behind your back. But at the head of the stairs you get the better of him—instead of being able to force you outdoors, you flip him over your shoulder and he bounces all the way down the flight [howls of tense, delighted glee from all group members]—he lands at the bottom in a heap, and you dust your hands together and say over your shoulder, "That's nothing compared to what you'll get if you try that again," and you go back to your room and go to sleep without being at all bothered.

It is not necessary that the alternative conclusion have a humanistic outcome if that's not the way the victim feels. Revenge is what is important now, although perhaps a "humanistic" reaction that takes account of the offender's problems may develop later. The opinion of one (female) psychiatrist, that the incest victim should at least forgive and ideally forget the episodes, strikes many ex-incest victims as quite unrealistic and totally undesirable.

The group may provide a particular type of openness by virtue of it's being a group of peers, even though the victim may have disclosed to a few chosen outsiders previously.

> Member 1: I can look at anyone in the group and know that I'm not alone, that they went through the same thing, that I don't have to explain anything. I don't have to justify—they *know* that I was a victim and not an offender. They *know* what it means to feel miserable and to hate yourself and to blame yourself. They *know* how many years you have suffered. It doesn't last a year and then go away, which is the model I was operating under.

> Member 2: I don't know how "enjoyable" a group session is; it's frustrating, but we laugh a lot. It's unhappy laughter, but it's laughter that comes from being in the same situation, going through the same rotten thing, and somehow being able to laugh about it together.

Member 3: There's a lot of "in group" humor. If somebody outside the
group made some of the cracks we make, I'd be furious!

Member 4: It's victim humor. I'd want to claw somebody in the face who
made a crack about incest. I'd hate them. But when one of us
makes a crack, it's just a howl. In the group we accept our
experiences and start from there. We're not ashamed of our
feelings, or of ourselves.

Sexuality

The unresolved issue of trust may be observed particularly in subsequent
sexual relationships. Two factors from childhood incest identified by the
group as influencing sexuality were low self-esteem and subjective response.
The frequency of prostituting fantasies and/or actions has been previously
discussed. Another concern is the frequency in which the women described a
lack of subjective sexual response, as through orgasm. Women reported being
unable to focus on their own sexual pleasure and therefore "faking" orgasm.
Sometimes the trust issue surfaces ("It's very, very hard to believe that a man
really cares about you. It's almost impossible."), and other times the
exploitation issue is major ("You figure he must be using you in some kind of
secret, sneaky way."). In the following example, the woman emphasized her
identification with the "pathology" of the offender.

Sometimes I have trouble relating to men who are "healthy" sexually.
When they don't insult you, when they don't force sex on you, you don't
know how to handle it. You think there must be something wrong with
them. But now I'm having an affair with a man who is emotionally
"healthy" and I keep wanting to do something to make him insult me. I
think he just must be hiding his contempt for me.

A woman may be troubled by flashbacks to the childhood memory of
incest during her adult sexual activity. The feeling of revulsion to the sexual
contact with the offender may recur in subsequent willing sexual encounters
("My husband touched me on the shoulder the way my father did and I
shuddered.").

Sexual activity, including whatever sexual arousal may have occurred in
the child, may be associated with fear, coercion, and pain. At the time of the
abuse/assault, the victim may have been trying to disassociate herself from
her body.

The revulsion may be felt toward heterosexual contact in general. At
least one-third of the women in the three support groups identified themselves
as lesbian in sexual orientation. Even with a change in sexual orientation,
childhood sexual exploitation may interfere with the sexual response of
lesbian women.

Influence of Incest
on Other Relationships

Child/Adolescent Peer Relationships. While other children are busy exploring their sexuality and maturing social relationships, the victim's attention is diverted to guarding her secret. As one woman stated:

> At slumber parties when they were talking about holding hands with boys, I was terrified they would see through my feigned ignorance and somehow magically know I had had sex with my father.

Another women described her perceptions of how she felt her friends viewed her:

> Because I had this big secret, and was spending my time on secret meetings, some of my friends labeled me as a "loner" and a "weirdo." I felt very disconnected from my peers' lives. And it's only been in the last few years that I trust friends and have normal peer relationships.

Family Relationships. The developmental issue of family integrity can be markedly disrupted by an incest experience. In one group there was prolonged discussion of a sense of sadness that the incest had happened, that this was "what our families were like." The bitterness about the very word *family* was raised as the group worked on the issue ("I want to choke whenever I say 'my family.' The word is a bitter travesty to me."). One observation was that in many families everyone just takes for granted some assumptions about family life. In incest families, this is not the case. And one woman stated:

> The family thing increases all the feelings that women generally have. I'd be pretty certain in saying that just because these are the people that society says are supposed to give you all your support and your strength they've done just the opposite to you. They've taken that away from you. I think all of us have a rather cynical attitude toward families.

SUMMARY

In summarizing the group experience, as women in groups validate each other, their experience, and themselves, the secrecy that supports stigma wanes. Disclosure may begin for many in the simple act of self-selecting for such a support group. The disclosure may extend to nongroup members during the course of the group's duration, and there is every indication that this process continues after termination. For example, women began to "go public" about their incest experiences as follows:

Some women at the Boston "Take Back the Night" march wore sashes saying, "I lived through a rape." Lili and I wore sashes saying "Incest Victim."

Another member of the support group reported her experience in disclosing her victimization:

I decided I wanted to live in a household with women and men, so I could have relationships with men on other than a sexual basis. When I interviewed these two guys to be a roommate, I told them I was an incest victim and I wanted to be able to freely speak about issues of violence and abuse. They both handled it pretty well, and I'm going to move in. Five months ago before the support group I wasn't even acknowledging it to myself.

A peer support group of adult victims of childhood sexual exploitation is apt to bring to light several issues of intense importance to all members. In addition, unresolved issues will arise that are common to the group. The etiology of unresolved incest trauma is guilt and self-blame. Freeing the repressed anger at the perpetrating family member and giving permission to express that anger enables the woman to move toward identifying unresolved developmental issues.

GENERAL INTERVENTION STRATEGY IN DEVELOPMENTAL CRISES

Developmental or maturational crises are typically encountered in adolescent and young adults, although at times a struggle with a specific maturational issue may continue far beyond young adulthood, as in the case of unresolved childhood traumas. In this type of emotional crisis, there is usually a clearly defined underlying issue (conflict) that represents an attempt to attain culturally defined criteria of emotional maturity (Baldwin 1977). Such crises are frequently presented as "another episode" in a pattern of relationship problems that have similar dynamics (of which the client may have varying levels of awareness) and in which the developmental issue involved has been instrumental in producing the crisis or preventing adaptive resolution.

Coons (1971) has defined several of the most important developmental issues such as trust, autonomy, independence that currently face young adults and that must be resolved adaptively in order to be deemed "mature." Treatment methods such as crisis therapy for resolving developmental conflicts have been conceptualized for individuals (Oxley 1973) and for young couples for whom developmental issues are becoming an increasing part of the caseload of community mental health centers and of university mental health services and counseling centers, as well as among paraprofessionally staffed crisis counseling services.

The basic intervention strategy for developmental/maturational crises is to conceptualize the underlying issue instrumental in producing the crisis situation in a relationship, and to define more adaptive means of responding to the other person in the area of greatest ambivalence (i.e., means that reflect the focal issue). Emphasis is placed on defining patterns in relationships that are determined by this underlying issue, on conceptualizing the issue clearly during the crisis contact, on defining its etiology/dynamics, and on developing more adaptive interpersonal responses. As the client is supported by the therapist, the client is encouraged to respond more adaptively to the crisis situation, while the dynamics that have produced maladaptive responses in the past are worked through. Although, in crisis intervention, material from the past is used sparingly and only as related to the present crisis, the Class 4 type of crisis represents a unique opportunity to blend present interpersonal difficulties that represent a focal dynamic issue (with its etiology in the past) into an effective growth experience for the client.

In maturational/developmental crises, there is a tendency by young adults to represent their crises within the framework of major social conflict, controversy, or ambivalence. For example, in the 1960s many developmental crises were presented within the context of drug use and counterculture values, whereas in the 1970s there has been a clear shift to developmental crises becoming more frequently presented as sexuality-related problems (Baldwin 1975). Too often in crisis intervention there is response only to the manifest problem of the client, and developmental issues involved are missed or neglected.

REFERENCES

AMERICAN NURSES' ASSOCIATION, "A Report on the Hearings of the Unmet Health Needs of Children and Youths," Kansas City, Mo., 1979.

AYOUB, C., and D. R. PFEIFER, "Burns as a Manifestation of Child Abuse," in C. H. Kempe, ed., *Child Abuse and Neglect,* Vol. 3. London: Pergamon Press Ltd., 1979.

BALDWIN, BRUCE, *Sex-Related Problems: Reflections of Emotional Growth.* New York: Planned Parenthood Federation of America (Youth and Student Affairs), 1975.

CAULIFIELD, B. A., "Legal Questions Raised by Privacy of Families and Treatment of Child Abuse and Neglect," in C. H. Kempe, ed., *Child Abuse and Neglect,* Vol. 1. London: Pergamon Press Ltd., 1977.

COONS, F., "The Developmental Tasks of the College Student," in *Adolescent*

Psychiatry, Vol. 1, S. Feinstein, P. Giovacchini, and A. Miller, eds. New York: Basic Books, Inc., Publishers, 1971.

DEC, D., "The Abused Child, the Abusing Adult: A Non-Judgemental Attitude," *The Journal of Practical Nursing* (September 1978), pp. 25–29.

DEFRANCIS, VINCENT, *Protecting the Child Victim of Sex Crimes Committed by Adults.* Denver, Colo.: American Humane Association, 1969.

DREWS, K., "The Child and His School," in C. H. Kempe and R. E. Helfer, eds., *Helping the Battered Child and His Family.* Philadelphia: J. B. Lippincott Company, 1972.

ELMER, ELIZABETH, H. G. BENNETT, and C. G. SANKEY, "A State-Wide Child Abuse Training Program for Public Health Nurses," in C. H. Kempe, ed., *Child Abuse and Neglect,* Vol. 3. London: Pergamon Press Ltd., 1979.

Federal Bureau of Investigation, *Uniform Crime Reports.* Washington, D.C., 1970.

———, *Uniform Crime Reports.* Washington, D.C., 1976.

FONTANA, V. J., "The Abused Child," *Nursing Care,* Vol. 10 (November 1977).

FRASER, B. F., "Child Abuse in America: A de Facto Legislative System," in C. H. Kempe, ed., *Child Abuse and Neglect,* Vol. 3. London: Pergamon Press Ltd., 1979.

GEISER, ROBERT, *Hidden Victims.* Boston: Beacon Press, 1979.

GIARRETTO, HENRY, "Humanistic Treatment of Father-Daughter Incest," in R. E. Helfer and C. H. Kempe, eds., *Child Abuse and Neglect: The Family and the Community.* Cambridge, Mass.: Ballinger Publishing Co., 1976.

GARY, J. D., et al., "Prediction and Prevention of Child Abuse and Neglect," in C. H. Kempe, ed., *Child Abuse and Neglect,* Vol. 1. London: Pergamon Press Ltd., 1977.

HATTON, C. L., S. M. VALENTE, and A. RINK, *Suicide Assessment and Intervention.* New York: Appleton-Century-Crofts, 1977.

HERRENKOHL, R. C., et al., "The Repetition of Child Abuse: How Frequently Does It Occur?" in C. H. Kempe, ed., *Child Abuse and Neglect,* Vol. 3. London: Pergmaon Press Ltd., 1979.

House Hearings before the Subcommittee on Crime, House of Representatives, Serial #12, 95th Congress, 1st Sessions. Washington, D.C.: U. S. Govt. Printing Office, 1977.

JONES, C. D., and P. F. FOX, "American Educational Systems and Child Abuse and Neglect," in C. H. Kempe, ed., *Child Abuse and Neglect,* Vol. 3. London: Pergamon Press Ltd., 1979.

JORDAN, F. B., "Recognizing the Child Maltreatment Syndrome," *The American Operating Room Nursing Journal,* 27 (1978), 636–41.

KELLEHER, D. (Associate Justice Family Court of Delaware, testifying at the

Washington D.C. Hearings), "A Report on the Hearings of the Unmet Health Needs of Children and Youths." Kansas City, Mo.: American Nurses' Association, 1979.

KEMPE, C. H., and R. E. HELFER, eds., *Helping the Battered Child and His Family*. Philadelphia: J. B. Lippincott Company, 1972.

Louisiana State University School of Nursing and Southeast Louisiana Emergency Medical Services Council, Inc., in collaboration with the Emergency Department Nurses Association and the South Louisiana League of Nursing, "The Child in Crisis Conference." Metairie, Louisiana, 1979.

MARTIN, H. P., "Child Abuse and Child Development," in C. H. Kempe, ed., *Child Abuse and Neglect*, Vol. 3. London: Pergamon Press Ltd., 1979.

MUNDIE, G. E., "How You Can Help," *Nursing Care*, 10 (November 1977), 11–12.

National Center for Health Statistics, *A Study of Infant Mortality from Linked Records by Age of Mother, Total-Birth Order, and Other Variables*, Series 20, No. 14. Washington, D.C.: U.S. Govt. Printing Office, 1973.

———, *Monthly Vital Statistics Report, Summary Report, Final Natality Statistics*, 23, no. 115. Washington, D.C.: U.S. Govt. Printing Office, 1976.

NELSON, B. J., "The Politics of Child Abuse and Neglect: New Governmental Recognition for an Old Problem." in C. H. Kempe, ed., *Child Abuse and Neglect*, 3. London: Pergamon Press, Ltd., 1979.

OXLEY, G., "Short-Term Therapy with Student Couples,"*Social Casework*, 54 (1973), 216–23.

PECK, M. L., and R. E. LITMAN, "Current Trends in Youthful Suicide," in *Sociol Muerte*. Madrid: Trubuna Medica, Spring 1974.

SGROI, SUZANNE M., "Kids with Clap: Gonorrhea as an Indicator of Child Sexual Assault," *Victimology*, 2 (1977), 251–67.

SOLNIT, A. J., "The Rights of a Child in a Changing Society,"in C. H. Kempe, ed., *Child Abuse and Neglect*, Vol. 2. London: Pergamon Press Ltd., 1979.

10

CLASS 5: CRISES REFLECTING PSYCHOPATHOLOGY

Crises reflecting psychopathology include emotional situations in which preexisting psychopathology has been instrumental in precipitating the crisis. Or the situation may involve a state in which the psychopathology significantly impairs or complicates adaptive resolution. The clinician needs to be able to diagnose the psychopathology and adapt the therapy approach to include appreciation of the personality or characterological aspects of the client.

The examples of crises reflecting psychopathology would include clients presenting with borderline adjustment, severe neuroses, characterological disorders, or schizophrenia. The traditional diagnostic categories are essential to know in working with such a client.

The following discussion of the multiproblem family in crisis attempts to illustrate some of the points of Class 5 crises.

THE MULTIPROBLEM FAMILY IN CRISIS[1]

How do we identify the multiproblem family? What is important or unique in this type of family that makes its response to crisis different from any other family undergoing a crisis? How does one assess a multiproblem family, and

[1] This section, through p. 294, written by Carol R. Hartman.

what are the implications of the assessment in terms of intervention? What can be the expected outcome of efforts to assist such families?

In an attempt to answer these questions, it is useful to start with a definition of "multiproblem family." For the purposes of this chapter, a multiproblem family is a unit of parent(s) and children who have developed family patterns that, to a lesser or greater degree, impinge on the family's continued ability to cope with conflict and to develop and release its progeny to enter into age-appropriate activities within the family and external to the family. The frequency of stressful life events, the inefficient reaction to these stressful life events, and/or the failure to support individual transitional developmental tasks can be either causal or the consequence of the deficiencies within the family. The factors sustaining functional deficiencies within a family unit must be understood from three major sources. One is the surrounding social environment, which supplies the family with material resources and imparts information as to how the family is accepted into the larger social system; two is the extended kinship system of the nuclear family and what it supplies genetically, socially, and materially; and three is the family unit itself and what it teaches its members about themselves and the family as a whole, through its internal allocation of affective and material resources.

Despite tremendous environmental stressors, many families in difficult circumstances function in a strong, positive manner. These families may have their strength disrupted by external events, but with some relief from the pressure they can reestablish their ability to function. For example, a family may be disrupted when the father loses his job, but once he finds a job, the family resumes its productivity. This is in contrast to a family that never resumes its productivity, even though the father regains employment. What is implied here is that, despite intervention, the multiproblem family is a unit that does not readily regain its previous level of functioning because of a lack of resiliency in responding to the life stressors.

Why families lack this resiliency is not known. Theories and empirical studies associate many variables with dysfunctional families, including poverty, the effects of racism, genetics, unrelenting environmental stress (such as criminal activity in the street), deaths of loved ones, or a complex history of physical and/or mental illness in the family. What one can assume from these investigations of cause is that a family's probability of losing its resiliency to function in an adaptive, productive manner is increased the more the associated life stressors surround the family and the longer these stressors have impinged on the evolution of the family. Thus far, the assumptions advanced emphasize the association of life stressors with a lack of resiliency on the part of the family and an inability to regain productive equilibrium. Much of this definition leaves one thinking that the multiproblem family can only be identified after the fact, that is, after the crisis and intervention in terms of the crisis. But how does this definition help one identify a multiproblem family beforehand?

Although one may come upon a family in crisis and be able to discern many of the hardships the family has been subjected to in the recent past, the impact of these hardships is not always clear until there has been time spent with the family, detailing important events in its struggle for survival. Is there anything to be learned about a multiproblem family as it addresses a crisis? There seems to be some use in assessing how a family structures itself around a crisis. The patterning of the family can contain useful information by which a multiproblem family can be identified.

Family patterns that either enhance family life or detract from it may be viewed in terms of mentally healthy or mentally ill behavior. Assumptions of family dynamics underscore the premise that deviant behavior of a family member represents a total family problem, not just a problem of the individual. The pattern of response to an individual member's problem behavior reveals immediate information about the family's internal organization and how it maintains itself. The multiproblem family can literally fall apart in the face of one member's problem; the other family members can scatter, or they can mobilize factions that focus the blame for the problem on the particular member (scapegoating). Such immediately observable interactional activities can reveal important structural and organizational strategies in a family that are clues as to what interpersonal resources are available for the family's survival and as to what end the deviant behavior addresses.

The emphasis on family patterns in the definition requires investigation of a variety of points of view about family life as well as about family disorganization and individual psychopathology. The intention of this section is not to review this material, but, rather, to present a formulation of the most salient concepts from the literature and how they apply to understanding the multiproblem family in crisis.

Briefly, then, to move in our definition from relying totally on identifying what a multiproblem family cannot do for itself to what the multiproblem family does do, requires some discussion on how families structure themselves and how this structure is revealed in interactional behaviors among family members and to people outside of the family, and in the less obvious interpersonal structures each family member carries in his own head about himself in relationship to other family members and the family as a unit.

Families, despite cultural differences, share common properties that have the potential for the families' growth or demise. The tasks of family life must be addressed as a unit, and the wherewithal of how to address these tasks must be learned by the family members through a continuous process that strikes a productive balance between the rights and obligations of the individuals and the group. The family is the earliest conveyor of meaning and value. The family interprets who will sleep with whom, who will be naked and who will be clothed, who will do what work, who will have control over resources, who will have sex and who will not, who will be cared for and who will care for whom, who will have authority over material resources, and many more details of life. Some extremely important but less obvious tasks involve affective and attitudinal expressions such as how anger will be expressed, as well as pleasure, and to whom. It is out of this context of learning and teaching that family patterning occurs. When a crisis ensues, this patterning is tested in its flexibility to transcend itself and solve a problem. In rigid families this patterning can be threatened by demands for change. The threat can come about from external factors that impinge on an individual or on the family unit, or from changes within the family unit that require the mobilization of support for a member, such as a new baby coming into a family or a family member becoming physically ill. The demand for increased differential responding within the family also requires the maintenance of continuity, which is seen as essential for the integrity of the family. As suggested beforehand, multiproblem families lack these abilities and their responding is rigid.

Concepts of Family Life

Several important concepts have been derived from research on family life and from family therapy clinicians. These concepts address processes that aid in discerning rigid family patterns and include: differentiation, enmeshment/ disengagement, triangling, double bind, and qualification/disqualification (Minuchin, Rosman and Bader 1978). These concepts are derived from the structural schools of family therapy. The concept of differentiation appears to be an overriding concept of all schools of thought regarding development and family therapy practice.

Differentiation

The concept of levels of differentiation (Boszormenyi-Nagy 1965) describes the degree to which the family unit is fused or regulated by rigid, unspeakable rules of allowable and nonallowable behavior. Conversely, the concept may refer to the degree to which the individual has succeeded in defining those rules of interaction instilled in him or her by the family upbringing. The concept, therefore, is used to describe both the family unit and the individual who springs from it (Minuchin 1974). Subsystems of the family are defined, and these in turn define the limits between the individual family members. There are the parents and there are the children. There is the eldest child and there is the youngest. In addition to these roles, there are the processes of defining the interaction within the family as to what is allowable and what is not. A less differentiated family is locked into agreements among its members that check against the loss of any one family member. For example, the youngest son in a family, age nineteen, finds himself psychologically trapped in an urban apartment with his family. Also living in the apartment, in addition to his middle-aged parents, are an aunt and a dying grandmother. He has older married brothers and sisters who are living out of the house with their own children. He cannot stand the turmoil night after night. He threatens to leave home, work, and go to school. His mother becomes upset—"How can you leave me at this time?" His father takes him aside—"Please don't upset your mother." A brother-in-law, husband of his beloved elder sister, takes him aside and calls him selfish, thoughtless, and says he should stay even if the apartment is crowded. The young man, feeling guilty and wrong, remains with his parents. The young man lives with the fear that if he should assert himself, he can disrupt his family. Note the pseudomutuality. The family mobilizes and ensnares the youth. The tactics are effective and the binding is by guilt.

Relationships in a fused family such as this are marked by a pervasive self-centeredness. The members do not regard the individual personality needs of each member. They do not listen well to each other, and their tendency to manifest continual disappointment in one another is marked by their level of expectation and demand on one another. Each member carries an interpersonal context of the family in his head, and, in the fused family, there is little alteration of this set by the members through their interaction. Feeling manipulated by family members, blaming one's feelings on other family members, and thinking one's self responsible for the feelings of another family member restrict change in the family. Autonomous change is not accepted. Even though family members may reside in separate abodes, there is little toleration for the successes or failures in the group. More important, there is no clear way in which family members can air their feelings and allow for the emergence of individual personalities, with a true acceptance of their existence through an acknowledgment of their differences. Understanding the concept of differentiation allows for comprehension of how a birth of a baby can precipitate extreme emotional reactions in competitive sisters, and how these reactions can be fanned by the attitude of the parents accusing one sister of extreme jealousy while competing for the attention of the daughter with the baby without regard for her needs as a new mother. Thus multiproblem families, in part, can be identified by seemingly normal life events being associated with a moderate to severe degree of family and individual disorganization.

As suggested in this concept, the transactions within the multiproblem family are the clue to the family's level of differentiation, i.e., the lack of an ability to listen, self-centeredness, demandingness, inappropriate expectations, blaming or holding others responsible for how one feels, etc. This lack of differentiation can relate to the individual. For example, a young man (twenty years old) rallying to his sister's aid during her extreme depression, blames his mother for his sister's and his problems. He states several rules he has had to live by, which have been laid down by his mother: one, he is never to confide in anyone, and two, she will know everything he thinks. The mother disclaims the statement to her son which further confuses him. Another less dramatic yet frequent clue to fusion and its manifestation in the thinking patterns of an individual family member is the frequent reference to "we think or we feel." Patterns that aim to bind at the expense of differentiation abound.

Enmeshment/Disengagement

Salvador Minuchin (1967) views a family as an organization striving to function. For him, functioning comes from processes and activities that bind and separate family members. The two extremes are enmeshment and disengagement. When a family system does not attempt to bind, the system can be described as *disengaged.* The opposite descriptive state is enmeshment, where boundaries within the family system are diffuse. Most families fall in the middle of these two extremes, manifesting a number of binding and disengaging activities. Families under crisis may be characterized structurally by extreme movement in one direction or the other, rather than maintaining a balance between the two.

A multiproblem family will manifest, during a crisis, a more rigid adherence to one structural stance. Rigid behavior depicting disengagement can be illustrated in the case of a family where the 18-year-old son has phoned the clinic because he wants to kill himself. He has had problems with his thinking and feels that he is going crazy. A home visit is made, and none of the family members address the two visitors who enter the open door and go into the kitchen. The boy's mother says she is glad to have the visitors because her son is using up her medication (thorazine). The boy's father and brother are in another room watching TV. The mother goes out of the room to tell the boy that the visitors are there; she does not return. Two sisters walk in and out of the barren kitchen to get tea, and two cats come in, searching their empty bowls. This family depicts, in the extreme sense, a disengaged pattern of interacting. The lack of connectiveness appears to be increased in the face of one family member's need for mobilized support.

The other extreme response of a family is one of enmeshment, an overwhelming, nonproductive involvement among the family members. Families with this predominant style tend to have all members excessively affected by an event or one member's distress. Rather than mobilizing around a crisis situation by each member sorting out a function appropriate to the needs of the situation and his or her role in the family, you find chaotic clinging, hysterical reactions, or lack of mobilization to deal with an event. No boundaries identify parent and sibling systems. For example, when a client named Alice was thirteen, and her elder sister was seventeen, they both developed pneumonia. The mother had taken the girls to the doctor who, while treating them, underestimated the seriousness of their conditions. The father, a salesman, was on the road. The mother returned home from the doctor's with the girls, and Alice returned to school for a special class. The mother went out to purchase medicine from the drugstore. When Alice returned home in the afternoon, her sister was coughing up blood. Alice helped her sister to bed and waited for her mother to return. Within two hours the elder sister was dead. It took three days to contact the father. When he came home, the family met him at the door; no words were spoken; the family moved together as a unit and held one another and cried. From that point on however, family members did not discuss the sister's death.

Some ten years later, Alice came for help because of depression and confusion as to her life goals and where they were taking her. She had not moved out of the room she had shared with her sister, nor had the family talked together about the sister's death. As Alice explained it, it was too painful and she might hurt her father if she said anything. This family was enmeshed emotionally, although on the surface there were attempts at leading independent adult lives. Family members were employed, yet when the father was home, there was almost constant fighting. Although all complained about the gloomy atmosphere, especially when the father was home, each found himself compelled to remain in close proximity to one another, engaging in repetitive arguments over outside the home activities. The arguments covered over the grief of the sister's death.

Disengaging patterns and enmeshing patterns of family life do not by themselves define a dysfunctional family system. As indicated earlier, most families develop a repertoire of both types of patterning. One can see that enmeshing patterns are useful in bringing needed support to a family through the grouping of the individuals; by the same token, disengaging patterns allow for autonomy and freedom for individuals within a family system. What is suggested here is that the rigid patterning of interactional responses supporting one extreme or another does result in dysfunctional families; and in multiproblem families, there is a tendency to rigid patterning that becomes heightened in the face of a crisis. The implications of rigid patterning on intervention methods and on expected outcome will be discussed later, but for the moment it is suggested that the intervenors will have to take a more active role in mobilizing the family in activating individual members and in defining subsystems within the family.

Triangling

M. Bowen (1966) introduced the concept of triangling to the area of family work. Triangling involves three people. At times, a triangle involves two people against one, and at other times one person may be caught in the crossfire between the two other people. This is a special type of double binding and will be discussed in more detail later. According to Bowen (1966) and Gregory Bateson (1960a), the triangle is the smallest stable relationship system. Groups of more than three will form interlocking triangles (Elles 1967). Dyadic relationships are most unstable. If you note how long you can talk to one person before a third person is brought into the conversation, you can appreciate the human propensity to form a triangle.

In a multiproblem family, the communication set up in the triangling relationships assures that no two people will really deal with each other directly. In some situations, the triangling is double binding—for example, when a child cannot address one parent without challenging the other. A famous example of how an isolated couple used an imaginary son to form a triangle and fend off their conflicts is in Albee's play "Who's Afraid of Virginia Wolfe?" When triangling takes on a fixed process where no two people deal with each other and this is relied on to keep a balance in family relationships, you have a dysfunctional set. For example, in the family where the adolescent daughter died, the remaining daughter, Alice, referred to her mother as her "Philadelphia lawyer" who argued her case with the father all the time. This example also suggests a double bind because the daughter viewed herself as the black sheep of the family. She was conflicted because the father, although telling her repeatedly that he loved her, would assault her to the point of physical injury. The strength of the set in this example is demonstrated by the number of years that ensued following the eldest daughter's death before help was sought.

In a multiproblem family, one will find such sets, fixed, often in unshakable coalitions. Such coalitions have the potential both to enhance separateness and to promote needed binding in a family. However, when triangling perpetuates interpersonal misinterpretation, the result is confusion and vagueness. In rigid families with a low level of differentiation, there is much triangling that prevents clarification of differences and relationships.

Double Bind

The concept of double bind was developed by Gregory Bateson (1972) and others who studied the communication patterns of schizophrenic families. The significance of this concept rests on its relationship to the concept of differentiation. Basically, the double bind concept states, in terms of the more deviant consequences of the double bind, that an individual is continually punished for his correct discrimination of the context of communication and meaning directed toward him. The result is that the person gives up his accurate perception. Bateson offered the concept of double bind as being causal in the formation of schizophrenia. This has yet to be proven. However, this concept does help in the observation of communication patterns as to whether they go in the direction of enhancing differentiation of an individual within a family or whether they are restrictive (Bateson 1972).

The most disastrous effect from the double bind is that the individual, out of need and coercion, cannot escape the relationship. The individual must defer to the coercer. For example, Alice pleads with her father not to ask her personal questions for fear that he will not like what he hears. He complains that he is interested and she doesn't "trust him." She counters with, "You just get mad and hit me." "No I don't," he says. "It's just that you make me so angry and you shouldn't talk back to me that way. Daughters who love their fathers don't get angry with them."

Within the relationship, the individual is continually presented with paradoxical injunctions. No matter what the individual does, it is a "no win" situation. The person cannot do what is asked without breaking some rule that she/he is told not to break. Comments like "Don't be such a good girl" convey this confusion. In multiproblem families, communication is mainly in an action framework. Little attention is paid to content; rather, emphasis is on seeking out basic acceptance or rejection through verbal and nonverbal communication. This is why there is a tendency to acting-out behavior in multiproblem families, as well as an inability to resolve conflict among family members through negotiation and clarification. Language is used to bind through guilt, fear, or incrimination—leading to noisy nonproductive discussions. Double bind means the confusion of meaning at the covert level of intention and motivation and at the overt level of the manifest content of the message. Alice's father requests contact with his daughter, but he delivers a confused message as to his intentions and his ability to tolerate the girl's individuality. When she challenges the context of his request and the paradox, she is rebuked.

Qualification/Disqualification

Qualification is another dimension reflecting on the quality of the communication process (Bateson 1960). Qualifying statements are clear, congruent statements of fact and motivation (Bateson 1968). Disqualifying statements lack congruence, increase paradoxical meaning, and lead to vagueness. For example, a mother asks her adult son, "Are you going to be in town today?" If he answers, "Yes," and says no more, the mother may then ask, "What are you going to do?" He may answer, "Nothing, just work." She may end her line of questioning with "Oh!" The observer may interpret the mother's statement as a request to her son to come and see her if he is in town. On the other hand she may just want to know if he will be in town, or she may want him to pick up something for her and bring it to her. The incongruence between what the covert meaning of the question is and the overt meaning is apparent. By the same token, when we examine the response of the son, we are led to several speculations about the meaning of his communication pattern. He is not clear in responding to his mother. Both individuals disqualify the meaning of their communication, leaving each struggling to define the nature of their relationship to one another. This ambiguity stultifies interaction and lessens spontaneity and a healthy relationship where an individual can say what he means. Multiproblem family communication patterns are marked by disqualifying statements; that is, the individual family members are under great restraint, unsure of their relationships with one another and therefore not conveying what they mean, thus narrowing the use of language. Often what is blocked is the expression of genuine concern and positive feeling for one another. For example, Alice's father's constant autocratic, domineering, and at times threatening nature does not allow clear expression of genuine caring and warmth, and she is likewise restricted in her response to him.

Discussion of Family Concept.   These abbreviated descriptions of concepts in the field of family study and family therapy have been presented to elaborate on the definition of a multiproblem family. The concepts selected by no means exhaust the growing descriptive concepts emerging from the area of family work. They do, however, give some insight into the structure of relationships and how these operate in a multiproblem family and how one might observe restrictive verbal and behavioral patterns. This can aid the observer of families in crisis and can provide a basis for describing the family. The family can now be described not only by what it is not doing in time of crisis but by what it does do. It is suggested that multiproblem families will be identified by a low level of differentiation, extremes of enmeshment and disengagement, restrictive triangling, and an excess of relationship communication maneuvers marked by double binding and disqualification. An individual involved in crisis intervention with such a family will be sensitized to his tasks when vagueness persists and attempts to resolve the crisis fail because demands are made for people to shift in their relationships in ways they are not prepared for, nor is the family system prepared to support.

Example of Responses
by Multiproblem Families
and Suggested Intervention Strategies

Two cases will be presented to demonstrate the responses of multiproblem families to a crisis and the tasks and problems involved in intervening with them.

The D Family

Mrs. D presented herself at the local mental health clinic in an obvious state of depression. Clinging to her were her four children: Doddy (age 2), Bryant (age 3), Kattie (age 5), and Sally (age 6). The children were unkempt and waiflike in their appearance. Mrs D, smoking cigarettes one after another, stated that she wanted some Valium for her nerves. Mrs. D is 32 years old. She lives in the project with her husband Jim. She and her family (namely, three sisters, a younger brother, father, and mother) have been known to the multiservice center for more than fifteen years. Mrs. D, upon questioning, revealed that she felt things were just getting to be too much this morning and she decided to come to the clinic. Although she did not describe herself as depressed, questioning revealed that she had lost twenty pounds in the last month, and her sleeping was erratic. She, as well as the children, looked emaciated. Although the children clung to their mother, she made little effort to move toward them.

Three months before, Mrs. D had had a hysterectomy. She was upset with the care she had received when she came home. She had been promised homemaker service, and when the homemakers came to her apartment, they quit the next day. She attributed it to the fact that they were black and she was white Irish. A month later, she got in a row with her father who was an alcoholic. It seems that he came and stayed at her house, and she got tired of his drinking and sleeping on the sofa. Her husband was at home most of the day or out playing baseball. He was out of work. During this time, her three sisters were in and out of her apartment, as was her brother. All her siblings were on drugs or were drinking. Two sisters had children, and, presently, the state was stepping in to remove the children from them because of neglect and multiple injuries to the children that could not be clearly accounted for.

Shortly after her return home from the hospital after the hysterectomy, Mrs. D slashed her wrists. She was taken to the emergency room at the City Hospital, and her wrists were stitched. She was offered psychiatric services at the time, but she refused and complained that what she needed was help in the house. Again, help was sent to her, and again the help left shortly after they were in the home. Mrs. D was most defensive when questioned as to why they left, and the subject was dropped. She recounted a life full of struggle— pregnancy and a beloved child at sixteen years of age; marriage at eighteen and another child; then a divorce; then marriage to her present husband and two more children. At 20–24 years of age, she had had difficulty in her relationship with her husband. He often beat her. During this prior period (age 20–24) a social worker came to the house and, in time, all these children were placed in a home and eventually given up for adoption. Thus, Mrs. D forbade any investigation into the records at this time for fear her present four children would be taken away. She claimed that she had been abused by the authorities and her children were removed from her against her will. The only other member of the family who was mentioned was her mother. Her mother had a small apartment nearby and occasionally babysat for the present four children. Mrs. D also mentioned multiple agencies with which she was involved.

Discussion of D Family. Sorting through this myriad of stressful life situations, as well as the loosely structured life style, the following hypotheses were developed as to the present precipitating event. The hysterectomy seemed to be the triggering event for the depression as it manifested itself at this time. The surgery is assumed to have been a major stressor just in the adaptation required. However, it was speculated that the removal of the uterus and the termination of pregnancy at 32 offered further intrapsychic stress, the pain of which was not amenable to the drinking and drug-taking Mrs. D did on a regular basis.

In addition to a request to rid her of her personal pain, she was again asking for help so that she might maintain her family. In this request was the fear that she would be found lacking in her care of her children and have them taken away again. This fear was increased by the fact that she now could not reproduce and replace the children. What is more despairing in the plight of Mrs. D is that not only is she suffering but her children are at extreme risk.

By her own admission, the extended family relates in a diffused, vague, insensitive way to the boundaries and needs of each individual concerned, including themselves. The other members of the extended family thus offer little in the way of extended external support other than the familiarity of their presence and the momentary pleasure gained from their reinforcement of one another's outlet through drugs and alcohol.

The multiproblem nature of this family is most obvious. The task is to sort out what the priority crisis is at this time and determine what can be done, given the report of Mrs. D. Attempts to address her requests in the past have not seemed to fare too well. For some reason, maladaptive coping mechanisms seem to have been repeatedly chosen. These appeared to be drugs and self-destructive actions. At least on this occasion Mrs. D has chosen to seek more controlled drug intervention. Responding to the drug request presents certain problems for the professional. Here is a woman who admits to substance abuse, and she is surrounded by other family members who also abuse drugs. A drug must be given that will give her some relief but will not kill her if she should overdose. Her extended family does not seem able to help her because each one is having enough trouble holding him- or herself together. When asked if her husband could come in, she indicated that they had been fighting and she wished to separate from him.

Present abilities to cope and precrisis functioning do not appear to be very efficient or functional for either Mrs. D or her extended family. What is most important is that although outside agencies have been called into the family situation repeatedly, there has been little progress in the family's defining itself along more functional lines. Not only is there a diffused family system, but the external support system of agencies seems equally ensnared in the patterning of this family by virtue of long-term contact without resolution of problems. A list of all the agencies involved in the past five years was obtained at the first interview, and immediate efforts were made to contact the agencies and set up joint meetings with them. This was seen as essential not only for immediate support but to examine what could be done over a longer period of time.

Briefly, the following decisions were made. First, a psychiatric nurse was immediately assigned to Mrs. D. Second, acknowledgment of Mrs. D's request for drugs was done in a structured way. She was informed that she could try a limited supply of Valium. Her drug abuse problem was discussed, and arrangements were made for her to have a physical examination for possible use of antidepressant drug therapy. Third, a home visit was scheduled for the next day to help evaluate her homemaker needs. Fourth, permission was granted to contact all agencies presently involved with the D family. Mrs. D left, feeling reassured that her immediate requests were being addressed.

There is a contrast here between what had been hypothesized as the precipitant of the crisis and what was done immediately. The concrete immediate plans were aimed at reducing symptoms of personally reported pain and had the objective of stabilizing a deteriorating situation. In this case, the mother was the immediate focus of stabilizing efforts. The time lag between her hysterectomy and the symptoms of depression was great, and her insight into the dynamic implications seemed irrelevant at this time to her overwhelming stated need for help and her plea for care.

Questions were many. What has prevented past efforts to assist this family from taking hold? What are the possible strengths in this family? What are the risk factors for the children?

What Happened within the Next 24 Hours.   The next morning, while the worker was en route to the D family's apartment, Mrs. D and her children were met on the street, running toward the clinic. The worker picked them all up in the car and took them back to the clinic. Mrs. D had left her husband with the children while she went out with her sister during the previous evening. She did not come home at the stated time. When she did return, she found him sexually molesting the eldest daughter. Mrs. D was leaving the house early in the morning because she had called the police and feared her husband's reaction toward her. Crisis intervention at this time focused on separating Mr. D from the family and linking him up with a mental health worker and providing support for Mrs. D and her eldest daughter Sally.

Later Results.   The next two weeks demonstrated how a fragmented service system dealt with an undifferentiated family system, with the family members attempting to disengage from increasingly frustrating and conflict-ridden patterns. Incest, child abuse, along with drug abuse and physical fights, brought a variety of agencies into the family, each member bringing in its own agency. Mr. D had no apparent agency connected with him. Mrs. D had the health clinic, welfare, and now the mental health clinic. The children had some representation through the health clinic and the school. With the open acknowledgment of the abuse, the eldest child now had representation from the official child abuse agency. At the first court hearing, the judge (near retirement) viewed the situation and claimed that the daughter would have to testify against the father, and in the presence of Mrs. D, he claimed that the father had a right to his children and children needed "fatherly love." He set a trial at a later date; Mr. D was not held over or placed on bail. Mrs. D was irate. She was advised to take out a restraining order to keep her husband out of the household. This required that she travel to another section of town. When assistance was offered to do this, she refused, claiming the judge should have done something then and there, and that she would not let her daughter testify. Her fury was great, and agency personnel were angry with the mother and one another.

An emergency meeting was set up with the family (husband and wife) and the various agency representatives. At this meeting, it was apparent that Mr. D was disturbed and helpless in his attempts to defend himself. He kept saying that he didn't do anything but love this child, and then cry that he was sorry. As a consequence of this meeting, he made an agreement to remain at a friend's house and to stay away from the children, to talk with his mental health worker, and, at this time, to meet with his wife in the context of scheduled meetings with the mental health worker present.

After the couple's initial reaction to the pretrial hearing was discussed, the problem of the splitting and fighting among agency personnel was addressed in a continuation of the meeting after the couple left. Agency personnel argued for one parent over another, or for the children against the parents. The side-taking and the emotionality ran high. The worker with Mrs. D attempted to help the agency representatives see how their interaction replicated the family's method of dealing with problems. Gradually and begrudingly, roles and responsibilities were developed and defined and regular meeting times were established to try and provide external support and protection (within reason) for the nuclear family.

Some stability ensued for approximately a week and a half. Then Mrs. D began letting her husband stay overnight, and he eventually moved back. Agency personnel began to fragment over their diverse reactions to the family's behavior. Meetings of all personnel and the couple redefined ground rules. Two weeks after Mr. D returned home, he was again left with the children while his wife went off drinking. When she came back, the youngest child was bruised, and abuse was reported by Sally and the other children. Again there was an emergency court hearing. There was a different judge, and Mr. D was sent to a prison hospital for observation.

Again agency personnel were in conflict, taking sides, and then mobilizing to provide support to Mrs. D and the children. With Mr. D in the hospital, Mrs. D was better able to respond to external supports. Evaluations of the children were carried out; home help was provided; Mrs. D had her physical examination and was responding to an antidepressant medication regimen. Day-care programing was set up for the children, and Mrs. D began to talk a bit more about herself to the nurse.

However, subtle undermining of the supports soon began. The home-maker left. Mrs. D fought with the children's day care mother; Mrs. D had her sister and family over more frequently. Her brother was using her antidepressant medications. Mrs. D began to complain to the social worker (care and protection) about her services from the mental health clinic. The social worker started to set up meetings with Mrs. D at the time of her scheduled meetings with the nurse. The social worker dropped out of the agency meetings, and by the time Mr. D was released from the hospital for his trial, the total situation of external agency support had been replaced by Mrs. D's reengagement with her family.

Since Mrs. D had gravitated toward the social worker—because this individual had legal authority—a decision was made by the nurse to terminate her case at the mental health clinic in order to reduce the case splitting and to consolidate the relationship with the social worker. However, shortly after this change was made, the social worker left the employment of the state agency. The state agency was overextended, and a new social worker was not assigned. Mrs. D was left on her own except for the agency that had always provided the family with day-to-day needs of food stamps, clothing, and so forth. A worker from this agency maintained family contact and sought consultation from the psychiatric nurse. During the next year, a plan was devised to hospitalize the children to evaluate them for possible lead poisoning. While in the hospital the children were evaluated, and all were found to have suffered extensive physical and emotional abuse. The workers also documented the repetitive agency contacts over the last fifteen years, detailing efforts within the last year. The result was a court hearing, where the children were removed from the family, placed in residential treatment, and now all have been adopted.

Pathological Family Patterns.   The narrative of the D family graphically illustrates rigid, diffused patterns of interaction that go beyond the deviant behavior of any one family member. Families with this extreme pathology constantly move from enmeshed, fusing contact to disengaged patterns. The agency contacts could be expected to occur during periods of disengagement. But note what happened to agency personnel. The service system became entangled in the splitting and triangulating patterns. Power struggles ensued despite valiant efforts to counter them. Disqualifying communications of a verbal and nonverbal nature dominated. Objectivity was lost, and the distortions of the legal and human service systems added to the confusion. Ultimately, in a family system with such rigid patterns, the family self-destructs. The project worker and the street worker related to the family but remained disengaged. They were able to structure a course of action beyond the cyclic system. The effectiveness of their arguments rested on documenting the failure of repeated attempts to engage and alter the family system.

The J Family

The second family is presented to demonstrate effective intervention with a multiproblem family during a crisis. As already suggested in the D family, multiproblem families often seek agency contact or find agencies brought in to them at times of pathological states of disorder. The disorder is viewed as pathological in that it does not provide a distancing that allows for increased differentiation of the individuals. Rather, there is physical distance but strong underlying emotional fusion.

The J family consisted of Mrs. J, a 20-year-old daughter Pamela, a 16-year-old daughter Linda, and a 13-year-old son Jason. Mr. J had been out of the house and divorced from his wife for seven years. The basis of the divorce was martial incompatability with the precipitant event being the disclosure of his sexual involvement with his eldest daughter. After the divorce, Mrs. J became involved in a lesbian relationship with an older woman, Dottie. Six months prior to Mrs. J's arrival at the clinic, Dottie died of burns received in a fire started by a lighted cigarette she dropped on a sofa as she fell asleep. She had had a long history of alcoholism.

Mrs. J came to the clinic to request that "something be done to make my 13-year-old son do his part of the housework at home and to stop fighting with his sister Linda." Mrs. J complained that there was incessant fighting between the children and that Jason and Linda kept telephoning her at work to settle their fights. She was depressed about the fights, totally "fed up" with her son, and feeling that things had to change. Mrs. J revealed a striking disengagement from her role as a parent. She felt pressured by her children and saw no need for their demands. She was furious with her eldest daughter for not going to college. Pamela was living in her own apartment. Mrs. J worked in a hospital and was attending school. She was so angered by her children's demands that she planned a trip to Europe by herself, leaving the children to take care of themselves. In reflecting on her husband and marriage, she said she thought the marriage was a mistake right from the beginning.

Mrs. J made little connection between her depression and the loss of Dottie. She claimed that the children liked Dottie, and, although Dottie did have her problems, the fighting had seemed less when she was there. Dottie had tended to be involved in caring for the children and setting limits. Mrs. J was remarkable in her rigid interpretation of her life events and her overt and underlying fury. The focus of her rage was on her son Jason, and it seemed almost unmovable.

Assessment of the Crisis Situation and the Meaning of the Precipitating Event.   The crisis was viewed by the mother as being precipitated by the uncooperative behavior of the youngest child Jason. The crisis worker viewed the dilemma as resulting from a shift in the family system requiring the mother to parent her children. The fact that this woman and her children went through an experience of open incest in the family, a divorce, and then introduction of a female lover without seeking outside assistance (although Pamela did seek individual psychotherapy when she was eighteen years old), speaks to some stabilizing dynamics within the family. The loss of Dottie, therefore, needed to be examined. The mother seemed less sad at the loss of Dottie as a person to whom she felt deeply committed than as one who served as a stabilizing function in the family system.

The crisis was seen in interpersonal terms and family dynamic terms. First, Mrs. J was extremely vulnerable to her increasing rage toward Jason and seemed unaware of her potential for physically acting out against him. Systemswise, the loss of Dottie forced a disengaged mother into a closer relationship with her children. She entered their fights and formed a pathological coalition with her daughter Linda against her son Jason. It was thought that Linda emulated her mother's behavior toward Jason partially out of fear that her mother might attack her. Engagement was always in terms of conflict, and the war was escalating.

Individually, Mrs. J was depressed, enraged, defensive, and helpless in her rigid view of Jason. At this time, an intrapsychic formulation of her reactions toward Jason could not be fully developed because of the energy going into the conflict and Mrs. J's precarious defenses. Her attempt at separating from Jason and the other children by seeking outside help was respected.

A decision was made to bring the family together to see what could be done within this system to diffuse the escalating rage. This maneuver also addressed Mrs. J's request to "do something" with Jason. The meeting was scheduled for the next day.

Crisis Intervention in the Family System.   The first family meeting found the mother and Linda forming a marked coalition against Jason, who was being significantly scapegoated. The therapist managed, during this meeting, to ally herself with the mother and to diffuse, to some extent, the sibling attack on Jason by interpreting the conflict as between the mother and all the children. This was very difficult on two accounts: one, the greatest "payoff" was in scapegoating Jason—it was a pattern that had tremendous reinforcement;

two, the mother's behavior was so detestable to the therapist that it was hard to ally herself with the mother.

The second maneuver by the therapist was to get the whole family to agree to come for six sessions before the mother went on her vacation. The third step taken during this meeting was to explore what was good about the way the family worked. What came out was that each child had a paying job outside of the home, and that they contributed to the household as well as managing to provide their own spending money.

During the next six weeks, several emergency meetings had to be called, and tensions mounted as the mother's guilt and anger were increased as she prepared to leave. Maneuvers to focus all of the rage on Jason continued. However, the older daughter Pamela began to form a coalition with him, in which she acknowledged his efforts to contribute positively. Jason's major defense was to blame his sister Linda. Linda maintained a tight bond with her mother against Jason, and then when Pamela opened up her anger toward her mother for not giving enough love, acceptance, and kindness, Linda joined in her mother's attack on Pamela for being too dependent because she wanted these emotional interchanges.

The therapist worked hard at this point to negotiate the reasonableness of people needing one another, yet needing freedom, and suggested that part of Pamela's complaints might be because her mother did not seem to love her. The therapist also aligned herself with the mother's need for distance, but not at the expense of disqualifying what Pamela was saying to her. Linda began to lessen her attacks with mother on Pamela and Jason as her mother's departure came closer, and on a few occasions she joined with her siblings in their disappointment with what their mother could not do, e.g., express love and caring. Plans were made for the children to meet with the therapist during the mother's absence and to continue the family meetings after the mother returned.

The crises of rage toward Jason abated toward the end of six weeks, and the mother did leave money for the children. During her fourteen days in Europe the children managed quite well. However, two days after returning, the mother became so enraged with Jason over his dawdling in feeding his dog that she had this dog put to sleep (killed). Linda then became angry with her mother, and her mother turned on her and said she would do the same to her cat if she did not "shape up." The therapist was called and emergency meetings were set up. The mother and children were not openly at war, with Linda vacillating more toward a coalition with her siblings than with her mother. The death of the dog was discussed. A similar situation had occurred before. To ease tensions, Pamela agreed to have Jason stay with her on weekends if necessary. Gradually, the therapist helped them all to deal with the experience of reengagement after separation from the mother.

At this point the mother requested a special meeting, asking help for

Linda. Linda had said that she felt like killing herself. The therapist met with Linda and her mother. Linda was able to reveal that she said this because she was so angered at her mother's threat (to kill her cat) when she came back from Europe. It was thought that this might be the first time Linda expressed real anger and separation from her mother. Mrs. J listened and did not retaliate. The crisis assumed a promising turn. The children became more of a group. The mother, not attacked but supported by the therapist, began to listen to the children's complaints about her lack of mothering. This was reinterpreted in terms of differences in desire for closeness and independence. The scapegoating of Jason was reduced. Linda still appeared to be in considerable conflict in separating from her mother and joining her sibling group. However, the fighting and bickering at home, which had involved the mother at work, were greatly reduced. The children and mother began to talk about Mr. J and Dottie. In addition, the mother began to move out into a new personal relationship. At this point (approximately ten weeks later), the family agreed to continue in therapy with a new therapist as the crisis therapist terminated with the family.

Discussion.   The J family demonstrates the relationship of deviant individual behavior perpetuated by family structure and the dominant modes of "disqualifying" interpersonal communications. The locked-in patterning was so restrictive that tension increased beyond a tolerable limit. The degree of passion and the focus of the destructive forces were on Jason. The symbolic destruction of his dog underscored the intensity of feeling. Mrs. J's actions, upon her return, broke her underlying pathological connection with Linda. Linda was no longer exempt from her mother's fury through siding with her. Linda's threat of suicide brought Mrs. J to the therapist under entirely different circumstances from the original contact. The therapist, not underestimating the precarious control over rage, expanded the meaning of the events to a less negative dimension. She supported Mrs. J in her struggle to find a more reasonable approach to her children, and encouraged her efforts to set clear, consistent limits. The children came together, exerting peer pressure to live up to agreements rather than taking over pseudoparenting roles. Linda reduced the undercutting triangling. The crisis abated, and the family moved into conventional family therapy.

The two examples of multiproblem family crises illustrate how the ongoing dynamics of a family need to shift, not only to reduce a crisis but also to move the unit toward therapeutic interventions aimed at long-term efforts to increase differentiation within the family. The clinician has to be most active, playing many roles within the system until a functional arrangement is achieved. Family crisis, just as individual crisis, requires the reduction of tension and the establishment of a functional balance so that problem-solving capacities can take over. In multiproblem families, diffusions and rigid patterns often undermine symptom reduction efforts. The D family demonstrates the failure of structuring efforts, whereas the J family gives hope of a better outcome.

The theoretical concepts of differentiation, enmeshment, triangling, double binding, and disqualification were presented to add to the crisis worker's framework of assessing a family in crisis. When these concepts are coupled with an understanding about precipitants of personal crisis, insight is enhanced as to the coping potential of a family. Assessment of dysfunctional patterns gives the crisis worker more comprehension as to the possible impact of intervention efforts.

GENERAL INTERVENTION STRATEGY IN CRISES REFLECTING PSYCHOPATHOLOGY

Class 5 crises are very difficult for the crisis therapist to respond to effectively on a time-limited basis. In such crises, preexisting problems of the client become manifest, usually within a relationship context, and they trigger strong maladaptive reactions. These maladaptive responses are determined primarily by the underlying psychopathology present and the great vulnerability of the client, rather than by the situation itself. Such clients are likely to have poorly developed coping ability or to demonstrate previously learned maladaptive coping responses. These individuals are more likely than others to present periodically with emotional crises that result from their unresolved problems, and it is this lack of resolution that frequently impairs or complicates learning more adaptive responses to stress.

Crisis therapists often find that crises initially assessed as Classes 1 through 4, will upon closer examination be determined to be Class 5 crises. In Class 5 crises, the general intervention strategy is to support the client and to encourage attempts to respond to the present stressful situation as adaptively as possible. The general therapeutic goal is to reduce client stress to more tolerable levels as quickly as possible and thereby prevent decompensation or regression that may ever further complicate effective crisis resolution. It is unfortunate that clients presenting with this level of crisis often have very poor ego strength, will demonstrate resistance to adaptive change, engage in "games" with the therapist, or otherwise manipulate during the crisis therapy contact. At times it is quite difficult for the crisis therapist to assess underlying psychopathology without becoming entangled in other client problems. Effective response to Class 5 crises requires maintaining a clear focus on the present precipitating stress and working with the client primarily at this level.

It is in Class 5 crises that the traditional assessment and diagnostic skills of the clinician are most helpful in identifying underlying psychopathology and determining effective intervention strategies. The therapist must prepare such clients to accept the need for longer-term therapeutic intervention, and must facilitate referrals once the crisis contacts have been terminated. Some clients presenting with Class 5 crises are already in psychotherapy, but they are seeking immediate help from crisis services as an alternative to contacting their therapists. At times, such crisis contacts are an adjunct to the ongoing therapeutic process that has been sanctioned by the therapist.

To reiterate, it is essential in responding to this type of crisis that the therapist *not* become involved in underlying problems that cannot be resolved during crisis therapy. It is incumbent upon the crisis therapist to prevent diffusion of the focal emphasis of the crisis intervention process. The naive crisis therapist finds it easy to become quickly involved in the myriad of client conflicts (that are accurately perceived to be the "real" problems). The diffusion of the focus in crisis intervention may be encouraged (either overtly or covertly) by the client to the extent that the crisis contact loses its boundaries. When this occurs, the crisis therapist is likely to encounter problems with client dependency, with transference issues, and with separation issues that complicate positive termination and referral.

REFERENCES

BATESON, G., "Minimal Requirements for a Theory of Schizophrenia," *Archives of General Psychiatry,* 2 (1960a), 477–91.

———, "The Group Dynamics of Schizophrenia," in L. Appleby, J. M. Scher, and J. Cumming, eds., *Chronic Schizophrenia: Explorations in Theory and Treatment.* New York: The Free Press, 1960b.

———, "The Logical Categories of Learning and Communication." Position Paper to the Conference on World Views, Wenner-Gren Foundation, August 1968.

———, *Steps to an Ecology of Mind.* New York: Ballantine Books, Inc., 1972.

BOSZORMENYI-NAGY, I., "A Theory of Relationships: Experience and Transaction," in I. Boszormenyi-Nagy and J. L. Frano, eds., *Intensive Family Therapy.* New York: Harper & Row Publishers, Inc., 33–86.

BOWEN, MURRAY, "The Use of Family Therapy in Clinical Practice," *Comprehensive Psychiatry,* Vol. 7 (1966).

ELLES, G. W., "The Closed Circuit: The Study of a Delinquent Family," in G. Handel, ed., *The Psychosocial Interior of the Family.* Chicago: Aldine Publishing Company, 1967.

MINUCHIN, S., *Families and Family Therapy.* Cambridge, Mass.: Harvard University Press, 1974.

MINUCHIN, S., et al., *Families of the Slums*. New York: Basic Books, Inc., Publishers, 1967.

MINUCHIN, S., B. L. ROSMAN, and L. BAKER, *Psychosomatic Families: Anorexia Nervosa in Context*. Cambridge, Mass.: Harvard University Press, 1978.

PITTENGER, R. E., C. F. HOCKETT, and J. J. DANEHY, *The First Five Minutes: A Sample of Microscopic Interview Analysis*. Ithaca, N.Y.: Martineau, 1960.

WATZLAWICK, P., J. H. BEAVIN, and D. D. JACKSON, *Pragmatics of Human Communication: A Study of Interactional Patterns, Pathologies, and Paradoxes*. New York: W. W. Norton & Co., Inc., 1967.

11

CLASS 6: PSYCHIATRIC EMERGENCIES

Psychiatric emergencies involve crisis situations in which general functioning has been severely impaired. The individual is rendered incompetent or unable to assume personal responsibility. The client is unable to exert control over feelings and actions that he or she experiences. The clinician needs to be confident of his or her skills and abilities to manage out-of-control behavior of the client and/or to have adequate assistance available.

Examples of psychiatric emergencies include acutely suicidal clients, drug overdoses, reactions to hallucinogenic drugs, and alcohol intoxication. Individuals experiencing acute psychosis are also classified as psychiatric emergencies as well as people with uncontrollable anger and aggression. In general, these clients are dangerous to themselves as well as to others.

The following section describes the aggressive behavior of rape as symptomatic of a class 6 crisis. This type of crisis is represented by the rapist. The impact of rape behavior on the *victim* has been discussed as a Class 3 crisis in Chapter 8.

RAPE:
A SYMPTOM
OF PSYCHOLOGICAL CRISIS[1]

Rape is a serious crime. It is achieving sexual relations with another person against her or his will through physical force or threat of bodily harm. From a clinical perspective rape is also a symptom of psychological dysfunction. It is a distortion of human sexuality in that rape is the sexual expression of nonsexual needs. Although it is a sexual offense, rape is not motivated primarily by sexual desire. In the same way that an alcoholic is not drinking to quench a thirst, a rapist is not raping for sexual gratification. Just as an alcoholic has a drinking problem, a rapist has a sexual problem. Viewed from a psychological perspective, rape, like alcoholism, is a maladaptive effort to cope with life stresses and to solve unresolved life issues. It is pathological behavior, the result of defects in human development.

Rape is first and foremost an aggressive act. It is the sexual expression of aggression more than the aggressive expression of sexuality. In every act of rape both aggression and sexuality are involved, but it is clear that the sexuality becomes the means of expressing the aggressive needs and feelings that operate in the offender and prompt his assault. This aggression may take several forms and may serve several psychological purposes simultaneously. Rape is a complex act that serves a number of retaliatory and compensatory aims in the psychodynamic functioning of the offender. It may be an effort to discharge his anger, contempt, and hostility toward women—to hurt, degrade, and humiliate. Or it may be an effort to counteract feelings of vulnerability, worthlessness, and inadequacy in himself and to assert his power and competency—to control and exploit. It may also be an effort to deny sexual anxieties, insecurities, and doubts and to reaffirm his identity, strength, and virility. Finally, it may be an effort—in gang rape especially—to compete with other males and to retain social standing and membership status with them. Rape, then, rather than being primarily or essentially a behavioral expression of sexual desire, is in fact the use of sex to express anger, power, domination, exploitation, and retaliation. It is a pseudosexual act, complex and multidetermined, but addressing issues of hostility (anger) and control (power) more than desire (sexuality).

[1]This section through p. 312 is written by A. Nicholas Groth and Ann Wolbert Burgess and includes a condensation of material from *Men Who Rape: The Psychology of the Offender,* by A. Nicholas Groth, with H. Jean Birnbaum (New York: Plenum Publishing Corporation, 1979). Used with permission.

Three Basic
Psychological Components
of Rape

In every act of rape there are three basic psychological components: anger, power, and sexuality. All three factors are present, in varying degrees, in every sexual assault, but distinctive patterns of assault emerge depending on which factor is paramount or dominant in the dynamics of the offender. (See Table 11-1.)

Anger Rape

In some cases of sexual assault, it is very apparent that sexuality becomes a means of expressing and discharging feelings of pent-up anger and rage. The assault is characterized by physical brutality. Far more actual force is used in the commission of the offense than would be necessary if the intent were simply to overpower the victim and achieve sexual penetration. Sex becomes the means by which the offender can degrade his victim. It is a weapon he uses to express his anger and rage. It is his means of retaliating for what he perceives or what he has experienced to be wrongs suffered at the hands of important women in his life, such as his mother or his wife. Rather than seeking sexual gratification, he is seeking to hurt, punish, degrade, and humiliate his victim, and he sees sex as a weapon to be used to this end.

Anger rape appears unplanned and impulsive, and the offender, although recognizing he is in an upset, angry, and depressed frame of mind, generally does not anticipate commiting a sexual assault. Typically the anger rapist will report that he was not feeling sexually aroused at the time of the rape and may even have experienced some problems achieving or maintaining an erection during the assault (although he is not troubled by such impotency in his consenting relationships). His language is abusive (swearing, cursing, using obscenities, making degrading remarks), and the assault itself is of relatively short duration, sometimes over within a matter of a few minutes. The assault does discharge the offender's pent-up anger and provides temporary relief from his inner turmoil, even though he does not find the assault sexually gratifying. His anger spent, it will take time for it again to build to that critical point where he is prone to strike again, and therefore the sexual assaults of the anger rapist tend to be episodic. His motives are retaliation and revenge.

Table 11-1

Patterns of Rape

ANGER RAPE:
1. Aggression: more physical force is used than is necessary to overpower the victim; she is battered.
2. Assault is impulsive and spontaneous.
3. Offender's mood state is one of anger and depression.
4. Offenses are episodic.
5. Language is abusive: cursing, swearing, obscenities.
6. Dynamics: retribution for perceived wrongs, injustices, or "put-downs" experienced by the offender.
7. Assault is of relatively short duration.
8. Victim suffers physical trauma to all areas of her body.

POWER RAPE:
1. Aggression: uses whatever force or threat is necessary to gain control of victim and overcome her resistance.
2. Assault is premeditated and preceded by persistent rape fantasies.
3. Offender's mood state is one of anxiety.
4. Offenses are repetitive and may show an increase in aggression over time.
5. Language is instructional and inquisitive: giving orders, asking personal questions, inquiring as to victim's responses.
6. Dynamics: compensation for deep-seated insecurities and feelings of inadequacy.
7. Assault may be of an extended duration with the victim held captive for a period of time.
8. Victim may be physically unharmed; bodily injury would be inadvertent rather than intentional.

SADISTIC RAPE:
1. Aggression: physical force (anger and power) is eroticized.
2. Assault is calculated and preplanned.
3. Offender's mood state is one of intense excitement.
4. Offenses are ritualistic, typically involving bondage, torture, or bizarre acts, and are interspersed with other nonsadistic sexual assaults.
5. Language is commanding and degrading.
6. Dynamics: symbolic destruction and elimination.
7. Assault may be of an extended duration in which the victim is kidnapped, assaulted, and disposed of.
8. Victim suffers physical trauma to sexual areas of her body; in extreme cases she is murdered and mutilated.

Power Rape

In another pattern of rape, power appears to be the dominant factor motivating the offender. In these assaults it is not the offender's intent to harm his victim but to possess her sexually. Sexuality becomes a means of compensating for underlying feelings of inadequacy and serves to express issues of mastery, strength, control, authority, and identity. There is a desperate need on the part of the offender to reassure himself about his adequacy and competency as a man. Rape here allows him to feel strong, powerful, and in control of someone else. He hopes his victim will welcome and be impressed by his sexual embrace, in order to feel reassured that he is a sexually desirable person.

It is through sexual assault that the offender seeks to assert his mastery and potency and to reaffirm his identity. It is through rape that he hopes to deny deep-seated feelings of inadequacy, worthlessness, and vulnerability, and to shut out disturbing doubts about his masculinity.

Such offenses are preplanned, although the actual assault may be opportunistic in origin. Adult sexuality is threatening to such an offender since it confronts him with issues of adequacy and competency, and his mood state at the time of the assault is usually one of anxiety. The power rapist, too, does not find the offense sexually pleasurable since it never lives up to his fantasy, and he may experience a premature or retarded ejaculation during the assault. His language is instructional (giving orders and commands) and inquisitive (asking the victim personal questions), and the assault may be of an extended duration. Although the power rapist may claim that he was motivated by sexual desire, an examination of his offense typically reveals no effort to negotiate a consenting encounter—he then would not be in control— nor any attempts at foreplay or lovemaking. Instead his *modus operandi* is capture, control, and conquer. Not feeling in control of his own life, the power rapist attempts to compensate and deny his feelings of helplessness and vulnerability by having sexual control of someone else.

Sadistic Rape

In a third pattern of rape, both sexuality and aggression become fused into a single psychological experience known as *sadism*. Aggression itself is eroticized, and this offender finds the deliberate and intentional sexual abuse of his victim intensely exciting and gratifying. Such assaults usually involve bondage and torture, ritualistic behaviors, and symbolic victims (that is, the victims seem to share some common characteristic in regard to their appearance or profession). In some cases the offender is an individual who cannot achieve sexual satisfaction unless his victim physically resists him. He becomes aroused or excited only when aggression is present. He finds pleasure in taking a woman against her will, and, in extreme cases the sadistic rapist may murder his victim and mutilate her body. In less extreme cases he may, rather than have actual intercourse with her, use some type of object or instrument with which to rape her, such as a stick or bottle.

Assessing the Dangers and Underlying Causes of Rape

Regardless of the pattern of the assault, *every* rape will contain elements of anger, of power, and of sexuality, each of which must be carefully assessed to determine what danger the offender constitutes to the community. The greater his anger or contempt toward women (or men), the greater the risk of physical injury to the victim. The stronger his need for power and control or the more desperate his need for validation and reassurance, the greater the risk for repetition of the offense. And the more the anger and the power components in the assault are eroticized, the more the offender becomes a lethal risk to his victim.

Although sexuality is not the only—nor the primary—motive underlying rape, because of the offender's psychosocial development it becomes the means through which his interpersonal conflicts surrounding issues of power and anger become discharged. Rape is symptomatic of an intrapsychic crisis for the offender. It may result from a sudden and unexpected inability to negotiate life demands in a mature or adaptive fashion, or from a progressive and increasing sense of failure in this regard. It may be symptomatic of transient and extraordinary life stresses that temporarily overwhelm the offender's resources to manage his life (which, under ordinary circumstances, are usually adequate), or it may result from a more endogenous state of affairs in which the offender's psychological resources are developmentally insufficient to cope with the successive and increasing demands and stresses of life.

A crisis is frequently precipitated when the individual begins to experience the biopsychosocial impact of adolescence or when he is confronted with the responsibilities and life demands of adulthood. This crisis results from the overpowering threat such demands pose; the individual feels unequipped to meet or fulfill these demands. His rape offense is symptomatic of this internal or developmental crisis, and as with any symptom, the rape serves to defend against anxiety, to express a conflict, and to partially gratify an impulse. When life events impact on the offender in such a way as to activate underlying and deep-seated feelings and fears of helplessness and vulnerability, of worthlessness and emptiness, and/or of rejection and abandonment, sexual assault becomes his defense against the resulting pain. Depression is converted into aggression, and he counterattacks. The extent to which the offender finds most life demands frustrating, coupled with his inability to tolerate frustration and his reliance on sex as the means of overcoming his distress, makes the likelihood of his being a repetitive offender very high.

Rapist and Victim Versions of the Offense—Two Cases

A great deal can be learned about the rapist's perception of the charge of rape being made against him by comparing his version of the offense with the statement given by the victim. This issue was analyzed in a sample of 156 convicted rapists sent to the Massachusetts Center for the Diagnosis and Treatment of Sexually Dangerous Persons. Most rapists agreed with the victim's version (identical version); some minimized the amount of physical or sexual aspects of the assault; and others did not contest the account because they had no memory of the assault. In response to the question, "Why did you commit the rape?" offenders gave a variety of reasons: sexual impulses stated as desire, urge, curiosity; projection onto drugs or alcohol ("I don't know why I raped the girl. I was drunk. If I was sober, I wouldn't have gone along with anything like that."); psychological problems with the theme of power and control ("I wanted to prove myself a man." "I decided to show them—three victims—who was boss."); and mood state at the time of the rape ("I hate this girl because she is the cause of most of my problems."). Some offenders could provide no explanation for their actions ("I couldn't decide why I did it. I got the impression she didn't want to leave the car and I got aggressive.").

In most cases, the offender's version and the victim's version corresponded closely, but there were some discrepancies, usually over the amount of injury inflicted. Two cases will be provided here to illustrate the defense mechanism of minimization used by the power rapist and the anger rapist. In both of the two cases the offenders, who plea-bargained the assault, minimized the violence and sexual components. However, they did admit the rape. That is not always the case.

Case 1

Power Rapist's Version.   The rapist, a 26-year-old married man, was describing six assaults that had occurred over a two-month time period. This is the fifth assault version.

> This assault happened when my wife was away for a week. She wanted me to eat dinner with my folks while she was away because she was afraid something would happen, and sure enough it did. I was at the shopping center, and I saw this girl walking home through the back lot to her house.

I approached her with a knife, led her off into the woods, tied her up, and went around and picked her up with my truck. First I undressed her and I put back some of her clothing—just her skirt and blouse. Then I took her into the woods. I picked her up in my truck and took her home because I knew my wife wasn't there. I tied her up, called my parents and said I'd be a little late, and I went down there and ate and then I came back. When I first assaulted her, I think I asked her if she really enjoyed sex, and she said yes. Then as I undressed her she said she was having her period, but I didn't pay too much attention to that because the thought of it didn't bother me much, and, uh, I might add too that she was black. The police made a big deal out of this. I didn't think too much about it because I am in no way prejudiced. . . . I think she was bleeding heavier than I had seen a woman bleed before. I committed sodomy with her and then I noticed she was bleeding, and it started to bother me so I got her dressed again and took her to a wooded area and tied her hands loosely and I left her.

Victim's version (21-year-old married mother of one child)

I was leaving work on my supper break. I worked two shifts that day. It was about 4–4:30 P.M., and I had an hour and then was due back to work till 9 P.M. I was staying at home with my mother and could see her house from where I was walking. I had to cut across a parking lot and was walking down a dirt road when I heard a man walking behind me. I started walking faster and he did also. I looked back but the man looked away so I could not get a full look at his face, but he reminded me of the boy who lived across the street. He had dark glasses on—carried a bag, like a paper bag. He had work clothes on. I was feeling a bit nervous with him behind me so I slowed up to let him go by. He grabbed me on the shoulder—not enough to stop me. If I stopped, it was just for a minute. But then he said he had a knife at my back and I could feel it. He walked me to the field—it had tall grass. He also told me not to turn around. Because I had a glimpse of him and thought he was the kid next door, I first thought he was the kid fooling around. We had to go down an embankment, and I pulled away and yelled for my mother. I could see her sitting on the porch. He grabbed me real hard and pushed the knife into my back and told me not to try that again. That really scared me—that I couldn't get away and that this wasn't the kid across the street.

He kept walking me to a wooded area. He blindfolded me and never let me look at him. Then he told me to take off all my clothes. Then he tied my hands. He must have been looking at my body—he made some remarks about it and poked me in the stomach and said I was fat. I had my period and told him. I thought that might change his mind. It didn't. He just pulled the tampon out. Then he got behind me and lifted me up. I thought at first it was his penis entering me, but I don't think it really did. At the hospital they told me my perineum was lacerated and that he had used the knife handle. The doctor didn't think he had entered me vaginally.

He had gagged me and I was choking and so he loosened the gag a bit. He left me there tied and gagged for about twenty minutes, and then he came back. He dressed me—even put on my shoes. Then he put me over his shoulder and carried me to his truck. He put me in the front on the floor. As we were riding he hit me with something on my head and that really hurt. When we were to wherever he took me, he led me into the house. Then he took me downstairs to the cellar. He lay me on a table with my arms over my head and tied them to a post. Then he left me and after a while came back and shaved my pubic area. I was really scared. I thought he was going to cut me—like he was going to operate on me. I really thought I was going to be killed. He left me again, and I found I could raise up and I looked around and saw I was in the cellar near a washing machine. Upstairs I heard a lot of thumping and a cat screaming. I guess he was roughhousing with a cat. Then he came downstairs and led me upstairs to a bathroom. He sat me in the bathroom on the toilet. He took my blindfold off and then put two coins over my eyes and retied the blindfold. My clothes had been off since he had me on that table. He touched my breasts and then made me rest my head on the toilet seat. He sodomized me and ejaculated. I think that is the only time he ejaculated. After that he dressed me. He also stuffed toilet paper in me.

Then he put me back in his truck and took me to a wooded area. I was so scared—what was he going to do now? I wanted to try and get away, but I had been so scared from trying and failing the first time. I thought I was going to die now. Then he said, "Get out of the truck, Mrs. Jones from Ft. Devens." That made me think I knew him but later realized he must have gone through my purse and saw my name. He said, "I'll let you go this time if you count to 100." He drove off. I counted all the way to 100. I started walking up the dirt road. I was so scared I was going to run into him. I came upon a man, told him what happened, and he called my uncle.

This victim encountered additional trauma from the hospital and police staff. They did not believe she had been raped. The victim said,

The hospital physician had his doubts, and I later found out he really thought I had made up the story and that I had tried to give myself an abortion. They saw I was shaved, and the man had put merthiolate all over me. I was bleeding so much that they kept me at the hospital—they didn't know if the bleeding was from the laceration or from my period. The police did not believe me. They went back to the woods and found nothing. They also investigated me—found out my 18-month-old baby was born before my husband and I were married even though it was my husband's child. They found out my husband was in the military and in Virginia. I didn't go with him because we were trying to save some money before I moved down, so I was staying with my mother. They thought I was pregnant by another man and tried to have an abortion. The police said I had to take a lie detector test. My husband came right here when he heard about the rape. I was so worried that the lie detector test wouldn't show I was telling the truth, but when it did show I was telling the truth, people seemed more concerned about me. While I was in the hospital and my friends came to visit, I told them what happened. I later learned the police didn't think it happened because I was telling everyone. They thought someone who was raped would keep it quiet—thought I was making too much of it.

This case illustrates the excited mood state of the offender, the repetition of offenses and ritualistic patterns, and the sexual curiosity and extended duration of the assault, which added to the terror of the victim. This case also illustrates how perceptions and stereotypes are projected onto the victim by people who are supposed to help. Prejudgment rather than listening to the victim prevailed in this case.

Case 2

Anger Rapist's Version.   The rapist, a 25-year-old separated father of two children, describes the rape from his perspective.

I began drinking on the job around noontime and had a little more than usual, but it was mostly typical. I went home, showered, drank more, picked up my girl, went to a bar, and began drinking whiskey. Later in the evening my girl drove the car to her place, and I drove away. I was heading back to my house, but when I went to turn for my place, there was a car blocking the road. I got angry and began driving away. Was having thoughts of having sex and decided to go to a lady's house where I fixed her telephone the previous day. Arrived at the house, knew it was wrong, but overrode those feelings and cut her telephone wires with wire cutters and broke through two doors to get into her house. I knew I had passed the point of no return and couldn't stop and so went for her bedroom. I stood at the end of her bed for a few minutes, felt confused and dumbfounded. She woke up, recognized me, and asked why I was there. I tried to lift her nightgown and commotion began. Do not remember well what happened or what I said—it was all slow and methodical. We both got up—ended up on the porch with her wanting to leave and then sitting on a lawn swing chair. I told her about not knowing why I was there, about my marriage, and asked her to talk with me, which she wouldn't do.

Remembered strangling her, dragged her back to the bedroom, slapped her on the stomach—was mad she wouldn't talk with me. Put her on the bed, lifted her nightgown but didn't have an erection. Went to the kitchen and got a spoon and used it on her while masturbating to get an erection. Went back to the kitchen, hung the spoon up and zipped up my pants. She ran out of the house . . . don't remember having intercourse with her . . . got in my car and drove home.

Victim's version (62-year-old married woman).

Was in bed and fell asleep. The first thing I saw was someone going past the foot of my bed and coming swiftly toward me. I could faintly see the sideburns and moustache. He grabbed me and we struggled. He kept dragging me to the foot of the bed. I started talking. I told him I was old and had cancer. He stood up to drop his pants, and I grabbed the door and tried to get by him and out of the room. He grabbed me and threw me back down. We struggled some more. I kept telling him that I couldn't breathe, and I kept trying to talk him out of it. We struggled and he wasn't able to rape me at this point. He was on the inside of the bed and I was able to get out of the bedroom door. He caught me in the hall and we struggled. I was able to get to the back porch. I tried to talk him out of it. He said, "You recognize me, so I am going to kill you." He said that he was going to kill me and that he was going to rape me whether I was living or dead. At this point I was praying out loud and screaming. I kept passing out. At one point I asked him to go home to his wife. He said that he was separated and he had two kids, one five and one six.

He tried to rape me on the back porch but there wasn't enough room. he dragged and carried me back to the bedroom after he had beaten me up and I had no strength left. He said that he had seen doctors about his urges to rape people, but they couldn't help him.

He threw me on the bed and punched my buttocks. He had a metal object that he raped me with. He then turned me on my stomach and inserted his penis into my rectum. Then he turned me on my back again and attempted to use the metal object again. After the last attempt with the metal object I was exhausted and could no longer fight him off. He then lay on top of me and entered me with his penis. He did make penetration, but I am not sure if he had a climax. He wanted me to look at his private parts and then he wanted me to put his penis in my mouth. I did neither. I asked for water, which he wouldn't let me have. I begged for water. He said, "No" and said, "You old son of a bitch—you should have been dead a long time ago." We struggled again and I managed to get out of the door of the bedroom and ran to a neighbor.

This case illustrates the mood state of the offender, the amount of force and resistance used by the victim, the sexual dysfunction of the offender, conversation during rape, derogatory remarks, and the victim's coping patterns.

Denial of Rape by Offenders

Not all offenders admit to committing a sexual assault. Some offenders will give a qualified admission to some type of assault, and other offenders completely deny the sexual assault. Offenders who admit to some type of assault usually admit to physically striking the victim but deny any sexual component, as in the following case.

> The offender states he was at the victim's home earlier in the day. He left to buy some liquor. He says he got stoned at a bar and never returned to the girl's home. He states the girl persistently antagonized him and now recalls striking her about six times. He denies any sexual assault, although he states he was intoxicated and doesn't know what he really did.

Offenders who are convicted and who completely deny any type of forcible assault may state they have been falsely accused. They give various reasons as to what they perceived occurred and why the woman cried "rape." Some victims, offenders say, lie their way out of a sexual situation when they are discovered. These offenders claim that their victim was not forced but in fact consented to sexual relations and then felt pressured into alleging rape when it appeared their sexual conduct would be discovered by their parents, boyfriend, or husband. As one offender said:

> I picked up a married woman waiting for a bus. We drove around, finally parked, and had intercourse. She reported it when her husband discovered she hadn't been out with her girlfriend.

Some women, convicted offenders say, actually initiate sexual relations and then cry "rape." According to one offender; while at the beach with some of his buddies, some girls he knew from school approached and asked for money. According to the offender, the victim began fondling him, so they took a walk into the sand dunes and had sex. "She was known around school to be easy. She was willing, but later put on an act saying she was raped."

The police, some offenders say, have it in for them and put victims up to saying it was they who committed the rape—a "bum beef" in their eyes. Offenders also say some women cry "rape" to get revenge for some conflict in their relationship. In such cases, the offender perceives himself as the victim. In one case, the offender denied the rape charge and stated that he was living with the victim before the alleged offense. He states that she reported the incident because he threw her out of his apartment when he found her having sexual relations with a male friend in his bedroom. Some offenders say the rape may well have happened, but it was not they who committed the offense—they claim mistaken identity. As one offender said:

> Someone in Lowell looks like me—a guy named Murphy. I've been mistaken for other people many times. The victim described somebody else with a full set of teeth and taller than me.

Or, the rape may have happened, say another group of offenders, but they weren't even in the area. As one offender said:

> I was walking down the street when I saw a knife—the kind we use at work, on the sidewalk. I picked it up and put it in my pocket. A detective stopped me and called the squad car. They searched me, found the knife, and arrested me for this rape.

Assessment of the Psychological Crisis of Rape

From a psychological standpoint it is important to understand three major issues related to the commission of rape: (1) the general personality structure and characteristics of the offender, (2) the psychological issues lived out in the offense, and (3) the situational events or conditions that activated the assault.

Assessing the Precipitating Event

You should obtain the offender's account of the sexual offense that brought him to your attention as well as his account of any and every previous sexual offense committed by him. You should also explore the following aspects of each offense:

Premeditation: Did the offender preplan his offense? When did he become aware of such intentions? Was his intent intentional, opportunistic, or spontaneous?

Victim selection: What were the descriptive characteristics of the victim, that is, the sex, age, race, social relationship, situation, and physical characteristics? Can the offender describe his victim, and what specific characteristics does he focus on?

Style of attack: How did the offender gain access to his victim? How did he carry out the sexual assault, such as through deception, intimidation, force, or some combination of these?

Mood state: What was the offender's frame of mind at the time of the offense? How was he feeling?

Accompanying fantasies: Was the offender's assault preceded or accompanied by any specific fantasies? What was the nature of his thoughts? Does he have an interest in pornography? Does he eroticize nonerotic material? When did his rape fantasies first begin? Are they escalated by any specific stimulus?

Role of aggression: What role did aggression play in the commission of the offense? What form did this aggression take? How seriously was the victim injured?

Conversation: What type of conversation did the offender initiate? Were his remarks hostile, instructional, inquisitive?

Sexual behavior: What was the nature of the offender's sexual behavior and activity during the offense? What types of sexual acts did he demand or perform? Was there any ritualistic component to the sexual activity such as any sadomasochistic elements like bondage or terror tactics? How long did the assault last? How did the offender perform sexually? Did he experience premature ejaculation, have difficulty achieving an erection, or have retarded ejaculation? What was the offender's subjective sexual response?

Client's psychological request: How does the offender acknowledge his responsibility for his offense, or does he maintain that he is a victim of circumstance? Does he make a full admission, a qualified admission, or deny the charge?

Assessing the Precipitant of the Crisis

There may be contributing factors that acted to trigger the commission of the rape. Can the offender identify any sources of frustration, aggravation, or anxiety that prompted the offense? Was there some special event to which he responded by sexually assaulting his victim? Were there any vocational, economic, interpersonal, physical, or situational pressures that played a part in the offense? Is the offender experiencing marital discord, social isolation, or other conflicts? Are there threats to his feeling adequate and in charge of himself that might have precipitated his projecting such feelings onto a victim?

Assessing Present Coping Responses

An examination of the correlation between the offender's version and the victim's version of the sexual assault has important implications for the diagnostic assessment and treatment of the offender. It is impossible to accurately evaluate the offender without knowledge of the victim's perception of the offense. If the offender is interviewed without knowing the victim's version of the offense, a number of significant details may not be retrieved because of the offender's coping patterns. With both versions, the clinician can determine what the offender is able to relate, what he minimizes or distorts, and what he evades or denies. The greater the degree of correspondence between the victim and offender versions, the less questions are raised as to distortion, evasion, projection, or responsibility on the part of the offender. Qualifications may have implications regarding areas of conflict; for example, an offender may be comfortable with aggression but not with sexuality. The nature and quality of his defenses likewise have important diagnostic implications. For example, denial is fairly primitive, whereas repression suggests a higher-level conflict over impulse behavior. Prognostic issues are also raised: To what extent can the offender explore his feelings and observe his behavior, or to what extent must he avoid this and externalize responsibility for his actions? How much does he experience himself as a victim, as being helpless and adrift in a hostile world? How much understanding does he have of his feelings? And what are the nature and quality of his self-image and his empathetic perceptions of others, both men and women?

Assessment of Precrisis Functioning

It is important to gain information regarding the offender's repertoire of learned coping behaviors. What is his emotional style and way of communication with others? Who is in his social network? Whom does he feel closest to, and what is the quality of his relationships with others? What areas is he most vulnerable to, such as issues of power, anger, or sexuality?

Assessing Offender's Sexual Development

An absolutely crucial assessment area is the exploration of the offender's sexual development. How did the offender learn about human sexuality? Did he receive any formal instruction? What was the tone of his parents' attitudes toward sex? What was his religious teaching in this regard? How sexually knowledgeable or uninformed is he? What experiences has he had during childhood, adolescence, and adulthood in regard to masturbation or sexual activity with other males as well as with females? When was his first sexual experience? What were the circumstances surrounding the activity, the age, the social relationship of the partner? Who initiated the activity, and what was his reaction? Has he had any sexual experiences he considers unusual or unconventional, such as exposing himself, spying on others, incestuous experiences, sexual activity with animals, cross-dressing? Does he find himself sexually attracted to articles of clothing such as women's undergarments? Has he ever engaged in prostitution or in the manufacture of pornography? Does he like to participate in sadomasochistic practices?

Has the offender been married or involved sexually in an ongoing relationship? What is the quality of this relationship? Have there been extramarital involvements? Has he ever pressured or forced his wife or partner into unconventional sexual practices?

What is the offender's sexual preference as well as sexual orientation: heterosexual, homosexual, bisexual, asexual, pedophilic, etc? What are his customary sexual outlets? How sexually active is he? Is he reasonably comfortable with his sexual life style?

What are the nature and quality of his sexual fantasies? What types of sexually oriented material does he read or buy? Does he ever fantasize about or wish he were a woman? What are his sexual interests?

What sexual concerns does he have? Is he concerned about his virility, his genitalia, his sexual performance? Is he confused about his sexual urges? Does he have any sexual fears, phobias, or aversions? Has he had any sexual experiences that he found upsetting, confusing, or frightening? Has he witnessed disturbing sexual activity?

Related Areas of Client Assessment

It is also important to know to what extent the issue of sexual assault is compounded by the physical and/or mental condition of the offender. Is there any evidence that severe psychiatric problems (psychosis), mental deficiency, organicity, or addiction to alcohol or drugs may have served to diminish the offender's self-control and judgment at the time of his offense? What situational factors or events may have served to "disinhibit" the offender and release his sexual aggression? Was there a codefendent, weapon, or other factors present in the commission of the assault?

SUMMARY

The clinician needs a great deal of background information about the offender as well as information about the current offense in order to make a crisis intervention plan. This assessment should lead to some decision about the danger that this person presents to society in his current status. Careful team planning is necessary for a final disposition.

GENERAL INTERVENTION STRATEGY IN PSYCHIATRIC EMERGENCIES

It is the psychiatric emergency that has most commonly been associated with crisis intervention, mostly as a result of the work done by drug, alcohol, and suicide crisis centers in the last decade. In a psychiatric emergency, the individual in crisis is in a dangerous (to self or others) condition. Without effective (and quick!) intervention, the client faces serious medical or psychiatric consequences.

Effective treatment of psychiatric emergencies is often impaired by the individual's loss of consciousness or of his ability to function. In responding to such crises, use of informants is often desirable because of the client's condition, the urgency of the situation, and the need for rapid and accurate assessment of the medical or psychiatric condition. Fortunately, informants with knowledge of the situation often become involved in psychiatric emergencies and bring the client to a clinical services center or a medical facility.

General intervention strategy for psychiatric emergencies emphasize: (1) assessment of the client's medical or psychiatric condition as quickly as possible, (2) clarification of the situation that led to the emergency, and (3) mobilization of all medical or psychiatric resources necessary to treat the client's condition effectively. The more incompetent the client in a psychiatric emergency, the more emphasis must be placed on assessment of the medical or psychiatric condition in order to minimize adverse consequences by mobilizing treatment quickly. The crisis clinician, in many psychiatric emergencies, must have the capacity to work effectively in highly charged situations and to intervene appropriately, under often adverse conditions (e.g., uncooperative clients), with a less than optimal amount of information available. It is in the psychiatric emergency that the mettle of the crisis clinician is frequently tested to the limit.

Much has been written about appropriate and effective techniques for the assessment and management of a variety of psychiatric emergencies using the crisis model (Bartolucci and Dryer 1973; Resnik and Rubens 1975). In addition to responding to the acute dysfunction of the client in a psychiatric emergency, the therapist may also function as a coordinator of services once the acute phase has passed. Referrals are often needed, as well as intervention at the level of the client's family or other social unit, to provide reassurance and support and to facilitate reintegration of the client back into that unit. The crisis clinician may also work with the client in the postemergency phase of the intervention process to facilitate adjustment and to aid the client in returning to social and community life.

REFERENCES

BARTOLUCCI, G., and C. DRYER, "An Overview of Crisis Intervention in the Emergency Rooms of General Hospitals," *American Journal of Psychiatry,* 130 (1973), 953–60.

RESNIK, HARVEY, and H. RUBENS, eds., *Emergency Psychiatric Care: The Management of Mental Health Crises.* Bowie, Md.: Robert J. Brady Co., 1975.

POSTSCRIPT

DIFFERENTIATING CRISES

When the classification paradigm for differentiating emotional crises, as presented in Part Two of this text, is used in clinical practice, the crisis clinician is often faced with a crisis that initially appears to be one type but then turns out to be another. Perhaps the most frequently encountered example of this are crises presented as "dispositional" (Class 1) that, upon closer examination and exploration of the situation, are more appropriately conceptualized in Classes 2 through 6. As the clinician is able to make a more accurate assessment of the crisis, a plan for effective intervention strategy can be formulated.

In addition, in clinical practice, there are times when clients present crises that clearly fall into Classes 2 through 6, but these must be dealt with initially at the dispositional (Class 1) level because of existing circumstances. In such situations, there must be assessment of the crisis and then mobilization of both support and a referral for appropriate crisis (or other) therapy. Such circumstances might involve therapists who are unable to follow up on cases (e.g., vacation, no time available in case load, etc.) or who do not have adequate training to respond effectively to more serious types of emotional crises. One potential benefit of a classification paradigm for emotional crises is that it provides a model for therapists (and trainees) on which to base decisions regarding their ability to respond to a given crisis.

This paradigm for the classification of emotional crises can be useful both in the training for and practice of crisis intervention. Once the theoretical framework for crisis intervention has been taught, clinicians can apply the principles of crisis intervention to the special characteristics of each class of emotional crisis and thereby avoid many of the problems that befall the novice crisis therapist. Further, this framework for the assessment of "crises" (as contrasted to the "diagnosis" of the individual) is developed as a skill that is of essence to the effective crisis clinician. This structure for assessing crises may also help clinicians to feel more secure when learning this particular mode of therapy in which clinician responsibility and accountability are felt very keenly (Wallace and Morley 1970).

A second point that must be considered as inherent in learning the crisis approach, and in the use of this paradigm for the assessment of emotional crises, is its emphasis on coping mechanisms as responses to present stressful situations. Clinicians are usually well grounded in the mechanisms of ego-defense, but they have not been exposed at the same depth of understanding to the concept of coping in a more general context that includes the defense mechanisms (Paul 1966). Knowledge of both adaptive and maladaptive styles of coping with stressful situations or events is an important part of the clinical expertise of the crisis clinician, one that is often neglected in training.

Certain dimensions inherent in this classification paradigm are helpful in understanding the more subtle structure of this model. These dimensions have important implications for both crisis assessment and for effective crisis intervention. In moving from consideration of Class 1 crises to Class 6 crises, there are general trends in the direction of (1) proportionately more "individual" crises as opposed to "generic" crises (Jacobson, Strickley, and Morley 1968); (2) increasing levels of clinical training and sophistication of therapeutic skills to effectively facilitate adaptive crisis resolution; (3) a shift in the focus of crisis intervention from primary to secondary and finally to tertiary levels of prevention; (4) the likelihood that premorbid personality or psychopathology has been increasingly an important determinant of the emotional crisis; (5) a shift from reasonably well-adjusted individuals confronted with new situations to individuals who have experienced similar crises for which maladaptive coping behaviors have been learned; and (6) increased probability that referral for additional therapeutic intervention will be indicated following termination of the crisis contact.

This paradigm does not define specific intervention techniques nor dictate the therapist's personal style in crisis intervention. The crisis model can be incorporated into a variety of theoretical frameworks for therapy (Baldwin

1977). There is a general sequence of steps in the crisis intervention process, steps that have been defined by Jones (1968), further refined by Rusk (1971), and empirically validated in research by Beers and Foreman (1976). It is hoped that the model presented here for the classification of emotional crises can be integrated into the general structure of crisis intervention in ways that will promote development of more highly skilled crisis clinicians.

REFERENCES

BALDWIN, BRUCE, "Crisis Intervention in Professional Practice: Implications for Clinical Training," *American Journal of Orthopsychiatry,* 47 (1977), 659–70.

BEERS, T., and M. FOREMAN, "Intervention Patterns in Crisis Interviews," *Journal of Counseling Psychology,* 23 (1976), 87–91.

JACOBSON, G., M. STRICKLEY, and W. MORLEY, "Generic and Individual Approaches to Crisis Intervention," *American Journal of Public Health,* 58 (1968), 338–43.

JONES, W., "The A-B-C Method of Crisis Management," *Mental Hygiene,* 52 (1968), 87–89.

PAUL, L., "Crisis Intervention," *Mental Hygiene,* 50 (1966), 141–45.

RUSK, T., "Opportunity and Technique in Crisis Psychiatry," *Comprehensive Psychiatry,* 12 (1971), 249–63.

WALLACE, M., and W. MORLEY, "Teaching Crisis Intervention," *American Journal of Nursing,* 70 (1970) 1484–87.

BIBLIOGRAPHY

ABRAMS, RUTH, *Not Alone with Cancer.* Springfield, Ill.: Charles C Thomas, Publisher, 1974.

ADLER, F., *Sisters in Crime.* New York: McGraw-Hill, Book Company, 1975.

AQUILERA, DONNA, and JANICE MESSICK, *Crisis Intervention: Theory and Methodology,* 3rd Ed. St. Louis, Mo.: The C. V. Mosby Company, 1978.

ALDOUS, JOAN, "Children's Perceptions of Adult Role Assignment: Father-absence, Class, Race, and Sex Influences," *Journal of Marriage and Family* (February 1972), pp. 55–65.

ARMSTRONG, LOUISE, *Kiss Daddy Goodnight: A Speak-Out on Incest.* New York: Hawthorn Books, Inc., 1978.

AVILA, D. L., A. W. COMBS, and W. W. PURKEY, *The Helping Relationship Sourcebook.* Boston: Allyn & Bacon, Inc., 1972.

BABERO, G., and E. SHEEHAN, "Environmental Failure to Thrive," *Journal of Pediatrics,* 71 (1967), 639.

BAGUEDOR, EVE, *Separation, Journal of a Marriage.* New York: Simon & Schuster, 1976.

BAILEY, L., "Family Constraints on Women's Roles," in R. B. Knudsin, ed., *Women and Success: the Anatomy of Achievement.* New York: William Morrow & Co., 1974.

BLANE, MARY JO, "Marital Disruption and the Lives of Children," *Journal of Social Issues,* 32, No. 1 (1976), 103–18.

BARDWICK, J. M., Readings on the Psychology of Women. New York: Harper & Row, Publishers, Inc., 1972.

BARNARD, MARTHA U., BARBARA J. CLANCY, and KERMIT KRANTZ, *Human Sexuality for Health Professionals.* Philadelphia: W. B. Saunders Company, 1978.

BEARDSLEE, CLARISSA, "The Interaction between a Failure to Thrive Infant and His Mother," *Maternal-Child Nursing Journal,* Vol. 1, No. 1 (Spring 1972).

BECKER, H., "The Sorrow of Bereavement," *Journal of Abnormal and Social Psychology,* 27 (1933) 391.

BENEDEK, T., "Psychobiological Aspects of Mothering," *American Journal of OrthoPsychiatry,* 26 (April 1958), 272–78.

BENSON, LEONARD, *Fathering, A Sociological Perspective.* New York: Random House, Inc., 1968.

BEQUAERT, LUCIA H., *Single Women: Alone and Together.* Boston: Beacon Press, 1976.

BERNARD, JESSIE, *The Future of Marriage.* New York: Bantam Books, Inc., 1973.

————, *The Future of Motherhood.* New York: Penguin Books, 1975.

BERNSTEIN, L., and R. BERNSTEIN, *Interviewing: A Guide for Health Professionals.* New York: Appleton-Century-Crofts, 1974.

BIBRING, GRETA L., et al., "A Study of Psychological Processes in Pregnancy and of the Earliest Mother-Child Relationship," *Psychoanalytic Study of the Child,* 16 (1961), 9–72.

BIGNER, JERRY J., "Fathering: Research and Practical Implications," *The Family Coordinator* (October 1970), pp. 357–63.

BILLER, HENRY, and DONALD MERIDITH, *Father Power.* New York: David McKay Co., Inc., 1974.

BIRNBAUM, J., "Life Patterns, Personality Style and Self- Esteem in Gifted Family-Oriented and Career-Committed Women" Doctoral dissertation, University of Michigan, 1971.

BLACHER, R., "Reaction to Chronic Illness," in *Loss and Grief,* ed. B. Schoenberg. New York: Columbia University Press, 1970.

BLAESING, S., and J. BROCKHAUS, "The Development of Body Image in the Child," *Nursing Clinics of North America,* December 1972.

BLAUFORD, H., and J. LEVINE, "Crisis Intervention in an Earthquake," *Social Work,* 17 (July 1972), 16–19.

BLOOD, R. O., *Marriage.* New York: The Free Press, 1969.

BOHANNAN, PAUL, "The Six Stations of Divorce," in Paul Bohannon, ed., *Divorce and After.* New York: Doubleday & Co., Inc., 1970.

BORENZWEIG, H., "The Punishment of Divorced Mothers," *Journal of Sociology and Social Welfare,* 3 (1976), 291–310.

BOWLBY, J., *Child Care and the Growth of Love.* New York: Penguin Books, 1965.

———, *Attachment and Loss.* New York: Basic Books, Inc., Publishers, 1969.

BRANDWEIN R., C. BROWN, and E. FOX, "Women and Children Last: The Social Situation of Divorced Mothers and Their Families," *Journal of Marriage and the Family,* 36 (1974), 498–514.

BRAZELTON, T. B., BARBARA KOXLOWSKI, and MARY MAIN, "The Origins of Reciprocity: The Early Mother-Infant Interaction," in M. Lewis and L. Rosenblum, eds., *The Effect of the Infant on Its Caregiver.* New York: John Wiley & Sons, Inc., 1974.

BRISCOE, C. W., and J. SMITH, "Depression and Marital Turmoil," *Archives of General Psychiatry,* 29 (1973), 811–17.

BRODY, S., *Patterns of Mothering.* New York: International Univeristies Press, 1956.

BROWN, C., R. FELDBERG, and J. KOHEN, "Divorce: Chance of a Lifetime," *Journal of Social Issues,* 32 (1976), 119–33.

BROWNMILLER, SUSAN, *Against Our Will: Men, Women and Rape.* New York: Simon & Schuster, 1976.

BURGESS, ANN W., A. NICHOLAS GROTH, LYNDA L. HOLMSTROM, and SUZANNE M. SGROI, *Sexual Assault of Children and Adolescents.* Lexington, Mass.: D. C. Heath & Company, 1978.

BURGESS, ANN W., and LYNDA L. HOLMSTROM, *Rape: Crisis and Recovery.* Bowie, Md.: Robert J. Brady, 1979.

BURKHARDT, KATHRYN W., *Women in Prison.* New York: Popular Library, 1976.

BUTLER, SANDRA, *Conspiracy of Silence: The Trauma of Incest.* San Francisco, Calif.: New Gide Publications, 1978.

CALHOUN, L. G., J. W. SELBY, and M. F. KING, *Dealing With Crisis.* Englewood Cliffs, N.J.: Prentice-Hall, Inc., 1976.

CAPLAN GERALD, "Patterns of Parental Response to the Crisis of Premature Birth," *Psychiatry,* 23 (1960), 365–74.

———, *Principles of Preventive Psychiatry.* New York: Basic Books, Inc., Publishers, 1964.

———, *Prevention of Mental Disorders in Children.* New York: Basic Books, Inc., Publishers, 1961.

CAREY W., "Maternity Anxiety and Infantile Colic: Is There a Relationship?" *Clinical Pediatrics,* 7 (October 1968), 590–95.

CARLSON, CAROLYN, "Grief and Mourning," in *Behavioral Concepts and Nursing Intervention,* ed. C. Carlson. Philadelphia: J. B. Lippincott Company, 1970.

CARR, A., and R. SCHOENBERG, "Object-Loss and Somatic Symptom Formation," in *Loss and Grief,* ed. B. Schoenberg. New York: Columbia University Press, 1970.

CHAPMAN, JANE R., and MARGARET GATES, *The Victimization of Women.* Beverly Hills, Calif.: Sage Publications, Inc., 1978.

CHAPPEL, DUNCAN, R. GEIS, and G. GEIS, *Forcible Rape: The Crime, the Victim and the Offender.* New York: Columbia University Press, 1977.

CLARK, LINDA, "Introducing Mother and Baby," *American Journal of Nursing,* 74, No. 8 (1974), 1483–85.

COELHO, GEORGE V., DAVID A. HAMBURG, and JOHN E. ADAMS, *Coping and Adaptation.* New York: N.Y.: Basic Books, Inc., Publishers, 1974.

COHEN, F., and R. LAZARUS, "Active Coping Process, Coping Disposition and Recovery from Surgery," *Psychosomatic Medicine,* 35 (September 1973), pp. 4–8.

CORBEIL, MADELINE, "Nursing Process for a Patient with a Body Image Disturbance," *Nursing Clinics of North America,* March 1971.

CRATES, M., "Nursing Functions in Adaptation to Chronic Illness," *American Journal of Nursing,* Vol. 65, No. 10 (1965).

DEMPSEY, M., "The Development of Body Image in the Adolescent," *Nursing Clinics of North America,* December 1972.

DIXON, SAMUEL L., *Working with People in Crisis: Theory and Practice.* St. Louis, Mo.: The C. V. Mosby Company, 1979.

DONOVAN, MARILEE I., and SANDRA PIERCE, *Cancer Care Nursing.* New York: Appleton-Century-Crofts, 1976.

DOUVAN, E., and J. ADELSON, *The Adolescent Experience.* New York: John Wiley & Sons, Inc., 1966.

DRUSS, G. D., "Psychological Response to Colectomy," *Archives of General Psychiatry,* 20, No. 4 (April 1969), 419–27.

ELMER E., *Children in Jeopardy.* Pittsburgh: University of Pittsburgh Press, 1967.

ELMER, E., and G. S. GREGG, "Failure to Thrive: Role of Mother," *Pediatrics,* Vol. 25 (April 1960).

EPSTEIN, CHARLOTTE F., *Woman's Place, Options and Limits in Professional Careers.* Berkeley, Calif.: University of California Press, 1973.

ERIKSON, ERIC H., *Identity: Youth and Crisis.* New York: W. W. Norton & Co., Inc., 1968.

FINKELHOR, DAVID, *Sexually Victimized Children.* New York: The Free Press, 1979.

FISHER, E., *Divorce: The New Freedom.* New York: Harper & Row, Publishers, Inc., 1974.

FOGARTY, M. P., R. RAPPOPORT, and R. N. RAPPOPORT, *Career, Sex and Family.* London: George Allen & Unwin Ltd., 1971.

FORMAN, LYNN, *The Divorced Mother's Guide: Getting It Together.* New York: Berkley Publishing Corporation, 1974.

FORWARD, SUSAN, and CRAIG BUCH, *Betrayal of Innocence: Incest and Its Devastation.* New York: J. P. Tarcher, 1978.

FRIEDAN, BETTY, *The Feminine Mystique.* New York: W. W. Norton & Co., Inc., 1974.

GALLAGHER, ANN, "Body Image Changes in the Patient with a Colostomy," *Nursing Clinics of North America,* December 1972.

GEORGE, VICTOR, and PAUL WILDING, *Motherless Families.* London: Routledge & Kegan Paul Ltd., 1972.

GETTLEMAN, S., and J. MARKOVITZ, *The Courage to Divorce.* New York: Simon & Schuster, 1974.

GETZ, W. L., et al., "Paraprofessional Crisis Counseling in the Emergency Room," *Health and Social Work,* 2, No. 2 (May 1977), 57–73.

GINZGERG, E., *The Manpower Connection.* Cambridge, Mass.: Harvard University Press, 1975.

GINZBERG, E., and A. M. YOHALEM, *Educated American Woman: Self Portraits.* New York: Columbia University Press, 1966.

GLASSER, P. H., and L. N. GLASSER, eds., *Families in Crisis.* New York Harper & Row Publishers, Inc., 1970.

GLASSER, PAUL, and ELIZABETH L. NAVARRE, "Structural Problems of the One-Parent Family, *Journal of Social Issues,* 21 (1964), 98–109.

GOLAN, NAOMI, *Treatment in Crisis Situations.* New York: The Free Press, 1978.

GREEN, RICHARD, ed., *Human Sexuality: A Health Practitioner's Text.* Baltimore, Md.: The Williams & Wilkins Company, 1975.

GROTH, A. NICHOLAS, with H. JEAN BIRNBAUM, *Men Who Rape: Psychology of the Offender.* New York. Plenum Publishing Corporation, 1979.

HALL, JOANNE E., and BARBARA R. WEAVER, *Nursing of Families in Crisis.* Philadelphia, J. B. Lippincott Company, 1974.

HALTON, CORRINE LOING, SHARON MCBRIDE, and ALICE RINK, *Suicide: Assessment and Intervention.* New York: Appleton-Century-Crofts, 1977.

HETHERINGTON, E. M., M. COX, and R. COX, "Divorced Fathers," *The Family Coordinator,* 25 (1976), 417–28.

HILBERMAN, ELAINE, *The Rape Victim.* New York: Basic Books, Inc., Publishers, 1976.

HOFF, LEE ANN, *People in Crisis: Understanding and Helping.* Menlo Park, Calif.: Addison-Wesley Publishing Co., Inc., 1978.

HOFFMAN, L. W., and F. I. NYE, *Working Mothers.* San Francisco: Jossey-Bass, Inc., Publishers, 1975.

HOLMSTROM, LYNDA LYTLE, *The Two Career Family.* Cambridge, Mass.: Schenkman Publishing Co., Inc., 1972.

HOLMSTROM, LYNDA LYTLE, and ANN WOLBERT BURGESS, *The Victim of Rape: Institutional Response.* New York: John Wiley & Sons, Inc., 1978.

KAGAN, J., and H. MOSS, *From Birth to Maturity.* New York: John Wiley & Sons, Inc., 1962.

KENNEDY, J. F., "Maternal Reactions to the Birth of a Defective Baby," *Social Casework,* 51 (July 1970), 410–16.

KJERVIK, DIANE K., and IDA M. MARTINSON, eds., *Women in Stress: A Nursing Perspective.* New York: Appleton-Century-Crofts, 1979.

KOMAROVSKY, M., "Cultural Contradictions and Sex Roles," in J. M. Bardwick, ed., *Readings on the Psychology of Women.* New York: Harper & Row Publishers, Inc., 1972.

KUBLER ROSS, ELIZABETH, *On Death and Dying.* New York: Macmillan Publishing Co., Inc., 1969.

————, *Death: The Final Stage of Growth.* Englewood Cliffs, N.J.: Prentice-Hall, Inc., 1975.

LEAVITT, H. J., "Comment II," in M. Blaxall and B. Reagan, eds., *Women and the Workplace.* Chicago: The University of Chicago Press, 1976.

LEONARD, BEVERLY, "Body Image Changes in Chronic Illness," *Nursing Clinics of North America,* December 1972.

LINDEMANN, ERIC, "Symptomatology and Management of Acute Grief," *American Journal of Psychiatry,* 101, No. 2 (September 1944), 141–48.

LOPATA, H. Z., *Occupation: Housewife.* London: Oxford University Press, 1972.

LOWEN, A., *The Betrayal of the Body,* New York: Macmillan Publishing Co., Inc., 1967.

MACCOBY, E. E., and C. N. JACKLIN, *The Psychology of Sex Differences.* Stanford, Calif: Stanford University Press, 1974.

MANNINO, F. V., and M. F. SHORE, "Family Structure, Aftercare and Post-Hospitalization Adjustment," *American Journal of Orthopsychiatry,* vol. 44, no. 1 (1974).

MCKEE, R. K., *Crisis Intervention in the Community.* Baltimore, Md.: University Park Press, 1974.

MEISELMAN, KARIN C., *Incest: A Psychological Study of Causes and Effects with Treatment Recommendations.* San Francisco: Jossey-Bass, Inc., Publishers, 1978.

MENNING, BARBARA ECK, *Infertility: A Guide for Childless Couples.* Englewood Cliffs, N.J.: Prentice-Hall, Spectrum Books, 1977.

MISCHEL, W., "Sex-Typing and Socialization," in P. H. Mussen, ed., *Carmichael's Manual of Child Psychology,* 3 ed. New York: John Wiley & Sons, Inc., 1970.

MURPHY, LOIS B., and ALICE E. MORIARITY, *Vulnerability, Coping and Growth.* New Haven, Conn.: Yale University Press, 1976.

MURRAY, RUTH, "Body Image Development in Adulthood," *Nursing Clinics of North America,* December 1972.

NEWTON, N., and M. NEWTON, "Mothers' Reactions to Their Newborn

Babies," *Journal of American Medical Association* (July 21, 1961), pp. 181–207.

NYE, F. I., and L. W. HOFFMAN, *The Employed Mother in America.* Chicago: Rand McNally College Publishing Company, 1963.

OAKLEY, A., *Woman's Work.* New York: Vintage Books, 1976.

ORDEN, S. R., and N. M. BRADBURN, "Dimensions of Marital Happiness," *American Journal of Sociology,* 73 (1968), 715–31.

OWENS, C., "Parents' Response to Premature Birth," *American Journal of Nursing,* 60, No. 8 (1960), 1113–18.

PARAD, HOWARD J., ed., *Crisis Intervention: Selected Readings.* New York: Family Service Association of America, 1965.

PARKES, COLIN M., *Bereavement.* New York: International Universities Press, 1972.

———, "Components of the Reaction to Loss of a Limb, Spouse, or Home," *Journal of Psychosomatic Research,* 16, No. 5 (April 1971), 163–73.

PAYKEL, E. S., B. A. PRUSOFF, and E. G. UHLENHUTH, "Scaling of Life Events," *Archives of General Psychiatry,* 25 (1971), 340–47.

PAYKEL, E., et al., "Life Events and Depression: A Controlled Study," *Archives of General Psychiatry,* 21 (1969), 753–60.

PERETZ, D., "Development: Object-Relationships and Loss," in *Loss and Grief,* ed. B. Schoenberg. New York: Columbia University Press, 1970.

PETRILLO, MADELINE, and SIRGAY SANGER, *Emotional Care of Hospitalized Children.* Philadelphia: J. P. Lippincott Company, 1976.

POLOMA, M., and T. N. GARLAND, "Jobs or Careers?" in A. Michel, ed., *Family Issues of Employed Women in Europe and America.* London: E. J. Brill, 1971.

PURYEAR, DOUGLAS A., *Helping People in Crisis.* San Francisco: Jossey-Bass, Inc., Publishers, 1979.

RADA, RICHARD, ed., *Clinical Aspects of the Rapist: Seminars in Psychiatry.* New York: Grune & Stratton, Inc., 1978.

RAPPAPORT, R., "Normal Crisis, Family Structure and Mental Health," *Family Process* 2, No. 1 (March 1963), 68–80.

RESNICK, H. L. P., *Sexual Behaviors: Social, Clinical and Legal Aspects.* Boston: Little, Brown & Company, 1972.

RESNICK, H. L. P., and HARVEY L. RUBEN, *Emergency Psychiatric Care: The Management of Mental Health Crises.* Bowie, Md.: Robert J. Brady, 1975.

ROLLIN, BETTY, *First You Cry.* Philadelphia: J. B. Lippincott Company, 1976.

ROSSI, A. S., "The Roots of Ambivalence in American Women," in J. M. Bardwick, ed., *Readings on the Psychology of Women.* New York: Harper & Row Publishers, Inc., 1972.

————, "Transition to Parenthood," *Journal of Marriage and the Family,* 30 (1968), 26–39.

RUBIN, REBA, "Body Image and Self Esteem," *Nursing Outlook,* 16, No. 6 (June 1968), 20–23.

SCHOENBERG, B., ed., *Loss and Grief.* New York: Columbia University Press, 1970.

SCHOENBERG, B., and A. CARR, "Loss of External Organs: Limbs, Amputation, Mastectomy and Disfiguration," in *Loss and Grief,* ed. B. Schoenberg. New York: Columbia University Press, 1970.

————, "The Patient's Reaction to Fatal Illness," in *Loss and Grief,* ed. B. Schoenberg. New York: Columbia University Press, 1970.

SEITZ, P., and L. WARRICK, "Perinatal Death: The Grieving Mother," *American Journal of Nursing,* Vol. 74, No. 11 (1974).

SHEEHY, G. *Predictable Crises of Adult Life.* New York: E. P. Dutton & Co., Inc., 1976.

SHONTZ, FRANKLIN, "Body Image and Its Disorders," *International Journal of Psychiatry in Medicine,* 5, No. 4 (Fall 1974), 461–72.

SPECTOR, RACHEL E., *Cultural Diversity in Health and Illness.* New York: Appleton-Century-Crofts, 1979.

STEINZOR, BERNARD, *When Parents Divorce.* New York: Pantheon Books, Inc., 1969.

STERN, D. N., "Mother and Infant at Play: The Dyadic Interaction Involving Facial, Vocal, and Gaze Behaviors," in M. Lewis and L. Rosenbaum, eds., *The Effect of the Infant on Its Caregiver.* New York: John Wiley & Sons, Inc., 1974.

STRAUSS, ANSELM L., *Chronic Illness and the Quality of Life.* St. Louis, Mo.: The C. V. Mosby Company, 1975.

SUGAR, MAX, "Children of Divorce," *Pediatrics,* 56 (1970), 588–95.

SWITZER, D., *The Dynamics of Grief.* Nashville, Tenn.: Abington Press, 1970.

WALKER, MARCIA J., and STANLEY L. BRODSKY, *Sexual Assault: The Victim and the Rapist.* Lexington, Mass.: D. C. Heath & Company, 1976.

WEISMAN, AVERY D., *On Death and Dying.* New York: Behavioral Publications, 1972.

WEISMAN, AVERY D. and WILLIAM WORDEN, "Coping and Vulnerability in Cancer Patients," Boston, Project Omega, Harvard Medical School, 1976.

INDEX